D1526756

AFFECT AND COGNITION

The Seventeenth Annual Carnegie Symposium on Cognition

edited by
MARGARET SYDNOR CLARK
SUSAN T. FISKE
Carnegie-Mellon University

LEA Lawrence Erlbaum Associates, Publishers
1982 Hillsdale, New Jersey   London

Lawrence Erlbaum Associates, Inc., Publishers
365 Broadway
Hillsdale, New Jersey, 07642

Library of Congress Cataloging in Publication Data

Symposium on Cognition (17th: Carnegie-Mellon Univer-
        sity: 1981)
        Affect and cognition.

        Bibliography: p.
        Includes index.
        1. Affect (Psychology)—Congresses.   2. Cognition—
Congresses.   I. Clark, Margaret S.   II. Fiske, Susan T.
III. Carnegie-Mellon University.   IV. Title.
BF531.S92   1982   152.4   82-2492
ISBN 0-89859-212-7   AACR2

Printed in the United States of America
10   9   8   7   6   5   4   3   2   1

This book is lovingly dedicated to our parents
Mary Sydnor and Robert Allan Clark
and
Barbara Page and Donald Winslow Fiske

Contents

Preface

In late May, 1981, the 17th annual Carnegie Symposium on Cognition brought 16 cognitive and social psychologists to Carnegie–Mellon University. Their topic was affect and cognition. For only the second time, the Carnegie Symposium had been organized by social psychologists. John Carroll and John Payne chaired the first social cognitive symposium in 1975. Their conference came precisely at the time when social cognition was beginning to take root within social psychology. Since then, the area has blossomed. We hope that the present volume on affect and cognition proves to be as propitious as their volume.

Our decision to hold the symposium on affect and cognition had two sources. First, 2 years previously we had discovered a joint interest in this topic, stemming from separate projects we were involved in at the time. In our reading, we have found that many people have been considering emotion and cognition's relationship (or independence or identity)—some for a long time. However, much of their work is surprisingly uninformed by one another. Second, there has been a recent upsurge of interest in the interface between affect and cognition among psychologists in general. Both cognitive and social psychologists, especially those in social cognition, have been concerned over the fact that the researchers in those areas have lately focused on cognition to the exclusion of affect. Cognitive psychologist Donald Norman (1980) captured this concern clearly: "What is the role of emotion in cognition? We leave it to the poet, the playwright, the novelist. As people we delight in art and music. We fight, get angered, have joy, grief, happiness. But as students of mental events, we are ignorant of why, how." (p. 18) And similarly, although social psychologists have always been concerned with attitudes, attraction, stereotyping, and other affectively toned phenomena, the interface of affect and cognition in these contexts has never been clear.

Consequently, we designed the symposium to give researchers an opportunity for discussion and mutual inspiration. Cognitive and social psychologists seemed obvious choices for participants. Cognitive psychologists have always been the mainstay of the Carnegie Symposium, and social psychologists have traditionally been interested in affect. Of course, psychologists in other areas are interested in affect and cognition, and undeserving omissions are inevitable in such choices. Given the decision to invite both cognitive and social researchers, we initially sought an even balance between the two fields. However, as Norman has aptly observed, most cognitive psychologists have not been concerned with affect. Thus, more social than cognitive psychologists are represented in this volume. In retrospect, we think this imbalance accurately reflects an imbalance of interest in the topic between the two fields.

The speakers having been invited, it only remained to organize the conference and edit the ensuing volume. Many people helped to insure that both ran smoothly. Several worked the entire weekend during which the symposium was held, time that would otherwise have been theirs. Foremost among them is Betty Boal, who took charge of virtually every detail of running the actual symposium. She worked on the first Carnegie Symposium and has been running them ever since. We wonder if the Symposia would survive without her; she clearly deserves special thanks. In addition, Lou Beckstrom, Muriel Fleishman, and Sandy Milberg contributed considerable time, patience, and expertise toward insuring the success of the Symposium. We would also like to thank Ann Beattie, Robert Coulam, Bonnie Haseman, John Herstein, Jeannie Jessup, Richard Lau, Karen Matthews, Frederick Polner, Michael Scheier, William Sholar, and Barbara Waddell, all of whom helped in various ways. Finally, we are grateful to the participants themselves who made for a provocative and enjoyable 3 days and, we believe, good reading.

Margaret S. Clark
Susan T. Fiske
Carnegie-Mellon University

REFERENCE

Norman, D. A. Twelve issues for cognitive science. *Cognitive Science,* 1980, *4,* 1–32.

COGNITIVE UNDERPINNINGS OF AFFECT

1 The Structure of Value: Accounting for Taste

George Mandler
University of California, San Diego

"I know what I like."

—Zuleika Dobson

THESIS

It is assumed that evaluative cognitions are central to a psychological understanding of emotional experience. Three sources of value judgments are innate approach/avoidance tendencies, cultural predication, and the internal structure of the target event/object. Only the last of these is addressed in this chapter.

The basis of a structural analysis is found in schema theory and in the notions of schematic assimilation and accommodation. Schemas are representations of experience that guide action, perception, and thought. Schemas (and the resulting expectations) are developed as a function of the frequency of encounters with relevant instantiations. New encounters are evaluated against existing schemas, and the interaction between an event (evidence in the world) and a schema determines the perception, understanding, and organization of our environment. The congruity between an event and the relevant schema's *relational* structure is suggested to be the basis of some judgments of value. A prototype of evaluative cognitions is found in the congruity between the structure of an event and the most frequent instantiations of a schema; such congruity gives rise to valuations of familiarity, acceptability, and a basic sense of liking. This positive valuation of the familiar is based on congruity and assimilability, while incongruity and accommodative pressures lead to arousal and to evaluative states that may be either positive or negative.

Value is generally considered to be a conscious judgment. It is therefore necessary to consider the conditions under which conscious representations of values are constructed. Such constructions of phenomenal value need not incorporate any *conscious* representation of other features of the target event/object. Evidence that is presented to the individual activates a large number of analytic

3

processes, but only a subset of the results of these activations is available in consciousness.

Evaluative cognitions, although depending on different schematic features and structures, have the same functional status as descriptive cognitions. In combination with states of physiological (autonomic) arousal, they contribute to the subjective experience of affects and emotions.

THE PLACE OF VALUE IN A WORLD OF COGNITIONS

Value and Emotion

What is it about taste that is indisputable? What is in the "eye" of the beholder that confers beauty? How is a judgment about goodness or beauty derived from the representation of an event? How can such a representation, which is traditionally considered to be a bundle of attributes or features, give rise to an evaluation that seems to have no identifiable source?

My reason for trying to account for taste, for describing the structure of value, arises from a desire to complete an account that I began some years ago in *Mind and Emotion* (1975). I presented an analysis of emotional experience based on the interaction between physiological arousal and evaluative cognitions. The former contributes the gut aspect of emotions—their intensity and "bodily" feel; the latter deal with the "mental" feel of emotions—their quality and subjective content. I also wish to expand the domain of cognitive psychology into an area that has been both neglected and misunderstood. It has been neglected by cognitive theorists and misunderstood by those who wish to make distinctions between cognitions and some other aspects of human functioning. My intent is also motivated by a commitment to go "beyond phenomenology," to understand the psychological processes that underlie the common language and the common understanding.

The analysis of most emotional states seems to devolve on some evaluative cognition about the world and the self; these cognitions typically are represented in descriptions of the world or the self as hostile, pleasant, threatening, beautiful, sexy, or evil. Such evaluations combine with autonomic arousal to produce the emotional states described in the common language as anger, joy, fear, ecstasy, lust, or dread. Evaluations are complex events that arise out of the ongoing meaning analyses that are a continuous feature of human mental life. In the psychological literature, as in belles-lettres, these complex evaluations tend to be described in the common language of value. Threat, beauty, attraction, and uncertainty often become primitives in psychological theory; they are taken at face value. Although there have been attempts to describe the cognitive states that may underlie the use of certain "emotional" words, the effort has typically been either in terms of an invocation of fundamental, neural states (as seen, for example, in Darwin) or by reference to wants, desires, expectations, and evaluations (an early example being Leibniz).

The latter enterprise comes close to my own hopes for a psychology of evaluative cognitions. The analysis of emotional terms taken from the common language tends to become a linguistic undertaking, trying to find the semantic structure that is discernible upon careful analysis of the terms (e.g., Wierzbicka's (1972) analysis of the semantic primitives that construct emotion words). Analyses such as these are an important first step toward an understanding of the structure of the cognitions that are incorporated in subjective emotional states. I want to go a step further and provide a psychological analysis of the evaluations that are needed even for the semantic enterprise. I shall concentrate on the basic evaluative dimensions of good/bad, approach/withdrawal, like/dislike, etc. I deliberately include several referents here because it is not my purpose to explicate any *one* term of the common language. I do not believe that the concern of theoretical psychologists should be such explication. Rather, I see our role to be that of constructing reasonable statements about structures and processes that, if all is well, will generate some of the phenomena spoken about (vaguely and diffusely) in the common language (Mandler, 1975). One result of such an enterprise is the rejection of some psychological implications of our common language. Thus, it will become apparent that the representation of ''good'' does not have a symmetrical counterpart in the representation of ''bad'', but rather that these evaluations arise out of somewhat different cognitive events. Similarly, it will become obvious that ''liking'' and ''disliking'' are not poles on a single psychological dimension.

It is the function of the psychologist to make reasonable guesses (on the basis of observation and experiment) about the underlying structures of the human mind and to explore how basic processes produce observable consequences, including the common language and understanding. Thus, it is not my function or intention to explicate value terms, to determine exhaustively, for example, the psychological bases of the good or the beautiful. In short, one can either try to analyze the terms and usages of natural or common languages, or one can concentrate on the underlying psychological processes that, inter alia, generate such terms and usages. I have consistently taken the latter approach. However, such an analysis is not likely to explain completely the common experience, because the latter's complexity suggests that it is determined by a number of different interacting processes.

There exists a large, possibly innumerable, set of cognitive states that are evaluative and that contribute to emotional experience. Evaluative states include judgments of threat, danger, gain, achievement, self-esteem, and so forth. I confine my presentation to one class of these evaluative cognitions, a class that I believe to be basic to the phenomenal experience of liking, preference, acceptability. It is exemplified by the pervasive human characteristic to prefer the known to the unknown, the usual to the unusual, the familiar to the strange.

These cognitions arise out of a structural analysis that is primarily concerned with the congruity between events and schemas. Such an analysis deals with the representation of knowledge (cognition) in the broadest sense. And it is in this broad sense that modern cognitive psychology addresses the notion of cognitions—it includes anything that is said to be mentally represented. For this reason I have occasion to question a recent proposition of Zajonc's (1980), that cognition and affect (value) are subserved by different mechanisms.[1]

Value and Consciousness

I want to make sure that my use of the concept of cognition is clearly understood. In the literature of the past several decades, cognition and cognitive processes are often used to refer to conscious, thought-like processes. For example, when Zajonc (1980) quotes Wundt (1905) on the primacy of affect, it is clear that cognition is identified with conscious ideation. The Wundt quotation concerns the observation that affective elements move into consciousness (become conscious) before anything of the ideational elements is (consciously) perceived. In making a distinction between affect and cognition, Zajonc endorses Wundt's distinction between affective and ideational elements. However, what seems to be actually at issue is the attainment of consciousness of likes and dislikes (i.e., values) and of descriptive (ideational) elements.

If one accepts the notion, expressed earlier by Lashley and G. A. Miller, that conscious contents are—to a large extent—the *products* of cognitive processes, then it is reasonable to ask what gives rise both to the affects and to the ideas. I assume that cognitive processes are at work whenever information is processed and knowledge used or invoked. Among that knowledge is information about preference, about liking and disliking, about good things and bad things. The same underlying thought is surely implied by theories of decision (Kahneman & Tversky, 1979; Luce, 1959), which consider the final (conscious) choice or preference to be the result of (cognitive) processes that are not conscious at the time of the choice and may, in fact, never become conscious.

All this is more than a semantic quibble. Zajonc's colorful statement that "preferences need no inferences" can now be rephrased to read that "*conscious* preferences need no *conscious* inferences." Since I assume that inferences can be the result of nonconscious, theoretically postulated, processes, we can refine

---

[1]I have much respect for Robert Zajonc's chapter, particularly because I use it as a frequent foil. Whereas I disagree with most of his conclusions, I consider it a useful contribution. In fact, it goaded me to several of the propositions that I developed in the course of reading his and writing my chapter. I believe however that some of his discussion is clouded by conceptual confusions. I address some of these, such as the distinctions between cognitive and affective processes, between emotion and preference, and between evaluative terms and the events that give rise to them.

the problem further and ask what inferred structures and processes could be responsible for judgments of value?

To recapitulate: Conscious as well as unconscious, deliberative as well as automatic, processes can be "cognitive." To say that one "likes" something requires access to stored knowledge, unless one accepts a radical position that goodness is in the object. If it is the case that affective/cognitive judgments appear to be made without any conscious access to other "cognitive" processes, then we must examine what it is about valuation and consciousness that produces such phenomenal characteristics. Is the apparent "direct" access to feelings and judgments of value unique to valuation, or is it—as I shall argue—an instance of a more general characteristic of human thought?

EVALUATIVE ACTIONS: TYPES AND SOURCES

I need to distinguish three different sources of evaluative actions and to delimit the range of events to which I wish to apply the notion of the structural source of value. I chose to speak of evaluative *action* in order to be able to include such things as evaluative terms in language, evaluative nonverbal behavior such as approach/withdrawal and facial expressions, and other acts that are apparently based on evaluation or preference.

I exclude two classes of evaluation from this analysis. The first comprises *innate preferences*. These are evaluative actions that are based on apparently innate approach/avoidance tendencies. These, often species specific, dispositions are exemplified by the preference for an optimal temperature range (and the rejection of extreme cold and heat), the preference for sweet and the rejection of bitter substances, and the retreat from looming objects.[2]

The second set of evaluative actions and judgments that I exclude are those that are based on *cultural predication*. Culture is a powerful teacher of valuative judgments, primarily through the vehicle of the common language. It is through the process of acculturation that we "learn" that corn is (in the U.S.) or is not (in France) fit for humans, that spinach is "good" for you, that shaking hands with people is or is not "proper." Such valuations are not based on an examination of the object of interest, but rather the value is a predicate of the object—produced and maintained by cultural processes. Thus corn is said to be inedible because it is corn, not because of the way it tastes and looks.

There exist relatively few instances of innate valuation in comparison with the vast array of predicated values. However, the large number of the latter should

---

[2]It should be noted, however, that even these judgments are subject to changes in expectations and valuation as a function of prior experience and thus subject to a structural analysis (cf. Helson, 1964, and the general application of adaptation level theory).

not mislead us into believing that all or even most of valuative actions that are socially acquired are based on cultural predication. The kind of value I wish to address also depends to a large extent on social and cultural contexts. If the familiar, the normal, and the usual are indeed preferred, then it is clearly our culture, our social context, and our normal environment that define what will become usual and familiar. Familiarity comes about through extensive experience in the culture and not by social fiat like cultural predication.

I am concerned with those cases of valuation that require an examination of the target event but that are not instances of innate dispositions or cultural predication. I shall argue that the third kind of valuation, *structural valuation,* is based on a relationship between the structure of the target event and some stored mental representation—a schema.

What is an Evaluative Judgment?

By asserting that evaluations are cognitive events, we must try to distinguish between those cognitive events that are evaluative and those that are not. Clearly it is only a subset of knowledge/information/cognition that plays a part in emotion and affects[3]—the judgment that something is good or beautiful seems to be quite different from the judgment that it is hot or orange.

We start therefore with the apparent distinction between descriptive and evaluative terms, sometimes also incorporated in the distinction between denotative and connotative meaning.[4] Descriptive judgments seem to depend primarily on information that is "out there." Evaluative judgments apparently do not. We may agree that "the tree is green" but may argue whether "the tree is beautiful." Somewhere between these two are judgments that the tree is "old" or "sick." The value judgments seem to require something about "beautiful" that

---

[3]I restrict the term *affect* to emotion-like states; it certainly seems to operate as such in the common language. Terms that describe preferences (or likings) are evaluative cognitions; they may become affective when combined with a state of arousal.

[4]The most concentrated effort at finding a psychological basis for the distinction between connotation and denotation has been provided by Osgood and his associates (see Osgood, May, & Miron, 1975; Osgood, Suci, & Tannenbaum, 1957), who originally developed the semantic differential as a measure of connotative meaning but later abandoned the vague notion of connotation for the (less-vague?) use of affective meaning. According to Osgood et al. (1975), connotative (or affective) meaning is defined as judgment about an event: "relative to its superordinate [p. 394]," whereas a denotative judgment is: "relative to some standard at the same hierarchical level [p. 394]." Thus, a "small baby" is denotative (relative to babies), while calling a baby a "small one" (relative to human beings) is connotative. This attempt to move the concept of connotation from a merely operational level ("connotation is what connotation does") may be useful, but it does not quite capture the nature of evaluative (affective) judgments. It does describe a structural difference between two kinds of concepts, but it does not do justice to some of the evaluative judgments that are used in the work with the semantic differential. Does the judgment that one's father is "good" or "bad" necessarily require a judgment relative to parents, or to human beings, or to other fathers?

"belongs" to the speaker. Yet nothing is "good" or "beautiful" that does not have some "out there" characteristic on which we base such a judgment, and within a cultural/social group (i.e., within a group with common experiences) we can often agree on what is good and beautiful.

It appears that evaluative judgments cannot be reduced to some "objective" attributes of the object or event that is judged. I assume that the sense of "meaning" in the natural languages is reflected in the relation between the representation of an event (word, image, etc.) and other mental contents (see Garner, 1962; Mandler, 1967; Piaget, 1953 for some samples of this view). Such "meanings" can be distinguished from evaluative meaning. The former might, redundantly, be called semantic meaning, which is typically handled by reference to semantic networks, feature analyses, prototypes, etc. The latter, evaluative meaning, is apparently not dependent on such relations to other mental contents but is more properly addressed by the internal structure of the target event (i.e., relations *among* the features of an object become important).

Evaluative terms are applied to objects and events (or rather the representations of them), not on the basis of the presence or absence of their constituent features, but rather on the basis of an analysis of the structure of the event as such. For example, a tree may be called green because of the salience of its green leaves, but it is considered beautiful for reasons other than the mere presence of leaves (or a trunk or branches). The valuation is based on an appreciation of the relations among its features. A steak may taste salty because of the detection of excessive salt features, but it tastes good because of an appraisal of more than one of its features in some combination. Description and evaluation are not dichotomous; they mark the end points of a *continuum*. As I indicated earlier, the "old" tree seems to be somewhat more than a description and not quite an evaluation. The continuum ranges from judgments based entirely on the presence or absence of certain features (red, hot, curved), to judgments that combine featural and structural characteristics ("That lake looks cold" or "He sounded tired"), and to judgments that are primarily dependent on structural, relational aspects of an object or event (the evaluative cognitions).

There still remains a problem that cannot be completely resolved at present. Both descriptive and evaluative judgments appear to rely to some extent on the internal structure of the reference event. Thus, an animal is called a horse not just because it has a head, mane, tail, legs, etc., but also because these elements occur in a particular configuration. These same configurations may be the occasion for calling a horse beautiful or not, but both kinds of judgments depend to some extent on the internal structure of the event. Clearly the descriptive judgment applies to a wide range of possible values of variables, whereas the evaluative judgment depends on a much smaller range. However, it is not quite clear where or how one can draw the line between the two kinds of structural characteristics. Evaluative judgments do seem to depend primarily on the internal structure. The same features will, in different configurations, occasion the same descriptive predicate "horse," but will give rise to two different evaluative predicates, e.g., "beautiful" or "ugly." Conversely, a particular configuration of features in an abstract painting may be found pleasing, and the identical configuration of different features may be equally pleasing. In both cases—the horse and the painting—it is the structure of the object, and not the presence or absence of certain features, that seems to determine its value. In other words, structure plays a very large role in evaluation and features a relatively smaller one, while in description and categorization, features as well as their structure have major determining functions.

We can now restate the focal argument about descriptive and evaluative judgments. Both description and evaluation depend on two sets of structures, the structure of the world as it is presented to the observer and the structure of prior experiences and current expectations that reside in the mind of the observer. Most judgments depend on some event in the world and a prepared organism. In that sense, descriptive (identifying) and evaluative actions are arrayed on a continuum of event/organism interactions. The mix of external (bottom up) evidence and organism (top down) expectations in the perception of objects and events can, of course, vary widely. Within that variation, evaluative judgments are influenced more by prior experiences and by structural relations than are descriptions or identifications. There is a large variety of instances that satisfy the criteria for being identified as a coffee cup, an automobile, a sonnet, or a violin sonata. However, there are fewer instances that satisfy the specific structural relations we demand of a comfortable coffee cup, an attractive automobile, a satisfying sonnet, or an acceptable sonata. There is a specific range of values of features and relations among features that are the most frequently encountered for a particular class of events or objects. In most cases it will be the objects/events that fall within those ranges that will generate the primitive judgment of positive value. Other cognitive structures will guide the appearance of other kinds of evaluations, as the structural requirements of the sonata or sonnet guide our esthetic judgments.

Although the most frequent instantiations of a particular schema will provide the basis for most of the primitive positive valuations, there will be cases where the general schema suffices as the basis for such judgments. For schemas that are idiosyncratic for an individual, the schema itself, and not some special instantiation, will determine the degree of congruity. The schema of a friend's physical appearance will, for example, provide the basis for congruity or incongruity. For generic social schemas (such as cups, tables, horses, trees, and cars), the specific personal schema, the idiosyncratic instantiation of the event, will frequently determine the congruity that guides evaluation.

This approach has a family relationship to the prototype approach to categorizations. According to Rosch's (Rosch, 1978; Rosch & Mervis 1975) approach to prototypes, a category can be defined as the class of instances that have a certain defined relationship to the categorical or class prototype. It is interesting to speculate whether social prototypes and positively valued instances show some degree of overlap. It is possible that the most frequently encountered instances of a category are also the most protoptypical ones. However, it is clear that this is not necessarily the case. For example, the prototypical fruit may well be the preferred fruit, but the prototypical occupation may not be the most frequently encountered one—namely one's own.

The phenomenal experience that evaluations are somehow contributed by the "self," while perceptions are driven by the evidence of the environment, is consistent with this interpretation of evaluative actions. To the extent that valuative judgments depend on the special subset of instances that satisfy the most frequently encountered samples, such judgments will vary from individual to individual and from group to group. Descriptive and identifying actions—by the process of socialization—necessarily depend on shared elements and structures. We may differ in what we expect an acceptable plant for our living room to look like, but we do not differ in what we expect to characterize houseplants in general. The structures that determine values will therefore show greater differences among people than will generally descriptive cognitive structures.

I have wandered afield from the focus of my analysis, extending my argument—for purposes of illustration—to a wide variety of evaluations, including judgments of beauty and function. Although I believe that structural descriptions lie at the heart of practially all evaluative judgments and actions, I intend to concentrate only on the simple kind of evaluation that I described earlier—the preference for the familiar. The basic evaluation that I address depends on the simplest relational characteristics; it is embodied in the unmodified use of "value," and in the pervasive ability of people to make judgments of "good" or of "liking" for all manner of objects.[5]

Interest and Appraisal

There exist first-order approximations to the problem of "good" that have been with us for some time. The most popular solution (from Spinoza to the contemporary behaviorists) is to explain the subjective sense of good in terms of something else—our interest, striving, wish, or approach. For example, in one of the

[5]Research with the semantic differential has claimed that three general factors of evaluation, potency, and activity account for most if not all connotative (affective) judgments. However, there is some evidence that the evaluative factor is the only truly general one. For example, Kim and Rosenberg (1980) have shown that in personality perception only evaluation is present in the data of all subjects. Potency and activity were: "simultaneously present in the data of less than half of the subjects." More generally, they note that there is: "little evidence for another universal dimension orthogonal to evaluation [p. 388]."

What is the evaluative factor? liking

more extensive attempts at a comprehensive theory of value, Perry (1926) argues
for the formula:

x is valuable = interest is taken in x.

Perry characterizes interest by expectancies that include not only cognitive elements but also attitudes of favoring or disfavoring the expected. A similar theme
is heard in an analysis of "good" by a contemporary linguistic philosopher (Ziff,
1960), who argues that: "this is what 'good' means: answering to certain interests [p. 247]." There are two possible interpretations of "interest." An object or
event may be "interesting," or it may be simply "of interest." In either case, if
value is a gloss on interest, then interest must be further examined. We wish to
know (from a psychological point of view) what it is that makes events interesting or of interest. Included in such an analysis will be the psychological factors
that make us favor some particular expected event or the realized event when it
occurs. It may turn out that whatever it is that makes us attend to or seek out
things is also what invests them with value.

There is an obvious distinction between the interestingness sense of "interest" and value. Interesting things are not always valued, and valued things are
not always interesting. A square coffee cup is probably interesting without being
valued, and a properly working tool may be valued without being particularly
interesting. The arguability of a distinction between interest and value suggests
the need for a more extensive analysis to which I return later in this chapter.

Perry also put the burden of interestingness (value) on the valuating individual
when he noted that evaluative predicates refer to specific relations into which
things "may enter with interested subjects." The interest here is ascribed to the
subject. It is as if individuals are always ready to extend their interests to some
selected objects; as if evaluative predicates are in readiness as they search for
appropriate objects. In contrast, I argue that the kind of interest that is involved
in value is the result of an *interactive* relationship between the object and the
subject. Only certain objects can be of interest (value) to certain subjects; people
do not scan the environment ready to bestow interest (value) on deserving events.

Evaluative judgments have often been subsumed under the concept of appraisal. Arnold (1960) specifically assigns to appraisal the estimative role of
telling whether something is good or bad. She asserts that appraisal is intuitive,
reflexive, and automatic, though her examples tend to deal with inborn approach/
avoidance tendencies such as children liking milk and disliking vinegar. However, according to Arnold, even appraisals that require some memory of past
encounters are based either on past approach/avoidance scenarios or invoke the
good/bad judgment as somehow given. In fact, for Arnold the knowledge of
good and evil is inborn and apparently lodged in the cortex of the limbic lobe
(1960, Vol. II, p. 34). Lazarus and his associates (e.g., Lazarus, Averill, &
Opton, 1970) have made extensive use of a cognitive interpretation of appraisal
that is based on the assumption of the immediate, unmediated apprehension of

meaning (see also Lazarus, 1981, and my later discussion of conscious and unconscious interpretation). Other uses of the appraisal concept have been less precise but none of them has, to my knowledge, inquired into the psychological basis of evaluative appraisals.

I conclude that evaluation and appraisal are judgments that cannot be grounded in consensually established sets of features or attributes of the target event, but rather they depend on relational, structural characteristics that require some match between the event and the schemas or expectations of the observer. I next describe specific theoretical propositions that incorporate such characteristics.

THE STRUCTURE OF VALUE

I start with a comparison with and contrast to Piagetian notions of assimilation and accommodation, relate the schematic approach to Gestalt approaches, and then discuss a schema-theoretic view in greater detail.

Value as Structure

There exist two quite distinct intellectual antecedents for a structural approach to problems of value. On the one hand there is the Gestalt movement which brought structural considerations into the mainstream of theoretical psychology—in direct competition with the then prevailing atomistic traditions. The other structuralist tradition is Piaget's, which itself derives from a longer tradition of structuralism within French intellectual history.

I suggested in *Mind and Emotion* that the process of matching an encountered event to an existing structure is similar to Piaget's concept of assimilation, while the discrepancy between the event and the structure is related to his notion of accommodation. Although such a comparison was evocative, it was quite incomplete.

Piaget (1970) uses assimilation to refer to the integration of "external elements into evolving or completed structures," whereas accommodation refers to the "modification of an assimilatory scheme or structure by the elements it assimilates [pp. 706–708]." Assimilation provides cognitive continuity and integration, while accommodation allows cognitive change.

I shall argue that whenever the analysis of an event fits an existing structural description (a schema), then the stage is set for a primitive positive evaluation. When no correspondence between schema and event is achieved (i.e., when some degree of incongruity is encountered), then further mental activity will determine whether a positive or negative evaluation will ensue. In other words, the simplest (and most primitive) kinds of judgments of value arise out of the structural congruity between event and schema. More complex mental activity is

required in the case of incongruity, and also for any valuative judgment that involves more than mere schematic congruity. Finally, whether a conscious judgment of value occurs at all will depend on a host of factors, most of them contextual and related to the intentions of the actor and the demands of the context.

Assimilation and accommodation are the processes that follow congruity and incongruity. Both of these should, of course, be considered to represent extremes of a continuum from complete congruity (and easy assimilation) to extreme incongruity (and extensive or even unsuccessful accommodation). In the case of the occurrence of schematic congruity, no important structural changes will take place. On the other hand, in the absence of a fit between evidence and expectation (schematic incongruity), assimilative and accommodative processes will be in evidence. I will discuss later how schematic incongruity can lead either to positive or to negative valuation. Incongruity may lead to the activation of a new schema that "fits" the new information. In this case the cognitive activity becomes positively valued. On the other hand, incongruity may make accommodation necessary. In that case the current expectations have been disrupted. In line with my previous presentations on that issue, I assume that the interruption of current tendencies and expectancies is an important condition for the initiation of autonomic arousal (Mandler, 1964, 1975). Such arousal sets the stage for emotional experiences (the real affects), but the evaluative cognitions that accompany the arousal determine the emotional quality.

For the Gestalt movement Wolfgang Köhler (1938) presented an extensive discussion of the problem of value from the point of view of structural psychology (though he would surely have objected to this locution). He placed value within the more general notion of requiredness, which is characteristic of both the phenomenal and the physical world. The Gestalten that shape our experiences *require* certain conclusions and perceptions. Value is one instance of the recognition of requiredness. In other words, the perception of value is formed by Gestalt qualities of the world and of our perceptions. Köhler (1938) concluded that what makes "requiredness compatible with facts" is the "observation that certain facts do not only happen or exist, but, issuing as vectors in parts of contexts, extend toward others with a quality of acceptance or rejection [p. 100]."[6]

---

[6]I read Köhler to say that value arises out of certain structural relationships (vectors), and that these relationships are constrained by the contexts in which they occur. Köhler notes that the world exhibits definite segregated contexts that "show properties belonging to them as contexts or systems." And: "given the place of a part in the context, its dependent properties are determined by this position [p. 85]." Requiredness may change historically. Thus, a few hundred years ago "no minor chords were acceptable as conclusions of any music [p. 97]." That situation has changed, suggesting the subjectivity of such a requiredness. However, historical change does not provide "subjectivity in the phenomenological sense." Value seems objectively real, whether forced by historical change or not. A preference for major over minor chords is just as objectively real as the preference for sweet over bitter substances. For Köhler, both kinds of value are required by the structure of the valued events.

The Gestalt tradition has fostered extensive and creative contributions to the topic of artistic production and appreciation that are consistent with the general point of view presented here. In the field of music, Meyer presented the basic argument against dividing affect and cognition in 1956. He also illustrated the role of expectations in esthetic appreciation. For example, Meyer (1956) speaks of "the intellectual satisfaction which the listener derives from continually following and anticipating the composer's intentions—now, to see his expectations fulfilled, and now, to see himself agreeably mistaken [p. 30]." And he relates affect to cognitions when he notes that: "Affect . . . is aroused when an expectation—a tendency to respond—. . . is temporarily inhibited or permanently blocked [p. 31]." Rudolf Arnheim's monumental contributions to the psychology of the visual arts are based on the belief that vision involves the apprehension of structure. His work defines a psychology of art and beauty, and it also comprehends beauty as being defined by the experience and expectations of the observer as well as being integral to the statement made by the artist.

Again I must note that these tangential discussions of the good and the beautiful do not imply that esthetic judgments are based on the kinds of factors that define the primitive kind of value I address in this chapter. I enter the comparison only because the good and the beautiful both arise out of a structural description that emphasizes the relations within a structure.[7] The complexities of the beautiful do, however, provide a useful bridge to the concept of interactive schemas that involve expectations, and conscious as well as unconscious processes, as the evidence from the surround interacts with the structures of the human mind. As Arnheim (1974) noted, in generalizing from vision to other mental activities: "All perceiving is also thinking, all reasoning is also intuition, all observation is also invention [p. 5]."

still what makes up structural characteristics of object or person

Schema Theory and the Structure of Value

I have suggested that the information that is accessed when a primitive liking/preference judgment is made is not (with the exception of innate preferences) any atomic information "available" in the object; it does not consist of any features or list of features. Nor is it more abstract information represented by classes, or categories, or concepts. The information that is accessed and that is or is not congruous with the evidence is the relational structure of a schema of the reference event. Congruity is assessed with reference either to a generic schema or to the personal instantiation of such a schema. I use the term *schema* to conform with current usage, but also to evoke similarities with Bartlett's and Piaget's usage. My own preference in recent years has been to refer to cognitive struc-

---

[7]This argument also suggests that there is more than social stereotype to the "What is beautiful is good" thesis (see, for example, Dion, Berscheid, & Walster, 1972). Both "beauty" and "goodness" depend to some extent on structural characteristics of the judged person.

tures, which I now include under the term schema. The concept of schema also overlaps with some aspects of Miller, Galanter, and Pribram's (1960) use of "plan" and "image."

Schemas are built up in the course of interaction with the environment. They are available at various levels of generality and abstraction. Thus, schemas may represent organized experience ranging from discrete features to general categories. For example, the available evidence may activate a schema of a horse's head, or alternatively a schema of a whole horse or the general "animal" schema. Such activation arises out of the concatenation of certain features (variables of a schema) such as the shape of the head and teeth, a tail, a mane, a certain size, a range of colors, etc. However, I may like that horse because of certain relations that exist, for example, among its head, mane, tail, size, and color.

I use schema here as a category of mental structures that organize past experience, and that includes Piaget's invention of the schema as structuring our experience and being structured by it. Rumelhart and Ortony (1978) have proposed four "essential characteristics" of schemas; I discuss here two of these that are directly relevant to the problem of congruity—the variables of schemas and their generic nature.

The variables of a schema are bound by different aspects of the environment for each occasion of the schema's activations. The schema has default values for most of its variables, and also more or less probable values and configurations of values. A default value defines the expected and normal value of a particular variable, in the absence of other evidence. Thus, the congruity between schema and state of the world will depend on the experience with particular variables and their values; some features of a table, a tune, a painting are more likely to produce congruity with table, tune, and painting schemas than will others.

The generic nature of schemas is, of course, most important to my argument. The schema that is developed as a result of prior experiences with a particular kind of event is not a carbon copy of that event; schemas are abstract representations of environmental regularities (see, for example, Franks & Bransford, 1971). Schemas vary from the most concrete to the most abstract; they are available for the perceptual elements of an event as well as for the abstract representation of its "meaning" or gist.[8] We comprehend events in terms of the schemas they activate, though we have different ways of talking about different kinds of comprehension. Perception is "comprehension of sensory input" (Rumelhart & Ortony, 1978); one kind of understanding is comprehension of semantic relations; preference involves comprehension of structural relations.

---

[8]I am using concrete and abstract here as essentially equivalent to specific and general. Though the distinction between these two sets of terms is potentially important, it does not interact significantly with my theme. For example, I have a concrete/specific schema for my wristwatch and an abstract/general schema for wristwatches, watches, and clocks.

What is referenced in the judgment of positive value is the congruity between the *relations* among the variables (nodes, embedded schemas) of a schema and the relations among those variables in the relevant event. Finally, it should be noted that generic schemas have modal (or even canonic) values of variables. As I have noted earlier, this property responds to the notion of schematic prototypes (Rosch, 1978) that affect the likely congruity of specific instances of objects and events.

Schemas operate interactively, that is, input from the environment is coded selectively in keeping with the schemas currently operating while that input also selects relevant schemas (cf. Marcel, 1982b; McClelland, 1981; McClelland & Rumelhart, 1981).[9] Whenever an event in the environment produces "data" for the schematic analysis, the activation process proceeds automatically (and interactively) to the highest (most abstract) relevant schema. Evidence from the environment activates potential schemas, and active schemas produce an increased readiness for certain evidence and decreased readiness (inhibition) for other evidence. The interaction between the contextual environmental evidence and the organism's available schemas constricts perception and conception to specific hypotheses, constructions, and schemas.

Most, if not all, of the activation processes occur automatically and without awareness on the part of the perceiver/comprehender. When and under what circumstances do we become aware of any part of the processing stream? We must find at least a tentative answer to that question because clearly there are some aspects of processing (at the most elementary feature level) that are never conscious, while the structures that concern us in the search for value often are represented in consciousness. What is of interest here is not automatic reaching for desirable objects, but rather conscious judgments of liking or preference.

Marcel (1982a & b) has addressed this problem of consciousness for the general perceptual process. His view of mental structures is consistent with the one presented here—he is concerned with structures and the conditions under which they reach the conscious state (cf. also Mandler, 1975, Chapter 3). However, in contrast to the view that structures *become* conscious so that consciousness is simply a different state of a structure, Marcel sees consciousness as a constructive process; the phenomenal experience is a novel construction to which two or more activated schemas have contributed. Treisman and Gelade (1980) recently proposed a constructive view of focal attention that is very similar to Marcel's proposition.

A precursor of these views is the theoretical account contributed by Posner and his associates (Posner & Boies, 1971; Posner & Snyder, 1975). Their inves-

---

[9]It should be noted that I use the term *environment* very broadly to refer to any input to the mental system. Such input may, of course, originate from processes "inside" the organism, including proprioceptive, peripheral physiological, and other events.

tigation of automatic activation also distinguishes between automatic pathway activation and conscious processing. The conscious processing discussed by Posner and Snyder (1975) is "a mechanism of limited capacity which may be directed toward different types of activity [p. 64]." In that sense, they hold to the more traditional position that consciousness is "directed toward" an unconscious structure or process.

Marcel (1982b) notes that "that of which we are conscious are structural descriptions." We can be conscious only of experiences that are constructed out of activated schemas. We are not conscious of the process of activation or the constituents of the activated schemas.[10] A constructed conscious experience depends on the adequately activated schemas of one or more of the constituent processes and features. The advantage of postulating that several such activated schemas construct consciousness is that we thereby can achieve the phenomenal unity of conscious experience. Consciousness constructed from more than one activated schema takes advantage of alternate ways of viewing the world and also integrates some optimal amount of the available information. Marcel advances his hypothesis in order to argue that phenomenal experience is: "an attempt to make sense of as much data as possible at the highest or most functionally useful level possible." When a value judgment is sought—by an actor's intentions or by an experimenter's instructions—the "most functionally useful" level of abstraction is the relational aspect of a schema that is involved in a test of congruity. And even then what is constructed as a conscious, phenomenal accompaniment is not the awareness of congruity but the direct apprehension of value.

Finally, Marcel argues that as we learn to interpret the significance of a set of cues: "*we are aware of that significance instead of and before we are aware of the cues.*" Whereas Marcel's argument here was specifically intended for the phenomenon of category access without access to instantiation, it applies pari passu to evaluative judgments. Marcel and others (see Fowler, Wolford, Slade, & Tassinary, 1981; Intraub, 1981; Marcel, 1981a) have shown that, under some conditions of minimal attention to or exposure of instances of verbal or visual categories, there is evidence that people "know" (consciously) to which category a specific event belongs (e.g., furniture, landscape) without being able to identify which particular item (piece of furniture or specific scenes) they had witnessed. Similarly, unidentifiable words still have significant priming effects on subsequently presented material. A related finding is that by Parker (1977) in which semantic incongruity in a visual display was recognized (peripherally) even before the direct fixation of the incongruous object. Somewhat closer to

---

[10]The contrast is introduced by Marcel as a distinction between the results of activation processes and their records. Whereas the former are generally unconscious processes, it is the latter—the records of these processes—that may become available to consciousness.

evaluative judgments are the results reported by Posner and Snyder (1975). Proper names were paired with one to four "emotional" adjectives, which constructed a particular positive or negative evaluation of the proper name (e.g., "James is honest, loyal, mature"). Subsequently, subjects were required to respond whether a probe word did or did not match one of the adjectives presented, or they had to decide whether the probe word matched the emotional tone of the previous presentation. Erroneous "no" responses were more frequent to probes that matched the emotional tone of the name/adjective arrays than to probes that did not match the emotional tone. When subjects were specifically required to match the emotional tone of the probe word and the array, their reaction times were slower when the probe matched only the tone than when the probe was also a member of the original array. These reaction times converged when the arrays increased from one to four adjectives. The data suggest that impression schemas are constructed from the evaluative adjectives that function to a large extent as cultural predicates. These schemas influence the reactions to the probe words and become more easily accessible the more evidence has been presented for a particular schema (i.e., four consistent adjectives).

It is of course obvious that we are customarily conscious of events and objects in our environ in a constructed fashion; we are aware of the important aspects of the event but hardly ever are aware of all our potential knowledge of the event. Similarly, I would argue it is possible that one can know the value of an event (its congruity with some existing schema) before one is aware of the details of the event that is being judged. Such an approach is also consistent with those arguments that claim immediate access to complex meanings of events (e.g., Lazarus, 1981).[11] A similar disjunction between the awareness of structural and event-specific information has been reported for some clinical observations.[12]

I conclude that an intention (or instruction) to make a judgment of (positive) value and the subsequent judgment involves:

---

[11] These analyses respond to most of Zajonc's (1980) arguments for the separability of affective and cognitive judgments, as well as against the priority of affective (preference) reactions. More generally, some of the examples he cites (e.g., the "new look" in perception) have long been known to be amenable to analyses by parallel interactive processes (see, for example, Morton, 1969).

[12] Warrington (1975) reports on patients who could identify the category name of an object, but not the object name. Similarly, Sheinkopf (1970, cited in Osgood, May, & Miron, 1975) has shown that anomic aphasics, who have difficulty in naming and word finding, perform like normals in a visual–verbal synesthesia task (Osgood, 1960). In that task subjects are asked to relate words (nouns and adjectives) to visual alternatives displayed on cards (e.g., large versus small or black versus white circles, curved versus jagged lines). For example, subjects would pick colorful, clear, and white alternatives for HAPPY rather than colorless, hazy, and black alternatives. The fact that the performance of aphasics in this task is similar to that of normals suggests that they have no difficulty responding to some intrastructural aspect of an event, without being able to access the name of that object in consciousness.

1. An inspection of the reference event that initiates automatic processing, through various levels of schematic representation, of the evidence it presents.

2. A schema of the reference event that is activated both by the intentions of the actor and by the evidence present in the environment.

3. The evidence generated by the reference event and the generic schema that has been activated by the intention/instruction produces some degree of congruity.

4. A constructive process generates a conscious state that incorporates schema congruity, intentional states, and other relevant schematic evidence.

Value and Schema Congruity

The most primitive kind of judgment of positive value arises out of the congruity between our generic or personal expectations (the activated schemas) and the evidence presented by the world. The phenomenal experience is one of acceptability and familiarity, and it arises out of the congruity between the evidence and the relational structure of the activated schema. Such an experience can occur prior to, or in the absence of, any awareness of the constituent characteristics of the reference event.

It is obviously not the case that positive value arises only if there is a perfect "fit" between the evidence and expectancy (the schema). "Fitting" the evidence to our schemas is at times complex cognitive work. It will only rarely be the case that the expected relations among the features and the actual ones will map exactly one into the other. However, the general schematic system is one that not only tolerates such "noise" but is actually constructed with relatively wide bands of acceptability with respect to potential evidence. Within these bands judgments of liking will occur if there is some reasonable fit between evidence and schema, where "reasonable" may vary from one event class to another, and also from situation to situation. In fact, I assume that the congruity–incongruity distinction is arrayed on a continuum, with the mental system setting various criterial values beyond which discrepancy, for example, may be seen as intolerable. The same kind of continuity exists of course for the Piagetian assimilation/accommodation distinction. In the next section I discuss those cases where low levels of incongruity lead to arousal as well as to positive affect; for the present I am concerned only with those cases where congruity seems to be operating.

One must distinguish between congruity that leads to object identification and congruity that leads to the kind of primitive value that concerns me here. Congruity and assimilation of an object or event represent the classic case of object/ event identification. I know that an object is a table or that somebody is cooking an omelette because the events fit certain schemas (expectations) about tables and omelettes. However, whether a table is a "good" table or whether the omelette is being cooked "correctly" is clearly a different kind of judgment, even though both depend on the same mental representations of tables and omelettes. The identification of the events involves processing the features and attributes as well as their relations to each other, whereas the judgment of value is dependent primarily on the relationship among these features, not *that* it is a table, but how well its proportions etc. fit my expectations. It should be kept in mind, though, that identification and valuation represent extremes of a continuum of schematic processing.

For purposes of identification a wider band of values of variables will result in congruity than are acceptable for evaluative (relational) congruity. A table may have four legs of different lengths. Such a discrepancy falls within the bounds of acceptability for purposes of identification; but for purposes of making a judgment of positive value the discrepancy produces incongruity. This implies that evaluative judgments involve more cognitive effort, and at least more comparison processes, than do descriptive ones. We have accumulated reasonable evidence that such is the case. People take much longer to make simple judgments of "liking" familiar words than they do to make a judgment whether the letter string is or is not a word (Mandler & Shebo, 1981). These simple judgments of preference also conform to the relationship between familiarity and value (see below); high-frequency words are liked better than low-frequency ones.

The kind of value I have discussed is devoid of passion or fire. The most primitive values of familiarity and acceptability clearly are that; they are "cold." Heat becomes an effective component of values once we move beyond mere schematic congruity. But it should be noted that other, often much more complex, evaluative cognitions operate in a variety of situations that lead to important positive valuations. Joy and ecstasy involve such cognitions—but their discussion is, unfortunately, beyond the reach of this presentation.

Value and Schema Incongruity

Up till now I have concentrated on the positive value judgments that arise out of schema congruity. What happens when the world presents evidence that is inconsistent with existing schemas? What are the consequences of schema incongruity? Schema incongruity is a case of interruption of expectations and predictions. Such interruptions are a sufficient condition for the occurrence of autonomic nervous system (ANS) activity. ANS activity in turn determines the intensity of emotion or affect. The relations among interruption, arousal, and cognitive evaluations, as well as the adaptive significance of these structures and processes, have been previously presented and discussed extensively (see Mandler, 1964, 1975, 1979a, 1980b).

If it is the case that schema incongruity leads to ANS arousal, then such conjunctions will produce true affect (i.e., valuative judgments in conjunction with peripheral physiological arousal). Given some quantitative physiological arousal, the quality of an emotion (or affect) depends on an evaluation of the

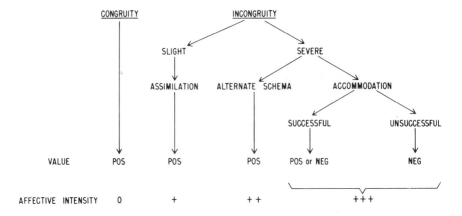

FIG. 1.   Several possible outcomes of schema congruity and incongruity in terms of both values and affective intensity. The resultant value is shown as either positive (POS) or negative (NEG). Degree of affective intensity is shown to vary from zero to +++.

meaning of the conditions and contexts in which individuals find themselves. Such a meaning analysis provides the "sign," the *quale* of the emotion. In the case of schema incongruity such a meaning analysis will depend—to a large extent—on the resolution of the incongruity, specifically on its assimilative and accommodative consequences.

Figure 1.1 shows some of the possible outcomes consequent upon schema congruity and incongruity. From left to right, the first case is one of extreme schema congruity, an instance of the "cold" positive value discussed previously. All the remaining cases assume some degree of discrepancy and arousal.

If we assume that the intensity of the emotion is a function of the degree of ANS arousal and that the latter depends to a large degree on how interrupting the eliciting event is, then emotional intensity depends on how much of a discrepancy (or incongruity) exists between what is encountered and what was expected. I argue therefore that assimilation results in relatively little arousal and therefore a low degree of affective intensity. If the existing schema can incorporate the new information without any major structural changes (e.g., when a new instance of a generic concept is assimilated), I would expect that there would be little disruption and—usually—a positive evaluative state. The latter will occur if for no other reason than that one of the immediate consequences of assimilation is that there does in fact exist congruity between the world and the slightly changed schema. In other words, in the case of assimilation we would expect judgments of positive value that are in fact slightly emotionally tinged. I shall return to this case in the discussion of interestingness; slightly incongruous events are usually interesting and positively valued. The second case in Fig. 1.1 illustrates this concatenation. Examples that come to mind are discoveries of generalizability of previous knowledge ("That's another kind of good cake"; or "I guess I can use the new variation of my old chess opening"; or "Joe doesn't look so bad without his beard").

If no assimilation is possible, if deep structural changes are necessary in order to accommodate the new information, then interruptions of expectation will occur, ANS arousal will be appropriately intense, and the intensity of experienced emotion (affect) will be a function of the arousal. Whether or not the quality of the experienced emotion will be positive or negative depends on a number of factors. Most of the times the affect will be negative, given the absence of structural congruity that could lead to a positive evaluation. More important however is the sense of helplessness that one experiences in the face of schematic incongruity and interruption. I have previously described helplessness—the unavailability of appropriate perceptions, thoughts, and actions—as the prime evaluative condition that leads to the subjective experience of anxiety. Other conditions of the disruptive situation may lead to other kinds of evaluative actions. If elimination of the disruptive event is possible, the evaluative quality may well be one of hostility (and lead to aggression); if the disruption is due to the loss of a person who has played a major role in supporting one's life actions, the evaluative quality will be one of grief (and see Mandler, 1975, for other examples). On the other hand, it is of course possible that the meaning analysis leads to positive evaluations, as in the case of finding a long lost friend, being given unexpected praise, etc. The important point is that schema incongruity can lead to emotions that may be positive or negative in their quality. An apposite example may be found in the positively valued concept of mastery and personal control, which indexes a situation that has been brought into conformity with the actor's expectations and intentions (Mandler, 1979a). In general, the quality of the emotion following incongruity will depend to a large extent on the broader evaluation of the context in which it occurs.

In Fig. 1.1 I have restricted myself to relatively simple examples. The third case (from the left) illustrates a situation in which incongruity occurs, but instead of major structural changes the solution is one of finding a different schema that fits the available evidence. In the simplest case this is an occasion of delayed congruity. However, the initial discrepancy has already initiated the course of arousal, and the newly found congruity occurs within that context. The value is positive and the arousal provides affective intensity for that positive value. At this point it is important to note the relative time course of assimilation/accommodation and of arousal. The peripheral autonomic nervous system is relatively slow; symptoms of arousal do not occur until 1 to 2 seconds after stimulus onset. In contrast, the time course of schema activation and access is usually much faster, probably in the range of 300 to 1000 msecs. As a result, conditions that produce arousal (such as discrepancies) will not have autonomic consequences until some 1.5 secs later. In the intervening time several cognitive events can and will have occurred. As a result, incongruity will have affective consequences for some time after the cognitive discrepancy or incongruity may have been repaired. The conscious construction integrates the persisting arousal with the current evaluative cognition (meaning analysis), and the resultant phenomenal affect may be intensely positive or negative, depending not on the fact of arousal but on the current state of evaluation.

The last two cases in Fig. 1.1 illustrate conditions in which accommodation—changes in the schematic structure—is forced by the evidence in the world. If the accommodation is successful, the evaluative state may be positive or negative, depending on the relation between the newly accommodated structure and the environmental evidence. Affect will be intense. If the accommodation is unsuccessful, if the system cannot adapt to the new circumstances, then the valuative sign will most probably be negative. The unavailability of an appropriate response to the environment is likely to generate an anxiety experience.

To summarize:

1. The evaluation of "good" based on schema congruity is a cognitive judgment with no arousal, no interruption or discrepancy.

2. Value judgments arising out of assimilation are typically positive judgments with a low degree of emotional intensity.

3. "Good" or "bad" judgments following disruption and accommodation involve arousal and therefore produce affective, emotional states.[13] Such an analysis seems to be consistent with an intuitive notion that negative judgments are usually affectively tinged, while positive judgments may be or not.

ASPECTS OF VALUE

Value and Interest

I now return to the question raised earlier about the relationship between interest and value. The commonsense notion of interestingness seems to involve encounters with events that are at least slightly incongruous or discrepant. Things are usually interesting or curiosity arousing because they deviate from the usual and the expected. In other words, events that are interesting may or may not be positively valued, though as noted earlier slight discrepancies that are easily assimilated are usually positively valued. The general topic of curiosity and arousal is one that is central to Berlyne's contribution.

---

[13]It seems not particularly useful to treat affect as synonymous with preference (Zajonc, 1980). The absence of liking is not, of course, dislike. And if there are features of events that determine preference, then there surely must be other sets of features that determine dislike or rejection. Would one have to search for rejecteranda just as for preferanda? How are these two classes of features likely to be related?

Daniel Berlyne's work was—to a large extent—an extension of Piaget's notion about schemas and their directive functions. Berlyne worked extensively on theoretical and empirical relations among arousal, effective thought, and the so-called collative variables (Berlyne, 1960). The latter include such phenomena as novelty, surprise, complexity, and incongruity, and Berlyne noted that conflict is an essential aspect of the operation of these collative variables. Whenever these effects are present, Berlyne assumed that they produce a hypothetical state of arousal. On the other hand, the accrual or acquisition of new information reduces the arousal (Berlyne, 1960, 1965).

With respect to evaluative judgments, Berlyne (1973) notes that "[t]here is a fair amount of work to suggest that judgments of how far stimulus objects are 'pleasing,' 'pleasant,' 'beautiful,' or 'good' reflect a common underlying . . . evaluative dimension. On the other hand, judgments of how 'interesting' objects are seem to reflect a quite different kind of evaluation. . . . Experiments . . . point, in fact, to two distinct kinds of evaluative judgments [p. 10]." Berlyne makes the distinction between interestingness and pleasingness in terms of stimulus complexity, with the former increasing with complexity and the latter reaching a peak at intermediate levels of complexity. What is important is that the distinction can be made and that it is related to structural aspects of the judged events.

Elsewhere Berlyne (1971) noted that simple or redundant patterns are pleasing, but uninteresting, whereas patterns that are both pleasing and interesting are complex patterns with distinct internal organizations. Clearly the former usually involve schema congruity, whereas the latter are more likely to require accommodation.

Berlyne assigns arousal functions to discrepant events that produce curiosity and interest. In the present framework I argue that positive value is tied to schema congruity, while interestingness is related to schema incongruity. Interesting things may be good or bad, and positively valued things may be interesting or not. The relations between positive value and interest will depend on the degree of arousal engendered by the interest creating incongruity and by the particular meaning analysis that is engendered by the situation.

Value and interest distinctions are also relevant to the frequent use of observation and fixation times to estimate preference, usually with nonverbal subjects. Is fixation (attention) time a good measure of preference between two events? Surely, longer fixation time for event A than for B implies that one prefers to look at A rather than B; but does that mean one would prefer to eat A, or own it, or play with it? Conversely, it is likely that increased interestingness of A over B would produce longer fixation time, but that does not mean that one would prefer A on some dimension other than its interestingness. Visual attention reflects a variety of different kinds of judgments, including good/bad evaluation and interestingness. If one restricts preference to the good/bad global evaluative dimension, then one must be particularly careful about fixation (attention) time, which may be a function of interestingness. Some "bad" things are clearly more interesting than some "good" things, and as a result fixation time would not tell us much about preference. Just consider the observation that gruesome events like automobile accidents seem to evoke rather intense attention and interest. Whereas preference and rejection (or approach and avoidance) are not arrayed on the opposite ends of a single continuum, both of them *are* related to structural (schematic) mappings.

Value and Familiarity

Familiarity—in the common language sense—is obviously involved with judgments of value. In fact, the most obvious and generally accepted notion about value is that we like what we know and are familiar with, that we tend to be suspicious about the new and the unfamiliar. The commonsense notion of familiarity seems to be very close to the notion of schematic congruity. Frequency of prior encounters with a class of events is exactly what we expect to be responsible for the construction of the relevant schema (cf. J. M. Mandler, 1979). Similarly, prior frequency of encounters is what is supposedly at the heart of familiarity. There are two aspects of the notion of familiarity that need to be distinguished, both in terms of their phenomenal differences and as a distinction between underlying processes. The commonsense notion of familiarity implies that there exists a representation (a schema) that "fits" the encoded event. The phenomenal counterpart of that conjunction is the experience of "knowing that" or "having seen (heard, etc.) that before." I refer to this sense of familiarity as familiarity$_1$, which also includes variations in degree of familiarity. The British flag is more familiar to me than that of Belgium; the word "table" seems more familiar than the word "gnu." However, I "know" both flags and both words; they are all familiar$_1$.

In addition to the experience of familiarity, and degrees of familiarity, there exists the experience of recency. The judgment of having recently encountered an event, regardless of its value of familiarity$_1$, is also related to the state of the event's schema. I have suggested previously (Mandler, 1979b, 1980a) that the phenomenal sense of recency is derived from the integration, the compactness, or the clarity of the representation of the event. Repeated encounters increase that integration and give rise to the sense of familiarity embodied in judgments of recency, which I call familiarity$_2$. The distinction is captured in our ability to distinguish recently encountered instances from among familiar groups of objects (such as books, faces, clothes).

The establishment of schemas for particular sets of objects and events is a function of prior exposure to instances of the schematically represented event of object. The judgment of value, as derived from schematic congruity, will therefore depend on the establishment of stable schemas for the class of events that is being judged. Value, in the current primitive sense, should be related to familiarity$_1$.

A relationship between a version of familiarity$_1$ and value has been demonstrated by Zajonc (e.g., 1968) in the so-called exposure effect. The exposure effect shows that, under some circumstances, increasing the sheer exposure to some events increases the probability that they will be "liked." Given that schemas probably need hundreds of exposures in order to be stably established, it is not surprising that exposure effects typically have not been demonstrated for familiar objects but rather with unfamiliar objects such as Turkish words and abstract paintings that activate few existing schemas (expectations). In general, however, it is important to note that the effect interacts with the pre-exposure status of the judged objects. If events are rated positively prior to additional exposures, subsequent presentations increase their positive evaluation. If however they are not "liked" during the initial judgments, then increasing exposure *increases the negative evaluation* (Brickman, Redfield, Harrison & Crandall, 1972; Mandler & Shebo, 1981). In terms of schema theory, I assume that objects that are liked originally have achieved some degree of schematic congruity, and further exposures increase the schematic "fit." For objects that are initially not liked, there does not exist a schema that is congruous with the evidence presented in the test objects. In that case the initial incongruity is only accentuated by repeated exposures to the incongruous event. Several of the experimental attempts to deal with this phenomenon are marred by a confusion between structural valuation and acquired predication (Burgess & Sales, 1971; Perlman & Oskamp, 1971; Zajonc, Markus, & Wilson, 1974). It seems at least premature to assume that the evaluative effects of repeated exposures are directly comparable with labeling an event as negative or positive (either by providing a label or by pairing it with a culturally defined positive or negative event).[14]

On the other hand, the typical recognition experiment in which individuals are asked whether a particular event is something that they have recently encountered requires judgments of incremental familiarity (i.e., familiarity$_2$). The recognition of recent occurrence, as distinct from the recognition of "knowing" the object at all, is based on an evaluation of recent renewed integration of the target event (see Mandler, 1980a; Mandler, Goodman, & Wilkes–Gibbs, 1982). It is also not surprising that judgments of prior frequency of exposure (that are proba-

---

[14]Prior exposure affects schemas, which in turn may determine preference, but there need not be a unique relationship between exposure and positive affect (Zajonc, 1980). Other effects of prior exposure have been shown, for example, by Hasher, Goldstein, and Toppino (1977) and Bacon (1979), who demonstrated that repeated exposure to simple propositional statements increases the likelihood that they will be judged as true. Bacon also showed that the association between repetition and belief was mediated by the subjects' judgment (obtained in a recognition test) that the item had been repeated, whether it actually was repeated or not.

bly derived from both familiarity$_1$ and familiarity$_2$), actual prior frequency, and preference (that depends on preexposure familiarity as well as on subsequent exposures) are not highly correlated (Matlin, 1971).

Both kinds of familiarity are properties of the representation of an event; they are context independent. The fact that familiarity experiences are independent of context is illustrated by the well-known phenomenon of "recognizing" a face or a scene without being able to determine where, when, or how we have encountered it before, or knowing who the person is. Based only on information contained within the representation of the event, it is possible to make the familiarity judgments. Other judgments of familiarity may, of course, be based on primarily contextual information. I have discussed elsewhere this elaborative, contextual information and its relation to the integrative context-free information (Mandler, 1980a).

Ceteris Paribus

It is important to repeat that my intent in this chapter has been to address only the analysis of the primitive evaluative cognition based on object and event familiarity. If I have wandered far into the psychological landscape in the course of this exploration, it should not mislead the reader into reading more into the analysis than I have intended. The evaluative actions based on sheer familiarity are both primitive and frequently overlaid by other needs, expectations, and values of the individual. The analysis of the many other evaluative cognitions that determine our affective lives will be needed before we can begin to understand the interactions among these mental events.

I have been primarily interested in the evaluative cognition that arises out of schematic congruity, *all other things being equal*. However, *ceteris* is very rarely *paribus*. Most of our values are complexly determined and overdetermined. We live in a flux of events that constantly changes the schemas that are being activated and used in our intercourse with the world, and that construct our phenomenal world. The value that arises out of familiarity is, in a sense, devoid of meaning; it arises entirely out of the structure of the valued event, not out of its relation to other knowledge. Most of our more complex values are dependent on the "meaning" of the valued object, on its relation to other knowledge and other valued objects and events.

The general proposition that relates increased acquaintance to positive value appears to be counterintuitive. For example, an immediate response to the notion that the old and familiar is positively valued is the thought that such events are typically dull and boring. First, we might note that the dull is not necessarily unvalued; it is certainly uninteresting, but interest and value are different dimensions. Furthermore, the search for knowledge and information instructs our mental life over and beyond the cozy ease of the familiar. For example, I have described in "Mind and Emotion" how the continuing examination of a work of art or music may consistently violate expectations and force us to construct new and instructive views (new accommodations) of the opera, the poem, or the novel.

Once more, I stress the multiplicity of values that enter our daily interactions. Any schema may include structural aspects of people's and events' functions, appearances, and behaviors. Congruity implies that our expectations about such functions and behaviors have been fulfilled. Note, however, that these behaviors themselves may have cognitive value on other grounds. For example, we expect nurses to provide care, conductors to collect our tickets, aggressive colleagues to be nasty. Having adapted to—formed schemas about—these regularities, we expect their functions to be fulfilled. When they are, the world is acceptable—it is as it should be; we have obtained schema congruity and are relatively comfortable with the behavior occurring as we expect it to happen. There may of course be other schemas operating, like not expecting people in general to be aggressive, or not having purchased a ticket for our trip. In general, however, any deviation from these schemas will produce arousal and accommodative pressures. When a nurse is uncaring or aggressive colleagues become kind or supportive, we are faced with incongruity and arousal. What is the likely quality of the affect or emotion that will emerge? That depends on the expectation evoked by other schemas. In the case of the aggressive colleague, caring behavior frequently activates a schema that expects caring; we seek love and affection. We may therefore react positively to the new behavior, but not so in the case of the uncaring nurse, whose unexpected behavior leaves us in a negative evaluative state.

How about the cases where the familiar is apparently unpleasant? The hostile colleague may be familiar—we face him daily. However, there is no net positive value; our valuation is dominated by the negative valuation accorded hostility and aggression. These negative values, quite a different kind than the values based on familiarity, overwhelm the positive valuation engendered by the person's sheer familiarity. Sometimes the positive value due to familiarity emerges despite some competing negative evaluation. Consider an ugly mauve couch that occupied a prominent place in one's parents' living room. Years later, the sight of that couch may well be the occasion for a positive response and subsequent nostalgic musings.

One motivation for the search for the new and for change can be found in the hierarchical character of schematic organizations. Schemas frequently serve as subgoals and subroutines for more general or abstract goals and expectations. A familiar and preferred action may cease to function as an appropriate subgoal for a more general schema and will be abandoned as other more appropriate completions are found for the higher-order expectation (need). The familiar local restaurant may (for example, because of a change of cooks) fail our expectations to have a good meal, or an old, comfortable (and liked) pair of shoes may finally be found to be beyond repair. Under those circumstances we do act in accordance with ''higher'' goals and give up the liked object.

Conversely, why don't we tire of our friends? Given that negative information about people is typically given more weight than is positive information, Rodin (1978) noted that our continued and increased liking of our friends seems paradoxical. She suggested that our continued affection is in part due to the fact that liking and disliking are not arrayed on a single dimension. I would add that, in addition, sheer familiarity would work against the effect of any negative information.

Finally, it is of course not the case that every expectation is the result of a familiar, highly organized schema, though clearly such schemas are the basis of expectations. We frequently construct expectations and predictions of the world, but the congruity between these expectations and the subsequent evidence is not necessarily valued on structural grounds (and the positive value that accrues to congruous—successful—predictions is a somewhat different cognitive evaluation). I may expect it to rain tomorrow, or that a friend will call, or that my favorite soccer team will lose, but these events are not expected on the basis of well-organized schemas that will produce structural value based on familiarity. On the other hand, the concept of interruption—which is independent of the notion of structural value—does apply to these cases, and failures of expectations and predictions do and will frequently occasion arousal and subsequent affect.

SOURCES AND CONSEQUENCES OF EVALUATIVE COGNITIONS

The Development of Value—Cultural and Individual

The cultural, social, and historical aspects of knowledge are carried to a large extent by valuative judgments. The ethnocentric view of other societies and cultures has as one of its origins the fact that green trees, red meat, warm dwellings, and sexual acts are the ''same'' for all people, for all members of the species. Since some of the gross descriptive characteristics of the world seem to be shared by all people, the ethnocentric inference assumes that all characteristics—including the evaluative ones—are so shared. Under that view, cultural/social variation involves a ''choice'' of how to deal with the facts of the world, but there are no fundamental differences in the way the world *can* be perceived. Yes, trees are green, meat is red and nourishing, a temperature of 18° C is more adaptive than 0° C, and some commonality in sexual activity is necessary for procreation. The way green trees are perceived, red meat is ingested, warm houses are experienced, and sexual acts are preferred will depend to a large extent on the structure of the invariants ''given'' by the environment. But how socialization?

we structure the tree, the meat, the house, and the sex act depends on the schema that we acquire for dealing with these "given" concatenations. The distinction made here involves the extremes of the continuum going from primarily descriptive to mainly evaluative functions of schemas; both aspects are driven by the structure of the world and by the structure of the (prepared mind.) The cultural/ social difference that seems ineluctable and so often incommunicable is the internal one—the evaluative outcome of the way common elements are structured in specific ways by individuals in different societies and groups. The "input" seems to be the same but the action and thought (and, most important, the accompanying experience) will depend on the way that input is structured (represented) by the experiencing individual. The kinds of relationships available for such structuring depend on the cultural–social experience of the person, on the "values" that can be and are imposed on the common experience. Thus, within the same culture, but as a result of different social experiences, the evaluative structure of a green tree, a steak, a comfortable house, and a sex object/subject may differ considerably. And that difference will hold beyond ties of common language and common "culture." Much of evaluation is a social phenomenon. Values are therefore not "relative," but rather they are specifically the outcome of the social milieu that structures our experience and produces values. The idiosyncratic variations within generic schemas that determine which particular events will be congruous and which not extends from individuals to social conditions and to cultures.

In discussing the effect of social/cultural milieus we must distinguish between context effects and historical determinants. It has been effectively argued that the action, perception, and thought of the individual are determined to a large extent by the specific context in which the event occurs. That position seems to imply that there are few if any "context free" perceptual, action, or thought structures. However, one can support such a view and still maintain the existence of context-free structures, such as relational schemas that determine simple values. The history of the individual in the social context determines what features and relationships are "allowed" to enter into evaluative structures. Thus, a judgment of value may be context free, but the kinds of such judgments that are possible for the individual are determined by his/her historical experience (or context).

The schemas that determine whether an event is positively valued or not are a function of individual histories. These histories, in turn, are determined by the social milieu that structures our world and by the expectations that we learn to impose on it. The development of these schemas can be studied in a variety of psychological and social contexts; it can be seen in the schematic representation of the memory abilities of young infants. Extensive research over the past 25 years has used differential looking and habituation techniques to demonstrate infants' ability to discriminate between new and old events (see Werner & Perlmutter, 1979, for a review). Sheer presentation of shapes and colors generates internal representations (or schemas) of the event. While the performance of adults and infants on recognition tests is inferred from different kinds of tasks, the underlying process is likely to be the same. Thus, the adult's response of "old" and "new" and the infant's differential fixation of old and new stimuli is based on the same activation of existing schemas, and on the assimilative relationship between the presented object and a previously stored representation.

Value and Consciousness

I suggested earlier, following Marcel, that consciousness involves an attempt to make phenomenal sense out of as much available data as possible. What is constructed in consciousness is a "functionally useful" structural representation that is in keeping with the available data as well as with the task at hand. In fact, one cannot make a distinction between available data and the demands of the task. The latter are just as much "available evidence" as is the sensory interaction with the physical evidence from the environment. We are—as Marcel notes—usually conscious of a construction from that involves the contribution from two or more underlying processes, an insight in keeping with Wolfgang Köhler's observation (1929) that we are not aware of constituent sensory elements but rather of perceptual units (wholes). Similar suggestions have appeared elsewhere. Broadbent (in press), for example, cites Flint (1979) to note that it is "not perceptual awareness . . . which is conscious; it is the process of going from the percept to the cognitive structure." I have previously suggested the importance of consciousness in choice and comparison processes and in reducing a world that is full of too many things to manageable phenomenal proportions that provide "short-hand" access to complex underlying processes.

Instructions, sets, and other "top down" processes that set into motion a requirement for different kinds of structures to be available in the conscious state interact with other evidence available to the mental system. Just as we are not continuously "conscious" of the fact that a table is a piece of furniture or a hamburger a meat dish unless a suggestion (such as these words) or request induces the constructions of the appropriate conscious state, so are we not necessarily aware of the possible valuative aspect of an event unless some internal or external event requires such a judgment. Schematic congruity is potentially available to make its contribution to such a judgment whenever it is situationally required or "functionally useful."

Value, Affect, and Consciousness

Finally, we turn to the construction of the unitary experience of emotion. I argue that the major processes that contribute to that particular conscious structure are peripheral autonomic arousal and evaluative cognitions. Just as value is a construction derived from the demands of the world on our expectations (schemas), so is conscious emotion constructed from value (in the broadest sense) and from the evidence of ANS feedback. Under some conditions the two component processes—cognition and arousal—may well be experienced as phenomenally distinct. The specification of the conditions under which value and ANS combine to form emotional experiences would take us far beyond the intent of this chapter. Evaluative cognitions include simple positive and negative values and a variety of other evaluations such as sexual attraction, harm doing and harm receiving, loss of loved ones, self enhancement, and many others. Emotional experiences are constructed from these valuations and ANS arousal to form a unitary experience, variously called love, fear, hostility, ecstasy, grief, and so forth.

There is one set of very primitive evaluative actions that deserves special attention—the evaluative signaling found in facial expressions. Most facial "expressions" are evaluative communications. They are early ones from an evolutionary point of view, and it is reasonable to believe that early human (and animal) communication dealt with value rather than with descriptive acts. The structure of facial communications is the basic evaluative/semantic structure of expressive communication (Ekman, 1977). Since all emotional experiences consist in part of evaluative components, and since it is primarily the evaluative aspect (not the arousal) that is visible or audible to the observer, we make the inductive leap that whenever we see or hear an evaluative expression we are in the presence of an emotional event. That is probably the source of the deeply held belief that facial expressions "express" emotions. It is not surprising that—given the evaluative nature of facial expressions—we ascribe emotional content to them. And it is similarly not surprising that evaluative expressions in other languages—verbal and gestural among them—are also seen as expressions of emotion or affect. We see the evaluative action and we infer the emotional experience behind it, despite the fact that we well know that value can be expressed without the phenomenal emotion. I believe that this particular configuration, as in the case of facial expressions and of statements of preference, is at the root of the confusion between value and affect. Affect involves value but to be phenomenally valid it requires more than that—namely arousal. We can, therefore, without violating either experience or theory, be content with an analysis of value and preference in cognitive terms.

CODA

Zuleika Dobson did not know much about music but she "knew what she liked." I have argued that she would not only know what she liked because she could construct the conscious state of positive valuation, but also that her liking was solidly based on her knowledge of her world. It is the structure of that knowledge that makes it possible for us to like things without knowing why it is that we like them. We not only know what we like but we also like what we know. Our values are structured by our past history, by the society that prescribes certain experiences and certain combinations (structures) of events. In that sense there is no accounting for taste—it is both phenomenally obvious and frequently publicly indefensible. But we can account for the existence and the structure of taste. Value, taste, and beauty are in the mind of the beholder as it structures the world and is structured by it.

ACKNOWLEDGMENTS

Preparation of this chapter was supported in part by National Science Foundation Grant BNS 79–15336. I am deeply grateful to William Kessen, Jean Mandler, and Andrew Ortony for extensive comments on an early draft of this chapter. Their comments are largely responsible for improving the structure of my argument, though only I can be responsible for residual failures. I also thank the members of my seminar on emotion for their critical and constructive reactions to the initial presentation of this chapter.

REFERENCES

Arnheim, R. *Art and visual perception: A psychology of the creative eye—The new version.* Berkeley: University of California Press, 1974.

Arnold, M. B. *Emotion and personality* (Vols. I & II). New York: Columbia University Press, 1960.

Bacon, F. T. Credibility of repeated statements: Memory for trivia. *Journal of Experimental Psychology: Human Learning and Memory,* 1979, *5,* 241–252.

Berlyne, D. E. *Conflict, arousal and curiosity.* New York: McGraw-Hill, 1960.

Berlyne, D. E. *Structure and direction in thinking.* New York: Wiley, 1965.

Berlyne, D. E. *Aesthetics and psychobiology.* New York: Appleton–Century–Crofts, 1971.

Berlyne, D. E. The vicissitudes of aplopathematic and thelematoscopic pneumatology (or The hydrography of hedonism). In D. E. Berlyne & K. B. Madsen (Eds.), *Pleasure, reward, preference.* New York: Academic press, 1973.

Brickman, P., Redfield, J., Harrison, A. A., & Crandall, R. Drive and predisposition as factors in the attitudinal effects of mere exposure. *Journal of Experimental Social Psychology,* 1972, *8,* 31–44.

Broadbent, D. E. From the percept to the cognitive structure. In A. D. Baddeley & J. Long (Eds.), *Attention and performance* IX. Hillsdale, N. J.: Lawrence Erlbaum Associates, in press.

Burgess, T. D. G., II, & Sales, S. M. Attitudinal effects of ''mere exposure'': a reevaluation. *Journal of Experimental Social Psychology,* 1971, *7,* 461–472.

Dion, K., Berscheid, E., & Walster, E. What is beautiful is good. *Journal of Personality and Social Psychology,* 1972, *24,* 285–290.

Ekman, P. Biological and cultural contributions to body and facial movement. In J. Blacking (Ed.), *Anthropology of the body.* London: Academic Press, 1977.

Flint, C. R. *The role of consciousness in memory.* Unpublished doctoral dissertation. Oxford University, 1979.

Fowler, C. A., Wolford, G., Slade, R., & Tassinary, L. Lexical access with and without awareness. *Journal of Experimental Psychology: General,* 1981, *110,* 341–362.

Franks, J. J., & Bransford, J. D. Abstraction of visual patterns. *Journal of Experimental Psychology,* 1971, *90,* 65–74.

Garner, W. R. *Uncertainty and structure as psychological concepts.* New York: Wiley, 1962.

Hasher, L., Goldstein, D., & Toppino, T. Frequency and the conference of referential validity. *Journal of Verbal Learning and Verbal Behavior*, 1977, *16*, 107–112.

Helson, H. *Adaptation level theory*. New York: Harper & Row, 1964.

Intraub, H. Identification and processing of briefly glimpsed visual scenes. In D. F. Fisher, R. A. Monty, & J. W. Senders (Eds.), *Eye movements: Cognition and visual perception*. Hillsdale, N. J.: Lawrence Erlbaum Associates, 1981.

Kahneman, D., & Tversky, A. Prospect theory: An analysis of decision under risk. *Econometrica*, 1979, *47*, 263–291.

Kim, M. P., & Rosenberg, S. Comparison of two structural models of implicit personality theory. *Journal of Personality and Social Psychology*, 1980, *38*, 375–389.

Köhler, W. *Gestalt psychology*. New York: Liveright, 1929.

Köhler, W. *The place of value in a world of facts*. New York: Liveright, 1938.

Lazarus, R. S. A cognitivist's reply to Zajonc on emotion and cognition. *American Psychologist*, 1981, *36*, 222–223.

Lazarus, R. S., Averill, J. R., & Opton, E. M. Jr. Toward a cognitive theory of emotion. In M. B. Arnold (Ed.), *Feeling and emotion*. New York: Academic Press, 1970.

Luce, R. D. *Individual choice behavior*. New York: Wiley, 1959.

Mandler, G. The interruption of behavior. In D. Levine (Ed.), *Nebraska Symposium on Motivation: 1964*. Lincoln: University of Nebraska Press, 1964.

Mandler, G. Organization and memory. In K. W. Spence & J. T. Spence (Eds.), *The psychology of learning and motivation: Advances in research and theory* (Vol. I). New York: Academic Press, 1967.

Mandler, G. *Mind and emotion*. New York: Wiley, 1975.

Mandler, G. Thought processes, consciousness, and stress. In V. Hamilton & D. M. Warburton (Eds.), *Human stress and cognition: An information processing approach*. London: Wiley, 1979, (a)

Mandler, G. Organization and repetition: Organizational principles with special reference to rote learning. In L. G. Nilsson (Ed.), *Perspectives on memory research*. Hillsdale, N. J.: Lawrence Erlbaum Associates, 1979. (b)

Mandler, G. Recognizing: The judgment of previous occurrence. *Psychological Review*, 1980, *87*, 252–271. (a)

Mandler, G. The generation of emotion: A psychological theory. In R. Plutchik & H. Kellerman (Eds.), *Theories of emotion*. New York: Academic Press, 1980. (b)

Mandler, G., Goodman, G. O., & Wilkes–Gibbs, D. The word frequency paradox in recognition. *Memory and Cognition*, 1982, *10*, 33–42.

Mandler, G., & Shebo, B. J. *Knowing and liking: An experimental comparison*. Paper presented at the 1981 meeting of the Society of Experimental Psychologists, Eugene, Oregon.

Mandler, J. M. Categorical and schematic organization in memory. In C. R. Puff (Ed.), *Memory organization and structure*. New York: Academic Press, 1979.

Marcel, A. J. Conscious and unconscious perception: I. Experiments on visual masking and word perception. *Cognitive Psychology*, 1982, in press. (a)

Marcel, A. J. Conscious and unconscious perception: II. An approach to consciousness. In preparation, 1982, (b)

Matlin, M. W. Response competition, recognition, and affect. *Journal of Personality and Social Psychology*, 1971, *19*, 295–300.

McClelland, J. L. Networks of interacting processors as models of perception and memory. Unpublished manuscript, 1981.

McClelland, J. L. & Rumelhart, D. E. An interactive activation model of context effects in letter perception: Part I. An account of basic findings. *Psychological Review*, 1981, *88*, 375–407.

Meyer, L. B. *Emotion and meaning in music*. Chicago: University of Chicago Press, 1956.

Miller, G. A., Galanter, E. H., & Pribram, K. *Plans and the structure of behavior*. New York: Holt, 1960.

Morton, J. Interaction of information in word recognition. *Psychological Review*, 1969, *76*, 165–178.

Osgood, C. E. The cross-cultural generality of visual–verbal synesthetic tendencies. *Behavioral Science*, 1960, *5*, 146–169.

Osgood, C. E., May, W. H., & Miron, M. S. *Cross-cultural universals of affective meaning*. Urbana: University of Illinois Press, 1975.

Osgood, C. E., Suci, G. J., & Tannenbaum, P. H. *The measurement of meaning*. Urbana: University of Illinois Press, 1957.

Parker, R. E. *The encoding of information in complex pictures*. Unpublished doctoral dissertation. University of California, San Diego, 1977.

Perlman, D., & Oskamp, S. The effects of picture content and exposure frequency on evaluation of negroes and whites. *Journal of Experimental Social Psychology*, 1971, *7*, 503–514.

Perry, R. B. *General theory of value; Its meaning and basic principles construed in terms of interest*. Cambridge: Harvard University Press, 1926.

Piaget, J. *The origin of intelligence in the child*. London: Routledge & Kegan Paul, 1953.

Piaget, J. Piaget's theory. In P. Mussen (Ed.), *Carmichael's manual of child psychology* (Vol. 1, 3rd ed.). New York: Wiley, 1970.

Posner, M. I., and Boies, S.W. Components of attention. *Psychological Review*, 1971, *78*, 391–408.

Posner, M. I., & Snyder, C. R. R. Attention and cognitive control. In R. L. Solso (Ed.), *Information processing and cognition: The Loyola symposium*. Hillsdale, N. J.: Lawrence Erlbaum Associates, 1975.

Rodin, M. J. Liking and disliking: Sketch of an alternative view. *Personality and Social Psychology Bulletin*, 1978, *4*, 473–478.

Rosch, E. Principles of categorization. In E. Rosch & B. B. Loyd (Eds.), *Cognition and categorization*. Hillsdale, N. J.: Lawrence Erlbaum Associates, 1978.

Rosch, E., & Mervis, C. Family resemblances: Studies in the internal structure of categories. *Cognitive Psychology*, 1975, *7*, 573–605.

Rumelhart, D. E., & Ortony, A. The representation of knowledge in memory. In R. C. Anderson, R. J. Spiro, & W. E. Montague (Eds.), *Schooling and the acquisition of knowledge*. Hillsdale, N. J.: Lawrence Erlbaum Associates, 1978.

Sheinkopf, S. *A comparative study of the affective judgments made by anomic aphasics and normals on a nonverbal task*. Unpublished doctoral dissertation, Boston University, 1970.

Treisman, A. M., & Gelade, G. A feature-integration theory of attention. *Cognitive Psychology*, 1980, *12*, 97–136.

Warrington, E. K. The selective impairment of semantic memory. *Quarterly Journal of Experimental Psychology*, 1975, *27*, 635–657.

Werner, J. S., & Perlmutter, M. Development of visual memory in infants. In H. W. Reese and L. P. Lipsitt (Eds.), *Advances in child development and behavior* (Vol. 14). New York: Academic Press, 1979.

Wierzbicka, A. Emotions. In A. Wierzbicka, *Semantic primitives*. Frankfurt: Athenäum, 1972.

Wundt, W. *Grundriss der Psychologie*. Leipzig: Wilhelm Engelmann, 1905.

Zajonc, R. B. Attitudinal effects of mere exposure. *Journal of Personality and Social Psychology Monograph*, 1968, *9*(2, Part 2, 1–28).

Zajonc, R. B. Feeling and thinking: Preferences need no inferences. *American Psychologist*, 1980, *35*, 151–175.

Zajonc, R. B., Markus, H., & Wilson, W. R. Exposure effects and associative learning. *Journal of Experimental Social Psychology*, 1974, *10*, 248–263.

Ziff, P. *Semantic analysis*. Ithaca, N. Y.: Cornell University Press, 1960.

2 Attraction and Emotion in Interpersonal Relations

Ellen Berscheid
University of Minnesota

Social psychologists interested in unraveling the mysteries of interpersonal attraction have rarely turned to theory and research on emotion for inspiration and aid (see Berscheid, in press-b). This is true despite the fact that the subject of interpersonal attraction is commonly defined as the study of how people "affectively respond" to one another. This chapter first addresses the question of why this is so, or how it is that interpersonal attraction investigators have managed to almost wholly avoid the subject of emotion despite the fact that virtually all would agree with John Bowlby (1973) that: "affectional bonds [between people] and subjective states of emotion go together" and "many of the most intense of our human emotions arise during the formation, the maintenance, the disruption, and the renewal of affectional bonds [p. 40]."

The neglect of emotion within the interpersonal attraction area is worthy of some discussion because it is, for one thing, a curiosity—a curiosity that newcomers to the social psychology of interpersonal attraction do not understand, and laypersons, who turn to us for an understanding of the affective phenomena that occur in their own personal relationships, most certainly do not understand. But for another thing, and perhaps most importantly, those of us interested in interpersonal attraction have a great deal of conceptual work to do on the construct of "attraction." This has become painfully apparent as more and more of us turn to the investigation of attraction phenomena as they occur in their natural context, that is, in ongoing relationships with past histories and anticipated futures. In this conceptual work, the emotion theorists have a great deal to offer us. As illustration, this chapter also briefly discusses how the application (see Berscheid, in press-a) of one general framework for viewing emotional phenomena, namely, George Mandler's (1975), illuminates some of the puzzles and paradoxes of emotional phenomena as they occur in close relationships—puzzles and paradoxes that interpersonal attraction researchers have had a great deal of trouble thinking about, let alone doing anything with empirically.

But before we can really get very far in the conceptual work that needs to be done to understand people's affective responses to one another, and before we can take full advantage of new theoretical approaches to the problems of interpersonal attraction, the ghosts of the past that continue to haunt the way we think about affective phenomena in social relationships must be exorcised. This exorcism requires, I believe, that we retrace our steps in order to reach some understanding of how the psychology of interpersonal attraction arrived at its present emotionless—and, I argue, relatively affectless—state.

The Traditional Conceptualization of "Attraction" and Some of its Consequences

Thus, the first question to be answered about this curious state of affairs is "Who performed the frontal lobotomy on interpersonal attraction?" The villain in the piece can be fingered very quickly: It is the traditional construct of "attitude"— our most honored and revered construct. As Allport (1954) said, and all introductory social psychology texts continue to maintain, it is "the most distinctive and indispensable concept in contemporary American social psychology [p. 43]." "Attitude," of course, has been the "construct of choice" of social psychologists for decades; no matter what the problem of interest, it has been likely to have been conceptualized as a problem of attitude.

Interpersonal attraction has proved to be no exception to the rule; the construct of interpersonal attraction has been wholly identified with the construct of attitude as is apparent in all surveys of the way in which attraction has been conceived. Such statements as that by Berscheid and Walster (1978): "almost all theorists agree that interpersonal attraction is a positive or negative attitude toward another person [p. 1]," and Huston and Levinger's (1978), in their recent *Annual Review* article, that: "interpersonal attraction, as defined by social psychologists, refers to . . . attitudinal positivity [p. 1]" are typical. And, unfortunately, after saying that attraction is a positive or negative "attitude" toward another, few of us have felt it necessary to say anything more. Having quickly disposed of the problem of conceptualizing attraction to everyone's apparent satisfaction, we have serenely gone about our empirical business.

But that business now shows the deep and, I think, rather bizarre imprint of our marriage to the attitude construct—for in allying ourselves with that construct, we have unquestioningly accepted the many assumptions that go along with it. These assumptions, we now belatedly realize, appeared only in the fine print of our contract with the attitude construct, and some did not explicitly appear at all.

Some of these assumptions, and what I believe their impact has been upon our current state of knowledge of interpersonal attraction, are outlined below. In bringing these assumptions forth for inspection, I am mindful that the attitude construct is currently in trouble and that various salvage operations and the construction of revisionist and even neorevisionist attitudinal formulations are proceeding apace (Ajzen & Fishbein, 1980; Fishbein & Ajzen, 1975). That is all to the good no doubt (although the hardhearted among us might say it's time we just threw the rascal out), and it may be that the thrashings and groans we hear from the attitude area signify rebirth rather than death. But in any event, these new formulations have yet to make any real inroads in attraction research. More importantly, many of the assumptions that underly the construct of attitude have acquired a life of their own and are thriving, not only in the attraction area, but also, one suspects, in the new social cognitive area as well.

The first of the many assumptions carried by the attitude construct has to do with constancy and stability. Katz and Stotland (1959) have argued, for example, that the concept of attitude has endured because: "the practical need for taking account of behavior does call for some stability and for some identifiable affective–cognitive elements which can be related to social behavior and to social situations. Hence, the concept of attitude is introduced to allow for the fact that cognitive and affective organization can achieve stability and some degree of constancy [p. 428]."

Second, "attitude" has traditionally been conceived as having three conceptually distinct components; namely, that infamous trio, cognition, affection, and conation. The "cognitive" component has referred to the ideas or beliefs held about Person X, the object of the attitude; the "affective" component has referred to the emotions and feelings experienced in association with the object of the attitude; and the "behavioral" component has referred to the actions (or "action tendencies") that are directed toward Person X (see Oskamp, 1977, p. 10).

In recent years, however, and as Oskamp (1977) points out, some theorists have questioned whether the distinction is worthwhile (McGuire, 1969), and many have resolved the question by simply focusing upon the "affective" or "evaluative" aspect of attitude (Fishbein & Ajzen, 1972). Thus, it has been the predisposition to respond in a "favorable" or "unfavorable" way toward the object of the attitude that has been increasingly stressed in attitude theory and research. This is also the component that has been stressed in the conception of attraction as an attitude, or as "a favorable or unfavorable predisposition to respond to another."

A third assumption, as these definitional statements imply, is that one's attitude toward Person X, or one's attraction toward another, is either favorable *or* it is unfavorable—it is one or the other (or somewhere in between on this dimension, for example, "neutral").

Fourth, this last assumption combined with the first implies that this favorable (or unfavorable) attitude, or response disposition, toward Person X is relatively stable across time and situations.

And, fifth, because affect has been conceptually separated out from certain thoughts about Person X (especially from beliefs about the properties possessed by X), and separated out, too, from actions or "behavioral intentions" directed toward X, the construct of attitude carries the implication that these beliefs and actions may be profitably conceived as "affectless" in themselves. In practice, however, it has carried a somewhat different implication; that is, it is commonly recognized that beliefs are often affectively tinged (that, for example, the properties believed to be possessed by X have positive or negative "affective loadings") and that actions similarly are often affectively colored. But where do cognitions and actions then get their affective quality? The only answer seems to be: "From spending a lot of time hanging around their comrade, the 'affective component,' in that stable mental conglomerate called 'attitude toward X' (or in that little cognitive storage bin that has X's name on it)." But wherever they get their affective color, the fifth assumption the construct of attitude has carried is that the favorability of beliefs about Person X, the positivity of the emotions and feelings experienced in association with X, and the favorability of the actions directed toward X are generally of *one* single affective quality—favorable or unfavorable.

If anyone doubts that this has been the interpretation of the attitude construct by social psychologists investigating interpersonal attraction, one need only look at the history of research on the determinants of affiliation—or the determinants of an individual's attempt to place himself in close physical proximity to another or otherwise attempt to interact with another. Until only very recently, an isomorphism has been assumed between attraction and affiliation; that is, attraction, or liking another, has been traditionally conceived as both necessary and sufficient for affiliation to occur (see Berscheid, in press-b). It has only been with some reluctance that we've recognized that our subjects in attraction experiments are very much like ourselves in that they spend time, often a lot of time, attempting to interact with people they basically don't like very much and, conversely, frequently won't walk across the street to see someone they *do* like.

Sixth, this last assumption of affective harmony in the "attitude toward X" kingdom rests upon another, and that is that the determinants of the affective quality of beliefs about another are identical (or overlap importantly) with the determinants of the affective quality of the emotions that other precipitates, and these, in turn, overlap importantly with the determinants of the affective quality of the actions we direct toward the other (for example, whether we attempt to approach or avoid them). And so, the inevitable conclusion has been that to determine the nature of the affective component of the attitude, to determine whether the disposition toward X is favorable or unfavorable, it matters little which of the three components—beliefs, emotions, or actions toward X—we focus upon.

How a thing is measured depends on how it is conceived. Because it is the so-called "affective component" of the attitude toward Person X that is of interest, attraction is customarily measured on a simple bipolar scale where the respondent is asked "How much do you like X?" and instructed to respond on a dimension ranging from, say, "+3," or "Like Very Much," to "−3," "Dislike Very Much." This is commonly called an "affective appraisal." Another measure that is sometimes used as a substitute for this, or used in conjunction with it, is one where the respondent is asked to indicate his or her beliefs concerning Person X's properties (that is, the respondent is asked "How 'kind' [or 'industrious' or other adjective] is X?"), and then the known "affective loadings" of the properties ascribed to X (many of which have been determined by Anderson, 1968) are toted up or combined in some manner to arrive at the "affective value" of X to the respondent. These are also commonly called "affective appraisals," or sometimes "cognitive appraisals," or even sometimes "cognitive affective" appraisals. Thus having determined the respondent's "attitude" toward X, or at least the nature of the affective component, we now know a great deal about the respondent's cognitions about X, his or her emotions and feelings toward X, and his or her actions toward X—or so the traditional attitude construct has led us to believe.

And, indeed, such measures have seemed to serve perfectly fine for over two decades of attraction research. But to understand why they have seemed perfectly fine one also has to understand something about the nature of the social relationship that typically exists between the respondent and Person X for whom the affective appraisal is obtained. Specifically, one has to recognize that Person X—including his or her dispositional properties and other qualities—is *personally irrelevant* to the respondent; that is, Person X is irrelevant to the respondent's welfare, is irrelevant to the future satisfaction or deprivation of his or her needs, is irrelevant to the fulfillment of his or her plans and goals. In sum, Person X is irrelevant to the respondent's life. Person X is irrelevant because he or she does not and never did exist (that is, the person who is "kind" and "industrious" is clearly a figment of the experimenter's imagination); is irrelevant because the person does exist (and respondents know *that* for sure because they have before them a photo, perhaps of a certain level of physical attractiveness), but they do not know the person's name and, in fact, are assured that the person exists thousands of miles away and is unlikely to ever be encountered; is irrelevant because Person X does exist and is there in the flesh (or at least is reflected on a video screen), but the respondent knows that he or she has never encountered the person before, and, as soon as the questionnaire is completed and the two points or two dollars are secured, he or she is unlikely to ever encounter the person again.

According to Huston and Levinger's (1978) recent review of the attraction literature, such persons, whom I have labeled "personally irrelevant," constitute the stimuli for over 80% of all the affective appraisals made in interpersonal attraction research. We know, then, a good deal about the determinants of such so-called affective appraisals toward personally irrelevant people and at least some of the behaviors to which they seem to be predictive. And, generally, those behaviors *are* of the congruent affective quality we expect; that is, people tend to say that they would prefer to work with the "kind" and "industrious" person on some unknown future task, and so on.

Now all this seems perfectly fine until armed with this knowledge about interpersonal attraction, we venture out of the soft twilight of the laboratory into naturalistic settings—until we turn to look at affective phenomena as they occur in the context of ongoing relationships. What we see there is not perfectly fine; it is perfectly dreadful to anyone weaned on the attitude construct, for it is nothing we were led to expect by our assumptions of affective harmony and stability in "attitude toward X."

What we see is people who love each other (or at least they say so, on their bipolar affective appraisals) literally beating each other about the head and shoulders, as those who investigate family violence are documenting (Straus & Hotaling, 1980). We see people experiencing the most intense positive emotion in association with persons whom they indicate, on the ubiquitous "kind" and "industrious" adjective checklist, to be neither "kind" nor "industrious," but rather thoroughly unreliable scoundrels, and, conversely, we see persons giving the most glowing appraisals to a person they have just decided to dump in the divorce court—"a prince of a fellow," she says, "but I no longer wish to associate with him." We see people approaching and maintaining contact with others whom they *say* they despise and with whom, we observe, they experience emotions that are predominantly negative in quality. We see people, curiously enough, terminating relationships with another *not* because they experience negative emotions in association with the other, but rather because they experience no emotion at all—that is, we see some people regarding the absence of emotion as a bad thing and the occurrence of even negative emotion as a good thing, signifying that the relationship is alive and vital. That's what we *see*.

And what we *hear* is people asking a lot of questions about all this: "How can you love someone and hate them at the same time?"; "How can I be so much 'in love' with someone I really can't stand?"; "I like her so much, why can't I fall in love with her?"; "Why do I always wind up behaving badly toward the people I love?," and so on and on.

What we see and what we hear, in short, is a dazzling mixture of affective tones associated with the responses directed toward, precipitated by, or otherwise associated with Person X; that is, that diverse (and in the case of close relationships—voluminous) domain of an individual's behavior that has X as its principal referent appears to be not of *one* homogeneous affective tone, favorable *or* unfavorable; it is of many. The thoughts, beliefs, emotions, and actions—centered around X—frequently appear to be affectively heterogeneous, even at a single point in time and certainly across time.

And so, as one turns from examining affective phenomena as they occur in naturalistic settings, the focus radically changes from accounting for stability and constancy in affective behaviors toward X to accounting for instability and inconstancy. And this, I suspect, is no accident. Because as we turn from the laboratory to naturalistic settings, we turn from trying to understand the affective quality of behaviors directed toward irrelevant persons to those that are directed toward *personally relevant* persons; such stimulus persons are relevant in that their properties and their behavior often determine whether the respondent shall eat tomorrow or not, keep a job or lose it, and sometimes even whether he or she shall live or die. They are relevant to the respondent's personal survival and welfare.

And this is interesting because if there is one thing on which the emotion theorists have spoken with one voice and consistently emphasized through the years since Darwin, it is that one's affective reaction to another depends importantly, if not exclusively, on the implications that the other is perceived to have for "*my* personal survival and *my* welfare"—for *my* needs, *my* goals, and *my* plans (see Plutchik & Kellerman, 1980, for a review of some contemporary theories of emotion); that is, the emotion theorists remind us that this is the very *source* of our affective reactions to other people and objects.

The emotion theorists remind us of something else, and that is that our responses to our physical and social environments virtually *always* have an affective quality, as is illustrated by the results of studies that have examined the dimensions that underly our symbolic representations of people and objects in our environment and our interactions with them. As Osgood and his associates (Osgood, Suci, & Tannenbaum, 1957) have amply documented, the evaluative or "good/bad" factor appears to be the theme of all human languages, or, as they (Osgood, May, & Miron, 1975) say: "We humans are still animals at base. What is important to us now, as it was back in the age of Neanderthal man, about the sign of a thing, is, first, does it refer to something *good* or *bad* for me (is it an antelope or a saber-toothed tiger)?"

That statement, however, does not exhaust the possibilities: Person X may be "good for me" or "bad for me" or he or she may be "irrelevant" to me. And if they are irrelevant to me, then they probably don't have much affective value to me. And so, on any kind of affective dimension they should fall somewhere in the "neutral" middle. Further, as long as they *stay* irrelevant to me, they should also stay fairly constantly in the neutral middle.

Some Conclusions for the Investigation of Interpersonal Attraction

This analysis of the traditional mode of conceptualizing and investigating interpersonal attraction leads to several conclusions:

First, irony of ironies, one may conclude that the study of people's affective responses toward each other primarily has been undertaken in settings in which the responses examined have been almost wholly severed from their affective

roots. If one believes that the affective nature of the responses that are precipitated by, associated with, or directed toward another have their primary source in
the implications that other (e.g., their properties or behaviors) is perceived to
have for the individual's welfare and survival, then one doesn't exclusively study
the determinants of the affective quality of those responses in settings in which
the stimulus person is personally irrelevant to the individual and which, then,
probably prompt responses of neutral affective quality.

Second, if one believes that the affective quality of responses toward another
are rooted in the way in which the stimulus person's properties interlock with the
individual's needs, plans, and goals, then one immediately suspects that the
stability or instability of an individual's affective behavior toward another very
much depends on whether the other person's relevance to these needs, goals, and
plans changes, and that when the interlock changes the affective reaction changes
also. One also immediately suspects, then, that changes in affective reaction to
another tend to occur primarily for two reasons: (1) Either the properties of
Person X have changed (e.g., new information has been received about X that
revises or adds to the old, thereby changing the way in which X interlocks with
current needs and plans); or, (2) all that information in the "storage bin" marked
X may stay precisely the same, but the needs and plans have changed, and thus
the way in which X interlocks with them has changed. (This last is illustrated by
the common answer to the old plaint "What did I do to cause your feelings about
me to change?," which is "You didn't do anything; it's not *you,* it's me"—or,
more bluntly put, "My plans changed and now you're irrelevant." Ellis and
Harper's (1961) "rational emotive" therapy, it might be mentioned, seems to be
partially based on this general principle, for a negative affective charge to another is often modified by leading the individual to see that the other person is
really quite irrelevant to their safety and welfare.) If this analysis is correct, then
the affective quality of all those things in the "Person X cognitive bin" are likely
to stay stable only if: X stays the same; the individual's needs and plans stay the
same; both change in tandem, thereby preserving the interlock; or X is irrelevant
and remains irrelevant, to these.

Third, because X is rarely irrelevant to these needs and plans in ongoing
relationships, especially close relationships (since these people are virtually by
definition personally relevant), and because people's needs and plans change
over time and the properties of the other person also often change, we probably
shouldn't *expect* affective stability and constancy in behavior toward X over time
in relationships in naturalistic settings.

Neither should we expect affective harmony among behaviors directed toward, precipitated by, or associated with Person X at even a single point in time
in such settings. The answer to the question of "good for me" or "bad for me"
depends on the answers to another, and that is "good for what?" or "bad for
what?" And the answers to those may be that X is good for some things and bad

for others. Person X, for example, may be "industrious" and that property may be good for some of my plans and bad for others. It seems doubtful, in other words, that that particular piece of information about X has one "affective loading" for me; rather, it may have many. And that trait "industrious" is especially unlikely to carry the same affective loading across stimulus persons; "industrious" is a very *good* property for my secretary to have and a very *bad* property for my Internal Revenue Service auditor to possess. It is hard to know, then, where these "abstract" affective loadings of traits really come from and what they mean.

Fourth, one may conclude that turning our attention to personally relevant stimuli, and thus to questions of the instability and inconstancy of the affective reactions such people seem to prompt, is not a bad thing for us to do; that is, if we believe, as Kurt Lewin did, that the best way to understand the dynamics of something is when it is moving and changing, then we shouldn't restrict ourselves to situations in which it is guaranteed to remain static and stable—or restrict ourselves to constructs that presume such stability.

Finally, one suspects that it is misleading to talk about "affect toward X" as if it were some *thing*—lying like a little lump in a mental storage bin marked "X." One of the most unfortunate legacies of faculty psychology and the traditional construct of attitude is that "affect" is so often used as a noun, not an adjective (as an examination of the way the term *affect* is used in introductory social psychology texts reveals). It seems no more profitable to imply that there is a thing called "affect" than it is to imply that there is a thing called "red." There are red walls, red paint, red light, and red faces; "red" is an adjective, not a noun. Similarly, there are "affective" behaviors and events in the sense that they can be placed on a good/bad continuum or are perceived by the individual (or an observer) to have the quality of goodness or badness; that is, there are behaviors and events (including thoughts, emotions, actions) that, for the individual, are perceived to be good/bad, pleasant/unpleasant, favorable/unfavorable, preferred/nonpreferred, rewarding/punishing, to be approached/avoided, or somewhere in between on these continuums. But because the good/bad dimension appears to permeate *all* our transactions with the environment, one suspects that the class of "nonaffective behavior" may be relatively empty, and thus to even speak of "affective behavior" may not be very useful. It may also be misleading, because the faithful modification of the word "behavior" with the adjective "affective" implies that such distinction is necessary—that we importantly need to distinguish "affective behavior" from "nonaffective" behavior (which, worse, usually gets translated as being "cognitive behavior," following the traditional distinction between these). Of course, if by "nonaffective" behavior we mean to distinguish behavior that falls in the middle of the good/bad continuum, or is affectively "neutral," from behavior falling at the extremities of the continuum, then we are led to think about the kinds of people and objects that prompt such behavior—which, as has been argued here, are probably personally irrelevant people. But one wants to understand, even then, what determines whether they change to being relevant or whether they stay irrelevant.

In sum, one may conclude that an understanding of interpersonal attraction and its dynamics—perhaps of all affective phenomena—lies in understanding the affective heterogeneity of the behaviors that have Person X as their principle referent. If so, then many of the most interesting questions about social affective phenomena currently lie buried under the assumption that Person X prompts one affective response (or all the responses prompted are of one affective tone).

These questions also lie buried under our use of such bipolar scales as that included on the Locke–Wallace marital-satisfaction scale (Locke & Williamson, 1958), where respondents are instructed that the value of ''+35'' should be reserved for ''those few who experience extreme joy or felicity in marriage'' and ''0'' should be endorsed by ''those few who are very unhappy in marriage.'' And they duly place their checkmark. We *do* ask, more frequently now, what the predictive utility of that checkmark is. And ''not much'' is too often the answer, which is one of the reasons the attitude construct is in trouble. But we don't ask how in the world they managed to place their checkmark in the first place. They always do manage, of course. As Jenkins (in press) has pointed out in his Nebraska Symposium paper, ''Can We Have a Fruitful Cognitive Psychology?''; the ''universal machine'' almost always performs the task set before it.

But how do they do it? Do the respondents have some consensual notion that all marriages are supposed to be happy, and this ''theory'' of theirs helps determine their response? Do they review their history of emotional events in the marriage and, if so, what do they remember? For example, how much do such reviews, if they are made, depend on their mood at the moment, as Bower (1981) and Clark and Isen (in press) suggest? Is it really true, other things being equal (including mood at the moment of response), that affectively positive events are better remembered than negative events, and both of these are better remembered than affectively neutral events as some have argued (Matlin & Stang, 1978)? Or, rather, is it true, as still others have argued, that the personally aversive behaviors of another, such as a spouse, are selectively tracked and remembered better than affectively pleasant behaviors (Weiss, Hops, & Patterson, 1972)? And, if they do review their emotional history, what is their metatheory of emotional events? That they signify nothing—nothing relevant, anyway, to the ''satisfactoriness'' of the partner or of the marriage? (One suspects that the husband who, when his wife pointed out that they had been fighting a lot recently, said, ''Yes, but what does this have to do with our loving each other or the goodness of our marriage'' is not unusual; she apparently had a different metatheory and thought it had something to do with it, for she filed for separation.) Or, do they believe that emotions of *any* kind signify a satisfactory marriage, and no emotion signifies an unsatisfactory one? Or, finally, do their ''affective appraisals'' depend not importantly on their emotional experiences in the relationship at all?

We do not know where these appraisals come from in relationships in which the respondent has voluminous amounts of information about X of varying affective qualities that have been received over some time, often long periods of time, and in relationships in which the *ways* Person X is personally relevant to the respondent has also probably changed in that time. It is doubtful, however, that we'll find out looking at so-called affective responses to personally irrelevant people or by making some of the assumptions we've been making.

Emotion in Interpersonal Relationships

I have blamed the identification of the construct of attraction with the construct of attitude for the fact that we have proceeded as we have. There is, however, something else—another reason why the social psychology of interpersonal attraction is relatively affectless, and why it glides past the psychology of emotion as two ships in the night. To an outsider, that door in psychology's corridor entitled "The Psychology of Emotion" carries a skull and cross-bone warning for many psychologists that says, "Enter at Your Own Risk." Historically, emotion has had the reputation of being a particularly perilous swamp, where explorers are more likely to be swallowed up than they are to emerge enriched for the experience. This is a shame, for some contemporary emotion theorists have laid down easily traversable highways across the domain and have a great deal to offer those of us interested in interpersonal attraction, especially in affective phenomena in close relationships—the place where I believe the most intense and dramatic of the affective phenomena occur. In particular, George Mandler's framework, as it is outlined in *Mind and Emotion* (1975), seems particularly well-suited to allow one to think about questions of emotion as they occur in relationships. To illustrate, the remainder of this chapter outlines some aspects of an application of Mandler's framework to the problem of emotion in close relationships (Berscheid in press-a).

I do not use the word "emotion" loosely. At the least, the problem of emotion in close relationships should not be confused with the more general problem of understanding the many kinds of affective phenomena that occur in close relationships. For reasons I've just described, the general question of affective behavior in close relationships (or anywhere else) is probably far too broadly formulated for anyone to do anything with. Even paring down the problem to emotion (or to emotional "events") isn't easy, because there is the problem of defining emotion and the amazing variety of referents for that word today. For example, those "affective appraisals" discussed earlier are sometimes called "emotional appraisals" or "feeling appraisals," and any preference for one thing over another (like vanilla over chocolate) is sometimes called an "emotional preference." And even within the emotion literature itself, "feelings" are often tacitly accepted to be "little emotions" (see Candland, 1977), thereby making the presumption that they have the same determinants (but these being more potently in force in the case of emotions and more weakly in the case of feelings). Because I suspect that "feelings" aren't really little emotions (and in this agree with Clark and Isen, in press), I want to make it clear that by "emotion" I mean an event, and an event that is accompanied by a perceived increase in autonomic nervous system arousal in the individual and by that arousal being interpreted by the individual with some sort of emotional label.

Further, by "emotion in a relationship," I mean that some event associated with the partner has precipitated that arousal increase. I, then, am interested in predicting the occurrence of "hot emotion" in close relationships and take it as a given that this prediction does not necessarily depend on such things as the individual's general global appraisal that the other possesses good or bad properties or depend on the affective qualities of the actions the individual has heretofore directed toward the other. Also (and for reasons I've already mentioned), I make no assumptions about the likely effect the occurrence of these emotional events may have upon the affective quality of any future global affective appraisals the individual might make of the other, or upon the affective quality of certain actions they might direct toward them in the future. Undoubtedly, emotional events sometimes enter into these, but I would not now presume to know how.

The aspect of Mandler's framework that makes it so easy to think about the occurrence of emotion in close relationships is his "interruption hypothesis"; that is, if you accept the Schachterian notion that a perceived increase in arousal is necessary for the experience of "hot emotion," if that is accepted as a necessary though not sufficient condition for the occurrence of an emotional event, then it is important to know what kinds of events cause ANS discharge. Mandler theorizes that these are *interruptive* events. And in discussing what it is that may get interrupted for an individual, Mandler importantly highlights the individual's organized behavior sequences and higher-order plans. And suddenly it becomes easy to think about emotion in relationships because the concepts of organized behavior sequences and higher-order plans—specifically, the *meshing* of two people's organized behavior sequences and plans—are integral to the concept of close relationship.

Although the concept of "relationship" between two people has been conceived in many ways, when these definitions are distilled, they all refer to the fact that two persons who are in a relationship with one another have some sort of causal impact on each other's behavior; that is, some events associated with the other (for example, a certain action performed by the other) cause a change in the state of the individual (for example, a change in their physiological state, a change in their cognitive state, and/or a change in their actions). They cause a change from what that state otherwise would have been had the event associated with the other not occurred. The substance of a relationship between two people, then, lies in the causal interconnections between them. A "close" relationship has been conceived (Kelley, Berscheid, Christensen, Harvey, Huston, Levinger,

Peplau, & Peterson, in press) as one in which the causal interconnections between the individual's chain (or series) of behavioral events over time and the other's chain of events over the same time dimension are: (1) *frequent* (e.g., there are many points of causal impact); (2) *strong* (e.g., the impact the other has on the individual is great); (3) *diverse* (e.g., the other has causal impact upon many different kinds of events for the individual). Thus, the closeness of a relationship is conceived to lie in the frequency, strength, and diversity of the causal interconnections between one individual's chain of events over time and another's chain of events.

If the substance of a relationship lies in the causal interconnections that exist between the individual and the other, and if arousal is a necessary condition for the experience of emotion, and if we entertain the proposal that interruption is a sufficient, and possibly necessary, condition for the occurrence of arousal, then it follows that for the individual to experience emotion "within" the relationship, some event in the other's chain must interrupt something in the individual's chain of events.

What is there to be interrupted? Mandler, as noted, calls special attention to the fact that some of the events in the individual's chain are intrachained; that is, they are causally connected to one another. Some of these are "highly organized behavior sequences" that tend to be emitted as a unit; that is, when the first behavior occurs, the rest tend to follow, the behaviors in the sequence show little variation both in their order of occurrence and in their nature from one occasion to another, and they tend to be performed rapidly and automatically. Further, some of the events in the individual's chain are intrachained in that they are part of higher-order plans. It is the interruption of these intrachain behaviors, Mandler hypothesizes, that sets the conditions for the experience of emotion. If so, then a necessary condition for emotion to be experienced within a relationship is that some of the events in the other's chain must be causally connected to intrachain events within the individual's chain—to some of his or her organized behavior sequences and plans, for example.

The existence of between-chain causal connections to intrachain behavior sequences, then, can be hypothesized to be a necessary condition for emotion to occur within the relationship. Such interchain causal connections can be conceived to be necessary, but not sufficient; they are not sufficient because between-chain causal connections to intrachain event sequences are not always interruptive—indeed, they may facilitate and augment the individual's performance of the next events in the sequence. For example, many domestic routines in daily marital life and in other close relationships provide instances where the individual's intrachain behavior sequences could not be performed well, if at all, were it not for the occurrence and appropriate timing of the other person's responses, which help stimulate and make possible the next response in the individual's sequence. Such mundane tasks as getting the kids ready for school, social entertaining, and sexual activities are examples where many intercon-

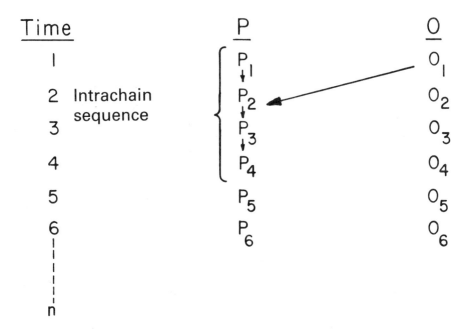

FIG. 2.1.   Illustration of a meshed interchain causal connection to an intrachain event sequence, satisfying a necessary condition for P to experience emotion within the relationship.

nected highly organized behavior sequences may be performed without the slightest interruptive hitch. We would say that the highly organized behavior sequences of the individual and the other are well-*meshed* (see Berscheid, in press-a); that is, each person facilitates and augments the performance of the other's sequences (see Fig. 2.1). Meshed sequences should not be an occasion for emotion in the relationship; as long as they run off without interruption, no increase in arousal should occur, and, thus, a necessary condition for emotional experience is not satisfied.

Sometimes, however, interchain causal connections to intrachain sequences are *nonmeshed,* or disruptive of them; that is, some event in the other's chain prevents the remainder of events in the individual's sequence from occurring, or they distort the strength, the form, or the sequence of the remaining responses (see Fig. 2.2). These nonmeshed interchain causal connections *should* be the occasion for emotion in the relationship.

The extent to which interchain connections to intrachain events exist may be hypothesized to define the extent of the individual's *emotional investment* in the relationship—or his or her *potential* for experiencing hot emotion in the relationship. One may think of an individual's emotional investment in a relationship,

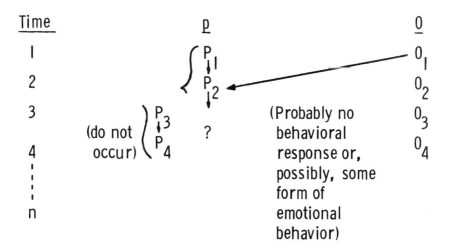

FIG. 2.2.   Illustration of an non-meshed interchain causal connection interrupting an interchain event sequence, thus satisfying a sufficient condition for P to experience emotion within the relationship.

then, as the extent to which that individual is hostage to interruptions from events in the other person's event chain (either events that *do* occur, in the case of nonmeshed interchain causal connections, or events that may *not* occur in the future, in the case of currently meshed interchain causal connections).

The degree to which a person is emotionally invested in a relationship obviously does *not* necessarily correspond to the frequency or intensity of emotion the individual may actually experience in the relationship on a daily basis. If the relationship is characterized by a great number of well-meshed causal interconnections, there should be little occasion for the experience of emotion within the relationship. But the potential for emotion exists—and should the partner die or otherwise no longer facilitate and augment those behavior sequences, they all become *unmeshed,* and the individual is interrupted indeed. Meshed interchain causal connections, then, can be thought of as the hidden ticking emotional bombs in a relationship; they explode when they are severed and when the individual experiences a great deal of interruption in the performance of those behavior sequences and plans.

Rather than further elaborate this conceptual scheme, which is elaborated elsewhere (Berscheid, in press-a), I shall briefly point out some of the demonic paradoxes, puzzles, and conundrums that have traditionally haunted the topic of emotion in close relationships that this particular application of Mandler's interruption hypothesis has the virtue of banishing:

First, it makes clear the degree of "closeness" of a relationship is not usefully conceived or determined by the frequency, hedonic sign, and intensity of emotion that the principals experience within the relationship on a daily basis. We have for too long bought the popular notion that close relationships are characterized by the perpetual experience of the hot emotions of joy and elation—or, at the least, by a lot of hot emotion. It then comes as a surprise to us, and to the individual involved, that the severest emotional reactions are often experienced after death or separation from partners in relationships that have heretofore been characterized by very little emotion. In fact, the two persons may *never* have experienced strong emotion in the relationship (e.g., in cases in which the meshing occurred gradually). This scheme suggests, in other words, that experienced emotion is not a useful classificatory variable of closeness.

Second, because highly organized behavior sequences tend to recede in conscious awareness, become automatic and unthinking, it becomes explicable why the severity of emotional reaction to separation from the partner often comes as an unpleasant surprise to the individual. We may hypothesize, in fact, that individuals may typically underestimate their emotional investment in relationships of some duration. And it follows, then, that those global affective appraisals we are prone to have them make of their partner probably don't reflect emotional investment very well either.

Third, and relatedly, this scheme allows us to differentiate between relationships that are emotionally tranquil because the two persons have few interconnections to intrachain event sequences (as in "parallel marriages," for example) and relationships that are emotionally tranquil because there are many such interconnections, but they are well-meshed.

And then, finally, there are all those other mysteries. Why, for example, obstacles posed to a relationship often seem to heighten passion and the experience of "hot" emotion; insofar as obstacles are by definition interruptive, that would seem to make great good sense. Or why one can heartily dislike someone but, at the same time, see them as the source of hot emotion, perhaps sometimes positive emotion; a person need not possess admirable character qualities to have interruptibility power, as Phillip in Maugham's *Of Human Bondage* reminds us. Or why the converse is true—why liking another, or perceiving that they have many positive attributes, doesn't necessarily mean they have the power to interrupt and thus to cause an emotional experience.

Or, in sum, this analysis suggests why it would be a good idea for those of us interested in affective phenomena in social relationships to stop assuming that an individual has *one* affective predisposition toward another. And also why it might be useful to stop assuming that the domain of interpersonal attraction can be usefully identified with a particular *type* of behavior, specifically "affective behavior" as opposed to "nonaffective" behavior. Insofar as one is interested in predicting an individual's affective responses to another, one first has to select the particular behavior for which one wants to learn more about its affective direction (positive/negative) and intensity (strong/weak). The choice of behavior is particularly important if one does not presume that any other behavior directed toward the other necessarily has the same determinants of affective tone.

What the emotion theorists have to offer us, then, is a reminder that if one is interested in affective phenomena in social relationships, one must study them in their context of a person's needs, aspirations, and goals, and how another person impinges on these. But those of us who have been trying to understand social relationships also have something to offer those interested in emotion: As Bowlby (1973) put it, anyone interested in emotion ultimately: "finds himself confronted by problems of affectional bonding: what causes bonds to develop, what they are there for, and especially the conditions that affect the form their development takes [p. 40]."

ACKNOWLEDGMENTS

The author wishes to thank Bruce Campbell, Steve Gangestad, and, especially, Eugene Borgida, all of the University of Minnesota, for their helpful suggestions during the preparation of this chapter, as well as George Mandler for his previous comments on several issues treated here.

REFERENCES

Ajzen, I., & Fishbein, M. *Understanding attitudes and predicting social behavior.* Englewood Cliffs, N. J.: Prentice–Hall, 1980.

Allport, G. W. The historical background of modern social psychology. In G. Lindzey (Ed.), *Handbook of social psychology* (Vol. 1, 1st ed.). Reading, Mass.: Addison–Wesley, 1954.

Anderson, N. H. Likableness ratings of 555 personality–trait words. *Journal of Personality and Social Psychology,* 1968, *9*, 272–279.

Berscheid, E. Emotion. In H. H. Kelley, E. Berscheid, A. Christensen, J. Harvey, T. Huston, G. Levinger, E. McClintock, A. Peplau, D. R. Peterson, *Close relationships.* S. F.: Freeman, in press.

Berscheid, E. Interpersonal attraction. In G. Lindzey & E. Aronson (Eds.), *Handbook of social psychology* (3rd ed.). Reading, Mass.: Addison–Wesley, in press. (b)

Berscheid, E., & Walster, E. H. *Interpersonal attraction* (2nd ed.). Reading, Mass.: Addison–Wesley, 1978.

Bower, G. H. Mood and memory. *American Psychologist,* 1981, *36*, 129–148.

Bowlby, J. Affectional bonds: Their nature and origin. In R. S. Weiss (Ed.). *Loneliness: The experience of emotional and social isolation.* Cambridge, Mass.: M.I.T. Press, 1973.

Candland, D. K. The persistent problems of emotion. In D. K. Candland, J. P. Fell, E. Keen, A. I. Leshner, R. Plutchik, & R. M. Tarpy, *Emotion.* Monterey, Calif.: Brooks/Cole, 1977.

Clark, M. S., & Isen, A. M. *Toward understanding the relationship between feeling states and social behavior.* In A. Hastorf and A. M. Isen (Eds.), *Cognitive social psychology,* New York: Elsevier, in press.

Ellis, A., & Harper, R. A. *A guide to rational living.* Englewood Cliffs, N.J.: Prentice-Hall, 1961.

Fishbein, M., & Ajzen, I. Attitudes and opinions. *Annual Review of Psychology,* 1972, *23,* 487–544.

Fishbein, M. & Ajzen, I. *Belief, attitude, intention, and behavior: An introduction to theory and research.* Reading, Mass.: Addison–Wesley, 1975.

Huston, T. L., & Levinger, G. Interpersonal attraction and relationships. *Annual Review of Psychology,* 1978, *29,* 115–156.

Jenkins, J. J. Can we have a fruitful cognitive psychology? In H. E. Howe, Jr., & J. H. Flowers (Eds.), *Cognitive Processes: Nebraska Symposium on Motivation,* 1980, Lincoln: University of Nebraska Press, 1981.

Katz, D., & Stotland, E. A preliminary statement to a theory of attitude structure and change. In S. Koch (Ed.), *Psychology: A study of a science 3.* New York: McGraw-Hill, 1959.

Kelley, H. H., Berscheid, E., Christensen, A., Harvey, J., Huston, T. L., Levinger, G., Peplau, A., Peterson, D. R. *Close relationships.* S. F.: Freeman, in press.

Locke, H. J., & Williamson, R. C. Marital adjustment: A factor analysis study. *American Sociological Review,* 1958, *23,* 562–569.

Mandler, G. *Mind and emotion.* New York: Wiley, 1975.

Matlin, M. W., & Stang, D. J. *The Pollyanna principle: Selectivity in language, memory, and thought.* Cambridge, Mass.: Schenkman, 1978.

McGuire, W. J. The nature of attitudes and attitude change. In G. Lindzey & E. Aronson (Eds.), *The handbook of social psychology* (2nd ed., Vol. 3). Reading, Mass.: Addison–Wesley, 1969.

Osgood, C. E., May W. H. & Miron, M. S. *Cross-cultural universals of affective meaning.* Urbana: University of Illinois Press, 1975.

Osgood, C. E., Suci, G. J., & Tannenbaum, P. H. *The measurement of meaning.* Urbana: University of Illinois Press, 1957.

Oskamp, S. *Attitudes and opinions.* Englewood Cliffs, N. J.: Prentice–Hall, 1977.

Plutchik, R., & Kellerman, H. *Emotion: Theory, research, and experience.* New York: Academic Press, 1980.

Straus, M. A., & Hotaling, G. T. (Eds.). *The social causes of husband–wife violence.* Minneapolis: University of Minnesota Press, 1980.

Weiss, R. L., Hops, H., Patterson, G. R. A framework for conceptualizing marital conflict. In L. A. Hamerlynck, L. C. Handy, & E. S. Mash (Eds.), *Behavior change.* Champaign, Ill.: Research Press, 1972.

3

Schema-triggered Affect: Applications to Social Perception

Susan T. Fiske
Carnegie–Mellon University

Since moving to Pittsburgh, I have encountered a new stereotype. It purportedly describes a "mill hunk," that is, the prototypic steel worker. A mill hunk, so the stereotype runs, can be male or female but is invariably macho and raunchy regardless of gender. A mill hunk always drinks Iron City beer, watches every Steeler game, and wears a t-shirt in all weather. Research in social cognition has had much to say about how such stereotypic information is represented and processed. For example, my mill-hunk stereotype is stored as an abstracted generic example, not as a collection of all the steelworkers I have ever known, although the stereotype does contain specific examples too. I am likely to ignore information irrelevant to the stereotype, so, for example, whether or not a particular mill hunk is athletic will not catch my attention. On the other hand, I will notice wildly discrepant information—a mill hunk who is also a Shakespeare scholar—and if allowed time to mull it over, I will recall the discrepant information. If I do not have time to elaborate on the information encountered, I will tend to recall only consistent information—a mill hunk who reads Hustler magazine. This research on social cognition and stereotyping is ably reviewed elsewhere (Hamilton, 1979; Hastie, 1981; Taylor & Crocker, 1981).[1]

A reading of the social cognitive literature indicates that practically nowhere in such cognitive analysis of stereotyping is affect addressed. Yet affect is the very reason stereotypes matter. Pigeonholing a person to fit one's oversimplified beliefs is certainly an issue, but prejudice is another, more serious issue. Clearly, a cognitive analysis does not aim to address affect, by definition. But this chapter

---

[1]To avoid possible misunderstanding, note that the steelworker stereotype is only an example, a generally-held stereotype that I myself do not endorse.

argues that cognitive social analysis can and should address the processing of affect.

So far, social cognition has borrowed heavily from cognitive psychology for its theories and methods and, in so doing, implicitly has accepted its major goals and shared its major omissions, some of which are inappropriate to social settings (Fiske, 1981; Higgins, Kuiper, & Olson, 1981; Zajonc, 1980a). In social cognition the current strategy has been to push cognitive explanations as far as possible, to see where they illuminate new ground not clarified by previous approaches. Cognitive explanations are not new in social psychology (Allport, 1954; Heider, 1958; Smith, Bruner, & White, 1956), but this widespread enthusiasm for explanations in terms of cognitive process is recent (Taylor, 1981; Zajonc, 1980a). Further, the new cognitive approach uniquely emphasizes careful specification, measurement, and manipulation of the steps intervening between input and output, using new methodologies especially designed for the purpose (Taylor & Fiske, 1981). Hence, social cognitive research relies heavily on direct measures and manipulations of attention, information search, memory, and inference. In addition to new methods, new models are either borrowed from cognitive theory or developed specifically in a social context, but informed by advances in cognitive theory. In all this, social cognition implicitly or explicitly accepts the assumptions of cognitive psychology.

To explain the thinking processes of individual people in isolation—the main task of cognitive psychology—one need not consider interpersonal perception. But to understand expressly social phenomena virtually demands the consideration of affect, which considerably complicates the cognitive analysis. The implications of integrating affect into social cognition is the major focus of the research reported here.[2] To anticipate, our position is that the origins of both affective and cognitive reactions to other people together lie in the individual's accumulated prior experiences; interpersonal affect and cognition both depend on abstracted individual history.

An example illustrates the current approach. Imagine walking down the street and encountering someone who exactly resembles your high-school sweetheart. Instant affect can surface from such an encounter. Moreoever, such experience-based affective reaction can occur prior to other "cold" knowledge that surrounds that person (e.g., that the person actually lives in another city, or that the sweetheart is now an ex, or that the person never would have worn a three-piece suit). The point is that one can react strongly to people, simply because they remind one of somebody or fit a prior configuration, but such a reliance on prior experience as cuing affect does not presuppose retrieval of all the facts. Such

---

[2]It is not true that social psychology as a whole has neglected cognition and affect. Some examples of social psychology's many forays into interpersonal cognition and affect are reviewed by Fiske (1981). It *is* true, however, that the subarea most suited to examining the processing of interpersonal affect has neglected thus far to do so. It is to this point that the chapter is addressed.

ideas have arisen elsewhere as affective resonance (Tomkins, 1980), as Freudian transference or as stimulus generalization. Here, however, the focus is explicitly cognitive: We are concerned with how interpersonal affect and cognition each are processed and how they interface. In short, how might human information processors deal with affect? The position to be taken here is that they process affect the way they process anything else—efficiently, if not "accurately." When new information can be fit to old affectively laden knowledge, then the person has available an immediate affective response.

Nevertheless, sharing an origin need not imply that affective and cognitive responses must depend on each other, a point proposed by Zajonc (1980b) and that we develop shortly in an interpersonal context. In arguing for the distinctions between affect and cognition, Zajonc has proposed that they may be entirely separate systems. In contrast, the current hypothesis is that affect and cognition both are cued by matching stimuli to abstracted prior experiences, but that affect may be processed differently than more "cognitive" knowledge.

One might argue that affective reactions are just another cognition. The final word is not in yet, but, until then, it is presumptuous to equate them. First, affect has been treated de facto as a separate phenomenon. In cognitive psychology's neglect of it, the implicit assumption is that affect is distinct. Further, affect operates at a different level than cognitions do. The same affective dimensions (e.g., positive–negative) apply to many more stimuli than does any single cognitive dimension. Affect thus is at a higher level than most cognitions, because it is a common feature of so many stimuli. Finally, Zajonc (1980b) has presented evidence that affect is accessed quickly, almost at the level of perception and categorization, and earlier than other more "cognitive" knowledge. Thus, it seems unreasonable to assume them equivalent a priori.

Before proceeding, it is also important to clarify the distinction between evaluation and affect. The present research sometimes equates evaluation and affect, but that is conceptually a first approximation. Evaluations and preferences are simple valenced judgments. Affective reactions involve separate, sometimes uncorrelated, positive and negative dimensions (Abelson, Kinder, Peters, & Fiske, 1982; but see Russell, 1979, for an opposing view). Affect also implicates an arousal or activation dimension (e.g., anger versus depression; contentment versus delight; see Russell, 1978). Simple evaluation measures ignore both the possible independence of positive and negative dimensions and neglect the activation dimension as well. However, affect and evaluation are highly correlated, and in some laboratory settings unaroused evaluative judgments are the best one can obtain. It remains an empirical question whether the results generalize, and this research is a first step in that direction.

To give some perspective to the current model, it is helpful to present the currently available alternatives. Given these, the chapter next describes the model we believe to be operating. Then, the next section describes our program of research, which applies this model to close relationships, voting, and stereotyping.

MODELS OF INTERPERSONAL AFFECT

The models implicit in much person perception research represent affective and evaluative reactions as piecemeal processes. In cognitive terminology, they are data-driven or bottom-up. In such a model, affective reactions are based on the information given. Bits of information, each with its own valence, accumulate independently. On demand, the valenced information is retrieved and summarized algebraically (either by summing or averaging). This *retrieval-based, piecemeal model* posits that affective judgments are made only when demanded, and it predicts that affect will depend on memory for the relevant data. For an illustration, consider evaluating a new next-door neighbor. This model presumes that one has only a neutral reaction until the need arises to evaluate the person. When an affective response is required, one first recalls the neighbor's various behaviors and attributes, representing, say, how noisy, friendly, neat, and gossipy the person seems. One abstracts out the evaluative component of each attribute, combines the evaluations, and produces a memory-based affective response that reflects all the available pieces. This model most clearly underlies the work of Fishbein (1967) and Norman Anderson (1981). For example, in one analysis of impression formation stated by Anderson (1981): "immediate judgment thus resulted from an integration of information stored in memory and recalled by the occasion [p. 365]."

However reasonable this might seem, the plausible idea that recall determines affective reactions has not been established. It has become clear that the affective impact and memorability of data are independent. For example, Dreben, Fiske, and Hastie (1979) found no correlation between an item's weight in evaluation and its probability of recall. Further, recall and evaluation yielded unrelated serial position curves and were differentially affected by various task manipulations. Several others (Anderson & Hubert, 1963; Fiske, Kenny, & Taylor, 1982; Love & Greenwald, 1978; Riskey, 1979; for a review, see Fiske, 1981) also have obtained evidence for the independence of evaluations and recall. It seems possible that evaluation and memory are, in fact, rather independent systems. It is becoming increasingly implausible to believe that an efficient information processor would separately store each instance of raw data, retrieve the lot, and evaluate. Thus, the rather cumbersome retrieval-based piecemeal model seems untenable.

An alternative data-driven or piecemeal model does not rely on retrieval. In the *on-line piecemeal model,* evaluation is presumed to be a primary component of perception (Osgood, Suci, & Tannenbaum, 1957; Zajonc, 1980b). Perceivers assess each input "on-line," as it is received (Fiske, 1980). They assimilate each input's evaluation as it is encoded, add it into the cumulative summary, and retrieve that summary affective judgment upon demand. In this view, people gradually accumulate and modify an affective reaction, changing it with each new bit of data; each input separately contributes to the outcome, at the time it is encoded. In our example, the new neighbor would constantly evoke affective responses from people in the neighborhood. Every behavior and every attribute would contribute to the running evaluation score, at the time that each feature was perceived. Affect, then, is constantly updated, and memory for the data is irrelevant, once the affective components are distilled and contributed to the running total or average. This model has been most clearly expressed again by Anderson (1981): "subsequent behavior provides additional information that is evaluated and integrated in the same way as the earlier information. In this view, the attitude is a dynamic entity, continuously modified by incoming information [p. 365]." This essentially analog, on-line model of affect suggests that affective impact is irrelevant to recall for the data on which the affect was based and is consistent with the findings reported earlier, that recall and evaluation are independent. Unfortunately, this model ignores the growing literature on complex information processing.

Both piecemeal models posit processes that do not consider the architecture and capacity of human cognition. Taken literally, such algebraic processes would strain the capacity of short-term memory. The sequence of events in an Andersonian version of the on-line model would include: retrieve initial evaluation, weight it, multiply them together, keep both the weight and the product in active memory, evaluate new information, weight it, multiply them together, keep both the weight and the product in active memory, add the two products, add the two weights, divide the products by the weights. Clearly, such mental gymnastics represent an unreasonable model of people's impression formation processes.

Even taken less literally, the piecemeal models still presuppose considerable inefficiency if they do not allow for combining information into patterns that facilitate encoding, recognition, and retrieval; these are crucial features of human cognition. Anderson (1981) again is the most explicit and articulate representative of the piecemeal alternative. He addresses the issue of complex units by assigning both evaluation and weight at the level of "molar unitization"; that is, a complex stimulus, such as a familiar configuration of nonverbal cues, could be integrated as a single unit. This solution, however, merely passes the buck; the problem is transferred to evaluation at the level of the compound stimulus. It leaves open the question of how the individual components interact and how such a complex pattern itself elicits an evaluative or affective response. More generally, the piecemeal models do not tackle the issue of *how* people assign affective responses to individual features or combinations of features.

Most importantly, the piecemeal models do not address the possibility of category-based affective responses. The models implicitly assume that each stimulus is a unique new encounter, with affective reactions to be calculated afresh, ignoring prior experience with other instances of the same category. The models are usefully called piecemeal because they are feature oriented and do not easily admit to category-based perception and evaluation. Thus, in their strictest form, they ignore the clear implications of categorization and of inferences that go beyond the data given, instead positing an entirely data-driven affective response.

A schema-based model of affect could incorporate current assumptions about the structure and capacity of human perception and cognition. Considerable evidence has amassed to show that people draw on structured prior knowledge—known collectively as schemata—to facilitate information processing. Bartlett (1932) defined a schema as: "an active organization of past experiences, which must always be supposed to be operating in any well-adapted organic response [p. 201]." Schemata are generic knowledge structures, abstracted from experience with instances, and they contain richly interconnected information about the attributes of the most usual instance (see also Rumelhart & Ortony, 1977). Thus, the contents of the mill-hunk stereotype earlier described could be represented schematically as the set of interconnected expectations about the more crucial features of a typical instance. Roughly summarized, schema research shows that schemata aid memory for schema-consistent information (Hastie, 1981; Taylor & Crocker, 1981); increase confidence in schema-consistent recognition (Cantor & Mischel, 1979); enhance memory for schema-consistent information that was in fact never presented (Bower, Black, & Turner, 1979); and, further, guide inferences and predictions (Schank & Abelson, 1977). Schema-based social information processing has been amply demonstrated elsewhere, although empirical and conceptual ambiguities plague the area (Fiske & Linville, 1980). The bottom line is that, if one is explicit about one's process model, the concept usefully describes the simplified perception of new inputs that can be fit to abstracted prior experience.

Implicating schematic processes in interpersonal affective responses is a novel extension of the schema concept.[3] Simply put, affect is assumed to be stored with the generic knowledge structure. The affect is available immediately upon categorization, so evaluations and affect are cued by categorization, that is by fitting an instance to a schema. In this view, a perceiver first comprehends an input, by assimilating it to an existing knowledge structure, and then evaluates the instance on the basis of the affect linked to the schema. The model diverges critically from the piecemeal models in two respects. First, affect is stored at the top level of the schematic structure. Without access to all the category's features and their respective evaluations, affect is linked to the initial act of categorization. Second, the model explicitly recognizes that affect may generalize from

---

[3]Tesser's (1978) model of self-generated attitude change and Linville's (1982) model of schema-based evaluative extremity also presuppose that feelings are a function of the schema evoked. Nothing here disputes either Tesser's or Linville's model, but the emphases differ. Both their models are concerned specifically with the extremity of evaluative responses, Tesser as a function of time, Linville as a function of schema complexity. Neither of these factors are particularly relevant here.

experience with prior instances to the category as a whole and thence back to new instances; that is, affective responses are often category based.

A crucial question remains behind: How is affect linked to the schema in the first place? Various processes likely operate in initial affective responses to individual stimuli. The first time a novel stimulus is encountered, its components may be evaluated and their evaluations combined, piecemeal fashion. Or, later, one may introspect on one's past behavior, abstracting over instances of one's behavior to infer one's evaluation of a particular stimulus (Bem, 1972). Or one may be conditioned to the individual stimulus, either classically or instrumentally. Whatever the process, the point is that the affect is ever after linked to the entire category, along with the relevant cognitive information. Neither cognitive nor affective associations are linked just to the originally encountered individual instance.

To return to the mill-hunk example, then, after I decide how I feel about individual steelworkers, by whatever process, I perceive and evaluate them as a category. The affect initially may be based on my own preference for Iron City beer, the Steelers, and t-shirts, but my response is not stored that way. Stereotypic or schema-based evaluation is a summary of many component evaluations, so it is an efficient affective processing device. Thus, when a stereotypic label is applied, it carries the implicit weight of its inferred or actual components. The affective impact of categorization derives from its being a proxy for quantities of other information; as an evaluative summary, it is more affectively informative than any individual item at a lower conceptual level. Of course, each attribute may carry its own affective implications and originally have combined to produce the summary affective reaction stored with the schema. Moreover, individual items of information, such as isolated attributes, may continue to have affective impact, as the cumulative impression is continually modified. The important point is that the affective reaction does not presuppose access to the schema's component attributes. Comparing this model further to the piecemeal approaches, then, schema-based affect combines both retrieval and on-line processes; that is, the affective reaction is retrieved from memory upon access to the schema, but the initial reaction and modifications of it are processed on line. The distinction between retrieval and on-line models evaporates in schematic processing.

RESEARCH ON SCHEMA-TRIGGERED AFFECT

The prediction unique to this model is simple: Schematic match determines affective responses. To the degree that an instance is perceived to fit the schema, it will receive the affect linked to that category. Otherwise, the instance receives moderate positive affect, by default, pending its possible categorization as a good example of something else. There is much evidence that the default evaluation of other people is moderately positive, all other things being equal (Matlin & Stang, 1978). In a program of research designed to investigate the main hypothesis, we have explored schema-triggered affect in the initiation of close relationships, in forming impressions of politicians, and in campus stereotyping. No single study entirely proves the point. Together the message of these studies encourages the use of this approach, as we hope to show.

All three applications of the model have followed a roughly similar strategy. First, we explored the contents of the relevant person schema and discovered the affect linked to it. This preliminary stage usually involved gathering norms from the relevant population as to the consensual perceptions or stereotypes of a given category of people. The second step was to present subjects with stimulus people who varied in their degree of match to the schema. The matches among these should elicit schema-triggered affect, whereas the mismatches should not.

The Initiation of Close Relationships

In collaboration, Ann Beattie, Sandra Milberg, and I were interested in the old-flame phenomenon as an example of schema-triggered affect (Fiske, Beattie, & Milberg, 1981). It is a common observation about one's friends that they repeatedly get attracted to the same type of person. (Of course, it's never that way for oneself.) We hypothesized that people develop idiosyncratic schemata for their own particular kind of mate. Their category for the sort of person they are attracted to might include information about appearance, personality, interests, and the like. Certainly, such a (same-)old-flame category is affectively laden. Consequently, when one encounters a person who is a good match to the old-flame schema, the attendant affects are triggered, based on one's accumulated prior experiences. Further, the schema cues expectations and behaviors based on previous encounters. Thus, the old-flame schema, when triggered, becomes self-fulfilling. Of course, in this sense, it is one of a long line of such self-fulfilling stereotypes (see Darley & Fazio, 1980, for a review).

Our research strategy began with assessing the contents and affect linked to old flames among our subject population. First, we constructed a personality inventory consisting of traits our pretest subjects thought most relevant to close relationships. This ''Princeton Personality Inventory'' (PPI) consisted of 17 traits: fun, adventurous, honest, sensitive, strong willed, intelligent, trusting, athletic, commensensical, polite, listens, romantic, respectful, sense of humor, trustworthy, understanding, and gentle. In addition to invoking old flames by personality profiles, we also presumed that most undergraduates would have patterns of attraction to certain physical types. For simplicity, we used women subjects and collected slides showing undergraduate men of varied appearance. Thus, the old-flame schema could be evoked along two dimensions: personality profile or photograph. It only remained to assess each individual's idiosyncratic experience and tailor a stimulus person to fit her type of guy, in personality and appearance.[4]

To do this, we told undergraduate women subjects that we were studying their impressions of people they had known in the past, would meet in the present, and expected to meet in the future. To serve this first alleged purpose, the women completed the PPI for three well-known people: themselves, a same-sex best friend, and a past or current romantic partner. Then they engaged in the alleged second part of the study, forming impressions of people they were just meeting. This actually was a filler task that consisted of observing a bland videotaped getting-acquainted conversation between two male students, after which the subjects completed two more PPI's and some recall measures.

During the 30-minute filler task, the experimenter constructed each subject's tailor-made stimulus person from her own romantic-partner profile. Each subject's own ratings were reproduced on scales of a different format (continuous 120-mm lines instead of 7-point Likert scales) and in a different sequence of the 17 standard PPI traits. This enabled us to construct for each subject an unrecognizable copy of her own old-flame profile. No one expressed the slightest suspicion on this score during debriefing.

In addition, we ascertained each subject's old-flame physical type. Under the guise of the third part of the study (people they expected to meet in the future), we asserted that they would be paired with some male volunteers in a later part of the research. Because physical attractiveness has an impact on whether people get along, we said, it was important to know their own personal reactions to the male volunteers' appearance. We emphasized that we were not interested in consensual physical attractiveness (i.e., would he be suited to appear in a scotch ad), but in whether he was "the type of guy you have been attracted to in the past."

After collecting these "base-line" measures, the experimenter made a show of randomly assigning subjects to rate only one of the stimulus people. The women, in fact, received the photograph of someone they had rated either very high or very low as physically their "type of guy," and they received the personality profile either of someone they themselves had described as an old flame or of someone else's old flame. Subjects thus were randomly assigned to receive one of four levels of match to their own idiosyncratic old-flame schemata (personality match or not, combined with appearance match or not). Surprisingly, as noted, no one recognized this fact.

---

[4]This assumed that our college-age subjects had all had romantic involvements already. This assumption did not appear problematic, at least to the extent that no one was willing to admit a problem in filling out the scale. Even if an undergraduate had never experienced a mutual romantic involvement, it is still likely that she would have experienced one-way involvements (crushes). The theory should hold equally well for unrequited attractions.

We hypothesized that subjects would react positively, given a total match, in which both personality and photo fit their own old-flame type.[5] A total nonmatch should elicit little effect. The partial matches (appearance match or personality match but not both) were a puzzle. It was not clear a priori how subjects would react, but we did expect to elicit some affect from the partial matches, in contrast to the total nonmatches who should elicit essentially no affect.

One set of dependent measures asked subjects to predict how the stimulus person might make them feel, rating their own affective responses on 15 adjectives derived from Roseman's (1979) structural theory of emotion. The affects included six positive adjectives (liking, happy, proud, hopeful, relief, and sympathy) and nine negative (afraid, sad, regret, unease, angry, disgusted, frustrated, shame, and disliking). The raw affect ratings were averaged to yield a positive and a negative index.

As can be seen from Fig. 3.1, total matches on both appearance and personality elicited much positive affect and little negative affect, exactly as predicted. The partial match results also are rather intriguing. Partial matches elicited moderate positive affect—especially those who matched on appearance but not on personality. *And* partial matches elicited moderate negative affect as well. These people, who were "close but not quite right," elicited more fear, sadness, regret, unease, frustration, and the like than did the total matches. So they elicited ambivalence, in contrast to the clear positive affect triggered by the total matches. Finally, nonmatches elicited little affect of either kind.

The affect results should be especially interesting if they are echoed by behavioral choices; that is, if subjects act on their schema-triggered feelings, then the schema becomes self-fulfilling. To test this, we provided subjects with their choice of settings in which to meet with the male volunteers. As predicted, they most often chose to meet with the total matches in "an informal gathering some evening," the setting most conducive to romantic involvement. As for the partial matches, the women preferred to meet with them in a more task-oriented setting ("a work group in a laboratory setting"). Presumably, a task setting would be less involving than an explicitly social setting, but it would still allow them to seek additional information, thus resolving the ambiguities of the partial matches. Not surprisingly, subjects had little desire to meet with the nonmatches in either setting. The neutral setting showed no effects, as would be predicted.

This study's results are of primary importance when taken in contrast to alternative models. The piecemeal models do not easily explain configural re-

---

[5]This assumes that their associations to past romantic involvements are primarily positive. In this study, this seemed to be the case, because most subjects rated their past romantic partners at or above the scale midpoint on positive traits. In subsequent research (Fiske, Beattie, & Milberg, 1981), we have found that positive prior experiences cue positive affect and negative prior experiences cue negative affect.

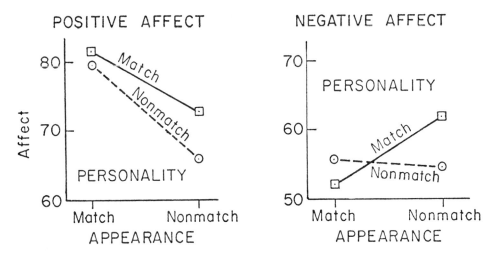

FIG. 3.1.   Positive and negative affect as a function of personality and appearance match to old-flame schema (Fiske, Beattie, & Milberg, 1981).

sponses, that is, the interaction effects in which partial matches do not simply fall in between total matches and nonmatches.

The most straightforward explanation seems to be that when a new person is a good match to one's prior category, the person elicits the affects and actions linked to the schema. One alternative, however, does remain unassailed by these data. It is possible that subjects prefer anyone who is a good fit to their own prior knowledge and expectations. In this view, the affect is not evoked by affect

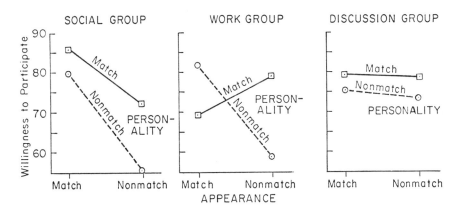

FIG. 3.2.   Choice of interaction setting as a function of personality and appearance match to old-flame schema (Fiske, Beattie, & Milberg, 1981).

stored with the schema, but people simply favor familiar examples and dislike messy ambiguity. The next set of research addresses this issue and applies schema-triggered affect to a different interpersonal knowledge domain.

Forming Impressions of Politicians

In order to differentiate between schema-triggered affect and the hypothesis that poor fit (lack of familiarity) simply causes discomfort, one needs a negative schema. If good fit to a negative schema causes negative affect and poor fit causes positive affect, that constitutes evidence for schema-based affect and against the idea that ambiguity simply causes the discomfort. Consequently, some of our research needed to draw on a negative stereotype and assess reactions as a function of match to it.

The political domain turns out to be well-suited to this enterprise. There is a shared set of knowledge about politicians, and the stereotype is rather negative. Moving from idiosyncratic schemata (old flames) to consensual ones (politicians) brings us to mass person perception, in which everyone is forming impressions of the same stimulus people. Again, the research required two steps: assessment of the schema's content and affect, followed by presentation of targets who varied in degrees of schematic fit, to see if good fit uniquely triggers the affect associated with the category.

In the first step, then, we (Fiske, Milberg, Destefano, & Maffett, 1980) collected undergraduates' shared conceptions about the nature of politicians. These include assumptions about both personality and appearance. According to the average student, a typical politician:

> smiles all the time, as if he's in a good mood even when he is not, so people never know when he means it. He tends to pose, being concerned with appearances and putting on a front. His colleagues describe him as warm and friendly.
>
> His life revolves around his career. He is an average worker, does only what is expected, nothing more or less, and worries about keeping his job. He will do what other people want in order to maintain his position; he cares desperately about what people in general think of him. He is informed and often in the spotlight; he enjoys speaking in groups. He is vain and very ambitious, and basically concerned only for himself. He rather thinks he has all the answers.
>
> He enjoys going out to social functions, mingling and greeting people; he is very outgoing. He dislikes arguing with people and he avoids controversy. His opinions are noncommital and middle-of-the-road; he is often swayed by pressure. Almost all the time his actions appear above question. However, on occasion he has been known to be somewhat untrustworthy.[6]

---

[6]Interestingly enough, this personality stereotype about the abstract category of politician, which was obtained from undergraduates, is echoed by the general public's stereotype of the central traits shared by the actual forerunners for President (Kinder, Peters, Abelson, & Fiske, 1981).

Undergraduates' politician stereotype also contains information about the appearance of typical politicians. Accordingly, we were able to obtain several photographs that exemplified politicians and several that were discrepant with the politician stereotype.

Having identified the contents of the politician schema and knowing that it triggers negative affect (Fiske, Milberg, Destefano, & Maffett, 1980; Sears, 1976), the prediction of the schema-triggered model again is that a good fit will cue the affect linked to the schema, but this time that affect is negative. Lack of fit again should moderate reactions, but this time in a positive direction.

In this study, match to the politician schema was manipulated, first, by appearance. Subjects were given either a stereotypic politician photograph or an atypical politician photograph. Second, subjects were told that the target was either a politician, a business executive, or a person. All subjects were given the same personality description, which consisted of half politician attributes (as shown previously) and half nonpolitician attributes. Thus, the written materials were ambiguous and could be interpreted as consistent with the politician stereotype or not, depending on the label and photograph.

In addition to the manipulations of appearance match and label, the political realm necessitates a third independent variable. Previous work (Fiske & Kinder, 1981) indicates extreme variability in levels of prior knowledge about politics, and such variability importantly influences political cognition. In this context, if the label *politician* cues little stored knowledge about politicians, there may well be no effect of schematic match or nonmatch. Novices who do not possess the schema will not notice the lack of fit. Consequently, the effects are predicted to hold only for the relative political experts among our undergraduates. Using a scale of political expertise and involvement developed in another context (Fiske & Kinder, 1981), we divided the subjects into relative experts and novices.

As predicted by a schematic model, novices do not show the effects of complex prior knowledge on affective reactions.[7] For the novices, the *label* politician was simply always a liability, regardless of appearance. In contrast, the *appearance* of a politician elicited positive affect among the novices, regardless of label (see Fig. 3.3). The two independent effects of appearance and label do combine to produce an affective response, but they do not exhibit the configural effects of schematic good or poor match.

The experts, on the other hand, do show schematic processing. Given the labels *executive* or *person,* the political or nonpolitical appearance of the photographs makes little difference, because they are irrelevant. However, once the relevant schema is cued by the label *politician,* an appearance that matches the

---

[7]Affect and evaluation measures were combined into a single index in this particular study, to simplify reporting. All the negative affects were subtracted from all the positive affects to form an overall affect scale. The evaluation measure was then combined with this scale to yield the summary index. Results do not differ crucially if reported separately.

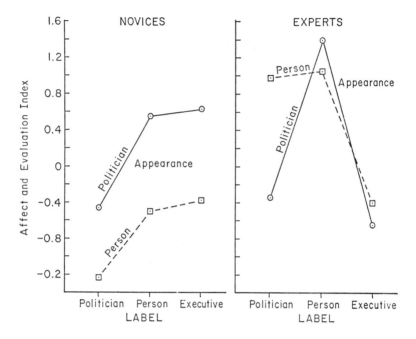

FIG. 3.3.   Affect and evaluation as a function of appearance and label match to politician stereotype (Fiske, Milberg, Destefano, & Maffett, 1980).

stereotype costs its possessor considerable damage. A politician who looks like one is not at all favored by those who know about politicians. However, if his appearance is a poor match to the negative politician schema, he does not elicit the schema-based affect. In sum, then, schematic match cues the associated affect for those who possess the relevant schema.

One possible criticism of these results is that they are limited in generality and pertain only to hypothetical politicians. Perhaps, given the complexities of reacting to actual political candidates, the politician schema would have little impact. Political image makers certainly would profit from knowing the generality of this effect, and we also were curious. Consequently, around the time of the first 1980 primaries, we conducted an experiment using as stimuli the actual frontrunners for President. At the time, they were the incumbent (Carter), two Republicans (Reagan and Bush), and two Democrats (Kennedy and Brown).

Again, the research required setting up degrees of schematic match. How to do this was another problem. Clearly, we could not label the Presidential frontrunners as anything other than politicians, nor could we change their appearance. So we manipulated their perceived fit to the politician schema along personality dimensions. The politician description generated earlier was presented as an intimate portrait of the candidate, written by a reporter who had shared the campaign trail with him. A third of the subjects received the politician description attributed to one of the five front-runners. The remaining two thirds received one of two control descriptions. One was exactly opposite to the politician description (extremely competent, not at all ambitious, very introverted, scrupulously honest); this "antipolitician" was rather a saint, extreme and peculiar. Consequently, another control was created by asking subjects where the "ordinary person" falls on each of the relevant attributes (i.e., moderately competent, somewhat ambitious, relatively extroverted, usually honest). That description turned out a nebish, a rather nondescript character. Thus, each of the five front-runners was rotated through each of the three personality portraits: politician, antipolitician (saint), and ordinary person (nebish). Each subject received only one description of only one candidate.

Subjects again were undergraduates, and their affective reactions were assessed by the standard adjective list. The affect results showed the predicted disadvantage to prototypic politicians; they consistently elicited less positive affect and more negative affect than did the nonpoliticians (see Fig. 3.4). This result is particularly striking when one considers that it held for such well-known national candidates.

Of equal or greater interest is that the personality descriptions influenced actual vote intentions. None of the respondents were much interested in voting for the candidates described as stereotypic politicians. Democratic voters preferred the rather unrealistic, saintly antipolitician, whereas Republican voters

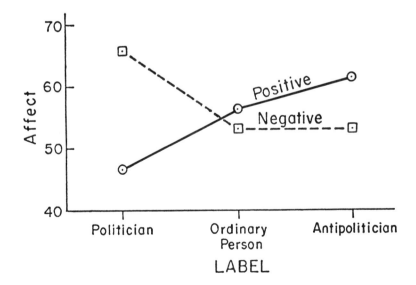

FIG. 3.4. Affect as a function of politician stereotype (Fiske, Milberg, Destefano, & Maffett, 1980).

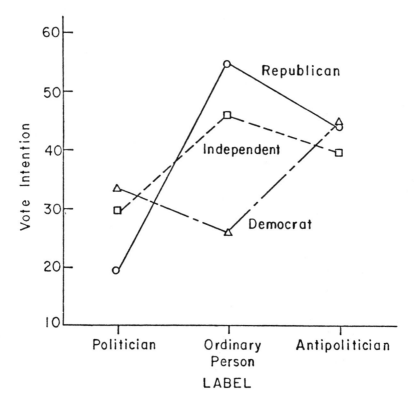

FIG. 3.5.   Vote intention as a function of politician stereotype (Fiske, Milberg, Destefano, & Maffett, 1980).

preferred the ''ordinary person,'' who was nondescript to the point of being a nonentity. Independents fell between the Republicans and Democrats (see Fig. 3.5). Of course, in addition, voter and candidate party combined to predict party-loyalty voting, but the description effects were of an almost comparable magnitude. Even the incumbent Carter was not immune to the detrimental effects of the politician stereotype.

To sum up the political research, then, the consensual politician schema contains richly interconnected information about the appearance and personality of typical politicians. When a hypothetical or actual politician is described as a good or a poor instance of the negatively tinged schema, his reputation suffers or improves accordingly.

Campus Stereotypes

Both previous sets of research argue for the schematic-match hypothesis on the grounds that degree of fit to an affectively laden schema determines whether the instance receives the affect linked to the schema. Both argue that the entire configuration's degree of fit determines affective responses. Thus, individual items do not combine additively but instead interactively. For example, if both appearance and personality fit one's category for an old flame or a politician, then schema-triggered affect, either positive or negative, results. If the fit is partial, affect moderates toward neutral or slightly positive.

A stricter test of the configural effects of schematic processing requires a different approach than that of the first sets of research. This involves the preliminary scaling of individual components to allow a more pointed differentiation between a piecemeal and a schematic account. The critical design must hold constant the evaluations of the component pieces of information, and it must vary only the consistency or inconsistency of their configuration. If the overall reaction changes as a function of the combination, in ways predicted by schematic fit, then the piecemeal model is weakened.[8] The next study did precisely that. Moderately negative campus stereotypes were combined with moderately positive behaviors, each of which was consistent or inconsistent with the stereotype. By holding component evaluations constant and varying only the consistency of the combination, the study constitutes a strong test of the schematic hypothesis.

As before, the study began by assessing the contents and affect linked to the target schemata. We (Fiske & Gup, 1980) found four campus stereotypes that fit our design specifications, as is clear shortly. At Carnegie–Mellon, there are two pairs of interlocking, mutually exclusive student stereotypes. The first pair of consensual stereotypes is artist and engineer (familiarly known as "fruits" and "vegetables"). Behaviors consistent with the artist stereotype (such as smoking marijuana, or perching in a tree to play the flute) are discrepant with the engineer stereotype. The reverse is also true: Engineers allegedly "nurd out" all night in the computer room ("vegetable garden") and wear dull, dated, mismatched clothes, whereas an artist allegedly never would. For generality, we used a second pair of mutually exclusive stereotypes; these were homosexual (gay) student and member of the Reserve Officers Training Corp (ROTC). The ROTC group stereotypically is involved in traditionally male pursuits (football and women), whereas the gay group stereotypically is involved in nontraditionally male pursuits (cooking and flower arranging). Upon collecting norms from undergraduates, then, two pairs of mutually exclusive negative stereotypes and attendant neutral behaviors were identified.

---

[8]This distinction sounds dangerously like the controversy in person perception, starting with Asch (1946), in which meaning change (Zanna & Hamilton, 1977) and averaging (Anderson, 1974) were pitted against each other. Meaning-change advocates argued that halo effects resulted from a semantic or evaluative change in the meaning of peripheral traits caused by the overall configuration of traits. The algebraic approach argued that such effects can be explained by changing the relative weights of the component attributes. This issue was declared unresolvable (Ostrom, 1977). The point here is different, however. Here, neither the evaluative nor the semantic meaning of individual attributes is argued to change. Nor is it predicted that an averaging model will easily explain the data, as is seen.

TABLE 3.1
Stimulus Photographs[a]

Pair[b]	Label Slide	Behavior 1	Behavior 2
1.	*Engineer.* Target wears blue t-shirt: "Carnegie Tech civil engineers give a dam!"	*Nurd.* Target wears short, out-of-fashion pants; carries calculator and glasses; shirt is short-sleeve, button-down, too big.	*Terminal.* Target working at computer terminal; school books littered about.
	Artist. Target sits with paint box and portfolio case.	*Flute.* Target stands in tree playing recorder.	*Joint.* Target sits on a couch, lighting a hard-rolled marijuana cigarette.
2.	*ROTC.* Target wears green fatigues.	*Date.* Target dressed up, helps woman on with her coat.	*Football.* Target stands outside, posed to throw football.
	Gay. Target wears black t-shirt with silver letters: "Gay Rights Now."	*Wok.* Target is in plant-filled, well-equipped kitchen, cooks with a Chinese wok.	*Flowers.* Target sits at a dining-room table arranging straw flowers in a glass vase.

[a]Each stimulus person always was presented first in a plain face photo not described here.

[b]Each pair of stereotypes is interlocking; that is, behavior consistent with one stereotype is discrepant behavior for the other stereotype within the pair. This unconfounds the discrepant/consistent manipulation from slide content.

The design, then, was simple. Stimulus materials were slides showing each of the eight behaviors described earlier (two consistent behaviors per stereotype). The stereotypes also were presented photographically. For example, the engineer wore a pale blue t-shirt that said "Carnegie Tech civil engineers give a dam," and the gay student wore a silver on black t-shirt that said "Gay Rights Now." Given four stereotype slides and eight behaviors, each subject could then see two consistent and two inconsistent stimulus people. (Table 3.1 describes the stimuli and the matching process.) In addition, the stereotype slides were presented either before or after their matched behavior pair. Because this order manipulation had no impact, it is not discussed further.

Subjects' evaluations of the stimulus people were assessed on a scale of "general likability."[9] As before, the prediction was that good match to the negative stereotype would cue negative affect, whereas poor match would not,

---

[9]This study was conducted before we began using the more sensitive, continuous measures of affect noted elsewhere in this chapter. Results were nonsignificant on a quick and dirty affect checklist we were using at the time. Consequently, this study's reported results used a bipolar evaluation measure of general likability, which should be highly correlated, although not identical, with affect.

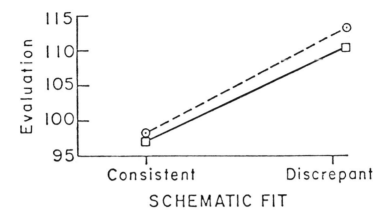

FIG. 3.6.   Evaluation fit between stereotype and behavior (Fiske & Gup, 1980). Upper line represents stereotype-behavior presentation sequence; lower line represents the reverse sequence.

even holding constant the component evaluations. As Fig. 3.6 shows, schema-consistent targets in fact were liked less that schema-discrepant targets, given negative schemata and moderate behaviors. The crucial point bears repeating: The evaluations of the components were held constant; it was the schematic fit of the ensemble that triggered the evaluative response.

SUMMARY AND CONCLUSIONS

A schema-triggered model of interpersonal affect makes several claims about our perceptions of others. First, other people are represented as instances of categories. There are consensual categories at the cultural level, as in the generic politician stereotype. Understanding the likes of Reagan, Carter, and Kennedy comes in part from shared prior knowledge about the personality and appearance typical of our nation's politicians. There are also consensual categories at the subculture level. Campus stereotypes include knowledge about the behavior to be expected of preppies and hippies, engineers and artists, gays and ROTC recruits. Finally, there are idiosyncratic categories, as in the old-flame schema. This includes, again, expectations about personality and appearance consistent with one's past experiences. At each level, the term schema captures the process of matching new information to old, of fitting an instance to an abstraction. Alternative terms, such as stereotype, do not explicitly evoke the matching process.

The model makes a second claim: Affect is linked to categorization. Given good fit to the schema, the instance elicits the schema's affect. Good examples of politicians and nurds trigger negative affect, whereas good examples of old flames trigger positive affect. Partial matches—in which the schema has been evoked but the fit is poor—trigger moderated affect, an ambivalent combination of positive and negative. Thus, both moderate positive and moderate negative affect are directed toward potential dates who have the "right" personality or the "right" looks but not both. And, in another realm, politicians who do not look or act like the typical politician are given benefit of the doubt and a moderately positive evaluation. Finally, engineering nurds who act atypically spontaneous and creative are preferred to those who simply work hard, as would be expected. All the partial matches elicit moderated affect compared to the total matches. Further, nonmatches elicit little affect of any sort. The ordinary person evokes little reaction unless a specific schema has been triggered.

The model ventures a third claim, namely that affectively triggered schemata are guides to action. In the case of prototypic politicians, one votes against them. In the case of prototypic old flames, one seeks them out in a social rather than task-oriented setting. Other research indicates similar category-based behaviors: People seek information that will support their expectations (Berscheid, Grazanio, Monson, & Dermer, 1976; Snyder & Cantor, 1979), treat people according to those expectations, and elicit the expected reciprocal responses (Snyder, Tanke, & Berscheid, 1977; Word, Zanna, & Cooper, 1974). Such self-fulfilling prophecies are particularly important when affectively tinged expectations are repeatedly confirmed and hence persevere. Clinicians, for example, devote lifetimes to uncovering and changing their clients' more destructive self-fulfilling expectations.

In sum, then, interpersonal schemata are usefully viewed as a network of knowledge, affect, and plans that are richly interconnected. In arguing this point of view, we must keep sight of the alternatives: piecemeal approaches in particular. Several results reported here weaken such attribute-oriented analyses. First, in the old-flame study, partial matches elicited an ambivalence not easily explained by the combined valence of the individual components; that is, the positive affect *does* roughly fit a piecemeal approach: Two positive attributes elicit extremely favorable reactions, a positive plus a neutral attribute elicits moderately positive reactions, and two neutrals elicit little reaction. In particular, however, negative affect *does not* follow a piecemeal model; that model would predict the reverse ordering for negative affects, which result does not occur. Instead, two positive attributes and two neutral attributes both elicit low negativity. One positive and one neutral elicit increased negativity. It is difficult to imagine how algebraic combinations, however weighted, would account for this pattern.

A second test of results that discredits the piecemeal perspective is in the final study reported. That study was explicitly designed to hold component evaluations constant, while manipulating only their schematic consistency or discrepancy. An algebraic model that manipulates relative weight as a function of the combination could assign lowered weight to part of the discrepant information and thus mimic the obtained results. But such an interpretation has an ad hoc quality, because it is unclear before the fact which component will be discounted and which heavily weighted. Further, as soon as an algebraic model begins to adjust for the configuration of components, it admits that some sort of complex prior knowledge shapes such relative weighting. Schematic models label and explain such expectations.

Finally, and most conceptually important, the piecemeal models do not attempt to be cognitively reasonable. They do not explain how people might actually process component evaluations into a summary reaction. Although such algebraic gymnastics might conceivably operate for combining, say, just two components into an overall attitude, it has yet to be explained how people would manage to process complex, piecemeal, evaluative information. Quite possibly, later efforts will elucidate plausible internal processes, but at present, the piecemeal models are simply outcome oriented and ignore cognitive mechanisms.

This latter lack undercuts explanations in the stimulus generalization terms of learning theories. While reinforcement models of attraction (Clore & Byrne, 1974; Lott & Lott, 1974) and of attitudes (Staats & Staats, 1957) have gathered much support, they deal mainly with the case of consistent instances (i.e.,liking someone who is rewarding) or presume all instances identical to the original. They are mute on the mechanisms of generalizing over varied instances to categories and vice versa. Nor do social conditioning models address the issue of partial matches. Instead, attitude objects are assumed to fit or not fit broader categories. A schematic approach explicitly lends itself to analyzing ambiguous and partial fits.

We can speculate about the origins of affectively laden schemata, and even less is known about how knowledge structures change through exposure to exceptions and inconsistencies. Various applied literatures offer strong bets, for example, about how to change stereotypes through contact with outgroups or how to alter maladaptive patterns through clinical intervention. If the social schema literature is going to come out of its cognitive ivory tower, it will profit much from such consultations.

ACKNOWLEDGMENTS

This chapter has benefited from the helpful comments of Eugene Borgida, Margaret Clark, Jane Costello, Barbara Fiske, Donald Fiske, Reid Hastie, David Klahr, Jill Larkin, Richard Lau, and Patricia Linville.

REFERENCES

Abelson, R. P., Kinder, D. R., Peters, M. D., & Fiske, S. T. Affective and semantic components in political person perception. *Journal of Personality and Social Psychology, 1982, 42,* 619–630.

Allport, G. W. *The nature of prejudice.* Reading, Mass.: Addison–Wesley, 1954.

Anderson, N. H. Information integration: A brief survey. In D. H. Krantz, R. C. Atkinson, R. D. Luce, & P. Suppes (Eds.), *Contemporary developments in mathematical psychology* (Vol. 2). San Francisco: W. H. Freeman, 1974.

Anderson, N. H. Integration theory applied to cognitive responses and attitudes. In R. M. Petty, T. M. Ostrom, & T. C. Brock (Eds.), *Cognitive responses in persuasion*. Hillsdale, N. J.: Lawrence Erlbaum Associates, 1981.

Anderson, N. H., & Hubert, S. Effects of concomitant verbal recall on order effects in personality impression formation. *Journal of Verbal Learning and Verbal Behavior*, 1963, 2, 379–391.

Asch, S. E. Forming impressions of personality. *Journal of Abnormal and Social Psychology*, 1946, 41, 258–290.

Bartlett, F. *Remembering: A study in experimental and social psychology*. Cambridge, Mass.: Cambridge University Press, 1932.

Bem, D. J. Self-perception theory. In L. Berkowitz (Ed.), *Advances in experimental social psychology* (Vol. 6). New York: Academic Press, 1972.

Berscheid, E., Graziano, W., Monson, T., & Dermer, M. Outcome dependency: Attention, attribution, and attraction. *Journal of Personality and Social Psychology*, 1976, 34, 978–989.

Bower, G. H., Black, J. B., & Turner, T. J. Scripts in memory for text. *Cognitive Psychology*, 1979, 11, 177–220.

Cantor, N., & Mischel, W. Prototypes in person perception. In L. Berkowitz (Ed.), *Advances in experimental social psychology* (Vol. 12). New York: Academic Press, 1979.

Clore, G. L., & Byrne, D. A reinforcement-affect model of attraction. In T. L. Huston (Ed.), *Foundations of interpersonal attraction*. New York: Academic Press, 1974.

Darley, J. M., & Fazio, R. H. Expectancy confirmation processes arising in the social interaction sequence. *American Psychologist*, 1980, 35, 867–881.

Dreben, E. D., Fiske, S. T., & Hastie, R. The independence of item and evaluative information: Impression and recall order effects in behavior-based impression formation. *Journal of Personality and Social Psychology*, 1979, 37, 1758–1768.

Fishbein, M. A consideration of beliefs, and their role in attitude measurement. In M. Fishbein (Ed.), *Readings in attitude theory and measurement*. New York: Wiley, 1967.

Fiske, S. T. Attention and weight in person perception: The impact of extreme and negative behavior. *Journal of Personality and Social Psychology*, 1980, 38, 889–906.

Fiske, S. T. Social cognition and affect. In J. Harvey (Ed.), *Cognition, social behavior, and the environment*. Hillsdale, N. J.: Lawrence Erlbaum Associates, 1981.

Fiske, S. T., Beattie, A. E., & Milberg, S. J. *Schema-triggered affect: Cognitive schemas and affective matches in the initiation of close relationships*. Unpublished manuscript, Carnegie–Mellon University, 1981.

Fiske, S. T., & Gup, D. *Effects of stereotype-behavior timing and consistency on attention, evaluation, and memory*. Unpublished manuscript, Carnegie–Mellon University, 1980.

Fiske, S. T., Kenny, D. A., & Taylor, S. E. Structural models for the mediation of salience effects on attribution. *Journal of Experimental Social Psychology*, 1982, 18, 105–127.

Fiske, S. T., & Kinder, D. R. Involvement, expertise, and schema use: Evidence from political cognition. In N. Cantor & J. Kihlstrom (Eds.), *Personality, cognition, and social interaction*. Hillsdale, N. J.: Lawrence Erlbaum Associates, 1981.

Fiske, S. T., & Linville, P. W. What does the term schema buy us? To appear in *Personality and Social Psychology Bulletin*, 1980, 6, 543–557.

Fiske, S. T., Milberg, S. J., Destefano, T. T., & Maffett, S. *Schemas and affect in political person perception*. Unpublished manuscript, Carnegie–Mellon University, 1980.

Hamilton, D. L. A cognitive-attributional analysis of stereotyping. In L. Berkowitz (Ed.), *Advances in experimental social psychology* (Vol. 12). New York: Academic Press, 1979.

Hastie, R. Schematic principles in human memory. In E. T. Higgins, C. P. Herman, & M. P. Zanna (Eds.), *Social cognition: The Ontario Symposium* (Vol. 1). Hillsdale, N. J.: Lawrence Erlbaum Associates, 1981.

Heider, F. *The psychology of interpersonal relations*. New York: Wiley, 1958.

Higgins, E. T., Kuiper, N. A., & Olson, J. M. Social cognition: A need to get personal. In E. T.

Higgins, C. P. Herman, & M. P. Zanna (Eds.), *Social cognition: The Ontario Symposium.* Hillsdale, N. J.: Lawrence Erlbaum Associates, 1981.

Kinder, D. R., Peters, M. D., Abelson, R. P., & Fiske, S. T. Presidential prototypes. *Political Behavior,* 1981, *2*, 315–337.

Linville, P. W. The complexity-extremity effect in age-based stereotyping. *Journal of Personality and Social Psychology,* 1982, *42*, 193–211.

Lott, A. J., & Lott, B. E. The role of reward in the formation of positive interpersonal attraction. In T. L. Huston (Ed.), *Foundations of interpersonal attraction.* New York: Academic Press, 1974.

Love, R. E., & Greenwald, A. G. Cognitive responses to persuasion as mediators of opinion change. *The Journal of Social Psychology,* 1978, *104*, 231–241.

Matlin, M., & Stang, D. *The Pollyana principle.* Cambridge, Mass.: Schenkman, 1978.

Osgood, C. E., Suci, G. J., & Tannenbaum, P. H. *The measurement of meaning.* Urbana: University of Illinois, 1957.

Ostrom, T. M. Between-theory and within-theory conflict in explaining context effects in impression formation. *Journal of Experimental Social Psychology,* 1977, *13*, 492–503.

Riskey, D. R. Verbal memory processes in impression formation. *Journal of Experimental Psychology: Human Learning and Memory,* 1979, *5*, 271–281.

Roseman, I. *Cognitive aspects of emotion and emotional behavior.* Paper presented to American Psychological Association, 1979.

Rumelhart, D. E., & Ortony, A. The representation of knowledge in memory. In R. C. Anderson, R. J. Spiro, & W. E. Montague (Eds.), *Schooling and the acquisition of knowledge.* Hillsdale, N. J.: Lawrence Erlbaum Associates, 1977.

Russell, J. A. Evidence of convergent validity on the dimensions of affect. *Journal of Personality and Social Psychology,* 1978, *36*, 1152–1168.

Russell, J. A. Affective space is bipolar. *Journal of Personality and Social Psychology,* 1979, *37*, 345–356.

Schank, R., & Abelson, R. *Scripts, plans, goals, and understanding: An inquiry into human knowledge structures.* Hillsdale, N. J.: Lawrence Erlbaum Associates, 1977.

Sears, D. O. *Positivity biases in evaluations of presidential candidates.* Paper presented to American Psychological Association, 1976.

Smith, M. B., Bruner, J. S., & White, R. W. *Opinions and personality.* New York: Wiley, 1956.

Snyder, M., & Cantor, N. Testing hypotheses about other people: The use of historical knowledge. *Journal of Experimental Social Psychology,* 1979, *15*, 330–342.

Snyder, M., Tanke, E. D., & Berscheid, E. Social perception and interpersonal behavior: On the self-fulfilling nature of social stereotypes. *Journal of Personality and Social Psychology,* 1977, *35*, 656–666.

Staats, C. K., & Staats, A. W. Meaning established by classical conditioning. *Journal of Experimental Psychology,* 1957, *54*, 74–80.

Taylor, S. E. The interface of cognitive and social psychology. In J. Harvey (Ed.), *Cognition, social behavior, and the environment.* Hillsdale, N. J.: Lawrence Erlbaum Associates, 1981.

Taylor, S. E., & Crocker, J. Schematic bases of social information processing. In E. T. Higgins, C. A. Herman, & M. P. Zanna (Eds.), *Social cognition: The Ontario Symposium.* Hillsdale, N. J.: Lawrence Erlbaum Associates, 1981.

Taylor, S. E., & Fiske, S. T. Getting inside the head: Methodologies for process analysis. In J. Harvey, W. Ickes, & R. Kidd (Eds.), *New directions in attribution research* (Vol. III). Hillsdale, N. J.: Lawrence Erlbaum Associates, 1981.

Tesser, A. Self-generated attitude change. In L. Berkowitz (Ed.), *Advances in experimental social psychology* (Vol. 11). New York: Academic Press, 1978.

Tomkins, S. E. Script theory: Differential magnification of affects. In H. E. Howe, Jr., & R. A. Dienstbier (Eds.), *Nebraska Symposium on Motivation* (Vol. 26). Lincoln: University of Nebraska Press, 1980.

Word, C. O., Zanna, M. P., & Cooper, J. The nonverbal mediation of self-fulfilling prophecies in interracial interaction. *Journal of Experimental Social Psychology,* 1974, *10,* 109–120.

Zajonc, R. B. Cognition and social cognition: A historical perspective. In L. Festinger (Ed.), *Retrospections on social psychology.* Oxford University Press, 1980. (a)

Zajonc, R. B. Feeling and thinking: Preferences need no inferences. *American Psychologist,* 1980, *35,* 151–175. (b)

Zanna, M. P., & Hamilton, D. L. Further evidence for meaning change in impression formation. *Journal of Experimental Social Psychology,* 1977, *13,* 224–238.

4

Affective Consequences of Complexity Regarding the Self and Others

Patricia W. Linville
Yale University

Extremity or variability of affect is a fundamental aspect of human affective experience. By affective extremity I mean the degree to which a person's moods and social evaluations vary across time, stimuli, or situations. For instance, consider a college senior who applies to a number of top law schools. Over Christmas she receives her LSAT score, which is 50 points above her expectation. Her mood is euphoric. She experiences an inflated self-appraisal. Shortly after, she receives her fall grade report. Her fall grades are much poorer than she expected, a real blow to her prospects for admission to a top law school. Her mood is now bleak, almost depressed. Her self-appraisal is severely deflated. This example illustrates how moods and feelings about oneself vary over time. It also illustrates the role of changes in circumstances as causes of affective variability. There are, however, individual differences in the degree of affective variability. To continue this example, another woman with the same academic record and the same hopes for law school admission responds very differently to receiving the same good and bad news. After receiving her LSAT scores, she feels really pleased; after learning of her fall grades, she feels mildly dejected. In short, her mood and self-appraisal vary less in response to good and bad happenings in her life.

Variability of affect applies not only to feelings about the self but also to feelings about others. For example, a white male professor sits on a law school admissions committee. When evaluating the folders of women, blacks, or other minorities, his ratings appear to be quite extreme or variable. That is, when these applicants have strong credentials, he gives them very high ratings; when these applicants have mediocre or weak credentials, he gives them very low ratings. When evaluating the folders of white males, however, his ratings appear to be

79

more moderate or less variable. He gives moderately high ratings to white males with strong credentials and only moderately low ratings to white males with mediocre or weak credentials.

How can we explain these observations of affective variability? When psychologists theorize about mood and social evaluation, they tend to emphasize *unidirectional* effects and biases. Consider how people feel about themselves. Research on self-esteem, for example, often characterizes some people as being consistently high in self-esteem and others as being consistently low. In fact, a major objective of research on individual differences is to find stable unidirectional biases that predict behavior. Consider next how people feel about others. Here too theories of stereotyping have emphasized unidirectional biases, either systematically favorable or systematically unfavorable, toward members of a social group. That is precisely what is meant by such terms as racism, sexism, or ageism. Ingroup–outgroup theories have also emphasized a unidirectional bias; namely, people are more favorable toward ingroup than outgroup members (Brewer, 1979; Wilder, 1980).

The theories that have been devised to explain such unidirectional biases cannot account for the extremity or variability of an individual's moods or evaluations—for variability is an inherently bidirectional phenomenon. This chapter presents a model and research suggesting that extremity in mood and evaluation is tied to cognitive structure, and specifically to the *complexity* of knowledge structures that guides the processing of information about the self and others. The basic argument is that *simplicity* in one's thinking about a domain is associated with more *extreme* affective reactions within that domain; greater *complexity* in one's thinking is associated with more *moderate* reactions. This hypothesis is used first to explain feelings about others and second to explain feelings about the self. The first section of this chapter presents a framework and theoretical model. The second section focuses on affective reactions to others, summarizing previous work on the link between complexity and stereotyping. The remainder of the chapter applies this model to feelings about the self, reporting current work on the link between self-complexity and variability in mood and self-appraisal.

In closing this introduction, I would like to clarify the use of the term *affect* in this chapter. The term affect has several meanings. As illustrated in the present volume, it may refer to mood or a feeling state, evaluation, or the interruption of attention and subsequent arousal. The present research specifically focuses on mood and evaluation. Although there are differences between the two, the present model makes the same predictions for both. Therefore, to make this chapter more readable, the generic term affect is used to encompass both mood and evaluation.

COMPLEXITY OF KNOWLEDGE STRUCTURES

According to the present model, affect results from a process that is in part determined by the structure of the representation of information we have about ourselves and others. This structural organization is critical because it guides the processing of information that can give rise to affect. People's knowledge in many domains may be thought of as being comprised of rich sets of features, and beliefs about the relationships among these features. People notice what sets of features tend to occur together within a category, and they store in memory this co-occurrence information about feature combinations (see J. R. Anderson, Kline, & Beasley, 1979; Hayes–Roth & Hayes–Roth, 1977). This information is organized into knowledge structures (e.g., schemas, implicit personality theories) that embody such beliefs concerning the association among features. Similarly, people's knowledge of themselves, others, and social groups may be thought of as being organized into feature sets and relationships among feature sets. People use these integrated structures to guide their processing of new information about themselves (e.g., Kuiper & Derry, 1981; Markus, 1977; Rogers, 1981) and others (e.g., Cantor & Mischel, 1979; Cohen, 1981; Snyder & Uranowitz, 1978; Taylor, Fiske, Etcoff, & Ruderman, 1978).

The present work concerns one aspect of social knowledge structures—their complexity. Complexity can be thought of in a number of ways depending on one's choice of representation. Thus the meaning and operationalization of complexity will vary across different representations. To speculate within several frameworks, complexity may have the following meanings. In a multidimensional spatial representation (e.g., Rosenberg & Sedlak, 1972), greater complexity may be interpreted in terms of a greater number of dimensions. In a feature set representation (e.g., J. R. Anderson, Kline, & Beasley, 1979), greater complexity may mean a greater number of features or feature sets, lower redundancy of features, or greater feature articulation. In a hierarchical feature tree representation (e.g., Sattath & Tversky, 1977), greater complexity may be represented in terms of a greater number of levels in the hierarchy, a greater number of conceptual nodes, or greater distances between nodes. Finally, in a semantic network structure (e.g., J. R. Anderson, 1976), greater complexity may be defined in terms of a greater number of nodes or more interconnections among nodes. Thus within each model, complexity has similar but not isomorphic meanings. And these speculations certainly do not exhaust the possible definitions. These speculations do point out the fact that the concept is multifaceted, model-specific, and somewhat fuzzy. Most of my work has assumed that people represent stimuli in terms of a set of features. For example, in my research on knowledge structures for social groups, complexity was measured in terms of the number of independent features underlying a person's thinking about members of a specific group, this number being represented by a convenient statistical measure (see

Linville, 1982; Linville & Jones, 1980). In my recent research on self-knowl-edge structures reported in this chapter, I use both this measure as well as a measure of the complexity of a hierarchical feature tree representation.

The present model treats complexity as domain specific. That is, a person may be simple in thinking about some domains but complex about others. For example, a person may be complex regarding psychologists yet simple regarding politicians. That is, the person may distinguish among clinical, developmental, cognitive, physiological, and social psychologists yet simply distinguish among liberal and conservative politicians. Whereas the exact degree of generalizability of complexity across different domains remains an open question (for reviews see Crockett, 1965; Goldstein & Blackman, 1978; Scott, Osgood, & Peterson, 1979), what does seem clear is that complexity is in part domain specific, with degree of complexity dependent on the type and amount of familiarity and experience regarding a specific domain. Empirical evidence supports this assumption. Greater information about nations was positively correlated with greater dimensionality for nations; and dimensionality was higher for well-known acquaintances than for little-known others (cited in Scott et al., 1979). A course in comparative government increased the dimensionality of students' ratings of nations (Scott, 1969); and Princeton seniors used more underlying dimensions in rating local slang than did freshmen (Friendly & Glucksberg, 1970). Given the domain specific quality of complexity, what are the likely affective consequences?

Complexity–Extremity Hypothesis[1]

The present model focuses on the link between this cognitive factor, the com-plexity of the knowledge structure used in thinking about a domain, and an affective factor, the extremity of responses to stimuli or information in that domain. First consider what is meant here by the term affective extremity. Greater extremity does not refer to a consistent tendency to rate stimuli more extremely in only one direction, but rather to rate stimuli more extremely in both directions, either more positively or more negatively depending on the favorability of information about the stimulus. For the case involving two stimuli in a domain, one favorable and the other unfavorable, the range or difference between one's rating of the favorable and unfavorable stimulus provides a mea-sure of extremity. For the case involving a set of three or more stimuli, the variance of one's overall ratings across the set of stimuli provides a useful measure of extremity.

---

[1]See Linville (1982) for a more detailed discussion of the present complexity notion; of its relationship to prior concepts and to other stereotyping research; and of the theoretical assumptions underlying the basic complexity–extremity hypothesis.

The basic hypothesis of the model is as follows: The less complex a person's representation of a given domain, the more extreme will be the person's affect regarding stimuli in that domain. In other words, if the representation is simple, that is, a person's thinking is in terms of fewer nonredundant features or aspects, affect will be relatively extreme. When the representation is more complex, affect will be more moderate.

This hypothesis follows from three observations: First, in areas of life where people have greater experience or familiarity, they develop more complex knowledge structures and thus use in their thinking more features or aspects in a nonredundant fashion. For example, when faced with stimuli from that domain, they encode or interpret it in a more complex fashion. Second, the greater the number of nonredundant aspects a person uses in thinking about a domain, the less likely it is that a given stimulus will be perceived as consistently good, or consistently bad, in all respects. Thus the more things one considers about a person, the less likely one is to find that person consistently good in all aspects, or consistently bad. And third, this tendency to perceive a stimulus as good in some respects yet bad in others (that is, to use categories comprised of mixtures of good and bad attributes) will have a moderating effect on affective ratings. It will if one's overall reaction to a stimulus results from a process of weighing the pros and cons across component attributes that can be well-approximated by a weighted averaging model. In many evaluative contexts a weighted average model provides an excellent approximation to human judgment (N. H. Anderson, 1974; Slovic & Lichtenstein, 1971). Some other evaluative processes could produce this complexity–extremity effect, but not all evaluative processes could. A simple summation process (Fishbein & Hunter, 1964), for instance, would not. To summarize, the more nonredundant aspects or features used, the more moderate the judgments.

For example, consider the perceptions of general ability or performance (see Fig. 4.1). A person complex in this domain might separately encode intellectual ability, motivation, and leadership. A simple person might collapse these and encode them as a single attribute, for example, general ability. Thus the simple person may perceive others as high or low in general ability, whereas the complex person is more likely to perceive others as high in certain respects, low in others. The simple person does not have many categories for fine distinctions, so he may assimilate the information to one of his extreme categories. In this example, the simple person perceives only two types of general ability, whereas the complex person perceives eight types. For the simple person, the categories are evaluatively extreme in one direction or another; but for the complex person, one quarter of the categories are extreme and the other three quarters are mixed or relatively moderate.

In general, with n independent binary attributes, there are 2^n possible categories and only two will be good or bad in every respect. The other categories will consist of mixtures of good and bad attributes; for instance, high in intellectual

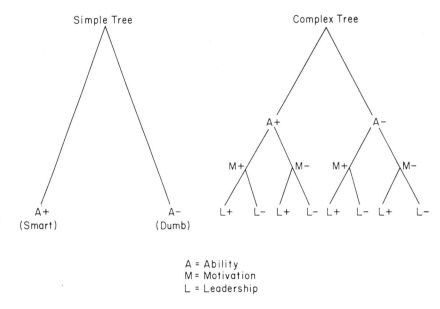

A = Ability
M = Motivation
L = Leadership

FIG. 4.1.   A simple and complex tree for representing general ability. A = Ability, M = Motivation, and L = Leadership.

ability and motivation but low in leadership. Assuming that each category is roughly equally likely to be used, the proportion of stimuli that will be categorized as either good in all respects or bad in all respects is $2/2^n$. Thus the proportion of extreme categories declines rapidly as n increases. This will tend to be the case even if the categories are not equally likely. So the person with a complex knowledge structure will tend to perceive a stimulus in terms of a mixture of good and bad attributes. Thus if the evaluation process has the qualitative properties of the weighted averaging model, the complex person will be less extreme on the average in his evaluations within the domain than a person with a more simple knowledge structure.

To illustrate, consider the perceptions of ability example in Fig. 4.1. Suppose that both perceivers assign a value of "1" to an attribute perceived as high, and a value of "0" to an attribute perceived as low. Next assume that the perceiver forms an overall evaluation of each individual by averaging across the values of each attribute. The simple perceiver using only one attribute will assign a rating of 1 to his A$^+$ category and a rating of 0 to his A$^-$ category. The complex perceiver using three attributes will assign a rating of 1 to his A$^+$ M$^+$ L$^+$ category, .667 to his A$^+$ M$^+$ L$^-$ category, .333 to his A$^+$ M$^-$ L$^-$ category, and so forth. Suppose that the complex and simple perceivers rate the ability of eight randomly selected individuals. And assume that the attributes are independent so that from the complex perceiver's point of view there is one of each of his eight types. From the simple perceiver's view, there are four of each of his two types. The ratings of the simple perceiver will be 1, 1, 1, 1, 0, 0, 0, 0; and the ratings of the complex perceiver will be 1, .667, .667, .333, .667, .333, .333, 0. In comparing these two sets of ratings, note that the average rating by both perceivers is .5. On the average then the complex and simple perceivers are equally favorable. But they differ in the extremity, or more precisely, the variance of their ratings. For the simple perceiver, the variance is .25; for the complex perceiver, the variance is .083. Thus the simple perceiver is more extreme or variable on the average than the complex perceiver.

AFFECT TOWARD OTHERS

In previous research I applied this basic model to stereotyping and intergroup biases, examining people's affective responses to various social group members. The main hypothesis to be tested was that the more complex a person's representation of a social group, the less extreme will be that person's evaluations of members from that group. The basic complexity–extremity prediction, that greater complexity results in less extreme evaluations, has been tested in three different ways. First, complexity for a social group was measured as an individual-difference variable and correlated with extremity of evaluation for members of that group. Second, complexity was manipulated indirectly through ingroup–outgroup status, and the differences in extremity of evaluations for ingroup and outgroup members were observed. Finally, complexity was directly manipulated through task instructions, and again the effect on extremity of evaluation was observed. The design and results of each of these converging tests of the hypothesis are summarized in the following sections.

Complexity as an Individual-Difference Variable

To examine the impact of people's complexity regarding social groups, Linville (1982) correlated an individual-difference measure of complexity with extremity of evaluation. College-age males participated in two sessions, the first to obtain a complexity measure regarding a social group and the second to obtain evaluations for members of that group (see Fig. 4.2 for design and main results). In the first session, they performed a trait sorting task designed to assess the complexity of their thinking regarding older males. Subjects sorted 33 traits into groups according to which ones they thought belonged together. They were instructed to think about males in their 60s and 70s while sorting the traits. A subject's trait sort was used to calculate his complexity score regarding older males. This complexity score may be interpreted as the number of independent conceptual attributes underlying that subject's trait sort (see Linville, 1982 and Scott, Osgood, & Peterson, 1979, for a more detailed description of the measure). In the

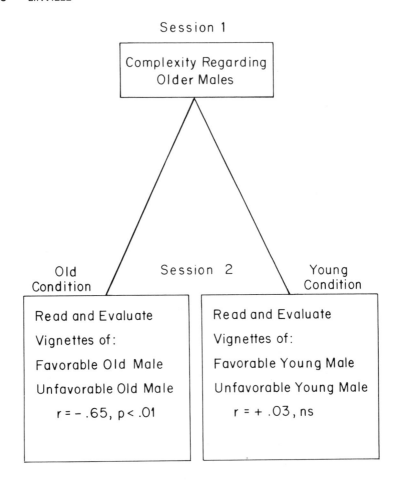

FIG. 4.2.   Design and main results for the age-based stereotyping study (Linville, 1982). Correlations are between complexity regarding old males and evaluative extremity for old and young males.

second session, 3 weeks later, these same subjects read and evaluated vignettes describing two older males. One older male was described by a vignette that was favorable in content, the other by a vignette that was unfavorable. Evaluative extremity was measured for each subject as the difference between his rating for the favorable and the unfavorable older male. According to the complexity–extremity hypothesis, greater complexity regarding older males (measured in session one) should result in less extreme evaluations of older males (measured in session two). And, in fact, the complexity and evaluative extremity scores were strongly negatively correlated ($r = -.65$, $p < .01$, $n = 15$, all tests are two-tailed, see Fig. 4.2). Those simple in their thinking about the category of older males were more extreme in their evaluations of individual older males. Further analyses showed that as predicted those simple in their thinking about older males were both more favorable toward the favorable older male ($r = -.43$, $p < .11$) and more unfavorable toward the unfavorable older male ($r = +.50$, $p < .06$). (Because the present theory predicts the direction of each correlation, one-tailed tests are in principle justified; thus the two-tailed tests reported here are conservative.) These results directly support the hypothesis using measures of overall affective reaction, liking, and various trait ratings.

The present model assumes that complexity and its effects are at least partially domain specific. That is, complexity regarding a specific domain influences evaluations of stimuli most strongly from that domain. Alternatively, complexity regarding one interpersonal domain may reflect a general personality or intellectual trait and therefore be associated with evaluations of stimuli in other interpersonal domains. To test this, the other half of the subjects read and evaluated these same vignettes that were now attributed to college-aged males. Consistent with the present domain specificity assumption, complexity regarding older males was not associated with evaluative extremity regarding college-age males ($r = .03$).

Complexity as an Ingroup–Outgroup Status Variable

In the ingroup–outgroup status studies, high or low complexity was indirectly manipulated by manipulating the ingroup–outgroup status of the target person to be evaluated. If people tend to have more complex representations of their own groups than of other groups (and in fact trait sorting data support this assumption, Linville, 1982; Linville & Jones, 1980), then people will evaluate outgroup members more extremely than ingroup members. In other words, if people have relatively simple representations regarding outgroups, and if simple representations result in more extreme evaluations, then it follows that people will evaluate outgroup members more extremely than ingroup members.

As discussed earlier, the fundamental interpretation of evaluative extremity involves the range or variance of a person's overall ratings across a set of stimuli. This is in contrast to most approaches to intergroup biases that make no prediction about extremity as defined here, but rather predict uniform biases (usually negative) toward certain groups. The present model is neutral regarding when such membership main effects will arise. But in the absence of a group membership main effect, and when two target persons are chosen so that one is favorable and the other unfavorable, evaluative extremity will take the form of a polarization effect. Thus polarization is simply a special case of the extremity prediction. That is, when the information about a member is favorable, the outgroup member will be evaluated more favorably than the ingroup member; when the infor-

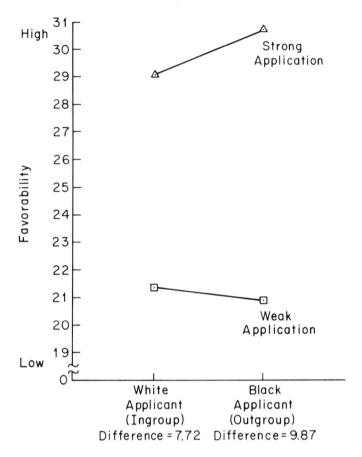

FIG. 4.3.   Mean ratings of favorability as a function of the race and favorability of the target person (Linville & Jones, 1980).

mation is unfavorable, the outgroup member will be evaluated more unfavorably.

This hypothesis was tested in two series of experiments using race, sex, and age as ingroup–outgroup variables. The first series looked at race and sex as group variables (Linville & Jones, 1980). White students read and evaluated several law school applications that contained incidental information on the race and sex of the applicant. In addition, we varied whether the application was strong or weak in quality. The results support the outgroup extremity or polarization prediction (see Fig. 4.3). When reading a strong application, white subjects rated a black applicant (outgroup) higher than a comparable white applicant. When reading a weak application, they rated a black applicant lower than a comparable white applicant. Similar results were obtained for cross-sex (outgroup) pairings on one dimension—leadership. Male subjects viewing a female applicant, and female subjects viewing a male applicant, were more extreme in their ratings than when rating an applicant of the same sex (see Fig. 4.4).

The second series of studies used age as the ingroup–outgroup variable (Linville, 1982). College-age males read and evaluated vignettes describing two separate people. One person was described by a favorable vignette, the other by an unfavorable vignette. For half the subjects, both vignettes were attributed to college-age males; for the other half, both were attributed to males in their late 60s. A pretest sample of subjects rates neither vignette as more likely to describe a younger than an older male. The results support the outgroup extremity hypothesis: Young male subjects evaluated older males more extremely than young males of their own age. When the vignette was favorable, the older man was rated more positively than the younger one. When the vignette was unfavorable, the older male was rated more negatively than the younger one (see Fig. 4.5). Thus subjects were not uniformly more positive or negative toward older males or blacks (that is, outgroup members) as some research would suggest. They were simply more extreme in their affective and evaluative reactions. Recently,

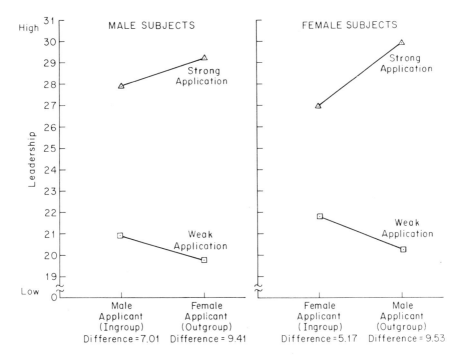

FIG. 4.4.   Mean ratings of leadership as a function of the sex and favorability of the target person (Linville & Jones, 1980).

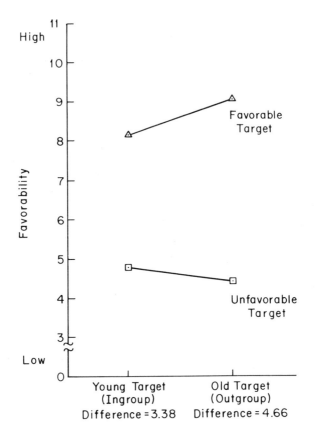

FIG. 4.5.   Mean ratings of favorability as a function of the age and favorability of the target person (Linville, 1982).

we found that older male subjects evaluated younger males more extremely than older males (Linville & Salovey, 1982).

Complexity as a Directly Manipulated Variable

Finally, the complexity–extremity prediction was tested by directly manipulating complexity through task instructions that induced subjects to adopt a simple or complex orientation toward a set of stimuli. The first study involved reading and evaluating several law school application essays, each describing why the applicant wished to attend law school (Linville & Jones, 1980). One of the essays was quite strong in quality, whereas another was relatively weak. The subject was asked to think about the essay in terms of several features for a brief time period prior to making one favorability rating of the essay. It should be noted that the subject never rated nor expected to rate the essay on the individual features. In the high-complexity condition, six features were listed for the subject to think about before rating the essay (e.g., motivation, writing style); in the low-complexity condition, only two features were listed, with all possible permutations of the six taken two at a time included. As predicted, those in the low-complexity condition made more extreme ratings, more extremely favorable toward the strong essay and more extremely negative toward the weak essay, compared to subjects in the high-complexity condition who were more moderate.

Using a similar design, subjects in another study (Linville, 1982) tasted and evaluated five different types of chocolate-chip cookies ranging in quality. Subjects thinking about two features (e.g., how buttery, chewy) were more extreme in their favorability rating of each cookie than were those thinking about six features. That is, they demonstrated a higher variance across their five-cookie ratings, compared to subjects in the high-complexity condition who were more moderate or demonstrated a smaller variance across their five-cookie ratings (Linville, 1982). Thus degree of complexity is situationally malleable and affects ratings of social as well as nonsocial stimuli, even cookies.

Summary and Implications for Stereotyping and Intergroup Relations

This research program provides three conceptual replications of the basic complexity–extremity relationship. Less complexity—either measured as an individual-difference variable, assumed in terms of perceptions of outgroups, or manipulated through task instructions—resulted in more extreme ratings. Thus there are parallel findings for dispositional, group membership, and manipulated complexity. This cross validation involving both dispositional and manipulated complexity was designed to provide a stronger empirical support for the hypothesized underlying mechanism.

These results suggest that degree of affect regarding social group members may be at least partially determined by the structure of cognitive representations of social categories. These representations guide the processing of person information that gives rise to affective or evaluative reactions. Intergroup affect is tied to cognitive structure, and specifically to the lack of complex interpretive mechanisms for processing information about less familiar social groups. In other words, we make "quick and dirty" and affectively laden responses to members of less familiar groups.

In relating this work to more traditional work in stereotyping, these results do pose one puzzle. Why does the present research find a polarization pattern, whereas many other studies find only a group membership main effect? For example, people are more negative toward older than younger persons (see Lutsky, 1980; McTavish, 1971), and subtly more negative toward blacks than whites (see Crosby, Bromley, & Saxe, 1980; McConahay & Hough, 1976; Pettigrew, 1979). First note that the range or extremity prediction can coexist with a group membership main effect, thus complementing rather than contradicting motivational theories. For instance, Americans may be biased against Russians, that is, on the average more favorable toward Americans than Russians. Despite this main effect, they may still demonstrate a greater range or *variability* in their overall ratings of Russians. That is, they may perceive a greater difference between a good and bad Russian than between a good and bad American. However, the findings reported here took the form of a polarization pattern with no race, sex, or age main effect. There are several methodological differences between the present research and other paradigms that may account for these empirical differences. First, in much of the stereotyping research, the only information that a subject receives about the target person is a group membership label (e.g., race, sex, religion, or age). In the present paradigm, subjects received a richer, fuller description of the target person. The attribute of interest, the target's race, sex, or age, is embedded in a context with other attributes and behaviors. Second, in the ingroup favoritism research, researchers rely on groups arbitrarily created in the laboratory, and subjects receive little information about a target beyond the ingroup or outgroup status of the target. The present paradigm relied on established group categories that allowed subjects to draw on prior knowledge structures associated with these categories. Third, most intergroup-relations research does not actually allow a test of an extremity prediction because subjects do not rate a set of target persons varying in favorability as well as group status.

With little information other than group membership per se on which to base feelings or evaluations, a group label may cue an affective bias associated with the group membership or status, resulting in prejudice or a main effect. One reasonable speculation then is that affect is cognitively stored with the group label (see also Fiske, this volume). With richer information about a target, however, group membership also evokes a knowledge structure that provides a basis for processing further information about the target. It is the interaction of rich data about a target person with a prior knowledge structure (simple or complex) that results in the complexity–extremity effect.

AFFECT TOWARD THE SELF

The work described previously focused on affective and evaluative judgments of others. More recently I have applied this same model to moods and self-appraisal. Assume that affect about the self results from the same basic processes as affect toward others. Then we would expect that those with a simple cognitive representation of the self will be more extreme or variable in their moods and self-appraisals. In other words, those with simple self-representations will experience higher "highs" and lower "lows" than those with complex self-representations. Greater complexity regarding the self moderates moods and self-appraisals. This hypothesis is developed and tested in the remainder of the chapter.

But before developing this hypothesis in more detail, it is first necessary to be more specific about the nature of self-representations and the meaning of self-complexity.

The Self as a Cognitive Domain

The remainder of the chapter presumes the existence of a complex cognitive structure that abstractly represents information about the self. This *self-representation* develops to help organize and keep track of vast amounts of self-relevant information and is evoked to help process new information about the self.

Content and Complexity of the Self-Representation. What is represented about the self in memory? The self may be viewed as a system of nodes in a memory network with associative links connecting various aspects or concepts comprising the self. The self-representation is likely to include information about specific past events and behavior (e.g., I cried at my sister's wedding), as well as abstractions developed from repeated behavior (e.g., I cry easily). These abstractions may take various forms such as general traits, features, scripts, or roles. Research on self-description suggests that these abstractions include such defining features as category membership in formal and informal groups ("female, black, student, liberal")[2], physical characteristics ("green eyes"), general traits ("independent"), behavior ("I write lots of letters"), talents ("cello player"), preferences ("a passion for chocolate"), intellectual abilities ("good at mathematics"), autobiographical recollections ("happy childhood"), goals ("to be respected"), relations with others ("socially unpolished"), and others' feelings toward the self ("my parents are proud of me") (see Gergen, 1971; Gordon, 1968; McGuire & Padawer–Singer, 1976; Robinson, 1976). The spontaneous self-descriptions of children reveal that with increasing age they define themselves in terms of social categories more than specific individuals (McGuire & McGuire, in press). In addition, affect and appraisal of the self are represented ("I'm happy because I maintain good friendships").

Two speculations about the self-representation are of particular interest here. First, the self-representation is *complex* relative to representations of most domains. Several unique qualities of the self-representation point to its richness and high degree of differentiation. First, we probably possess a greater amount of information about the self relative to other domains. This enormous data base demands more elaborate organization, differentiation, and inference to function in a relatively efficient manner. Second, self-relevant information in the environment is relatively salient and easily gains our attention (e.g., Moray, 1959). Third, self-observations vary across many situations and persons, thus increasing

---

[2]Illustrations throughout this chapter were taken from actual spontaneous self-descriptions of subjects in a pilot study.

the differentiation of possible attributes and behaviors. For example, a person may note that he is shy in large classes, yet outgoing in smaller seminars. The tendency to make more situational than dispositional self-attributions (Jones & Nisbett, 1971) is compatible with this type of differentiation. Fourth, much of our general information (e.g., about individuals, social categories, specific encounters, places) is probably linked to some degree with the self, both because of motivations to monitor possible consequences for the self and because of the constant presence of the self in experiences where such data is encoded. As the old saying goes, "No matter where you go, there you are." Finally, the domain of the self is relatively affect laden, adding to its complexity and elaboration. Self-knowledge is associated with evaluative appraisal (e.g., "I feel successful in my work") and feelings (e.g., "I feel happy with my closest friends," "I feel angry when a friend is late"). Here the knowledge base is most intimately associated with the affective system.

A second related speculation is that the self-representation is multifaceted. Whereas the exact form of self-knowledge and self-complexity remain an open question, what does seem clear is that people think of themselves in terms of multiple aspects (see also Gergen, 1971; Goffman, 1955; Gordon, 1968; James, 1892; Sullivan, 1953). The self-representation is not an indivisible or unitary cognitive structure but rather a structure housing many concepts corresponding to various roles and situations. For instance, a woman may have an assortment of interpersonal roles (e.g., lawyer, friend, mother) or psychological roles (e.g., competitor, supporter, nurturer). These two types of self-roles may be linked. For example, she may view herself as competing with opposing lawyers, supporting her friends, and nurturing her child.

This emphasis on multiplicity is supported in part by the various aspects used by people in self-descriptive tasks. Certain aspects are obviously more central than others. Self-aspects are not all salient at the same time; attribute distinctiveness increases the accessibility of an attribute (see McGuire & Padawer–Singer, 1976). People may feel good about themselves in certain respects but not in others. Some aspects are unrelated, having little relation to one another. Certain aspects are even contradictory. The following self-description by Lyndon Johnson (cited in Gordon, 1968) illustrates this multiple, complex quality of the self-representation: "I am a free man, an American, a United States Senator and a Democrat, in that order. I am also a liberal, a conservative, a Texan, a taxpayer, a rancher, a businessman, a consumer, a parent, a voter, and not as young as I used to be nor as old as I expect to be—and I am all those things in no fixed order" (p. 123).

Self-aspects vary in the type and degree of affect associated with them. For example, the spontaneous self-description of one subject includes various aspects, some with positive affective associations ("I am proud of being independent"), others with negative associations ("I dominate conversations but feel uncomfortable about it"), and still others that are mixed ("I am basically open-minded but feel embarrassed about several bad prejudices''). How people feel about themselves varies over time and circumstances, depending partly on the particular dimension activated or on new self-relevant information. For example, a fellow may feel good when thinking about himself as a student but not as an athlete. Success in one area enhances our feelings about ourselves in that area, whereas failure diminishes these feelings.

The present model assumes that people differ in the degree of complexity of their self-representation. Why might this be the case? Just as other knowledge structures develop through processes of generalization and discrimination (see J. R. Anderson, Kline, & Beasley, 1979), so too the self-representation is likely to develop over time with use and increased information. People learn to conceptualize themselves in varying ways through varying roles, behavior, situations, or relationships. With an increase in the range of experiences relevant to the self (e.g., social, professional, family, aesthetic, physical), a person not only has the opportunity to differentiate or abstract more nonredundant features, but this may actually be necessary in order to efficiently process self-relevant information in a variety of areas, to efficiently discriminate among an increased number of roles and interpersonal situations, and to respond quickly and appropriately. Thus greater self-complexity is likely to be linked with greater and more varied experiences and situational demands. Consistent with these speculations, research indicates that with an increase in age, an individual's self-concept and self-evaluations become more differentiated and more abstract (Montemayor & Eisen, 1977; Mullener & Laird, 1971). Similarly, Linville (1982) and Linville and Jones (1980) have shown that people have more complex knowledge structures about more familiar social groups.

Affective Consequences of Self-Complexity

What might we expect to be the consequences of self-complexity? I am interested in the link between a cognitive factor, self-complexity, and an affective factor, variability in mood and self-appraisal. Casual observation suggests that people differ substantially in how much they respond to positive or negative happenings in their lives. Some people's moods swing dramatically in response to the ups and downs of daily life. Others are relatively unaffected. How can we account for this observation? The basic hypothesis developed here is that greater self-complexity results in less extreme or variable moods and self-appraisals. Why might we expect this to be so? Note that the stereotyping section centered on variation in evaluations of a set of others. Here we are concerned with variations over time in evaluations or feelings about a single entity—the self. This requires a slightly different kind of explanation.

This hypothesis follows from three assumptions. First, people differ in the complexity of their self-representations. Those who are complex either have more independent aspects in their representation or maintain greater distinction among the various aspects. Second, the more complex the self-representation, the less likely a person is to feel uniformly good or uniformly bad about all aspects of the self at any one time. With a more complex self-representation, an event that causes a change in feelings about one aspect of the self is less likely to "spill over" and change feelings about other aspects of the self. For example, if a scientist gets a paper rejected and has a simple self-structure in which professional aspects are closely tied to family aspects and social aspects of the self, then the negative affect associated with professional failure is more likely to activate these other areas. With a more complex self-structure, other areas that are not closely tied to one's professional self are not activated and thus are not as affected. By maintaining distinctions between various aspects of the self, the impact of favorable or unfavorable information is localized. It is much less likely then that a person will feel uniformly good or uniformly bad about all self-aspects. And third, if overall mood or self-appraisal can be approximated by some process of "averaging over" different aspects of the self, then those higher in self-complexity will tend to be less extreme or variable in mood and self-appraisal than those lower in self-complexity.

To illustrate this logic, consider a man who has four conceptually independent self-aspects (e.g., school, athletics, male friendships, relationships with women). If an unpleasant experience occurs in one (e.g., his girlfriend breaks up with him), then the unpleasant feelings will impact on only one quarter of his self-concept. Now consider a man who fails to make a sharp distinction between this male and female relationships; so in effect he has three distinct aspects (school, athletics, relationships). Here the unpleasant feelings will impact on one third of his self-concept, a much higher proportion of his total self. Kelly (1955) and Gergen (1971) also discuss the possible association between cognitive differentiation and mental health. Two experiments were designed to test these ideas. But first, how might we operationalize the concept of self-complexity?

Measurement of Self-Complexity

Although the exact structure of the self-representation is unknown and in some sense unknowable (see J. R. Anderson, 1976, pp. 4–15), an examination of self-descriptions leads to the following speculations: There appear to be clusters of features that define distinct aspects of the self. Members of a cluster appear to share common properties or superordinate features and are perceived closer to each other than to features in other clusters. Whether these organizing properties are roles, traits, or behavior, and whether and how they are hierarchically organized remain open questions. But as a first approximation, the present research measures the self-representation in two ways—one assuming a set of features or traits and the second a hierarchical feature tree composed of self-roles. The meaning of self-complexity varies somewhat across these measures.

In the feature set representation, self-complexity may be interpreted in terms of the number of independent conceptual features used to think about the self. To measure self-complexity defined in this way, the trait sorting method used to study complexity regarding social groups was adapted. Subjects receive 33 traits, each one on an index card. The traits were chosen to represent a wide range of dimensions that people use to think about themselves. Subjects are instructed to think about themselves and to sort the traits into groups representing traits that they think belong together. Each pile might represent a different aspect of the self. Subjects can form few or many groups, can put a trait in more than one group, and do not have to use all the traits. Each subject receives a score for self-complexity based on his or her trait sort. The statistical measure used is an information theory measure that may be interpreted as the minimum number of independent binary attributes needed to reproduce the trait sort. This is not to indicate that people think in terms of independent binary attributes. It is simply a useful statistical measure of the richness or complexity of a trait sort. In general, subjects find the task meaningful and interesting, and all form at least several groups, often reusing the same trait in several different groups. Table 4.1 illustrates an actual trait sort produced by one subject. In this particular case, the subject herself later provided the labels that appear above her trait groupings. This prototypic sort suggests the following speculations about self-representation. The self is multifaceted, including categories related to specific superordinate traits (e.g., creative), roles (e.g., with friends, alone), and evaluatively organized aspects (e.g., bad traits). Also, the self includes aspects that are often contradictory (e.g., both lazy and industrious, quiet and outgoing), and the same trait may vary in connotation depending on the particular self-aspect (e.g., relaxed and quiet versus relaxed and playful).

The second measure of complexity assumed a hierarchical tree representation of the self. One reasonable measure of the complexity of such a tree is simply the number of nodes in the tree. The greater the number of nodes in a tree, the more complex the structure. This measure reflects both the number of levels in a

TABLE 4.1
An Example of One Subject's Trait Sort and Her Category Labels

Creative	Alone	With Friends	Real World Survival	Bad Traits
Industrious	Relaxed	Relaxed	Outgoing	Lazy
Reflective	Reflective	Playful	Rebellious	Impulsive
Imaginative	Quiet	Softhearted	Assertive	Unorganized
Individualistic		Affectionate	Mature	Not Studious
Humorous		Humorous	Competitive	
Unconventional				

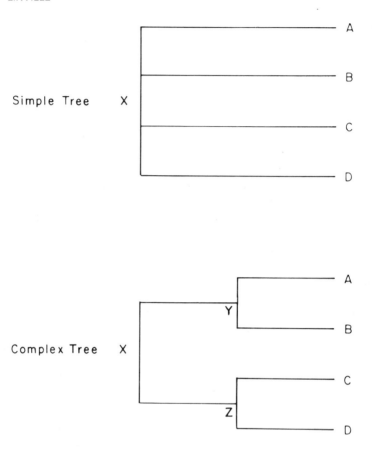

FIG. 4.6.   A simple and complex tree.

hierarchy and the amount of differentiation at each level. For example, the simple tree in Fig. 4.6 has four terminal nodes (A, B, C, D) and one superordinate property or node (X). The more complex tree in Fig. 4.6 also has four terminal nodes and one superordinate property but, in addition, has two intervening properties or nodes (Y, which is common only to A and B; and Z, which is common only to C and D).

A measure of self-complexity defined in this way was obtained by asking subjects to make similarity ratings of various self-roles. Each subject receives 10 self-roles (i.e., myself as a student, friend to women, leader, socializer, daughter, on a date, friend to men, in my career, alone, and when I fail.) These roles were chosen for their frequency and distinctiveness from a list generated by a pretest sample of women. Each subject is encouraged to interpret the roles in ways that are meaningful to her. She then rates how similarly she views herself in

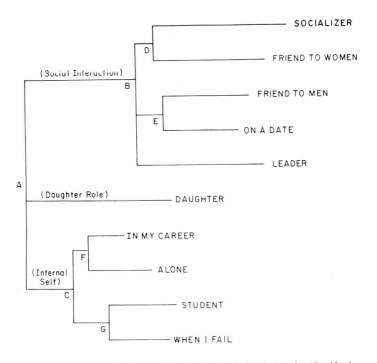

FIG. 4.7.   An example of one subject's additive similarity tree for 10 self-roles. Each vertical line represents a nonterminal node in the tree and can be interpreted as the features shared by all nodes in that cluster.

terms of each possible pair of self-roles. This similarity data is analyzed using the ADDTREE program developed by Sattath and Tversky (1977), which constructs an additive similarity tree structure whose leaves represent the rated objects (here representing the 10 self-roles). The dissimilarity between two self-roles corresponds to the length of the horizontal path joining them. Thus the tree illustrates the similarity between self-roles and yields a hierarchical clustering structure for these self-roles. Figure 4.7 illustrates an actual tree produced by ADDTREE using the similarity data of one subject. Each vertical line represents a nonterminal *node* in the tree[3] and can be interpreted as the features shared by all roles in the cluster, and by them alone. The length of a horizontal line may be thought of as the distinctiveness of the cluster. In this particular case, the subject was later shown her computer-generated tree, and she provided the following labels for her

---

[3]The use of a vertical line to denote a node is confusing at first, but it simplifies drawing a tree with exact branch lengths because all branches can be drawn with horizontal lines. The ADDTREE program draws trees in this fashion.

clusters: (1) social interaction; (2) daughter role; and (3) internal self. The tree shown in Fig. 4.7 has seven nonterminal nodes (labeled A to G) and 10 terminal nodes (self-roles), or 17 nodes in all, giving it a complexity score of 17. Whereas ADDTREE has not previously been used to analyze self-representations or to generate individual-difference measures of complexity, its use for these purposes seems intuitively appealing.

An inspection of the self-role trees across a number of subjects indicates that the roles do appear to cluster in logical groupings. For example, the roles "socializer," "on a date," and "friend to men" frequently cluster together, thus sharing common features. "Leader" and "in my career" likewise frequently cluster together. The role "daugher" is often isolated or clusters with "when I fail." "When I fail" also frequently clusters with either "alone" or "student." In addition to these common groupings, the wide variety of tree structures as well as their ideographic nature suggest a rich data base for possible clinical usage.

Response To Feedback: Empirical Evidence

The arguments developed previously suggest that people who are high in self-complexity will change less in their overall mood and self-appraisal in response to a positive or negative experience in one aspect of their lives. To test this prediction, a study was conducted to measure both self-complexity as well as affective changes after success or failure feedback (Linville, 1981b). First, each subject (all males) completed the trait sorting task, putting traits together that tended to go together in terms of himself. From this task a self-complexity score was obtained for each subject. The subject then filled out a mood scale, a self-evaluation scale, and a self-esteem scale. The self-evaluation scale included such characteristics as motivated, logical, sensitive, and intelligent. The subject answered the items as he felt right at the moment. The scales were presented on a computer terminal and were counterbalanced for order. After answering the last item, a bogus error message appeared on the subject's terminal screen. While the experimenter supposedly checked on the meaning of the error message, the subject completed an embedded figures task, described to him as an analytical task related to intelligence. The analytical test was then graded in front of the subject, followed by bogus feedback in which he was told that his performance was either in the top or bottom 10% of those taking the test. Finally, the experimenter explained to the subject that the error message indicated that the computer had gone down, losing his data. She then asked the subject to fill out the initial scales again as a favor to her. All subjects believed the computer breakdown story, and all repeated the scales. The subject was told to answer the items as he felt right at that moment and not to be concerned with how he originally answered the items. The prediction is that those with a simple self-representation will change the most after feedback, that is, they will change the

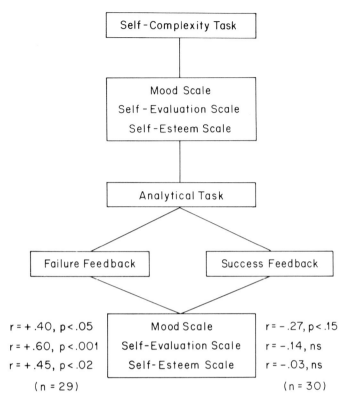

FIG. 4.8.   Design and main results for response to feedback study. Correlations are between self-complexity and change in mood, self-evaluation, and self-esteem.

most in a negative direction after failure feedback or the most in a positive direction after success.

The hypothesized relationship between self-complexity and affective extremity was tested and supported by correlating the self-complexity score obtained from the trait sorting task with change scores in mood, self-evaluation, and self-esteem, the change score being defined as the difference between these scores before and after feedback. The same pattern of results arose when initial scores were entered as a covariate in a multiple regression framework. A general affect index combining mood, self-evaluation, and self-esteem revealed that those with lower self-complexity had a greater drop in affect after failure ($r = .61, p < .0001$) and a greater but nonsignificant increase in affect after success ($r = -.28, p < .14$). In the failure condition, as predicted, those with lower self-complexity had a greater drop in mood ($r = .40$, $p < .05$, $n = 29$), in self-evaluation ($r = .60$, $p < .001$), and in self-esteem ($r = .45$, $p < .02$, see Fig. 4.8). In the success condition, those with lower self-complexity showed a greater but nonsignificant increase in mood ($r = -.27$, $p < .15$, $n = 30$) but not in self-evaluation ($r = -.14$, ns), or in self-esteem ($r = -.03$, ns). Examination of the change scores in the success condition suggests that the weaker results in this condition may be due to the fact that mood and especially self-evaluation and self-esteem did not change substantially after the success feedback. Many subjects in debriefing indicated that the success feedback meant little because they always do well on analytical tasks. Thus lower self-complexity was definitely linked with greater negative reaction after failure and only weakly linked, but in the expected direction, with greater positive reaction after success.

Mood Variability: Empirical Evidence

If those with higher self-complexity do experience less extreme mood swings, both in a positive and a negative direction, then one would expect those with higher self-complexity to experience less variability in mood over a period of time. The assumption is that most people have to deal with both positive and negative self-relevant experiences even over a brief period of time. The following experiment was conducted to test this in a natural setting (Linville, 1981a).

The study involved two phases. A group of college women first completed a task designed to measure their self-complexity. The task involved similarity judgments between 10 self-roles. The judgments of each woman were analyzed using the ADDTREE program (Sattath & Tversky, 1977) to obtain for each woman an additive similarity tree structure with clusters of self-roles. A self-complexity score was calculated for each woman by simply counting the number of nodes in her tree.

For each of the next 8 days, the subject filled out a mood scale. She chose one time of day and filled it out at that same time each day. She turned in her mood scale ratings each day, keeping no record of her previous ratings. The experimenter stressed an interest in possible mood differences among those entering and those finishing college, making no mention of an interest in mood variability.

The prediction is that those high in self-complexity will experience less mood variability. To test this prediction, a correlational analysis was performed involving the self-complexity score and the mood variability score of each subject. The mood variability score was calculated by first combining the mood items for one day into an index, with high numbers indicating more positive mood, then calculating the variance of this mood index across the 8 days. The results indicate that self-complexity, as measured in terms of the number of nodes in the additive tree structure, was negatively correlated with mood variability ($r = -.54$, $p < .002$, see Table 4.2). So, as predicted, those higher in self-complexity experienced less mood variability over an 8-day period. There was no significant relationship between self-complexity and the overall mean of the mood index.

TABLE 4.2
Correlations of Mood Variability with
Self Complexity

Mood Variability Measure	
Overall mood variance	$-.54^b$
Happiness variance	$-.45^b$
Activeness variance	$-.46^b$
Sadness variance	$-.47^b$
Aggression variance	$-.50^b$
Anxiety variance	$-.08$
Depression variance	$-.31^a$

[a]$p < .1$.
[b]$p < .01$.

Thus, as expected, simple persons were not more positive or more negative in their moods; they were simply more variable.

The mood scale was comprised of six subscales. The correlations between self-complexity and the variability of each of these subscales revealed the same predicted association. Those higher in self-complexity demonstrated less variability in happiness, activeness, sadness, depression, and aggression, but not in anxiety (see Table 4.2).

In concluding the discussion of these studies, let us return to the question of why self-complexity is negatively related to mood variability. Self-relevant information takes on an affective quality, having an impact on the relevant self-aspect. The central question involves the degree to which impact on one part of the self results in impact on other parts. Recall that self-complexity refers to the number of *different* aspects of the self, the aspects being distinct, nonredundant, and not highly correlated. To speculate, one immediate consequence of greater self-complexity is to limit the spillover of this affective impact on one aspect to other aspects of the self. With greater complexity, positive or negative changes in feelings about one aspect do not tend to color feelings about other aspects. This assumption, in combination with the assumption that general affect or feelings about ourselves reflect a weighted average of different aspects, results in the present association between greater self-complexity and lower mood variability. For example, suppose that a fellow gets cut from his junior high basketball team. If being a good basketball player is perceived to be quite separate from being a good baseball player or football player, or more generally from being an athlete, a leader, a friend to other fellows, or a good student, then the impact will be relatively local. If, however, all of these aspects are conceptually linked for him, then the impact will be more massive. If each role is simply an example of the general concept of himself as a competent male, then the unpleasant feelings for one is now an unpleasant feeling for all.

This argument is fundamentally analogous to the previous argument involving perceptions of social group members. In the case of social groups, independence of aspects results in less variability in feelings across different persons. In the case of the self, independence of self-aspects results in less variability of feelings about the self over time.

Assuming then a connection between complexity and degree of spillover, what does the number of nodes have to do with degree of spillover? One speculation is that intervening nodes dampen the spread of affect or feeling about oneself. The greater the number of nodes there are in a tree, the greater the number of nodes on the average between any two endpoints (here self-roles). For example, in Fig. 4.6 the simple tree has an average of one intervening node between any two endpoints, whereas the complex tree has an average of 2.33. To speculate further, if changes in feelings about one aspect of life spread from node to node through a tree-like structure, and if changes in feeling tend to get dampened at each node, then the more intervening nodes the less likely a change in affect concerning one aspect of life is to spill over to another aspect.

This dampening process has the effect of reducing the magnitude of the impact as one moves from one node or one level in the hierarchy to the next. At some point, of course, it will simply fail to have an impact at the next level of nodes. For example, suppose a student sets the curve in a math course. This has a substantial impact on her feelings about her math abilities. It produces a moderate improvement in her feelings about her general analytical skills and a smaller improvement in her feelings about her overall intellectual abilities. It perhaps has a slight impact on her feelings about her interpersonal insightfulness and absolutely no impact on her feelings about her troublesome backhand.

The actual mechanism for his spillover and dampening process remains unclear. Presumably, it could be accounted for by a spreading activation process (e.g., J. R. Anderson, 1976) in a network involving both semantic and affective nodes (see Bower, 1981; Clark & Isen, in press). Activation in the present model may be considered either an *affective spreading process* or an *inferential spreading process*. It is premature at this point to theorize beyond these speculations. Current research in progress hopefully will provide more definitive answers.

Relationships to Other Research on the Self

Classic theories of the self tend to emphasize affect (e.g., Cooley, 1902; Epstein, 1973; James, 1890; Kelly, 1955; C. R. Rogers, 1951; Snygg & Coombs, 1959). Recent cognitive models of the self, in contrast, tend to ignore affective, evaluative, and behavioral consequences (see Rogers, 1981, for an exception). They have instead focused on memory consequences involving encoding and retrieval (e.g., Bower & Gilligan, 1979; Kuiper & Derry, 1981; Markus, 1977; Markus & Smith, 1981; Rogers, 1981). The self-structure appears to be an active part of the information-processing system. This research provides accumulating evidence that the self-representation functions as a schema or prototype. For example, judgments about the self are made relatively quickly and confidently, and they are more easily recalled (for reviews see Kuiper & Derry, 1981; Markus & Smith, 1981; Rogers, 1981). Whereas other chapters in this book attest to the importance of affect in the memory system, most cognitive models of the self are strongly deficient in handling the affective quality of self-relevant processing. In contrast, the present work adopts a cognitive perspective on the self and focuses on affective and evaluative consequences.

The present cognitive model of the self differs from some other models in that first, it conceives of the self-representation in terms of multiple aspects or schemas; and second, it focuses on the consequences of individual differences in the self-representation. In these two respects, the present work resembles the work of Markus (1977). The present work differs from the work of Markus in several respects. First, her work focuses on memory consequences, whereas the present work focuses on affective consequences. Second, Markus measures the presence or absence of a schema for a single aspect of the self (e.g., independent, fat). The present work considers the interrelations among various aspects, in particular, measuring the number and the independence or distinctiveness of the various aspects.

Finally, the present view of multiple aspects of the self is in contrast to the conception of the self as a singular, global entity. Some research assumes a single, fixed self, measured in such terms as self-esteem or self-concept. Some clinical theorists assume that a unitary self is a mentally healthy self. The distinction is often drawn between a self that is fragmented, disconnected, and inconsistent and a self that is unified into a coherent, consistent, and constant whole (see also Gergen, 1971). In contrast, the concluding section suggests that a self comprised of many distinct aspects may actually have positive mental health consequences.

SUMMARY AND CONCLUSION

This research on self-complexity, together with previous work on complexity for social groups, indicates that the complexity of cognitive representation has affective and evaluative consequences. One study showed that those high in self-complexity experienced smaller swings in mood and self-appraisal following failure or success. A second study showed that those high in self-complexity experience less variability in mood over an 8-day period. These results parallel those obtained for evaluations of others reported in the first section of this chapter. In both cases, greater complexity was associated with less extreme affect or evaluation. The research reported here on the self, although encouraging, is preliminary. Present research is focusing on theoretical and measurement issues as well as applications of the model.

In conclusion, I would like to suggest some broader implications of the complexity–extremity link in mood and self-appraisal. First, examples discussed in this chapter suggest a sociological implication. Occupations differ in the degree to which they lead people to make distinctions between work and non-work aspects of the self. At one extreme there are professions like the priesthood in which one's work is one's life. Creative and scientific professions also encourage a merging of the professional and nonprofessional aspects of the self. At the other extreme are those who leave their work at their office door. The present model suggests that maintaining a distinction between various professional aspects, or between professional and nonprofessional aspects of the self, is conducive to less extreme affective variability.

Second, these results have possible clinical implications, suggesting a link between self-complexity and clinical depression. With a simple self-structure, negative happenings in one area of life are more likely to spill over and affect views of other self-aspects, affecting one's entire self-image and possibly leading to depression. For example, a life crisis such as divorce, death of a spouse, or an occupational failure will have a serious emotional impact on almost anyone. But a person high in self-complexity is more likely to be able to contain that impact, to maintain positive feelings about other aspects of his or her life. Thus high self-complexity may reduce the likelihood of serious depression in response to a life crisis. With a simple self-structure, one does not have the buffer of other positive aspects of the self that remain intact. With a more complex self-structure, these other aspects remain intact. Thus self-complexity may conceivably be a cognitive marker for distinguishing depression-prone individuals. Our present research is investigating these possibilities. One finding in the response to feedback study previously reported is suggestive of this association. The correlation between self-complexity and depression (as measured on the depression item of the mood scale) revealed that those lower in self-complexity were more depressed ($r = -.30$, $p < .02$).

These speculations may be extended to the area of physical illness. A recognition of the multiplicity of the self may be helpful in dealing with a health crisis. For example, upon learning of a serious illness, the identity of "patient" or "diabetic" may be evoked and then amplified by the continued experience of being ill. The continued recognition of other self-aspects such as dedicated teacher, good mother, and conscientious friend may be a factor in one's ability to live a useful and meaningful life within one's physical problems.

ACKNOWLEDGMENTS

The author would like to thank Margaret Clark, Jane Costello, Gregory Fischer, Susan Fiske, David Hamilton, Eric Johnson, and Miriam Schustack for their helpful comments on this manuscript; Michael Scheier for his helpful suggestions regarding the feedback study; and Alice Huber for her helpful comments and her aid in running the experiments. I would like to thank Philip Costanzo for asking me during my final orals what my stereotyping model implies about affect toward the self. This research was supported by a Sloan Foundation Postdoctoral Fellowship at Carnegie–Mellon University

REFERENCES

Anderson, J. R. *Language, memory and thought.* Hillsdale, N. J.: Lawrence Erlbaum Associates, 1976.

Anderson, J. R., Kline, P. J., & Beasley, C. M. A general learning theory and its application to schema abstraction. In G. H. Bower (Ed.), *The psychology of learning and motivation* (Vol. 13). New York: Academic Press, 1979.

Anderson, N. H. Information integration theory: A brief survey. In D. H. Krantz, R. C. Atkinson, R. D. Luce, & P. Suppes (Eds.), *Contemporary developments in mathematical psychology* (Vol. 2). San Francisco: Freeman Press, 1974.

Bower, G. H. Mood and memory. *American Psychologist,* 1981, *36,* 129–148.

Bower, G. H., & Gilligan, S. G. Remembering information related to one's self. *Journal of Research in Personality,* 1979, *13,* 404–419.

Brewer, M. B. Ingroup bias in the minimal intergroup situation: A cognitive-motivational analysis. *Psychological Bulletin,* 1979, *86,* 307–324.

Cantor, N., & Mischel, W. Prototypes in person perception. In L. Berkowitz (Ed.), *Advances in experimental social psychology* (Vol. 12). New York: Academic Press, 1979.

Clark, M. S., & Isen, A. M. Toward understanding the relationship between feeling states and social behavior. In A. Hastorf & A. M. Isen (Eds.), *Cognitive social psychology.* Boston: Elsevier, in press.

Cohen, C. E. Person categories and social perception: Testing some boundaries of the processing effects of prior knowledge. *Journal of Personality and Social Psychology,* 1981, *40,* 441–452.

Cooley, C. H. *Human nature and the social order.* New York: Scribner, 1902.

Crockett, W. H. Cognitive complexity and impression formation. In B. H. Maher (Ed.), *Progress in experimental personality research* (Vol. 2). New York: Academic Press, 1965.

Crosby, F., Bromley, S., & Saxe, L. Recent unobtrusive studies of black and white discrimination and prejudice: A literature review. *Psychological Bulletin,* 1980, *87,* 546–563.

Epstein, S. The self-concept revisited, or, a theory of a theory. *American Psychologist,* 1973, *28,* 404–416.

Fishbein, M., & Hunter, R. Summation versus balance in attitude organization and change. *Journal of Abnormal and Social Psychology,* 1964, *69,* 505–510.

Friendly, M. L., & Glucksberg, S. On the description of subculture lexicons: A multidimensional approach. *Journal of Personality and Social Psychology,* 1970, *14,* 55–65.

Gergen, K. J. *The concept of self.* New York: Holt, Rinehart, & Winston, 1971.

Goffman, E. On face-work: An analysis of ritual elements of social interaction. *Psychiatry: Journal for the Study of Interpersonal Processes,* 1955, *18,* 213–231.

Goldstein, K. M., & Blackman, S. *Cognitive style: Five approaches and relevant research.* New York: Wiley, 1978.

Gordon, C. Self-conceptions: Configurations of content. In C. Gordon & K. J. Gergen (Eds.), *The self in social interaction* (Vol. 1). New York: Wiley, 1968.

Hayes–Roth, B., & Hayes–Roth, F. Concept learning and recognition and classification of exemplars. *Journal of Verbal Learning and Verbal Behavior,* 1977, *16,* 321–338.

James, W. *Principles of psychology.* New York: Holt, 1890.

James, W. *Psychology: The briefer course.* New York: Holt, Rinehart, & Winston, 1892.

Jones, E. E., & Nisbett, R. E. *The actor and the observer: Divergent perceptions of the causes of behavior*. Morristown, N. J.: General Learning Press, 1971.

Kelly, G. A. *The psychology of personal constructs*. New York: Norton, 1955.

Kuiper, N. A., & Derry, P. A. The self as a cognitive prototype: An application to person perception and depression. In N. Cantor & J. F. Kihlstrom (Eds.), *Personality, cognition, and social interaction*. Hillsdale, N. J.: Lawrence Erlbaum Associates, 1981.

Linville, P. W. *Self-complexity and mood variability*. Unpublished manuscript, Carnegie–Mellon University, 1981. (a)

Linville, P. W. *Self-complexity and reactions to success and failure*. Unpublished manuscript, Carnegie–Mellon University, 1981. (b)

Linville, P. W. The complexity–extremity effect and age-based stereotyping. *Journal of Personality and Social Psychology*, 1982. *42*, 193–211.

Linville, P. W., & Jones, E. E. Polarized appraisals of outgroup members. *Journal of Personality and Social Psychology*, 1980, *38*, 689–703.

Lutsky, N. S. Attitudes toward old age and elderly persons. In Carl Eisdorfer (Ed.), *Annual review of gerontology* (Vol. 1). New York: Springer, 1980.

Markus, H. Self-schemata and processing information about the self. *Journal of Personality and Social Psychology*, 1977, *35*, 63–78.

Markus, H., & Smith, J. The influence of self-schemata on the perception of others. In N. Cantor & J. F. Kihlstrom (Eds.), *Personality, cognition, and social interaction*. Hillsdale, N. J.: Lawrence Erlbaum Associates, 1981.

McConahay, J. B., & Hough, J. C. Symbolic racism. *Journal of Social Issues*, 1976, *32*, 23–45.

McGuire, W. J., & McGuire, C. V. Significant others in self-space: Sex differences and developmental trends in the social self. In J. Suls (Ed.), *Psychological perspectives on the self*. Hillsdale, N. J.: Lawrence Erlbaum Associates, in press.

McGuire, W. J., & Padawer–Singer, A. Trait salience in the spontaneous self-concept. *Journal of Personality and Social Psychology*, 1976, *33*, 743–754.

McTavish, D. G. Perceptions of old people: A review of research methodologies and findings. *The Gerontologist*, 1971, *11*, 90–101.

Montemayor, R., & Eisen, M. The development of self-conceptions from childhood to adolescence. *Journal of Personality and Social Psychology*, 1977, *34*, 314–319.

Moray, N. Attention in dichotic listening: Affective cues and the influence of instructions. *Quarterly Journal of Experimental Psychology*, 1959, *12*, 56–60.

Mullener, N., & Laird, J. D. Some developmental changes in the organization of self-evaluations. *Developmental Psychology*, 1971, *5*, 233–236.

Pettigrew, T. F. Racial change and social policy. *Annals of the American Academy of Political and Social Science*, 1979, *441*, 114–131.

Robinson, J. A. Sampling autobiographical memory. *Cognitive Psychology*, 1976, *8*, 578–595.

Rogers, C. R. *Client-centered therapy*. Boston: Houghton Mifflin, 1951.

Rogers, T. B. A model of the self as an aspect of the human information processing system. In N. Cantor & J. F. Kihlstrom (Eds.), *Personality, cognition, and social interaction*. Hillsdale, N. J.: Lawrence Erlbaum Associates, 1981.

Rosenberg, S., & Sedlak, A. Structural representations of implicit personality theory. In L. Berkowitz (Ed.), *Advances in experimental social psychology* (Vol. 6). New York: Academic Press, 1972.

Sattath, S., & Tversky, A. Additive similarity trees. *Psychometrika*, 1977, *42*, 319–345.

Scott, W. A. Structure of natural cognitions. *Journal of Personality and Social Psychology*, 1969, *12*, 261–278.

Scott, W. A., Osgood, D. W., & Peterson, C. *Cognitive structure: Theory and measurement of individual differences*. Washington, D. C.: Winston, 1979.

Slovic, P., & Lichtenstein, S. Comparison of Bayesian and regression approaches to the study of information processing in judgment. *Organizational Behavior and Human Performance*, 1971, *6*, 649–744.

Snyder, M., & Uranowitz, S. W. Reconstructing the past: Some cognitive consequences of person perception. *Journal of Personality and Social Personality*, 1978, *36*, 941–950

Snygg, D., & Coombs, A. W. *Individual behavior: A perceptual approach to behavior* (rev. ed.). New York: Harper, 1959.

Sullivan, H. S. *The interpersonal theory of psychiatry*. New York: Norton, 1953.

Taylor, S. E., Fiske, S. T., Etcoff, N., & Ruderman, A. Categorical and contextual bases of person memory and stereotyping. *Journal of Personality and Social Psychology*, 1978, *36*, 778–793.

Wilder, D. A. Perceiving persons as a group: Categorization and intergroup relations. In D. L. Hamilton (Ed.), *Cognitive processes in stereotyping and intergroup behavior*. Hillsdale, N. J.: Lawrence Erlbaum Associates, 1980.

5 Comments

Charles A. Kiesler
Carnegie–Mellon University

I'll take my charge as the discussant of chapters on cognition and affect in its broadest sense. The collection of chapters in this volume represent (at least) two quite different theoretical—indeed metatheoretical—approaches and two quite different data bases. It would be difficult—narrow-minded in fact—to comment specifically on the chapters before me without considering the higher-level context in which they occur. That higher-level context itself can be seen in more than one perspective. At one level we are discussing competing theoretical explanations for complex human *phenomena,* a term chosen to be intentionally ambiguous. In this view, the work of, say, Zajonc, Bower, and Mandler offer theoretical explanations for empirical domains that overlap. To the extent that they do overlap, the theories compete, and one should not miss the opportunity to induce a confrontation. In the process of confrontation, however, we hope to reach another level of discussion; that is, one can see the participants in this volume as collectively engaging in a broad gauge attempt to understand more of human processes than has hitherto been tried in detail. The empirical and theoretical work on both cognition and affect have lived relatively isolated lives in social psychology, which used both constructs, but which until recently made little contact with more specialized approaches to each.

The next step is a difficult one. We are faced with several subareas of psychology that have in the past used different theoretical constructs, different independent and dependent measures, and various research styles. How is it we can assess what we "know" in ways that will point to fruitful lines for future research? One approach is to look at theoretical and empirical signposts—events and/or data that are difficult for other theories to explain and therefore challenge our thinking. Yet another is to look at the extreme theoretical cases, to deduce the most extreme implications from a given theory in order to juxtapose instances from competing theories. There is some overlap between these two kinds of approaches.

In this context we emphasize that theoretical interest should focus not on intermediate aspects of the theory but on the extremes. Intermediate aspects are easiest to assess from alternative points of view, and arguing over data bases that are simple to explain from alternative perspectives is not very fruitful.

At the simplest level both behaviorally and cognitively are the questions raised by Zajonc: Can the cognitive and affective systems be considered to be independent? Zajonc says they can and uses the phrase "preferences need no inferences." Mandler says "conscious preferences need no conscious inferences," but it is unclear to me what the function of the first "conscious" is. At the other end of an extreme degree of affect (which includes extreme behavioral and emotional responses but perhaps not extreme cognitive ones) are wars, heroism and cowardice, divorce, murder, suicide, demonstrations, revolution, and perhaps even Proposition 13. These are perhaps not good sites for experimentally testing theories of affect, but the implications for extreme settings must be reasonably straightforward.

The more complex settings are awkward to work with experimentally. It is often difficult to distinguish experimentally and theoretically between "simple" emotional reactions (devoid perhaps of cognitive content or instigation) and reactions to interruptions of complex but overlearned sequences. For example, if a spouse makes an obscene remark at a formal dinner party, is the other spouse's emotional reaction a simple conditioned one to the phrase, a reaction to the incongruity of the remark in that atmosphere, or the interruption of the sequence of that complex schema "dinner party"? Consider the variations of that basic theme: same remark, different person, same circumstances; same remark, same person, different circumstances, and so forth. It seems clear from that approach that all three interpretations contribute to the reaction but are difficult to disentangle both theoretically and experimentally. In this sense it is difficult to produce in the laboratory a simple emotional reaction devoid of cognitive content or to rule out that such cognitive content might provide a viable theoretical explanation. To a lesser extent the reverse is also true.

In general, it is difficult to test theory of the overlap between affect and cognition while successfully ruling out competing explanations. Most data on both sides—that is, affect is or is not governed by the same theroetical rules as cognition—are consistent with the theoretical position their proponents advocate, but not uniquely so. In my view, Zajonc's (1980) data are consistent with his position of two partially independent systems, but they do not rule out the possibility of only one. By the same token, Bower's (1981) data are consistent with one system, a unitary set of rules, but they do not rule out the possibility of two. Part of the problem is the different styles of research. Social psychology in general has always been very attuned to ruling out competing explanations by design, even when those explanations may be fairly naive and not well-grounded in alternative theories. Cognitive psychology is less accustomed to this technique, and studies in social cognition have often not met the methodological rigor that social psychology is accustomed to. I emphasize that the need for such rigor in dealing with complex alternative explanations occurs when one begins to do research with more complex and less-well-controlled phenomena. As long as one maintains total control over the experimental setting and the perceptions of the subject of the experimental materials, such methodological notions become less important.

In the discussion to follow I emphasize some data from social psychology relevant to the relationship of affect and cognition, which seem apparent to me at least to have significance for competing theoretical frameworks. In this discussion I use emotion and affect in the loosest sense, and we come back to that distinction in greater precision later.

For example, the earlier data do suggest that emotional reactions can be learned without conscious awareness. For example, Zanna, Kiesler, & Pilkonis (1970) conditioned both positive and negative reactions to specific words through pairing them with the offset and onset, respectively, of shock. The offset of shock, in Wolpe's terms, presumably produces a spread of positive affect. In using one linguistic concept to indicate the onset of shock and another to indicate offset, we can separate the two sources of affect. Zanna et al. found predictable physiological responses to the concepts, positive and negative, and found that it generalized to linguistically similar concepts. One reason for doing this experiment was that Zanna et al. felt previous studies of conditioning were loaded with demand characteristics; they wished to test whether such conditioning could occur under more strict methodological procedures. Although a subject could anticipate that the experimenter might think that a word used to indicate the onset of shock should be viewed negatively, it is unlikely that they would suspect that the offset should be viewed positively. It is also unlikely that they could control their physiological responses so consistently, such that it would be generalized to similar concepts. To the extent that such experiments can be regarded as studies of affect, they shed light on Zajonc's provocative proposal. Questions regarding emotions and affect have been sharpened recently, with the help of advances in physiological measurement and the technology of cognitive psychology. However, the change in the technology and the theoretical context makes it awkward to apply what we thought we already knew in this area. For example, for decades, social psychology has been using affective measures as its primary dependent measures. This is not the same thing as studying affect directly, but it is relevant to the general area. Studies of group cohesiveness, interpersonal perception and attraction, group decision making, and even such areas as dissonance, commitment, reactance, and equity theory have typically used evaluatively laden dependent measures. Over the course of the last 50 years, I estimate there are somewhere between 10 and 15 thousand experiments on such affectively laden measures. I'm not sure what to make of them in this context. It seems likely that we need to sort them over anew from an entirely different perspective. However, there are some conclusions that I think we can draw from such experiments regarding the relationship of affect and cognition.

For example, the meaning of emotional experience depends greatly on the context in which it occurs. The effect of context occurs partly in a direct sense, as in the Schachter and Singer (1962) experiments on the labeling of emotion. It can also occur indirectly as in dissonance experiments. When Pallak and I reviewed this literature several years ago (Kiesler & Pallak, 1976), we came to the conclusion that although arousal had seldom been measured directly it did seem apparent that dissonance manipulations (not the same as the theoretical construct of dissonance) were indeed arousing. Further studies by Zanna and Cooper (1974) and their colleagues have supported this conclusion. One can add to or subtract from the dissonance effect by leading the subject to expect, respectively, little arousal in a dissonance setting, or a lot of arousal. One can enhance the dissonance effect by using drugs that produce an aroused state (Cooper, Zanna, & Tave, 1978). I regard these two sets of data as empirical signposts. These are the kinds of data about which theories competing in the arena of the relationship of affect to cognition must offer reasonable explanations.

In applying the vast attitude literature, it is important to keep in mind that the study of attitude change has been a study of affect by and large, not cognition. From Rosenberg's original work (1956), in which he induced a change in affective state through hypnosis and found dramatic changes in cognition, it has been generally found that a change of affect more powerfully affects cognition than the reverse. Indeed, as Zajonc notes, the study of attitude change as a purely cognitive phenomenon has never been particularly effective. More generally, the resistance to external influence on attitude is only partly a cognitive phenomenon. For example, coaching people during World War II about techniques of propaganda did not increase one's resistance to propaganda. Although coaching did not increase resistance, it did affect subjects' recognition of propaganda.

Other social research has a more directly cognitive focus. In my own work, psychological commitment is seen to be a cognitive process. By itself, varying commitment will affect such things as the learning of related material (Salancik & Kiesler, 1971), but not attitude. However, when attacked, committed subjects are more likely to act on their beliefs, become more extreme attitudinally, and decrease interest in other information, whether pro or con. In that sense, perhaps commitment is a good site for studying the interplay of affect and cognition. Looking at the commitment research from a different perspective, one might speculate that cognitive phenomena only partly determine the degree of affect but can dramatically focus and channel its effects.

It is not a simple matter to account for the attitude data. One problem is that the cognitive representations of typical attitude objects are not well-articulated within or between systems. I once spent a frustrating year trying to study the relationships between complex attitude structures. The general idea was to do attitude change and commitment experiments on one complex structure and look at the effects of such manipulations on higher and lower levels within the structure as well as the effects on a logically related structure. I still think the idea is a good one, but I couldn't find any consistent attitude structures, let alone study their interplay.

Fishbein (Fishbein & Ajzen, 1975) has had more success dealing with attitude structures. His model and data stress the notion of independence of belief (cognition) and attitude (affect) in their joint impact on intention to behave. However, all the behaviors used in those experiments are very specific and clearly defined, and it is unknown what implications they have for this more general discussion (although Fishbein's method could have great utility here). Further, it is generally accepted within social psychology that the attitude–behavior link is weaker than the behavior–attitude link. Although this effect seems rather general in the experimental literature, it is perhaps difficult to understand in a context of cognitive representations of affect. I note also that neither the affective nor the cognitive side of the current theoretical discussion is paying much attention to behavior.

It is somewhat unclear exactly what we are to make of the implications of the data on attitude change for the current discussion. Berscheid in this volume has delivered a very effective rapier-like attack on the applications of the attitude concept to interpersonal attraction. Her data suggest very strongly that the applicability of the attitude concept to interpersonal attraction is severely limited to experiments with uninvolved others.

I go on at some length about attitude change because some of the cognitive representation of affective phenomena could be considered an implicit attack on the attitude-change literature. The attack is only implicit because the view seeks to explain similar phenomena but ignores the previous data base.

Part of the difficulty in explaining the attitude-change data using more cognitive models is the lack of match up and ease of translation among theoretical concepts. One particular villain in this drama is that of schema. I find the schema concept intuitively appealing in that it combines with suitable complexity the affective and cognitive aspects of the human orientation toward objects of the phenomenological field, but it is also frustratingly vague around the edges. Thorndyke and Yekovich (1980) see this weakness in terms of a lack of theoretical development, in particular, a weakness in the area of process specification. They regard schema-based theories as lacking in: (1) specification of the domain of knowledge for which the schemata exist and are used; and (2) specification of detailed processes that operate the utilization of the schemata. Pragmatically, in trying to apply this concept to social-psychological phenomena, we need better specification of how one can tell in advance which schemata would be salient and the degree to which the information or experiences of the subjects would be congruous or incongruous with it. The chapters here by Mandler, Linville, and Fiske all build on schema theory, and, in spite of my comments here, all provide thoughtful and interesting discussion.

Mandler's work in particular is powerfully stated and has been well-received by others (Strongman, 1978). There are several points I raise about this work that may be of more general interest. Mandler does not discuss innate approach/avoidance tendencies and "cultural predications." It is his right to narrow his discussion, of course, but I suspect that many and perhaps most strongly held beliefs are acquired in just such a noncritical way, and their violation or denial produces perhaps our strongest emotions. On the other hand, perhaps Mandler's concept of evaluative cognitions, and his assertion that they become affective when combined with a state of arousal, provide the easiest bridge to the existing social-psychological data base.

Mandler does go on to say that the interruption of ongoing plans, particularly highly organized ones, is a sufficient and probably necessary condition for the experience of emotion. I have several related thoughts here. Let's assume that a person has undergone a number of experiences in which the interruption of ongoing plans produced emotion. If so, then it may also be true that the person subsequently begins to infer that the experience of emotion is a cue that such interference has occurred and therefore might use emotion as an impetus to replan or reorganize. This notion might well provide a basis for interpreting some of the data we have discussed. If the experience of emotion itself is an impetus to replan, then we might expect increased vigilance and attention, leading to increased receptivity to new information. The outcome would be a perceived need to replan or "explain" the emotion, through such techniques as attitude change and situational definitions. If we allow for the lack of recognition for the correct source of the interruption and possibly inaccurate perceptions of the interruption per se, we can see how such a process might underlie the results of Cooper, Zanna, & Tave and Schachter and Singer.

There are several related possibilities within social psychology. The focus of attention on self, as in Scheier's work, could be arousing partly because it is unusual, partly because it is an interruption of the stream of behavior. Barker's (1963) concept of the stream of behavior was explicitly a criticism of experimental work in social psychology. He felt that social-psychological experiments broke up into what he referred to as behavior tessarae, what was in real life an integrated sequence of behavior, and the effects of the experiments were therefore not generalizable to ordinary behavior. Note further that Barker's notion of the stream of behavior implies that we do not actively process much of the social information that we encounter in everyday life. Cognitive understandings of social behavior are less amenable to the criticism of Barker than are current social-psychological theories, partly because the experimental manipulations are less sharply defined and provoking.

Fiske has an interesting prediction related to this general area. She says that the schematic match determines the affective response; that is, to the degree that an instance is perceived to fit the schema, it will receive the affect linked to that category. This does raise an issue of how one develops the original affect and how it's maintained. However, it did make me think that cognitive therapy is one test of the cognitive approach to affect (Beck, 1967). In Beck's view, the subject or patient has inappropriate (or inappropriately severe) thoughts about self or relationships with others. The therapeutic style is to rethink, or to have new thoughts about, or to think differently about, or to have a new style of thought about people and objects around one. Indeed, in some paradoxical sense, one might think of the cognitive therapy of depression as using cognitive methods to increase the affective response to the environment. Linville comes at this issue in a somewhat different way in looking at the complexity of the self-image and mood swings. I'm not sure here which way the directionality goes. If one has developed a very extreme evaluation of an object, perhaps through a dramatic conditioning instance, would it be possible therefore to have a complex view of it?

I'm very impressed by Ellen Berscheid's chapter. She takes Mandler's notion of arousal following interruptive events a long way and applies them to interpersonal sequences as well as intrapersonal. She asserts that organized behavior sequences and higher-order plans are integral to the concept of close relationships, and their interruption produces great emotion. She lays out a well-organized and highly convincing reinterpretation of existing data on close relationships. Indeed, some of these ideas could be applied with considerable benefit to organization theory in the workplace.

There is yet another way to attempt a theoretical translation from cognitive theory to theories about attitudes and attitude change. Thorndyke and Yekovich describe the notion that levels in a representational hierarchy can be translated as importance, and that importance affects recall but not recognition memory. The concept of importance, and therefore hierarchical levels, may functionally relate to the concept of attitude. Attitudes cause objects to be seen as important or to stand out in the phenomenological field. Attitudes affect the interpretation of new information and the perceived relationships of old information. So, much like a higher-level node in a schematic structure, attitudes are "important," therefore recalled, and therefore perhaps become higher-level nodes. Further, the concept of hierarchical structure can help us understand how and why subjects develop and maintain inconsistent attitudes, and how information relative to more than one attitude is not necessarily thereby suitably encoded.

Certainly we have to discover ways of attending to the notion of the social context in which information is accrued. Sampson (1981), in discussing the process of internalization, notes the key role of other people in a social and historical context. As he quotes from Vygotsky: "an interpersonal process is transformed into an intrapersonal process" (p. 732). In this sense the basis for "I think" exists in the social world. To some extent the basis of "I feel" also exists in the social world. In questions of relationships of thinking and feeling, I emphasize that both have imperfect filters in the process of internalization. However, if the basis for what I think is imperfectly recognized by self, then certainly what I feel is even more so. This may be especially true for extreme affects. In a general article about cognitive psychology, Abelson (1981) draws attention to Tompkins' concept of the nuclear scene, in which the same strong emotional reaction occurs repeatedly in similar but not identical scenes. Abelson says that emotional experiences turn scripts into overgeneralized metascripts, but that's a description and not an explanation. A precise cognitive explanation for such powerful emotional reactions as a nuclear scene remains a challenge for an imperialistic cognitive psychology.

The detailed understanding of the relationship of affect and cognition is perhaps the core theoretical problem of psychology for the 80s. It is an important problem and one that has plagued psychologists and philosophers for centuries. These chapters represent a significant advance in our thinking.

REFERENCES

Abelson, R. P. Psychological status of the script concept. *American Psychologist*, 1981, *36*, 715–729.

Barker, R. G. (Ed.). *The stream of behavior.* New York: Appleton–Century–Crofts, 1963.

Beck, A. T. *Depression: Causes and treatment.* Philadelphia: University of Pennsylvania Press, 1967.

Bower, G. H. Mood and memory. *American Psychologist*, 1981, *36*, 129–148.

Cooper, J., Zanna, M. P., & Tave, P. A. Arousal as a necessary condition for attitude change following induced compliance. *Journal of Personality and Social Psychology*, 1978, *36*, 1101–1106.

Fishbein, M., & Ajzen, I. *Belief, attitude, intention, and behavior: An introduction to theory and research.* Reading, Mass.: Addison–Wesley, 1975.

Kiesler, C. A., & Pallak, M. S. The arousal properties of dissonance manipulations. *Psychological Bulletin*, 1976, *83*, 1014–1025.

Rosenberg, M. J. Cognitive structure and attitudinal affect. *Journal of Abnormal and Social Psychology*, 1956, *53*, 367–372.

Salancik, J. R., & Kiesler, C. A. Behavioral commitment and retention of consistent and inconsistent attitude word pairs. In C. A. Kiesler, *The psychology of commitment: Experiments linking behavior to belief.* New York: Academic Press, 1971.

Sampson, E. E. Cognitive psychology as ideology. *American Psychologist*, 1981, *36*, 730–743.

Schachter, S., & Singer, J. Cognitive, social and physiological determinants of emotion. *Psychological Review*, 1962, *69*, 379–399.

Strongman, K. T. *The psychology of emotion.* New York: Wiley, 1978.

Thorndyke, P. W., & Yekovich, F. R. A critique of schema-based theories of human story memory. *Poetics*, 1980, *9*, 23–49.

Zajonc, R. B. Feeling and thinking: Preferences need no inferences. *American Psychologist*, 1980, *35*, 151–175.

Zanna, M. P., & Cooper, J. Dissonance and the pill: An attributional approach to studying the arousal properties of dissonance. *Journal of Personality and Social Psychology*, 1974, *29*, 703–709.

Zanna, M. P., Kiesler, C. A., & Pilkonis, P. A. Positive and negative attitudinal affects established by classical conditioning. *Journal of Personality and Social Psychology*, 1970, *14*, 321–328.

II
COGNITION AND AFFECT: APPLICATIONS AND BEHAVIOR

6

The Integration of Emotion and Cognition: A View From the Perceptual-Motor Theory of Emotion[1]

Howard Leventhal
University of Wisconsin, Madison

INTRODUCTION

The objective of this chapter is to describe the interrelationship of emotion and cognition. This task would be simple if the words referred to specific entities: They do not. Rather, they refer to two sets of phenomena (experiences and overt behaviors) that are products of complex underlying processes. To relate emotion to cognition means, therefore, that one must describe and then link the processes that generate them. The first step in this task is to describe the basic assumptions and the framework guiding my approach. Following this background material, I present a perceptual–motor model of the processes assumed to underlie emotion. The model is compared to other theories of emotion, and a limited number of supportive empirical findings are presented. The next section deals with the link between emotion and cognition in a substantive area: that of illness cognition. In that final section of the chapter I develop a number of ideas about the workings of an emotion–cognition system.

Basic Assumptions

There are seven important assumptions underlying my approach to emotion and cognition. The first is that subjective experience, typically indexed by verbal

[1]The health related research reported in this paper and the preparation of this manuscript were supported by grants #HL24543-02 and NIC 061-26-8191. I would like to express thanks to my associates and students for many of the ideas here included, to Dr. Cal Izard for pressing me to explore the interrelationships of emotion and illness processes, and to Andrea Straus for careful reading of the entire manuscript and clarifying discussions of specific ideas.

report, is the appropriate and best starting point for the study of emotion. Subjective states are the central phenomena or data defining the presence of an emotional state and its type (fear, anger, joy, etc.).

My second point is that emotional states can be regarded as a form of meaning: They have significance for the person experiencing and expressing them (Peters, 1970). Their meaning has two aspects: they "say" something about our organismic state (i.e., they meter its moment-by-moment readiness), and they "say" something about the environment. For example, there are negative meanings, such as FEAR, which tells us we are confronting a danger and that our ability to master it is doubtful; ANGER, which tells us we are confronting insults or threats that have aroused us and that we are ready to attack and master; DISGUST or NAUSEA, which tells us we are confronting bad-tasting and bad-smelling objects; and SHAME and GUILT, which tell us we are confronting the misbehaviors and hurt esteem that we wish to hide. The positive affects also have their objects and action impulses that comprise their meaning. I think it is obvious that emotion categories are categories of meaning, and I believe that most category theorists would agree (see, for example, Eibl–Eibesfeldt, 1980; Ekman, Friesen, & Ellsworth, 1972; Izard, 1971, 1977; Plutchik, 1962, 1980; Tomkins, 1962, 1963, 1980). Weiner's (in press) finding of clear, predictable associations among causal dimensions of success, control, and affect supports this assumption. His attributional analysis says less, however, about emotion's other internal meaning referent. Affective signals also provide a moment-by-moment clue to the readiness of our biological machinery to fight, flee, reject, accept, and so on.

My second assumption implies that emotion itself is a form of cognition, especially if we assume that cognition is meaning. This leads into my third assumption: that there are several types of cognitive processes. Those we call abstract reasoning and perception form the two major categories within the domain of cognition, and they may be further divided to suit one's theory and data. My fourth assumption is that the perceptual processing system is where basic meanings develop, for this system constructs the world in which we dwell, the ground and figures in it, and our self (Gibson, 1950; Koffka, 1935; Köhler, 1947; Neisser, 1967). Reasoning or thought appears to be an abstract or symbolic way to represent events and relationships. It builds upon perception but is not completely dependent on it. Reasoning is a flexible though not particularly exhaustive way of representing events.

My fifth assumption is that emotion can attach to and interact with both perceptual and abstract cognition. I believe, however, that emotion is attached more swiftly and perhaps more permanently to sensory and perceptual cognition than to abstract cognition. This assumption is based on the idea, to be developed later on, that emotion is a form of automatic motor activity, and that most automatic motor behavior is controlled by concrete sensations and perceptions. Thus, a major problem in controlling emotional thought and behavior is the difficulty of controlling the perceptual processing system by means of reasoning or propositional thought.

My sixth major assumption is that meaning systems develop and change over time. This is obvious with respect to thinking. It is somewhat less obvious with respect to emotion and perhaps most open to dispute with respect to perception. The point is simple; the distress, anger, fear, joy, and interest of the neonate is not that of the infant, that of the infant not that of the child, and that of the child not that of the adult. These changes are not always simple or obvious (e.g., not just an increase in the size of vocabulary). They are also changes in the structure of thought. Emotion undergoes a developmental process involving changes such as those described by Piaget (1967, 1981).

My seventh and final assumption is that it is necessary to study the content of specific meaning systems if we are to deepen our understanding of the mechanisms underlying emotion as well as cognition and their relationship. To study emotion or cognition in the abstract would be like studying memory by investigating the learning of nonsense syllables, or considering chemistry without studying specific elements and chemicals. This is a guiding rule in our exploration of illness cognition.

The following section gives an overview of our processing model. It defines the approach by which my colleagues and I developed a more detailed theory of the processes that construct emotions. Empirical findings that suggested this approach are also described.

A FRAMEWORK FOR RELATING EMOTION AND COGNITION

Our basic framework developed from two separate sets of investigations: one on the effects of fear-arousing communications on attitudes and behavior, the other on the effects of preparatory communications on response to noxious (painful) stimulus situations. The results of these studies led to the following conception of the mechanism underlying the observed behaviors. The behavioral mechanism consists of two simultaneously active, parallel systems, one cognitive, the other emotional. Each of these systems is made up of two stages, an initial perceptual or representational stage and a second action-planning or coping stage (Leventhal, 1970). The perceptual stage takes the form of a perception and an abstract representation of the objective features of the external situation that is created in the cognitive system, and a feeling representation and its related expressive and autonomic reactions that is created in the emotional system. The action-planning or coping stage consists of response alternatives and their anticipated outcomes. The two systems, emotional and objective, function as self-regulating feedback mechanisms, one designed to control feelings, the other to control the objective features of these threatening situations. Because the two stages draw upon a common behavioral mechanism, the output of either system can be expected to appear in a sequence determined by features of the situation and the person.

Ideas put forth by a number of investigators influenced this formulation. The hypothesis of a sequence of stages for the appraisal of threat was stated explicitly by Janis (1962, 1974) and Lazarus (1966) and was embodied in Miller, Galanter, and Pribram's (1960) generalized model of a testing process (TOTE). Experimental support for stages and appraisal appeared in Sternberg's (1969) classic studies.

The results that first suggested the framework were generated in studies of the effectiveness of preventive health communications recommending such practices as using seat belts, stopping smoking, taking tetanus innoculations, and good dental hygiene. The communications were designed to vary the level of threat and to study its interaction with other variables such as specific action instructions (how to perform the recommended actions) and information on action effectiveness (Leventhal, 1970). The crucial experimental findings were those showing that variations in fear level failed to interact with other variables such as specific action instructions, although the combination of the two factors was critical if the communication was to change behavior and not just attitudes. For example, in three separate studies we varied the fear level of the message, with high-fear messages produced by color pictures or color movies showing the threats of injury and death from tetanus, smoking, unsafe driving practices, and so forth. We also created specific action instructions by giving our subjects maps and detailed plans to help them identify environmental cues for the actions specifically needed to protect against danger. Our high-fear messages quite consistently aroused more fear than the low-fear messages, generated more favorable attitudes toward quitting smoking, using seat belts, etc. but had minimal effects on behavior. What was important for behavior was combining a fear message, high or low, with an action plan (Leventhal, Jones, & Trembly, 1966; Leventhal, Singer, & Jones, 1965; Leventhal, Watts, & Pagano, 1967). Confirmation of these findings can be found in later studies by Rogers and his colleagues (Rogers, 1975, in press; Rogers & Deckner, 1975; Rogers & Mewborn, 1976).

Our studies of reactions to noxious stimuli further persuaded us of the general validity of these assumptions. First, the notion of parallel systems suggested that directing attention to the objective features of a noxious stressor (e.g., asking the subject to monitor the specific features of coldness, pins and needles, and numbness in a cold pressor test) could lead to an objective rather than an emotional representation of the stimulus and to declines in pain and distress (Leventhal, Brown, Shacham, & Engquist, 1979; Leventhal & Everhart, 1979). Second, the definition of stages also proved relevant as we found once again that action instructions were essential if we wished to alter overt, instrumental coping reactions in addition to reducing pain and distress. These effects were obtained primarily in field studies of distress and pain reduction in clinical settings. For example, Jean Johnson and I (Johnson & Leventhal, 1974) had a nursing student prepare half of a set of patients undergoing endoscopy by describing the endoscopic procedure and including information about the sensations they would experience during this diagnostic examination. The assumption was that concrete sensory cues that were interpreted as threatening would stimulate fear and distress. Preparation would allow the subject to attend to and process these cues as information, regard them as "normal," and gradually habituate to them. The other half of the group received descriptions of the procedure without information about the sensory features. Half of each of the groups was given instructions on how to breath and swallow during the throat swabbing and intubation. The results suggested that sensory information played a major role in reducing distress during the noxious procedure, and that action information was essential to affect performance, (i.e., tube swallowing). Johnson has obtained similar results in a study of postsurgical recovery (Johnson, Rice, Fuller, & Endress, 1978). Further confirmation came from our studies of women's reactions during childbirth: Paying attention to and monitoring sensory activity plays a critical role in self-regulation during stressful episodes when combined with information and skills for coping with the stressor (Leventhal, Shacham, Boothe, & Leventhal, 1981).

Our studies of pain and distress reduction supported our theoretical assumptions in two ways. First, the results were congruent with our theoretical expectations. Second, they allowed us to connect our ideas to a substantial body of neurophysiological and behavioral research on pain mechanisms. Neurological studies of pain show that the pain system consists of two (if not three) parallel conducting networks (Casey, 1973). One of large A fibers begins at the periphery and carries objective, stimulus information rapidly and directly to the spinal cord, where it ascends ipsilaterally and crosses at the cervical region to sensory areas in the cortex. The other system of smaller c fibers also begins at the periphery, than arrives at the cord, activates so-called t cells, and crosses immediately before ascending in ventro-lateral pathways (Melzack & Wall, 1965, 1970). These signals are widely dispersed in the reticular activating system, the hypothalamic and related midbrain areas, and the paramedial bodies of the thalamus before they ascend to the cortex. This latter system is considered an activating system and is richly supplied with opiate sensitive receptor sites (Snyder, 1977). These findings strengthened our commitment to the proposition that affect and cognition were generated by partially independent, parallel systems.

In summary, our early work persuaded us of the usefulness of conceptualizing the affect–cognition mechanism as two parallel, sequentially staged processing systems that acted as feed-back systems for regulating emotion and the control of noxious settings. Is this formulation reasonable? If the latency of response from our social-psychologist colleagues was a measure of our success, we would indeed have had reason to doubt the validity or utility of our formulation. Zajonc (1980) proposed a nearly identical formulation a decade later without reference to earlier models. However, we, too, found things to question. Indeed, the very notion of the independence of emotional and cognitive process defied reason and motivated us to delve further into the question of the relationship of emotion and cognition.

THE MEANING OF PARALLEL SYSTEMS

We have assumed a substantial degree of independence between the emotional and the intellective processing of information. If this is correct, it should be possible to study the process underlying emotional experience and behavior. What is the nature of this processing system?

Emotion is Emotion versus Emotion as Sensory and Motor Events

The first step toward an answer of the preceding question is to search the theoretical and empirical literature on emotion. It divides into two broad classes: studies based on theories that treat emotion as the product of nonemotional processes, usually a synthesis of cognitive and autonomic motor reactions, and studies that treat emotion as "real" or existant. The synthetic positions view emotion as a product of social learning; or argue that cognition gives it its feeling quality, because the autonomic response is not varied enough to create these differences. The realist positions view emotion as a product of specialized bio-logical mechanisms that are part of our evolutionary history (Izard, 1971; Plutchik, 1962, 1980; Tomkins, 1962, 1963, 1980). The former theories tend to build on rationalist conceptions of man (Cofer, 1972), whereas the latter build on an animal or impulse model.

Social psychology of the 1960s and 1970s was clearly dominated by synthetic views of emotion. Schachter and Singer's (1962) brilliant investigation set the stage for a generation of emotion researchers, when they looked at the behavioral and subjective consequences of the joint effect of a stooge's angry or euphoric behavior with injections with epinephrine and prepatory instructions. Mandler (1962) neatly summarizes the model with a jukebox analogy, which equates autonomic arousal with the jukebox motor and the behavior of the stooge with the recording: The emotional "tune" emerges from their combined activity.

The realist positions are of two kinds: (1) Darwin's evolutionary theory and later versions espoused by Izard (1971) and Plutchik (1980); and (2) neu-rophysiological models such as Cannon's (1927), Papez's (1938) and MacLean's (1958). For these theorists, emotion is a primary fact of experience (see Hebb, 1949; Leventhal, 1974). As Konorski (1967) states: "the experience of each emotion or drive has the attributes of unitary perception . . . pure fear, or pure anger, or pure sorrow are certainly familiar to everyone'' [p. 158].

Like James' (1884) preceding theory, synthetic theory is based on an outdated view of the human nervous system in which the brain is assumed to consist of sensory, motor, and association areas, with no areas specifically dedicated to the creation of ''emotional'' experience and behavior (James, 1890). This biased description of the nervous system undoubtedly reflects the investigators greater access to the outer, cortical areas of the brain in comparison to the deeper paleo-cortical and hypothalamic structures. The rationalistic bias of the 19th century may also have reinforced this view. Our conceptualization need no longer be confined by it; our model is constructed in line with the realist position.

Requirements of a Perceptual Motor Theory of Emotion

If distinct emotions are as familiar as Konorski and most laypersons would suggest, the process that gives rise to them must be identified. Moreover, every differentiation in emotional experience (and behavior) must be accompanied by a differentiation of the underlying psychophysiological process. What tasks must be performed by this ''independent'' emotional processing system, if it is to provide us with a satisfactory account of emotional phenomena? The following represents a minimum list of such requirements.

1. The system needs a ''primary'' mechanism to account for differences in the quality of emotional experiences. This primary mechanism should have the following capabilities:

(a) Operation early in life to allow for the perception of similarity and difference in emotional meaning across settings. In this way the growing child can learn to use social labels to identify emotional states.

(b) Selective response to situational stimuli so that emotional feelings or meanings (e.g., fear, anger, joy) are appropriate to the adaptive needs of the setting.

(c) Some degree of independence from learned or acquired emotional reactions. This is essential to allow for change in acquired feelings and the capacity to experience emotion in situations that would seem impossible given the individual's history. An example would be a dying cancer patient who experiences joy when treatment reduces pain and immobility for even just a few weeks.

Schachter and others (Russell, 1927; Sully, 1902) suggested that emotional qualities were determined by cognition because of the pertinent failure to locate a primary mechanism in the autonomic system. There is no need to review once again the controversy surrounding autonomic differentiation. But it is important to recognize that people on both sides, Jamesians and Schachterians, assumed that the experience and behavioral display of turbulent emotions was impossible in the absence of autonomic activity. If this assumption is false, the search for a primary emotional mechanism need not be confined to the autonomic motor system. This does not mean, of course, that autonomic activity does not enter into emotional experience.

2. The system needs to contain a memory mechanism to account for the connection of emotional experience and behaviors to perceptions and to allow for the development of new affective ties to perceptions. More specifically, this memory mechanism should:

(a) Combine subjective feelings and primary response components with perceptions of situations and actions (both autonomic and instrumental), so as to form emotional memory SCHEMAS.

(b) Allow for the blending of primary emotional meanings to form new and more complex emotional states.

(c) Be able to function automatically without the intervention of complex, intellectual evaluation.

3. The system must contain a mechanism for processing the abstract and volitional aspect of emotion. This includes two types of processing:

(a) The abstract representations of emotional situations and experiences so we can think about, discuss, and evaluate their meaning.

(b) The voluntary control of the instrumental, expressive, and autonomic components of emotional responding.

4. The system must have an attentional mechanism to describe the effects of changing the contents of consciousness on emotional processing and experience.

This is but a partial list of requirements. A more complete list would include a mechanism to account for the development of addictive behavior (Leventhal & Cleary, 1979). The list provided is sufficient, however, for a system that accounts for these processes will deepen our understanding of emotion. As I show later on, it will also help us understand illness cognition.

A MODEL OF EMOTIONAL PROCESSING

The proposed system consists of a hierarchy of three processing levels (Leventhal, 1979, 1980): (1) expressive-motor processing; (2) schematic or perceptual memory (i.e., a record, IN memory, of emotional situations, experience and reactions); and (3) conceptual or abstract memory for processing emotional experience and volitional behavior. The expressive-motor mechanism generates the basic set of subjective feelings and expressive reactions that make up the primary affective palette or our emotional vocabulary (Izard, 1971, 1977; Tomkins, 1962, 1980). Its action creates the perception of emotionally based similarities and differences between situations. It allows us to say "I felt frightened!" to situations that differed over many attributes and meanings. It allows the individual to rediscover "true" feelings, when social learning has forced a distortion in affective response to a class of situations. It is also the basis for affective communication within and across cultures. Finally, the system is structured so that different cues are keyed to different emotions (Garcia, 1981; Seligman, 1970; Tomkins, 1962).

The schematic or perceptual memory provides a record in memory of emotional episodes. It stores a representation of the features of the situation that provoked the emotion, a record of the emotion itself, perhaps like color memory (Hurvich, 1969, p. 503), and a record of motor responses including expressive, autonomic, and voluntary or instrumental actions. New situations reactivate these schematic structures without deliberation or conscious thought. Indeed, virtually all emotional behavior is brought into play by the activation of this type of implicit meaning system (Epstein, 1979).

Conceptual processing includes at least two types of process: (1) a verbal conceptual component; and (2) a performance component. The first includes the conclusions we draw as to the causes of typical emotion episodes as well as the internal events that accompany them, and what consequences can be expected. These expectations or rules can be expressed in verbal form, but this mechanism is not simply a verbal paraphrase of schematic memory! If it were, it would be an accurate parallel of schematic processes, but the verbal system often fails to abstract adequately or report features or processes at the schematic level.

The performance component consists of nonverbal codes for recognizing and enacting emotions. They are developed by active participation. The individual thrusts him or herself into emotional situations and, in response to real or imagined cues, deliberately enacts the expressive responses and instrumental behaviors associated with the feelings and their eliciting situation. This enactment generates a sequential or propositional code (see Lang, 1979; Pylyshyn, 1973), whose motor elements are abstracted from the perceptions in the emotional schemata. These elements are spatially arranged in the schematic code. An actor gains a degree of control over the automatic processing mechanism by representing the critical junctures or branching points of the automatic schematic codes in the sequential form of the performance code (see Carver & Scheier, 1981; Powers, 1973).

It is important to note that all mechanisms in the hierarchy function simultaneously. It is difficult, therefore, to parcel out their independent contributions to an emotional reaction in a specific situation. Indeed, it is not clear that traditional experimental procedures are adequate to the task. A more effective approach may be to hypothesize how each level of processing will contribute to emotional behavior in real world settings and to identify this contribution empirically. The next section presents some of the evidence that led me to propose each of the three mechanisms.

Evidence For An Hierarchal System

This review includes anatomical, neurophysiological, and behavioral data. It emphasizes the converging features of these diverse findings at the expense of detail. Let me turn first to the expressive motor system.

Expressive Motor System. There is both physiological and behavioral evidence to support the claim that facial expressions play a central role in emotional experience and behavior. They are obviously important for the communications of feelings and behavioral intentions (Andrew, 1965; Eibl–Eibesfeldt, 1970).

The evidence pointing to expressive motor behavior as the generator of feeling was first summarized by Silvan Tomkins (1962). He drew from two major types of data. One was anatomical and physiological evidence about the facial muscles; they are highly differentiated (Izard, 1971) and heavily supplied with neural connections to the hypothalamus (Gellhorn, 1964). Hence, they could be the source of primary affective experience. The other was the abundant data showing that people can accurately judge each other's facial expressions. This holds true whether they are from the same or different cultures. Moreover, people from different cultures produce the same expressions for specific emotional situations (Ekman & Friesen, 1971, 1975; Izard, 1971, 1977; Woodworth & Schlosberg, 1954). There is also evidence suggesting that situations that arouse a specific feeling produce common facial-muscle changes (Leventhal & Sharp, 1965; Schwartz, Fair, Mandel, Salt, Mieske, & Klerman, 1978; Schwartz, Fair, Salt, Mandel, & Klerman, 1976), and data also show that judgments of facial expression can be predicted from muscle patterns in the target faces (Ekman & Friesen, 1975). It has also been found that emotional expressions develop even in blind (and deaf) children, making clear that these patterns are innate and initially independent of external, social reinforcement (Eibl–Eibesfeldt, 1980; Fulcher, 1942; Goodenough, 1932). Finally, there is a substantial body of evidence suggesting that expressive patterns are stimulus specific, at least to a substantial degree. For example, in the infant, alertness, attention, and cycling movements are readily elicited by high-pitched vocalizations and the presence of the human face (Brazelton, Kozlowski, & Main, 1974), startle and aversion are elicited by approaching forms (Bower, 1971), and expressions of disgust are elicited by tastes and disturbances of the gut. We can see, therefore, that the expressive system is a good candidate for the generator of primary emotions.

It is less clear what role, if any, expressive motor activity plays in the generation of subjective feeling. James rejected the hypothesis that enacted expressions cause subjective feeling, though he believed they could readily block unwanted emotion (see James, 1890, and Pasquarelli & Bull, 1951). More recent studies generally confirm this state of affairs (Laird, 1974; Cupchik & Leventhal, 1974;

Tourangeau & Ellsworth, 1979). These findings, however, are only relevant to the hypothesis that emotional experience is generated by peripheral feedback from the facial muscles (see Tomkins, 1980). Facial motor activation of subjective emotion need not, however, depend on peripheral feedback but could be centrally located. There are few instances in which motor control can be adequately accounted for by simple, peripheral feedback models (Lashley, 1951). My alternative hypothesis is that the motor mechanism is always centrally located with peripheral information making a contribution to the guidance of central activity (Leventhal, 1979, 1980).

The Schematic-Emotional Mechanism.   The schematic code is a record IN memory of situations, subjective feelings, and motor reactions (expressive, autonomic, and instrumental) and is activated automatically, without deliberation. It is a first critical step in stimulus enrichment. It is also close to perception and preattentive or nonconscious (Broadbent, 1977). The early critics of James' theory of emotion, Angier (1927) and Dewey (1894, 1895), recognized that stimulus interpretation must occur swiftly and prior to autonomic arousal. This hypothesis is supported by the work of Lazarus (1966) and his colleagues, which demonstrates the effects of stimulus interpretation or appraisal on autonomic activity.

The multicomponent code of a schema integrates a variety of sensory information with motor representations. Included are features of the situation eliciting the emotion, the subjective experience itself (the emotion is coded in memory), and the expressive, instrumental and autonomic reactions (when present) linked with the emotional arousal. The code is an ANALOG, a record of a specific emotional episode. A generalized or prototypic code can also develop when the individual is exposed to multiple situations that arouse similar affective experiences (Posner, 1973).

There are many types of evidence converging to support the concept of schematic coding of emotional information. First, and best known, are studies showing that imagery stimulates autonomic arousal where verbalization fails to do so (Grossberg & Wilson, 1968; Lang, 1979). Words that can provoke emotional reactions (e.g., aggressive behavior) are typically high in concrete image value, whereas words equivalent in meaning but low in image value fail to do so (Turner & Layton, 1976).

Studies also show that arousal can initiate emotional reactions (Marshall & Zimbardo, 1979; Maslach, 1979) or sustain and intensify existant ones (Zillmann, 1978). Findings such as these suggest a substantial degree of symmetry in the relationship of the components of the schema.

Studies of intrusive imagery provide a third source of evidence for a link between imagery and emotion. Images of recent, vivid, disturbing experiences intrude on subsequent mental activity despite active effort to keep them out of mind (Horowitz, 1970). Such imagery can even intrude into dream processes during paradoxical sleep (Witkin & Lewis, 1967). Data from dream studies and psychodynamic interviews also suggests that threats can reactivate images of situations that were frightening in childhood, a phenomenon that has been labeled as "unrepression" (Janis, 1974). These observations reinforce the hypothesized symmetrical link between emotional reactions and imagery.

Other studies of dreaming show that vivid images occurring during paradoxical sleep are accompanied by eye movements, heightened cortical arousal, a variety of muscular changes, and appropriate emotional experience (Dement, 1965, 1972). Money (1960) has reported vivid sexual dreams and nocturnal emissions in paraplegics who no longer experience sexual arousal when awake. This suggests that schematically processed imagery is sufficient to provoke sexual arousal and experience. It is also clear that peripheral feedback affects the central process, because these paraplegics do not experience sexual arousal in the waking state. Powerful emotional reactions, rich in body sensations, are an integral part of the nightmares that appear during nonparadoxical or slow-wave sleep (Broughton, 1968).

Finally, there is a large body of neurophysiological evidence for our hypothesized schematic processing system (Tucker, 1981). This includes an extensive body of data showing greater involvement of right hemisphere processing in facial recognition (Moscovitch, Scullion, & Christie, 1976; Safer, 1981), recognition of facial expressions of emotion (Jaynes, 1977; Ley & Bryden, 1979; Suberi & McKeever, 1977), and recognition of emotional tones of voice (Haggard & Parkinson, 1971; Safer & Leventhal, 1977), and laughter and crying (Carmon & Nachson, 1973; King & Kimura, 1972). Anatomical evidence also indicates that norepinephrine-activated neurons that are linked with centers critical for emotional behavior (e.g., the medial forebrain and limbic areas of the brain) are more common and more widely distributed in the right rather than the left hemisphere (Tucker, 1981). The right hemisphere also has widely distributed motor innervation, which enhances its suitability as a site for joining perceptual and motor signals into schematic packages (Semmes, 1968).

The five classes of evidence point to a common conclusion: Structures exist for the schematic processing of emotion. However, the most persuasive data are those on the phenomenon of phantom pain. Phantom body parts may be experienced after surgical removal. They occur most often after the removal of limbs but can appear after the removal of almost any part of the body. The loss of the body part must be abrupt for the phantom to appear; gradual deterioration, as in leprosy, is not followed by the phantom experience (Simmel, 1962). It is the occurrence of pain in the phantom that strongly suggests that emotions can be stored in perceptual (schematic) memory. Pain is likely to appear in phantoms if there was pain and emotional upset prior to the loss (Melzack, 1973; Simmel, 1962). Case histories suggest that the type of pain stored in the phantom may be determined by the individual's emotional involvement with the injured part. For example, a soldier's leg was amputated after a sequence of events beginning with a fall and a severely sprained ankle and followed by a shrapnel wound to the leg, which then became painfully infected and gangrenous. The phantom that appeared following surgery incorporated the less-severe pain of the sprain, a selection related to his belief that the sprain was entirely responsible for his injury and loss. Phantom pain appears to be a clear example of schematic (pain) memory.

Nathan (1962) reports an ingenious demonstration by Hutchins and Reynolds of how pain memories can be stored without conscious participation. They applied a nonpainful electrical stimulus to the trigeminal nerve of patients who had dental work a week or two earlier under nitrous oxide or novocaine. The former analgesic reduces emotional distress without altering the sensory signals to the brain, whereas the latter blocks the transmission of impulses from the teeth to the central nervous system and prevents the formation of a pain memory. The electrical stimulus to the nerve recreated the pain of having one's teeth drilled for those patients who had received nitrous oxide but did not do so for the patients who had received the novocaine.

Phantom pain also illustrates the symmetrical relationship between imagery and emotion. A painful phantom that has been absent for months and even years may be reactivated by the occurrence of emotionally distressing life experiences (Melzack, 1973). Indeed, even discussing severely upsetting life experiences may activate the painful phantom experience.

The motor involvement in schematically generated emotional imagery is well-illustrated by the use of relaxation training for the removal of phantom pain. McKechnie (1975) reported a case in which relaxation was used to eliminate the increasingly severe pain produced by a phantom that became progressively more contorted. The schematic memory was not static!

Finally, phantoms are not reported in children under 6 to 7 years of age. It is not known whether the effect of age is due to the frequency of experience per se or to some cognitive developmental change. It is clear, however, that experience has different effects depending on the age of the individual.

Phantom pain illustrates virtually all the features of schematic processing. This should come as no surprise, because the system mediating pain experience integrates informational and emotional processes. The physical structures in the emotional part of the pain system are exceedingly complex and include processes involved in both positive and negative reward (MacLean, 1958; Milner, 1967) and are rich in opiate receptor sites (Snyder, 1977). The system also includes sites for the production of the neurotransmitter norepinephrine, and sites involved in cerebral activation, the maintenance of paradoxical sleep, and the appearance of vivid, dream imagery (Jouvet, 1967, 1969). Thus, the structures include separate reward and image-enhancing components that participate in the schematic organization of central nervous system functions.

The Conceptual Processing System.   Some aspects of conceptual processing are highlighted here, before a more complete discussion of this system in the following section on the interrelationship of the systems.

The conceptual system can be conceived of as a set of rules derived from social learning (direct instruction or observation) and self-observation. Four such rules for the conceptual processing of information about pain have been articulated (Leventhal & Everhart, 1979): (1) The pain–injury rule; this is the notion that pain implies injury or illness, and injury or illness implies pain. It can create considerable doubt about their sanity in patients with phantom pain (Melzack, 1973); (2) the magnitude rule; an hypothesis that more-intense pain implies more-severe illness or injury (Chaves & Barber, 1975); (3) the contingency rule; the notion that events immediately antecedent to pain onset are its cause; and (4) the distraction rule; the notion that pain can best be managed by distraction or ignoring it, and that attention to injury enhances pain.

Rules are important as they affect volitional processes such as the direction of attention and the initial steps to cope with emotionally provocative situations. These acts can effect later pain experience by bringing the subject into contact with stimuli he or she might otherwise avoid, and the stimuli may alter the activity of the schematic and expressive motor mechanism in unexpected ways. For example, the voluntary direction of attention to stimulation during the earlier phase of a noxious experience can reduce the intensity of pain and distress minutes later (Leventhal, Brown, Shacham, & Engquist, 1979). However, the subjects directing their attention in this manner may not anticipate this change or even realize it had occurred.

Evidence for the performance component of conceptual processing can be found in data on desensitization therapy. Lang has subjects imagine threat scenes, attend to their fear reactions, relax as soon as the fear appears, and report when they have achieved nonfearful states in response to a formerly frightening image (Lang, 1968). In his most recent work, Lang (1979) trains subjects to rehearse simple stimulus and response scripts prior to behavioral treatments for phobic conditions. A stimulus script consists of propositional statements describing threatening stimulus conditions but omitting reference to the individual's motor (expressive, autonomic, and instrumental) behavior. A response script consists of statements about the individual's reactions (sweating, deep breathing, muscle tension) to the stimuli. Subjects who are exposed to prior response training show much stronger autonomic reactions when they are asked to "imagine" specific threat scenes. This is an important first step in fear reduction, as relaxation to threatening images reduces fear only for those subjects who produced clear autonomic responses to imagery at treatment outset. Our model suggests that Lang's procedure first brings the expressive and autonomic reactions under volitional control, rather than automatic schematic control. Once the responses are under volitional control, voluntary imagery and relaxation practice can minimize these responses. Our interpretation of this effect is similar to Bair's

(1901) interpretation of learning volitional control over ear wiggling and other nonvolitional reactions (see Kimble & Perlmutter, 1970).

Interactions Between the Processing Mechanisms

Each of the processing levels integrates a set of components for generating emotional experience and behavior. The entire hierarchy is active during emotional behavior. Emotional behavior and subjective experience will vary, therefore, with changes in the relationship of the mechanisms. The system can generate congruent or incongruent feelings, they can be relatively balanced or one may dominate processing at a given moment, and so on.

The hierarchical model also makes clear the intricate relationship between emotion and cognition. The definition and complexity of cognition varies at each level of processing. Sensory–motor cognition involves features (a high-pitched voice) or simple wholes (a facial configuration), schematic cognition involves more complex relatively stable perceptual memories that also include contextual factors, and the conceptual-cognition level involves abstract, inferential processing. Because emotions, or "raw" moment-by-moment affective states, can be generated by all three levels but seem to be most powerfully controlled by the sensory–motor and schematic ones, it is little wonder that emotion and cognition appear to be independent. This independence, however, depends on one's definition of cognition. If we identify cognition with conceptual rules, emotion and cognition will appear independent, indeed. (This assumes the individual's emotional development is relatively primitive, Piaget, 1981.) If cognition includes perceptual schemata, the two systems seem less separate.

We have adopted two approaches to the study of this complex system. The first was experimental. Its goal was to detect the contribution of each of the three processing systems to emotional responding to humorous and noxious stimulus situations. The second approach was to study behavior during stressful illness or treatment episodes. Our aim here was to detect the influence of each level of processing on the way people construe and cope with such stressful episodes. In the remainder of this section the key findings from our laboratory studies are presented with emphasis on those findings that set the stage for our investigation of illness cognition.

Conceptual-Schematic Interactions. A variety of interactions between conceptual and schematic processing have been observed in our studies of adaptation to noxious stimulation. The response to such stimulation is an integration of emotional distress and sensory information, and the integration is dependent on the schematic (perceptual) coding of the noxious sensory cues (Leventhal & Everhart, 1979). The cues themselves will generate less pain if this integration is blocked. In an extended series of laboratory and field studies we have found that learning of the sensory features of a noxious event and then monitoring and processing these features facilitates distress reduction (Johnson, 1973; Leventhal, Brown, Shacham, & Engquist, 1979; Reinhardt, 1979; Shacham, 1979). Such features might be the numbness, tingling, aching, and change in skin color of ischemic pain, or the coldness, numbness, pins and needles, and tightness of skin due to cold pressor stimulation. These effects are visible in laboratory situations where exposure to the noxious stimulus lasts a minimum of 5 to 6 minutes. Briefer stimulus exposures do not show distress reduction to sensory information or sensation monitoring.

If we think back to our list of pain rules, we can see that how people think about pain runs counter to the effects of sensory monitoring. Our conceptual logic argues that pain is felt when one is injured or ill, that its severity is in proportion to the seriousness of the illness, and that it is best coped with by distraction. Our commonsense, conceptual representation of pain is unlikely to separate pain into sensory and emotional components, or to include three levels of emotional processing, let alone suggest that emotion and sensation are integrated by a preattentive schema. Indeed, what Melzack (1973) calls the "puzzles of pain" are puzzles only when we confuse our conceptual rules with the underlying pain mechanism (Leventhal & Everhart, 1979). Sensation monitoring reduces pain by altering unobservable, schematic processing. The monitoring may generate an objective, or nonaffective code of the sensory features and so stimulate or allow the more rapid appearance of stress-induced analgesia. Monitoring can also facilitate coping. Objective coding of the features of a noxious event can help one regulate one's reactions to it, if self-regulation is possible, childbirth being an example (Leventhal, Shachem, Boothe, and Leventhal, 1981).

We found that the vast majority of subjects were completely unaware of the beneficial effects of sensation monitoring. Fewer than 20% of our subjects spontaneously adopted monitoring as a strategy for distress reduction, and less than half of this group did so with the expectation that it would reduce their pain and distress. The remainder monitored because they could not voluntarily remove their attention from the pain (Reinhardt, 1979). When subjects were strongly urged to monitor, however, they did so and reported substantial pain reductions if the noxious stimulus lasted for more than 4 to 5 minutes (Reinhardt, 1979; Shacham, 1979). When asked if the monitoring helped, they usually said it did not, and that they would have greatly preferred to distract themselves from the noxious event.

In our study of the monitoring of labor contractions, most subjects were also unaware of the benefit of monitoring sensations for distress reduction (Leventhal et al., 1981). I am not suggesting that distraction is always unhelpful. Active efforts to distract oneself from a painful stimulus can be effective in reducing pain, but distraction must be maintained. Once it stops, the pain experience returns to the level of that of control subjects. In contrast, subjects who have monitored sensations and formed images of their reaction to the noxious stimulus continue to experience substantial distress reduction, both during the latter part of a 6-minute stress trial and on subsequent trials, even when they no longer consciously monitor the sensory features of the noxious stimulus (Shacham, 1979). Yet, these subjects seem totally unaware of the benefit of monitoring! They have not had the opportunity to compare their experience with monitoring to that with distraction.

Our pain studies have also shown that conceptual, cognitive sets can sensitize schematic processing. When subjects expected a noxious event to be painful, the expectation accessed emotional pain and distress schemata, and monitoring of sensory features did not produce reductions in reported pain or increases in skin temperature (Leventhal, Brown, Shacham, & Engquist, 1979). The pain studies show, therefore, a considerable degree of independence of schematic and conceptual processes. However, they also show that conceptual processes can facilitate objective schematic processing, if the conceptual instruction leads subjects to monitor the sensory features of the information. It may also block objective schematization if the subject follows a distraction rule or expects the stimulus to be intolerably painful. The conceptual system has a powerful effect on schematic processing by sensitizing schemata and by directing attention toward or away from critical cues. This can be restated in more traditional psychological language: Voluntary (conceptual) actions can produce stimulation that effects classical conditioning (see Furedy, 1979; Riley & Furedy, in press).

Research in our own and other laboratories points to a still more intimate and complex interaction between conceptual or volitional processes on the one hand, and schematic and sensory–motor on the other. These studies suggest that conceptual codes can be constructed to MATCH automatic, perceptual codes. This does not mean the two codes are identical. The matching process may involve a joining of the key features of the spatially arranged schematic codes with those of a sequentially organized (propositional) conceptual code. The key features would include junctures (onset instructions) for critical stimuli and response instructions. As the volitional code comes closer to a match with the automatic perceptual code, the actor is better able to control his or her affective reactions. Matching should have an important effect on short-term emotional states as well as the long-term potential for emotion. The availability of volitional codes to control emotional reactions in specific content domains, such as work stress or disease and dying, allows the individual to experience emotions in that area that could not be experienced otherwise. Cancer patients can develop a set of performance codes to deal with the fears and depressive feelings associated with advanced metastatic disease. Once this is achieved, the individual may derive pleasures from simple life events that a "normal" person would regard as impossible. An example would be that of a woman whose severe metastatic disease kept her bedridden and prevented her from performing the simplest of household tasks. She was very pleased when chemotherapy allowed her to walk to the kitchen to get a glass of water, even though she was aware that the remaining time was brief indeed.

The first of two types of research supporting the matching concept investigated the hypothesis that schematic and sensory–motor processing of emotion was closely associated with right-hemispheric function. The reasons for this were reviewed earlier. In a series of studies (Safer & Leventhal, 1977), we found that subjects were much more likely to use the tone of voice of the speaker than the content of the sentences to judge the emotional quality of tape-recorded passages when they were played to the left rather than to the right ear. Material heard over the left ear is initially processed by the right hemisphere of the brain. Evidence suggests, however, that musical practice generates left-hemisphere competence that resembles that of the right. Thus, highly skilled musicians are equally facile in melody identification with either hemisphere, whereas unskilled individuals show a clear left-ear (right-hemisphere) superiority (Bever & Chiarello, 1974).

On the basis of this finding and others showing that females are more apt to express and enact emotional scripts, Safer (1981) reasoned that female subjects would be more likely than male subjects to have developed volitional or left-hemisphere competence in emotional judgment. Female subjects should be able to process emotional information equally well with either the right or the left hemisphere. To test this hypothesis he used an emotional recognition task, in which subjects first saw a facial expression of an emotion in the center of their visual field (for 8 seconds) and then saw a second expression of emotion that was flashed for 50 or 150 msec to either the left or right visual fields. When subjects were asked to say whether the emotional expressions were the same or different, female subjects were found to be equally accurate in both left and right hemispheres, whereas males were considerably less accurate in their judgments when the second photograph was exposed in the right visual field (left hemisphere). In a second study Safer ruled out the hypothesis that the sex difference reflected a difference in the ability to judge the similarity of pictures or spatial patterns, rather than emotions. The methods in this study were identical to the first, except that subjects were asked to judge whether the two pictures were the same picture or different ones. Under these conditions, both males and females shows a right-hemisphere superiority in accuracy, females slightly more so than males. Hence, the equal left- and right-hemisphere ability shown by females in the first experiment was skill in judging emotion.

Safer's findings support the hypothesis that a volitional, affective code can be constructed in the left hemisphere that is parallel to the holistic and automatic code of the right.

The second type of research that supported the matching concept also studies sex differences in the organization of humorous emotion. Leventhal and Mace (1970) conducted a series of studies in which high positive correlations appeared between expressions of humor (smiles and laughter) and ratings of the funniness of a W. C. Fields movie for female subjects, and negative correlations appeared for males. The correlations were even stronger in conditions where subjects were urged to be expressive. Lang (1980) and his colleagues reported similar findings for the relationship between imagery and autonomic responses: Women showed much greater consistency among their imagery, their heart-rate responses, and their fear of snakes than did male subjects. The correlations between fear reports and heart rates were positive for women whether or not they were trained to make response propositions ($r - .51$ and $.46$, respectively); that is, to think of themselves touching snakes with their hearts beating, hands trembling and sweating, and so on. By contrast, males showed a near-zero correlation between heart rate and fear reports prior to training ($r = -.22$), whereas response training, the correlation increased to the same level as for women ($r = .43$). Training, therefore, was important in creating a volitionally controllable integration for male subjects.

The finding of greater consistency in female than in male subjects suggested that volitional and automatic components of emotional responding are more frequently matched in females than in males. It also led us (Leventhal & Cupchik, 1976) to propose that a match between volitional and automatic components would not only be simpler to achieve in female than male subjects but might also have a greater effect on the individual's subjective, emotional state. Creating a match could convert automatic emotional impulses and their associated feelings into intentional, nonemotional movements. We proposed, therefore, that monitoring of expressive motor behavior would undercut the spontaneity of response and reduce the subjective affect accompanying smiles and laughter in female subjects. This hypothesis was tested by having subjects monitor and rate their smiling and laughter immediately after exposure to a cartoon. The cartoons were rated for funniness immediately after the self-rating was completed. The results were clear. Female subjects rated all cartoon stimuli as substantially less funny when they first observed and rated their own expressions of mirth. Volitional anticipation of the expressive response appeared to have subtracted from subjective feeling, and this in turn led to a reduction in the rated funniness of the cartoons. As the rating task continued, many of the women found they could no longer discriminate good from poor cartoons. There was no parallel change for ratings for male subjects. This supports the hypothesis that the expression of mirth and ratings of the humorousness of cartoons are functionally related for female subjects and actually influence one another, whereas for men both are related directly to the stimulus and so are functionally independent.

These findings not only point to important sex differences in the organization of emotional response; they also suggest a way in which volitional motor codes might interact with spontaneously elicited motor behaviors in generating emotional states. It can be hypothesized that the spontaneous or perceptually generated expressive-motor impulses move in two directions, toward the expressive motor apparatus itself (i.e., the face) and toward a comparator in the voluntary motor system. Subjective emotional states would be experienced when an automatic, expressive motor impulse feeds forward into the comparator in the voluntary motor system and remains unmatched. The motor impulse is felt as externally provoked and uncontrollable when the individual was not voluntarily set to perform the expressive action. The quality of the feeling (anger, fear, joy, etc.) is determined by the pattern of the spontaneous discharge. If the individual is set to perform the expressive action, the motor impulse is felt as a signal that the actor has made a smiling, frowning, disgusted, etc. expression. Hence, when an expressive movement is anticipated, its successful completion is experienced as an action, just as we would feel the successful completion of an action if we reached for, grasped, and picked up a tea cup. (For more detail see Leventhal, 1979, 1980, p. 167–171.)

The feed forward hypothesis has implications for subjective emotional experience at a given instant and for the potential for varied emotional experience over time. Understanding the interaction between spontaneously elicited expressive motor behavior and volitional motor behavior provides a way of deriving predictions as to which emotion will be felt and the strength of the feeling at a given point in time. It is the long-term implications of the hypothesis, however, which are the most important and the least explored. In particular, the hypothesis suggests that as new knowledge is acquired, major changes can be expected in the individual's emotional life. New knowledge in this instance would refer to performance and conceptual knowledge, which allows the individual to anticipate situational stimuli and his or her automatic responses to them. The growth of an anticipatory system, particularly of the behavioral component (and this means one's action impulses) means that emotional reactions would cease to have an impulsive quality, and the individual would become more deliberate and controlled in response. For example, if the individual faces an unknown but terrifying threat, increasing knowledge of its stimulus features and acquiring the ability to anticipate emotional responses would gradually reduce impulsive terror and allow problem-solving behavior (Calvert–Boyanowsky & Leventhal, 1975). Once the individual achieves control over the automatically elicited terror, his or her capacity for emotional response would broaden and permit the experience of a variety of both positive and negative emotions. To return to an earlier example, cancer is dreadful, terrifying, and painful, and to an outside observer there is no joy to be found once one is so afflicted. But patients find joy even within the context of death from metastatic disease as they have developed differentiated schematic and performance codes. To the adapted patient, cancer is to be lived with, and positive and negative emotions can be experienced within this envelope of meaning. Of course, the stability is fragile and changes in the disease can all too easily disrupt the match of conceptual to automatic processes.

ILLNESS COGNITION AND THE PERCEPTUAL-MOTOR THEORY OF EMOTION

If we think about illness within a medical framework, we are likely to assume that illness is caused by some external or internal agent leading to a qualitative change in somatic processes, which generates in turn symptoms, the suspicion that one is ill, and information seeking from family, friends, or professionals to define the meaning of the symptom. Once a diagnosis and prescription are in hand, the patient adheres to treatment and is rewarded by a cure: the normalization of the underlying process and the disappearance of symptoms (see Leventhal, Zimmerman, & Gutmann, 1981; Zola, 1973). Although this sequence is not atypical of most infectious disease episodes, it is far from a complete picture of illness. Is a conceptual "script" of this type the primary mediator of health and illness behaviors? I propose that health and illness behavior is mediated by a system very similar to that which mediates emotional reactions. Central to this perspective is the belief that concrete cues and perceptual schemata identical to those used in automatic emotion processing play a critical role in the way people represent illness episodes and have an important effect on health and illness behavior. Hence, conceptual or normative scripts represent but one of the mediating systems underlying health and illness behavior and can be very much at variance with the schematic system that pushes behavior in a less thoughtful and more compelling way.

The Mental Representation of Illness Episodes

As an episode of illness unfolds, the individual will construct a mental representation of it that is a product of the available information and the structure of the processing system. Our studies of patients seeking medical care for "everyday" complaints (Safer, Tharps, Jackson, & Leventhal, 1979), of adherence to treatment for antihypertensive therapy (Leventhal, Meyer, & Nerenz, 1980; Meyer, Leventhal, & Gutmann, in press), and of patients in chemotherapeutic treatment for cancer (Leventhal & Nerenz, in press; Nerenz, 1979; Nerenz, Leventhal, & Love, in press; Ringler, 1981) suggest that illness representations are characterized by the following features, each of which include concrete and abstract elements:

   1. An identity: This includes the concrete features of the illness (body sensations, physical changes, etc.) and an abstract, label or diagnosis.
   2. A perceived cause: the belief that the illness episode is due to a specific external agent (germ, poison, etc.), to aging, or to one's own actions, as well as concrete images of specific instances (eating overly salted foods) of contact with an agent.
   3. Expectations about consequences: These may range from vague expectations of death, severe pain, and strokes to more benign thoughts such as distress, or soreness. These thoughts may be concrete or abstract.
   4. A time line: The expected duration of the episode may be a concept (e.g., a few days) or a specific image (e.g., I'll live till my grandchild is born).

The representation of the illness is also acompanied by emotional reactions and plans to engage in one or more coping reactions, ranging from "waiting to see what happens" to following prescribed treatments regimens. These are expected to change the disease process and alter the symptom experience. This section briefly describes the sources of information contributing to the representation and then discusses in some detail the operation of the schematic and conceptual systems in constructing it.

Sources of Information.   Three sources of information seem to influence the way patients construe their illness episodes. The first is the illness and its natural history. Each illness develops at different rates, generates different symptoms, goes into periods of quiescence, and re-emerges with at least some degree of regularity, though less is known about these patterns than one might expect.

The unfolding of the episode is also greatly influenced by the social context in which the disease develops. The very same symptomatology may be regarded as an unavoidable accompaniment of everyday living in one social context and be seen as a sign of mild, moderate, or even severe illness in another. For example, in his study of Welsh families, Robinson (1971) found that wives saw fatigue and irritability as a normal response to work stress in their husbands and a sign of illness in their children. It has also been found that symptoms are more likely to be interpreted as benign and medical care delayed when an ill person shares this information with a family member rather than with a friend. The social context has an important effect on the interpretation given concrete, bodily signs.

Third, the individual's past history leaves a host of interpretive structures that give meaning to bodily sensations. As was pointed out at the beginning of this section, we have all experienced bodily sensations and discomfort following specific events, had these symptoms labeled as illness, acted to treat them, and observed the disappearance of the symptoms over time. These experiences have left a residue of abstract (verbal and performance) and concrete knowledge in the form of perceptual or schematic memories, which interact with and interpret new stimulus material in building the representation of it.

The Mechanisms Active in Constructing the Representation.   Schematic and conceptual processes play a continuing role in processing illness information. Contextual information from family, friends, and practitioners is typically coded in verbal form. If the context provides examples of illness (e.g., cancer in a family member), the coding may be schematic. And if the practitioner requires the patient to review body sensation and rehearse responses to them, a performance code will be constructed to parallel and regulate automatic, schematic processes.

Sensations from the body, in this case the symptoms of illness, are also coded in conceptual form. We know and discuss our symptoms and how we react to and treat them. But sensations are first coded in perceptual memories that have many of the properties we have assigned to emotional, memory schemata. These schemata can be generalized prototypes of illness experience or structures representing particular classes of illness.

Symptom memories form the core of the schematic memory, and body sensations are the basic components of the schemas. They have quality (e.g., aching, burning, pulling) and are distributed over space and time. Because symptoms are under the control of the illness process and not readily controlled by the investigator, we know far less about the effects of symptom patterns upon behavior than we would like. Our ignorance is unfortunate when we realize that much of the behavior of patients is based on symptoms interpretations. For example, many patients confuse myocardial infarctions with gastric distress and, when they do so, may delay months or years in seeking professional help. Indeed, even patients who have had an MI may fail to recognize a recurrence when the symptom pattern on the second occasion deviates from the first. Because the MI is threatening, the sensory pattern of the initial attack seems to be indelibly etched in perceptual memory, and departures from this schema are discounted and attributed to other causes. Patients seem to behave as if they "know what an MI feels like" and are convinced that one would feel exactly as it did before!

The label or diagnosis attached to the symptom pattern forms a second, parallel focus for the interpretation and response to body sensations. Sensations labeled as cancer have quite different meaning than those labeled gastrointestinal distress. In the latter instance, well-learned performance conceptualizations are available to guide self-treatment behaviors. In the former instance, fear, defensiveness, and help seeking will compete for control over behavior. Hence, diagnostic labels and symptoms, or conceptual and concrete factors, define the core of the illness episode. Not surprisingly, patients typically recall their diagnosis and symptoms, although forgetting what it is they are supposed to do about them (Ley, 1979).

Hypertension: An Example of Discrepant Schematic and Conceptual Meanings.   A good illustration of conceptual and schematic codes in the representation of an illness episode is an example of illness behavior in which the two systems operate simultaneously and generate conflicting responses. It comes from a study investigating the behavior of patients with hypertension (Meyer, 1980; Meyer, Leventhal, & Gutmann, in press). We examined how patients represented their illness, how their representation developed, and how it influenced their coping behavior. Meyer interviewed about 375 people in six groups. The interview covered their beliefs about the symptoms that accompanied high blood pressure, their notions of the physiological mechanisms underlying it, their ways of coping with it, including their adherence to medication if on treatment, their beliefs about the causes of high blood pressure, and their expectations about how long treatment would have to continue and what its outcome would be.

The first, most striking finding emerging from this study was the substantial discrepancy between the abstract and concrete components of patient representations of high blood pressure. When asked, "Can people tell when their blood pressure is up?," 80% responded, "No, they cannot." But when asked, "Do you think you can tell when your blood pressure is up?," approximately 90% said, "Yes, I can tell." Not only did these patients say they could tell; they indicated what kinds of symptoms were indicators of blood pressure elevations. It was usually headache, dizziness, face flushing, or tension; heart beating was reported by patients new to treatment but not by those patients who had been in treatment 6 months or longer. These seemingly paradoxical responses were given by respondents who had been in treatment for a few months to several years. They were also given by respondents who had been in treatment in the past but had dropped out for 6 months or more and then returned to treatment. Their return was often motivated by the reappearance of symptoms. Only 71% of the patients new to treatment believed they could monitor elevations in their blood pressure, but 6 months later 92% of them said they could tell when their pressures were up, although they still clung to the statement that "People can't tell."

The patient's conviction that they can use body symptoms to tell when their blood pressure is elevated is not an idle belief. A substantial portion of those who monitor symptoms use them as a guide to vary their medications. Of those patients who felt that treatment had not reduced their signs of high blood pressure, only 31% were taking medication as prescribed. By contrast, 70% of the patients who reported that treatment had beneficial effects on their symptoms were taking medication as prescribed. These behavioral reports are also related to blood pressure control. A similar and equally dramatic result obtains when one looks at the newly treated patients: If they are not persuaded their symptoms are reduced, they drop treatment.

Patients are clearly responding to events at a concrete as well as an abstract level. They seem to deal with the discrepancy by assuming that they are different from other people. Doctors may know what happens to MOST patients, but the patients know what happens to them. Sickness means symptoms, and the absence of symptoms means successful treatment. Patients are also aware they are deviating from a normative rule: Over 60% spontaneously asked the interviewer not to tell the doctor when they were treating their blood pressure. The representation of the disease of hypertension includes a potent, concrete, symptomatic core, which in this instance prevails over abstract, verbal communication in directing behavior. It is also protected from public scrutiny.

It is obvious that this concrete, symptomatic component of the illness representation is analogous to the schematic component of emotional processing. Both include autonomic and other bodily features, both are caused by events such as stress, and both are short-lived and responsive to simple ministrations. It is no wonder that patients frequently have difficulty deciding whether they are ill or emotionally upset! This question lurks in many a patient's mind when he or she seeks medical care. The similarity of these schematic structures are elaborated later, but the analogy does suggest that concrete, schematic processing (or perceptual memory) is not unique to emotion. Indeed, it is reasonable to suggest that emotional processes share the concrete memory component along with other processes that involve perceptual memory (e.g., memory for position of chess pieces, Simon & Chase, 1973). It is important, therefore, to elucidate how concrete, schematic, illness cognition is linked to emotion.

Cancer Chemotherapy: An Example of Uncertainty and Distress. Chemotherapy is becoming one of the major tools in the effort to control cancer. Patients with malignant disease will be put on treatment protocols for 6 months to a year. The protocol involves a series of treatment cycles each of which lasts 3 to 4 weeks. A typical cycle would begin with an intravenous injection of several drugs, followed by a week of oral medication, followed by a second injection and another week of pills. The patient is typically off medication for 1–2 weeks before beginning the next cycle. The medications, both injected and oral, produce a variety of side effects ranging from nausea, tiredness, changes in sleep patterns, joint pains, and weight gain, to less-frequent effects such as mouth sores, weakness, rashes, and anorexia. Chemotherapy is not pleasant, but it is effective. In the previously fatal category of diffuse histiocytic lymphoma, for example, aggressive combinational chemotherapy appears to be curing 50% of cases (Schein, DeVita, Hubbard, et al., 1976).

Although chemotherapy is clearly difficult, the promise of survival and evidence of improvement in conditions ought and do make it tolerable. We have conducted a number of studies examining how patients respond to treatment. In one such study, Nerenz (1979) interviewed 60 patients suffering from lymphatic cancers and asked how they monitored the progress of their treatment, as well as what difficulties they experienced with it. He found a substantial portion (39 of 61) had palpable nodes that could be monitored to assess the effectiveness of the treatment. Twenty-one of these 39 patients had difficulty using nodes to monitor their treatment, however, because the nodes disappeared within 1 to 2 weeks after treatment began. Sixteen of the remaining 18 said the nodes had shrunk gradually; the remaining two reported no change. When the level of distress with treatment was compared for these groups, Nerenz found higher reports of distress for patients whose nodes had disappeared rapidly ($X = 5.90$) in comparison to those whose nodes had merely shrunk ($X = 3.14$; on 14-point scales). A careful examination of the data revealed that patients whose concrete signs of cancer had disappeared rapidly were extremely distressed if this concrete cue was replaced by abstract sources of information from physicians (Nerenz, Leventhal, & Love, in press).

It is not entirely clear why patients were so distressed at having to give up their concrete indicators of disease. One factor appears to be that the continuation of treatment conflicted with the notion they were cured. Several patients voiced this idea, which was consistent with the disappearance of the nodes. Whether this led to distrust of the practitioners, or fear that the cancer had spread to undetectable locations (why else would they still be treating it?), is unknown. But it is evident that the conflict between concrete sensory cures and more abstract information was a source of considerable distress.

Models of Illness.   Both the hypertension and cancer data show the importance of concrete, sensory information in defining illness states. The disappearance of such cues can cause a variety of problems—dropping out of treatment for newly treated hypertensives and distress with treatment for patients with lymphatic cancer. Discrepancies between body cues and abstract information about treatment are sources of difficulty for the patient, but it is not just the identity of the illness that is coded in both abstract and concrete form. Our cancer patients discussed the duration of their illness, its cause and its consequences in concrete terms. They expressed hopes of living to see events such as the marriage of children, attributed the illness to specific early experiences (contact with pesticides on the farm), and imagined the course of the disease would parallel that observed in friends and family. Having observed particularly malignant forms of the disease was a source of considerable stress and despair (Ringler, 1981). It is important to ask, however, whether these features are discrete or whether they cluster into meaningful forms, or models of disease.

Although we have a number of leads, we do not at this time have a clear answer to the preceding question. Steve Penrod and Daniel Linz have initiated a program of studies using multidimensional scaling to detect the basic features of illness cognition. In one study they asked undergraduate subjects to compare pairs of illness labels and found five dimensional solutions when these similarity judgments were analysed (Linz, Penrod, & Leventhal, 1981). Three of the dimensions corresponded to those found in our patient populations: cause, consequences, and time lines. The agreement is actually greater than this indicates because the causal factor divided into three dimensions in the MDS solution, and identity couldn't appear as a factor because it is built into the labels used for illness comparisons. Whereas multidimensional scaling generates more or less independent dimensions, we expect to find patterns in illness cognition. It is not clear whether the organization will focus on specific labels, or about dimensions (e.g., disease caused by external, infectious agents). We suspect that relatively tight organizations will occur around specific disease labels, but it is not unlikely that clusters of illnesses will share time lines and consequences. The cluster of diseases caused by external infectious agents, for example, may be seen as having short time lines and mild consequences. Whether they will share symptomatology is questionable. Many symptoms are perceived to be disease specific. On the other hand, those such as fever and pain are so general they cannot define an illness dimension. Evidence for this is already present in multidimensional scaling carried out under instructions to compare the labels on symptomatology: The first dimension is quite robust but not readily interpretable. Symptoms are symptoms and generate their own dimension.

The Link of Emotion to Illness Cognition

Several parallels and links between the processing of emotion and illness representations have been presented: The analogy between the two types of processing systems, the importance of schematic processing, and the effect of schematic and conceptual conflict on distress were the most important. Emotions, however, are linked to illness cognition in other ways.

Features and Emotions.   The conceptual content of illness cognition acts as a stimulus to emotion. The features of the representation, its identity, cause, and time lines, can elicit specific emotional states. The effects of identity are obvious. Cancer is far more fear provoking and depressing a label than infectious mononucleosis, and certain symptoms, such as lumps or bleeding, are far more threatening than others. Unusual behavior in a symptom can add to threat. If a tumor spreads upward from the breast or gut to the neck, a patient may become far more terrified than if it spread to a proximal area. The disease takes on awe-inspiring power by leaping about the body.

Emotions and illness representations are also linked together because their underlying schemata have common features. Body sensations from autonomic disturbances are part of both emotion and illness schemata. Hence, many such body states can be felt either as emotion or illness. If an emotionally generated body state is schematized and experienced as an illness, fluctuation in the emotion will be experienced as change in the illness. Stress and negative emotion in general (e.g. fear or anxiety) are very likely to be experienced as causes of illnesses such as high blood pressure and heart attack that are expected to include cardiac sensations which are autonomically mediated. Illnesses which are expected to be debilitating, such as the cancers, have body experiences overlapping with depression. The perceived link to emotion can have strong effects on coping strategies, many patients following stress-reduction programs to abet medical treatments. Finally, it is clear that the time line of the disease plays a strong role in feelings of depression. Depressed affect is often associated with recognition that an illness is chronic and progressive. This time line may provoke intense anger in younger people, who feel they have been denied their ''right to life'' and feel frustrated and angry in the face of death. It is doubtful that simple relationships of this sort will be adequate to describe the linkage of emotion to illness cognition, because specific dimensions may provoke varying affects depending on the constellation of features in the illness representation. This area is open for exploration.

Emotion and the Scanning of Features. Emotion may also impact on the organization of illness representations by affecting the order or sequence in which the individual scans or attends to specific features of the representation. If depression is linked to the representation of cancer, the individual appears likely to move her or his attention from the disease and its symptoms to the consequences and time line of the representation (a downhill slide to death). The angry patient, however, is likely to scan the features to define an agent or enemy suitable for attack. This brings attention from the illness to its causes and enhances receptiveness to treatment information and coping plans. Thus, depressive affect will promote a cognitive sequence that leads to a cul-de-sac in thought, a dwelling on the brevity of life and pain and its distress. Anger, on the other hand, appears likely to encourage an active, coping, cure-oriented pattern.

Scanning patterns or biases may have profound effects on receptivity to communication (Janis, 1962). Patients who are frightened and depressed are unlikely to attend to information about treatment and cause (Ley, 1977). Those who are angry seem more readily to assimilate curative or preventive information. However, other than the few studies reviewed by Ley (1979), we have little to guide us in our exploration of the effects of emotion on the scanning of the features of illness representations.

Emotion and Meaning Domains. We have suggested that illness representations become more differentiated and interrelated and include more performance as well as schematic and abstract–verbal cognition, as the individual has more experience with an illness. Repeated experience develops a rich cognitive domain, and the self is nested in a set of meanings involving the cause, symptoms, time line, and consequences of the illness. Associated with this representation is, of course, a history of emotional reactions and coping strategies. This history is also embedded in a meaningful set of social relationships. If we truly wish to understand the relationship of emotion to illness cognition, we must recognize that emotion is embedded in virtually every aspect of this meaning or knowledge system. Self-descriptions such as, ''I am a person with cancer,'' summarize complex, knowledge systems that are linked with emotional experience by schematic and conceptual processes.

We have observed an interesting change in this knowledge system as the cancer patient learns to live with his or her illness. The entire system appears to become encapsulated and segregated from prior self-knowledge. In its most extreme form, we see patients who take life on a day-by-day basis and no longer allow themselves to think back to times when they were active and well. Nor do they look forward to cures. Their pleasures and pains exist within a new envelope of meaning and are conditioned by this system of concrete and abstract expectations. Less-extreme versions of reorganization of the self in life are seen with patients who have accepted the disease and have reasonably good expectations for extended survival. They frequently express distaste for the trivial nonsense that occupies so much of life. Their wish is to fully experience their days and not lose valuable time in family or work squabbles, or worrying about material goods. They focus on essentials. Affects are experienced within such meaning systems. The meaning system sets limits on the possibility for emotional experience, and emotion can only be fully understood if it is considered within this total context.

FINAL COMMENTS ON EMOTION AND COGNITION

Our hierarchical model provides a complex view of the processes underlying the generation of emotional experience and behavior and of the links of emotion to cognition. Emotion is attached to simple perceptual cues, to perceptual or schematically organized experiences, and to more organized meanings. Our studies of illness cognition not only support the significance of concrete, schematic processes for the elicitation of emotion; they also suggest that emotion is linked to a variety of cognitive processes. These are the cognitive processes involved with the features of the representation and in the organization of the individual's self-perception in relation to a disease, the processes that create the meaning or knowledge domain that develops with illness experience. To treat the relationship of emotion to cognition as that of unbridled affect to cold cognition, as suggested by some investigators (Zajonc, 1980), is both misleading and a step backward. On the other hand, it is important to recognize, as both Tomkins (1962) and Izard (1971) have urged us to, the existence of primary, expressive motor processing, for it preserves the identity of emotional expressions and experiences over wide variations in knowledge. Hence, we also reject views that imply that emotion is nothing more than the attachment of autonomic arousal (or reticular activation) to knowledge (Mandler, 1975, in press). Yet we acknowledge what we see as the central theme of Mandler's contribution: Emotion is nested and integrated in meaning systems. The major objective of this chapter and of the extensive writings of Silvan Tomkins (1962, 1963) has been to spell out and provide examples of different types of emotion–cognition integrations.

Because I have focused on the processing of emotion and its link to illness cognition, I have ignored at least one extremely important aspect of emotion in my presentation. The perceptual motor model as presented appears to be fully compatible with the computer representation of the emotion-memory system, as so brilliantly depicted by Bower (Bower, 1981; Bower & Cohen, in press). Both presentations assume some type of emotion generator with emotion connected to specific cognitive entities. The feature of emotion overlooked in this perspective is that emotion is experienced both as a reaction to an object and as a reaction within the experiencing person. Hence, emotion not only informs us about feelings attached to perceptions and thoughts; it also informs us about our own moment-by-moment internal states, both in relation to perceived objects and with respect to potentials for action (see Leventhal & Mosbach, in press). In this respect emotion is very much like illness. Both tell us about the impact of conditions on our systems, and both tell us about the state of our systems. The experience of emotion, therefore, serves as an ongoing meter of our internal bodily condition and our capacity for different types of action. If we are angry, we have the capacity to attack, if fearful, the capacity to flee, if fatigued and ill, the need to rest, and so on. Awareness of emotion establishes a set of goals that relate to and are independent of our goals with specific objects. I may wish to attack, destroy, and be rid of a threat agent, but my fear and fatigue inform me I need to accept its presence until my resources can match the demands of coping. The moment-by-moment nature of this readout and its tendency to summate over many inputs (e.g., fatigue summates over a wide range of central and peripheral cues) makes self-observed emotional goals somewhat different from external, or objectively defined ones. If this aspect of emotion were represented in Bower's computer models, it would be in the form of electrical meters, circuit regulators, temperature gauges, and thermostats controlling the voltage and temperature of the computer. It is not part of his model. It is part of emotion. In short, understanding emotion is complicated by its varying position in self-regulatory systems. It is my hope to capture some of this complexity in describing the integration of emotion and illness cognition.

REFERENCES

Andrew, R. J. The origins of facial expression. *Scientific American*, 1965, *213*, 88–94.

Angier, R. P. The conflict theory of emotion. *American Journal of Psychology*, 1927, *34*, 390–401.

Bair, J. H. Development of voluntary control. *Psychological Review*, 1901, *8*, 474–510.

Bever, T. G., & Chiarello, R. J. Cerebral dominance in musicians and nonmusicians. *Science*, 1974, *185*, 537–539.

Bower, G. H. The object in the world of the infant. *Scientific American*, 1971, *226*, 30–38.

Bower, G. H. Mood and memory. *American Psychologist*, 1981, *31*, 129–148.

Bower, G. H., & Cohen, P. R. *Emotional influences in memory and thinking: Data and theory*. In M. S. Clark & S. T. Fiske (Eds.), *Affect and Cognition: The Seventeenth Annual Carnegie Symposium on Cognition*. Hillsdale, N. J.: Lawrence Erlbaum Associates, 1982.

Brazelton, T. B., Koslowski, B., & Main, M. The origins of reciprocity: The early mother–infant interaction. In M. Lewis & L. A. Rosenblum (Eds.), *The effect of the infant on its caretaker*. New York: Wiley, 1974.

Broadbent, D. E. The hidden preattentive process. *American Psychologist*, 1977, *32*, 109–118.

Broughton, R. Sleep disorders: Disorders of arousal. *Science*, 1968, *159*, 1070–1078.

Calvert–Boyanowsky, J., & Leventhal, H. The role of information in attenuating behavioral responses to stress: A reinterpretation of the misattribution phenomenon. *Journal of Personality and Social Psychology*, 1975, *32*, 214–221.

Cannon, W. B. The James–Lange theory of emotions: A critical examination and alternative theory. *The American Journal of Psychology*, 1927, *34*, 106–124.

Carmon, A., & Nachson, I. Ear symmetry in perception of emotional nonverbal stimuli. *Acta Psychologica*, 1973, *37*, 351–357.

Carver, C. S., & Scheier, M. F. *Attention and self-regulation: A control-theory approach to human behavior*. New York: Springer–Verlag, 1981.

Casey, K. L. Pain: A current view of neural mechanisms. *American Scientist*, 1973, *61*, 194–200.

Chaves, J. F., & Barber, T. X. Hypnotism and surgical pain. In M. Weisenberg (Ed.), *Pain: Clinical and experimental perspectives*. Saint Louis: Mosby, 1975.

Cofer, C. *Motivation and emotion*. New York: Scott, Foresman, 1972.

Cupchik, G. C., & Leventhal, H. Consistency between expressive behavior and the evaluation of humorous stimuli: The role of sex and self-observation. *Journal of Personality and Social Psychology*, 1974, *30*, 429–442.

Dement, W. C. An essay on dreams: The role of physiology in understanding their nature. In Barron, *New directions in psychology* (Vol. 2). New York: Holt, Rinehart, & Winston, 1965.

Dement, W. C. *Some must watch while some must sleep*. Stanford, Calif.: Stanford Alumni Association, 1972.

Dewey, J. The theory of emotion: (I) Emotional attitudes. *Psychological Review*, 1894, *1*, 553–569.

Dewey, J. The theory of emotion: (II) The significance of emotions. *Psychological Review*, 1895, *2*, 13–32.

Eibl–Eibesfeldt, I. *Ethology: The biology of behavior*. New York: Holt, 1970.

Eibl–Eibesfeldt, I. Strategies of social interaction. In R. Plutchik & H. Kellerman (Eds.), *Emotion: Theory, research, and experience*. New York: Academic Press, 1980.

Ekman, P., & Friesen, W. V. Constants across culture in the face and emotion. *Journal of Personality and Social Psychology*, 1971, *17*, 124–129.

Ekman, P., & Friesen, W. V. *Unmasking the face*. Englewood Cliffs, N. J.: Prentice–Hall, 1975.

Ekman, P., Friesen, W. V., & Ellsworth, P. *Emotion in the human face: Guidelines for research and integration of the findings*. New York: Pergamon, 1972.

Epstein, S. The ecological study of emotion in humans. In P. Pliner, K. R. Blankstein, & I. M. Spigel (Eds.), *Perception of emotion in self and others*. New York: Plenum, 1979.

Fulcher, J. S. "Voluntary" facial expression in blind and seeing children. *Archives of Psychology*, 1942, *272*, 5–49.

Furedy, J. J. Teaching self-regulation of cardiac function through imaginational Pavlovian and biofeedback conditioning: Remember the response. In N. Birbaumer & H. D. Kimmel (Eds.), *Biofeedback and self-regulation*. New York: Lawrence Erlbaum Associates, 1979.

Garcia, J. Tilting at the paper mills of academe. *American Psychologist*, 1981, *2*, 149.

Gellhorn, E. Motion and emotion: The role of proprioception in the physiology and pathology of the emotions. *Psychological Review*, 1964, *71*, 457–472.

Gibson, J. J. *The perception of the visual world*. Boston, Mass.: Houghton Mifflin, 1950.

Goodenough, F. L. Expression of the emotions in a blind–deaf child. *Journal of Abnormal and Social Psychology*, 1932, *27*, 328–333.

Grossberg, J. M., & Wilson, H. K. Physiological changes accompanying the visualization of fearful and neutral situations. *Journal of Personality and Social Psychology*, 1968, *10*, 124–133.

Haggard, M. P., & Parkinson, A. M. Stimulus and task factors as determinants of ear advantages. *Quarterly Journal of Experimental Psychology*, 1971, *23*, 168–177.

Hebb, D. O. *The organization of behavior*. New York: Wiley, 1949.

Horowitz, M. J. *Image formation and cognition*. New York: Appleton–Century–Crofts, 1970.

Hurvich, L. M. Hering and the scientific establishment. *American Psychologist*, 1969, *24*, 497–514.

Izard, C. E. *The face of emotion*. New York: Appleton–Century–Crofts, 1971.

Izard, C. E. *Human emotions*. New York: Plenum, 1977.

James, W. What is an emotion? *Mind*, 1884, *9*, 188–205.

James, W. *The principles of psychology* (Vols. I & II). New York: Holt, 1890.

Janis, I. L. Psychological effects of warnings. In G. W. Baker & D. W. Chapman (Eds.), *Man and society in disaster.* New York: Basic Books, 1962.

Janis, I. L. *Psychological stress.* New York: Academic Press, 1974.

Jaynes, J. *The origins of consciousness in the breakdown of the bicameral mind.* Boston: Houghton Mifflin, 1977.

Johnson, J. Effects of accurate expectations about sensations on sensory and distress components of pain. *Journal of Personality and Social Psychology,* 1973, *27,* 261–275.

Johnson, J. E., & Leventhal, H. Effects of accurate expectations and behavioral instructions on reaction during a noxious medical examination. *Journal of Personality and Social Psychology,* 1974, *29,* 710–718.

Johnson, J. E., Rice, V. H., Fuller, S. S., & Endress, M. P. Sensory information, instruction in a coping strategy and recovery from surgery. *Research in Nursing and Health,* 1978, *1,* 4–17.

Jouvet, M. The states of sleep. *Scientific American,* 1967, *216,* 62–72.

Jouvet, M. Biogenic amines and the states of sleep. *Science,* 1969, *163,* 32–41.

Kimble, G. A., & Perlmutter, L. C. The problem of volition. *Psychological Review,* 1970, *77,* 361–383.

King, F. L., & Kimura, D. Left-ear superiority in dichotic perception of nonverbal sounds. *Canadian Journal of Psychology,* 1972, *26,* 111–116.

Koffka, K. *Principles of Gestalt psychology.* London: Routledge & Kegan Paul, 1935.

Kohler, W. *Gestalt psychology.* New York: Liveright, 1947.

Konorski, J. *Integrative activity of the brain: An interdisciplinary approach.* Chicago: University of Chicago Press, 1967.

Laird, J. D. Self-attribution of emotion: The effects of expressive behavior on the quality of emotional experience. *Journal of Personality and Social Psychology,* 1974, *29,* 475–486.

Lang, P. J. Fear reduction and fear behavior: Problems in treating a construct. In J. M. Shlien (Ed.), *Research in psychotherapy* (Vol. 3). Washington, D. C.: American Psychological Association, 1968.

Lang, P. J. A bio-informational theory of emotional imagery. *Psychophysiology,* 1979, *16,* 495–512.

Lang, P. J., Kozak, M. J., Miller, G. A., Levin, D. N., & McLean, A. Emotional imagery: Conceptual structure and pattern of somato-visceral response. *Psychophysiology,* 1980, *17,* 179–192.

Lashley, K. S. The problem of serial order in behavior. In L. A. Jeffress (Ed.), *Cerebral mechanism in behavior.* New York: Wiley, 1951.

Lazarus, R. *Psychological stress and the coping process.* New York: McGraw–Hill, 1966.

Leventhal, H. Findings and theory in the study of fear communications. In L. Berkowitz (Ed.), *Advances in social psychology* (Vol. 5). New York: Academic Press, 1970.

Leventhal, H. Emotions: A basic problem for social psychology. In C. Nemeth (Ed.), *Social psychology: Classic and contemporary integrations.* Chicago: Rand McNally, 1974.

Leventhal, H. A perceptual-motor processing model of emotion. In P. Pliner, K. Blankenstein, & I. M. Spigel (Eds.), *Perception of emotion in self and others* (Vol. 5). New York: Plenum, 1979.

Leventhal, H. Toward a comprehensive theory of emotion. In L. Berkowitz (Ed.), *Advances in experimental social psychology* (Vol. 13). New York: Academic Press, 1980.

Leventhal, H., Brown, D., Shacham, S., & Engquist, G. Effect of preparatory information about sensations, threat of pain and attention on cold pressor distress. *Journal of Personality and Social Psychology,* 1979, *37,* 688–714.

Leventhal, H., & Cleary, P. Behavioral modification of risk factors: Technology or science? In M. L. Pollock & D. A. Schmidt (Eds.), *Heart disease and rehabilitation: State of the art.* New York: Houghton Mifflin, 1979,

Leventhal, H., & Cupchik, G. L. A process model of humor judgment. *Journal of Communication,* 1976, *26,* 190–204.

Leventhal, H., & Everhart, D. Emotion, pain and physical illness. In C. Izard (Ed.), *Emotions and psychopathology.* New York: Plenum, 1979.

Leventhal, H., Jones, S., & Trembly, G. Sex differences in attitude and behavior change under conditions of fear and specific instructions. *Journal of experimental social psychology,* 1966, *2,* 387–399.

Leventhal, H., & Mace, W. The effect of laughter on evaluation of a slapstick movie. *Journal of Personality,* 1970, *38,* 16–30.

Leventhal, H., Meyer, D., & Nerenz, D. The commonsense representation of illness danger. In S. Rachman (Ed.), *Medical psychology* (Vol. 2). New York: Pergamon, 1980.

Leventhal, H., & Mosbach, P. Perceptual-motor theory. In J. T. Cacioppo & R. E. Petty (Eds.), *Social Psychophysiology.* New York: Guilford Press, in press.

Leventhal, H., & Nerenz, D. R. A model for stress research and some implications for the control of stress disorders. In D. Meichenbaum & M. Jaremko (Eds.), *Stress prevention and management: A cognitive behavioral approach.* New York: Plenum, in press.

Leventhal, E., Shacham, S., Boothe, L. S., & Leventhal, H. *The role of attention in distress control during childbirth.* Unpublished manuscript, University of Wisconsin, Madison, 1981.

Leventhal, H., & Sharp, E. Facial expressions as indicators of distress. In S. S. Tomkins & C. E. Izard (Eds.), *Affect, Cognition and Personality.* New York: Springer, 1965.

Leventhal, H., Singer, R. P., & Jones, S. Effects of fear and specificity of recommendations upon attitudes and behavior. *Journal of personality and social psychology,* 1965, *2,* 20–29.

Leventhal, H., Watts, J. C., & Pagano, F. Effects of fear and instruction on how to cope with danger. *Journal of Personality and Social Psychology,* 1967, *6,* 313–321.

Leventhal, H., Zimmerman, R., & Gutmann, M. *Compliance: A topic for health psychology research.* Unpublished manuscript, University of Wisconsin, Madison, 1981.

Ley, P. Psychological studies of doctor-patient communication. In S. Rachman (Ed.) *Contributions to medical psychology.* Vol. 1. New York: Pergamon Press, 1977.

Ley, R. G., & Bryden, M. P. Hemispheric differences in processing emotions and faces. *Brain and Language,* 1979, *7,* 127–138.

Linz, D., Penrod, S., & Leventhal, H. *Lay persons' conception of illness.* Unpublished manuscript, University of Wisconsin, Madison, 1981.

MacLean, P. D. Contrasting functions of limbic and neocortical systems of the brain and their relevance to psychophysiological aspects of medicine. *American Journal of Medicine,* 1958, *25,* 611–626.

Mandler, G. Emotion. In R. Brown, E. Galanter, E. H. Hess, & G. Mandler (Eds.), *New directions in psychology* (Vol. 1). New York: Holt, 1962.

Mandler, G. *Mind and emotion.* New York: Wiley, 1975.

Mandler, G. The structure of value: Accounting for taste. In M. S. Clark & S. T. Fiske (Eds.), *Affect and Cognition: The Seventeenth Annual Carnegie Symposium on Cognition.* Hillsdale, N. J.: Lawrence Erlbaum Associates, 1982.

Marshall, G. D., & Zimbardo, P. G. Affective consequences of inadequately explained physiological arousal. *Journal of Personality and Social Psychology,* 1979, *37,* 970–985.

Maslach, C. Negative emotional biasing of unexplained arousal. *Journal of Personality and Social Psychology,* 1979, *37,* 953–969.

McKechnie, R. J. Relief from phantom limb pain by relaxation exercises. *Journal of Behavior Therapy and Experimental Psychiatry,* 1975, *6,* 262–263.

Melzack, R. *The puzzle of pain: Revolution in theory and treatment.* New York: Basic Books, 1973.

Melzack, R., & Wall, P. D. Pain mechanisms: A new theory. *Science,* 1965, *150,* 971–979.

Melzack, R., & Wall, P. D. Psychophysiology of pain. *The International Anasthesia Clinics,* 1970, *8,* 3–34.

Meyer, D. *The effects of patients' representation of high blood pressure on behavior in treatment.* Unpublished doctoral dissertation, University of Wisconsin, Madison, 1980.

Meyer, D., Leventhal, H., & Gutmann, M. Symptoms in hypertension: How patients evaluate and treat them. *New England Journal of Medicine,* in press.

Miller, G. A., Galanter, E., & Pribram, K. H. *Plans and the structure of behavior.* New York: Holt, 1960.

Milner, B. Discussion of the subject: Experimental analysis of cerebral dominance in man. In C. H. Millikan & F. L. Darley (Eds.), *Brain mechanisms underlying speech and language.* New York: Grune & Stratton, 1967.

Money, J. Phantom orgasm in dreams of paraplegic men and women. *Archives of General Psychiatry,* 1960, *3,* 373–383.

Moscovitch, M., Scullion, D., & Christie, D. Early versus late stages of processing and their reaction to functional hemisphere asymmetries in face recognition. *Journal of Experimental Psychology: Human Perception and Performance,* 1976, *2,* 401–416.

Nathan, P. W. Pain traces left in the central nervous system. In C. A. Keele & R. Smith (Eds.), *The assessment of pain in man and animals,* Edinburgh: Livingston, 1962.

Neisser, U. *Cognitive Psychology.* New York: Appleton–Century–Crofts, 1967.

Nerenz, D. R. *Control of emotional distress in cancer chemotherapy.* Unpublished doctoral dissertation, University of Wisconsin, Madison, 1979.

Nerenz, D. R., Leventhal, H., & Love, R. R. Factors contributing to emotional distress during cancer chemotherapy. *Cancer,* in press.

Papez, J. W. A proposed mechanism of emotion. *Archives of Neurology and Psychiatry,* 1938, *38,* 725–743.

Pasquarelli, B., & Bull, N. Experimental investigation of the body–mind continuum in affective states. *Journal of Nervous and Mental Diseases,* 1951, *113,* 512–521.

Peters, R. S. The education of the emotions. In M. B. Arnold (Ed.), *Feelings and Emotions: The Loyola Symposium.* New York: Academic Press, 1970.

Piaget, J. *Six psychological studies.* New York: Random House, 1967.

Piaget, J. *Intelligence and affectivity: Their relationship during child development.* Palo Alto: Annual Reviews, 1981.

Plutchik, R. *The emotions: Facts, theories, and a new model.* New York: Random House, 1962.

Plutchik, R. *Emotion: A psychoevolutionary synthesis.* New York: Harper & Row, 1980.

Posner, M. I. *Cognition: An introduction.* Glenview, Ill.: Scott, Foresman, 1973.

Powers, W. T. Feedback: Beyond behaviorism. *Science,* 1973, *170,* 351–356.

Pylyshyn, Z. What the mind's eye tells the mind's brain: A critique of mental imagery. *Psychological Bulletin,* 1973, *22,* 12–18.

Reinhardt, L. C. *Attention and interpretation in control of cold pressor pain distress.* Unpublished doctoral dissertation, University of Wisconsin, Madison, 1979.

Riley, D. M., & Furedy, J. J. Psychological and physiological systems: Modes of operation and interaction. In S. R. Burchfield (Ed.), *Psychological and physiological interactions in the response to stress.* Washington, D. C.: Hemisphere, in press.

Ringler, K. *Process of coping with cancer chemotherapy.* Unpublished doctoral dissertation, University of Wisconsin, Madison, 1981.

Robinson, D. *The process of becoming ill.* Boston: Routledge & Kegan Paul, 1971.

Rogers, R.W. A protection motivation theory of fear appeals and attitude change. *The Journal of Psychology,* 1975, *91,* 93–114.

Rogers, R. W. Cognitive and physiological processes in fear appeals and attitude change: A revised theory of protection motivation. In J. Cacioppo & R. Petty (Eds.), *Social psychophysiology.* New York: Guilford Press, in press.

Rogers, R. W., & Deckner, C. W. Effects of fear appeal and physiological arousal upon emotion attitudes and cigarette smoking. *Journal of Personality and Social Psychology,* 1975, *32,* 222–230.

Rogers, R. W., & Mewborn, C. R. Fear appeal in attitude change: Effects of a threat's noxiousness, probability of occurrence, and the efficacy of coping responses. *Journal of Personality and Social Psychology*, 1976, *34*, 54–61.

Russell, B. *An outline of philosophy*. New York: Meridian, 1960 (Original U. S. publication by W. W. Norton, 1927).

Safer, M. A. Sex and hemisphere differences in access to codes for processing emotional expressions and faces. *Journal of Experimental Psychology: General*, 1981, *110*, 86–100.

Safer, M. A., & Leventhal, H. Ear differences in evaluating emotional tones of voice and verbal content. *Journal of Experimental Psychology: Human Perception and Performance*, 1977, *3*, 75–82.

Safer, M. A., Tharps, Q., Jackson, T., & Leventhal, H. Determinants of three stages of delay in seeking care at a medical clinic. *Medical Care*, 1979, *17* (1), 11–29.

Schachter, S., & Singer, J. E. Cognitive, social, and physiological determinants of emotional state. *Psychological Review*, 1962, *69*, 377–399.

Schwartz, G. E., Fair, P. L., Mandel, M. R., Salt, P., Mieske, M., & Klerman, G. L. Facial electromyography in the assessment of improvement in depression. *Psychosomatic Medicine*, 1978, *40*, 355–360.

Schwartz, G. E., Fair, P. L., Salt, P., Mandel, M. R., & Klerman, G. L. Facial expressions and imagery in depression: An electromyographic study. *Psychosomatic Medicine*, 1976, *38*, 337–347.

Schein, P. S., DeVita, V. T. Jr., Hubbard, S. et al. Bleomycin, adriamycin, cyclophosphamide, vincristine, and prednisone (BACOP) combination chemotherapy in the treatment of advanced diffuse histiocytic lymphoma. *Annals of Internal Medicine*, 1976, *85*, 417–422.

Seligman, M. E. P. On the generality of the laws of learning. *Psychological Review*, 1970, *77*, 406–418.

Semmes, J. Hemispheric specialization: A possible clue to mechanism. *Neuropsychologica*, 1968, *6*, 11–27.

Shacham, S. *The effects of imagery monitoring, sensation monitoring and positive suggestion on pain and distress*. Unpublished doctoral dissertation, University of Wisconsin, Madison, 1979.

Simmel, M. L. The reality of phantom sensations. *Social Research*, 1962, *29*, 337–356.

Simon, H. A., & Chase, W. G. Skill in chess. *American Scientist*, 1973, *61*, 394–403.

Snyder, S. H. Opiate receptors and internal opiates. *Scientific American*, 1977, *236*, 44–56.

Sternberg, S. Memory-scanning: Mental processes revealed by reaction-time experiments. *American Scientist*, 1969, *57*, 421–457.

Suberi, M., & McKeever, W. F. Differential right hemispheric memory storage of emotional and non-emotional faces. *Neuropsychologia*, 1977, *15*, 757–768.

Sully, J. *An essay on laughter*. London: Longmans, Green, 1902.

Tomkins, S. S. The primary site of the affects: The face. In *Affect, imagery, consciousness* (Vol. 1). New York: Springer, 1962.

Tomkins, S. S. The positive affects. *Affect, imagery, consciousness* (Vol. 2). New York: Springer, 1963.

Tomkins, S. S. Affect as amplification: Some modifications in theory. In R. Plutchik & H. Kellerman (Eds.), *Emotion: Theory, research and experience* (Vol. 1). New York: Academic Press, 1980.

Tourangeau, R., & Ellsworth, P. X. The role of facial response in the experience of emotion. *Journal of Personality and Social Psychology*, 1979, *37*, 1519–1531.

Tucker, D. M. Lateral brain function, emotion and conceptualization. *Psychological Bulletin*, 1981, *89*, 19–46.

Turner, C. W., & Layton, J. F. Verbal imagery and connotation as memory induced mediators of aggressive behavior. *Journal of Personality and Social Psychology*, 1976, *33*, 755–763.

Weiner, B. *The emotional consequences of causal ascriptions.* In M. S. Clark & S. T. Fiske (Eds.), *Affect and Cognition: The Seventeenth Annual Carnegie Symposium on Cognition.* Hillsdale, N. J.: Lawrence Erlbaum Associates, 1982.

Witkin, H. A., & Lewis, H. B. Presleep experiences and dreams. In H. A. Witkin & H. B. Lewis (Eds.), *Experimental studies of dreaming.* New York: Random House, 1967.

Woodworth, R. S., & Schlosberg, H. Experimental psychology (rev. ed.), New York: Holt, 1954.

Zajonc, R. B. Feeling and thinking: Preferences need no inference. *American Psychologist,* 1980, *35,* 151–175.

Zillmann, D. Attribution and misattribution of excitatory reactions. In J. H. Harvey, W. Ickes, & R. F. Kidd (Eds.), *New directions in attribution research* (Vol. 2). Hillsdale, N. J.: Lawrence Erlbaum, 1978.

Zola, I. K. Pathways to the doctor—from person to patient. *Science and Medicine,* 1973, *7,* 677–689, 335–368.

7
Cognition, Affect, and Self-Regulation

Michael F. Scheier
Carnegie–Mellon University

Charles S. Carver
University of Miami

A group of businessmen are having a drink after work. One launches into a series of Polish jokes. Another man, who happens to be of Polish ancestry, becomes more and more irritated. As it happens, he and the first man must interact fairly regularly. He is thus quite aware of the fact that it is to their mutual benefit to get along. But as the anger continues to mount, he abruptly fires off a hostile retort. The others stare, incredulous, and he mumbles apologetically that he just lost his head for a moment.

A high school student has been asked to make a speech before the assembled student body. She has never faced that many people before, and she is very tense. As the anxiety mounts, she wonders whether she will be able to carry out her intentions. She takes a deep breath, reaffirms her conviction in her ability, and delivers the speech flawlessly.

The purpose of these two opening examples is to convey a sense of the kinds of processes that we have been studying in the laboratory over the past several years, though the research situations that we have investigated are perhaps more prosaic than these opening examples might suggest. The examples are illustrative because they share three characteristics: Both involve cognition, in one way or another. Both involve affect. And both involve overt behavior. That is, in each case, the cognitive and affective processes are ultimately linked with actions.

Overt behavior is, in a sense, a "silent partner" in the subject matter of this volume. It is important, but in the background, playing a role that is secondary to affective and cognitive considerations. But this silent partner actually represents the starting point of our own work. Eventually, our investigations led us to consider issues of affect and cognition, but to consider them by virtue of their involvement in action. Given the behavioral orientation of our work, the kinds of processes that are considered here might appear quite different from those considered in the other chapters comprising this volume.

The present chapter is organized into three parts. We begin by outlining the theoretical approach we have taken to understanding the process of behavioral self-regulation. Included in this context is a consideration of several specific ways in which affective and cognitive processes can impinge upon ongoing behavior. Following this, we describe some research that offers empirical support for a specific aspect of the model, an aspect that is intimately tied to affective experience. We close the chapter by raising for examination some issues concerning affect—in particular, some points at which our implicit assumptions appear similar to those made more explicitly by others.

THEORETICAL OVERVIEW: A CONTROL-THEORY APPROACH TO BEHAVIORAL SELF-REGULATION

Self-Focused Attention

The model of behavioral self-regulation that we find useful derives from two rather disparate sources. The first is a body of research findings concerning the behavioral effects of directing one's attention inward to the self. This research stemmed from Duval and Wicklund's (1972; Wicklund, 1975) theory of self-awareness, the essence of which can be stated quite succinctly. Duval and Wicklund assume that an inward focus of attention causes a person to compare his or her ongoing behavior or state to whatever standard has been made salient by the person's behavioral context. If a discrepancy is perceived between ongoing behavior and standard, then negative affect is assumed to be generated, one potential result of which is a tendency to alter the behavior so that it conforms more closely to the standard regulating it. Thus, self-focus is presumed to cause a closer correspondence between ongoing behavior and salient standards.

That such effects upon behavior do occur as a result of heightened self-focus seems now beyond dispute. The "matching-to-standard" proposition has found repeated support in a great many studies, in several different behavioral domains (e.g., Carver, 1974, 1975; Gibbons, 1978; Greenberg, 1980; Scheier, Fenigstein, & Buss, 1974; Wicklund & Duval, 1971). In brief, self-attention does seem to produce a closer match between behavior and the standard associated with it.

What has been a matter of greater controversy, however, is the precise mechanism by which such behavioral effects occur. As just noted, Duval and Wicklund assume that conformity is due to a negative drive state that is generated when intra-self discrepancies are perceived. Our own position on the matter derives from an examination of the processes of control theory, or cybernetics (Wiener,

1948). Control theory thus represents the second source of background to our analysis of behavioral self-regulation.

Control Theory

The principles of cybernetics are principles of self-regulating systems. They are applicable to systems of many types, including living systems as well as electromechanical systems. Indeed, among living systems, control principles seem applicable at a great many levels of analysis, which has led some theorists to suggest that control principles are ubiquitous in their functioning (see, e.g., Buckley, 1968; Kuhn, 1974; Miller, 1978; von Bertalanffy, 1968). Our own interest in control processes has been more parochial in scope, however. As a result, we limit ourselves here to a discussion of the utility of cybernetics in analyzing human behavior at the level of abstraction that is of greatest interest to our own area of psychology: personality and social. We begin by reducing control theory to its simplest element.

Feedback Loops. The basic unit of cybernetic control is the negative feedback loop (see Fig. 7.1). It is called negative or discrepancy reducing because its function is to negate or minimize sensed differences between two values. A feedback loop constitutes a closed loop of control and, as such, really has no beginning or end. It is perhaps most intuitive to begin describing its functioning, however, by examining what is labeled ''input function'' in Fig. 7.1 (the left box). The purpose served by the input function is the sensing of some existing state or quality.

This perception is then transferred to a second component of the loop, termed a ''comparator.'' This component is so named because its function is to compare the sensed value against a reference value, or standard of comparison. (Some readers may be more familiar with the comparison function under the designation ''test,'' the term used by Miller, Galanter, and Pribram, 1960, in their discussion of the behavior of feedback systems.) The ultimate outcome of the comparison process can take one of two forms: Either the sensed state matches the reference value or it does not. In either case, control is transferred to the next component of the loop, labeled here ''output function'' (what Miller et al., 1960, labeled ''operate''). The output function is behavior, in the most general sense of the word. As we see later, outputs are not always *literally* behavior, but they always have some impact on the system's environment (i.e., anything external to the system itself).

What action the output function calls for is dependent on the outcome of the comparison process. If the sensed value and standard of comparison are not discriminably different from each other, no alteration in action is called for. The system simply keeps doing what it has been doing. In contrast, if a discrepancy is sensed between the two values, an alteration in output is called for. The purpose of this alteration is to counter the sensed discrepancy, by bringing the existing

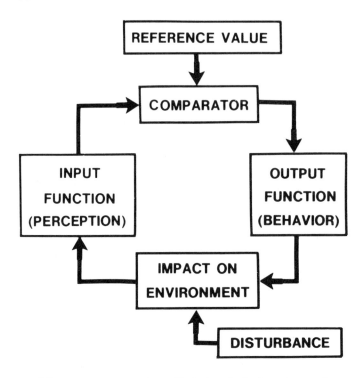

FIG. 7.1.   The feedback loop: The basic unit of cybernetic control.

state closer to the standard of comparison. The output function does not attain this goal directly, however, but does so by having an impact on the system's environment. Thus it is possible for outputs that might seem quite unrelated to the "present state" to have a major impact on that state, but an impact that is very indirect. As the present state changes, so too is there a change in the perception that constitutes the input function. This perception is compared anew to the reference value, and the cycle continues.[1]

Self-focus and Feedback Loops.   Having described the operation of a negative feedback loop, let us step back for a moment to draw a connection between the two preceding sections. In the first of those sections we described one of the

---

[1]We should note that our description of the negative feedback loop differs somewhat from that presented by Miller et al. (1960). Miller et al. suggested that congruity at the comparator stage leads to "exit," which frees the system for other applications. Our description suggests that control is always transferred to "operate," regardless of whether an incongruity exists at the comparator stage or not. The difference between descriptions stems at least in part from a broader conceptual question: specifically, whether feedback loops are better construed as cycling information and control in a sequential fashion or a continuous fashion. Treatment of this issue is beyond the scope of the present discussion (see Powers, 1973a, for an argument in support of the continuous-feedback model).

effects of self-directed attention—i.e., that such a state leads to a comparison between one's present behavior and whatever is salient as a standard of comparison. The result is a tendency to alter the behavior so that it conforms more closely to the standard. In the second section we described the essential elements of a feedback system: the comparison of a sensed present state with a reference value, and the output of behavior that compensates for any sensed discrepancy. The parallels between the two should by now be apparent. To be explicit about the matter, we view the focusing of attention inward to the self (when a behavioral standard is salient) as engaging a feedback loop. More specifically, we view self-focus as a precursor to the operation of the comparator of such a loop (see Carver, 1979; Carver & Scheier, 1981a, 1981b).

Behavioral Standards

The foregoing statement constitutes a first approximation to a cybernetic perspective on behavioral self-regulation. As such, it leaves several very basic issues untouched. Perhaps the *most* basic question is how to account for the existence of a behavioral standard, or reference value. It is at this point that cognitive considerations become more important—in particular, considerations about how it is that people organize their impressions of the world that they inhabit, and about what that organizational tendency implies.

Many theorists in cognitive psychology have for several years been working on models of the process of category formation. The various models differ from each other in ways that are quite fundamental (cf. Anderson, 1980); but for present purposes, what is most important is the models' similarities. That is, the models all share the assumption that people encode aspects of their experience more or less continuously, and that these internal records are organized in some fashion over time and experience (e.g., Franks & Bransford, 1971; Neumann, 1977; Posner & Keele, 1968; Reitman & Bower, 1973; Rosch & Mervis, 1975).

These implicit organizations—which are typically referred to generically as schemas (cf. Bartlett, 1932)—then have an influence on the "perception," or "recognition," or "categorization" of subsequent experiences. When aspects or attributes of a new experience are the same as aspects of the information coded into a knowledge structure, the new event seems to evoke the structure, wholly or partially. This results in an implicit or explicit *identification* of the experience, and enhanced access to *other* aspects of the knowledge structure. This may lead the person to be more likely to seek out and notice other schema-relevant aspects of the stimulus (e.g., Rothbart, Evans, & Fulero, 1979; Srull & Wyer, 1980; Wilder & Allen, 1978; Zadney & Gerard, 1974). It may even lead the person to assume the presence of stimulus characteristics that have not been explicitly observed (e.g., Bransford & Franks, 1971; Cantor & Mischel, 1977; Hastorf, Schneider, & Polefka, 1970).

What does this have to do with reference values for a feedback system? The answer is straightforward. Several cognitive theorists have explicitly assumed that knowledge structures can incorporate information that specifies action, as well as strictly descriptive information (see e.g., Rosch, 1978). Consider, for example, the category "apples." Apples are round, grow on trees, are often red, and you can eat them. Behavior. And another example, symposia are relatively formal gatherings, with erudite scientists present, and audience members commonly do either of two things: try to soak up as much information as possible from speakers, or try to think of difficult and/or embarrassing questions to ask the speakers. Again, behavior. (It should be obvious there is room for variability of responses, depending on what elements comprise the individual's knowledge structure regarding symposia, or apples, or whatever category is under consideration.)

As just mentioned, using a structure to recognize or construe an object, person, or event appears to make the rest of that structure more accessible. It seems sensible to suggest that if the structure incorporates or implies a behavioral prescription, then use of the structure also renders that information more accessible. If the behavioral information is accessed, we assume that it then becomes the reference value for the feedback system we have been discussing. Thus, people recognize their social (and nonsocial) surroundings, and (provided they have previously encoded behavioral information along with the other information) they thereby know how to act.

Is this reasoning viable? There is at least some evidence that it is. For example, Price (1974) had subjects rate the appropriateness of a series of behaviors occurring in a series of settings. He found a clear consensus that certain classes of actions were linked to certain classes of settings. Research on the association of behavioral prescriptions with environment categories appears to be limited to this type of data. But there is a greater diversity of research linking behavioral biases with classifications of *persons*. For example, arbitrary group assignments (i.e., the target person is made a member of the subject's group, or a different group) have had predictable influences on how subjects allocate money (Allen & Wilder, 1975; Billig & Tajfel, 1973). Racial categorizations lead to variations in behavior (Rubovits & Maehr, 1973), as do variations in perceived physical attractiveness (Snyder, Tanke, & Berscheid, 1977). Even perceiving the same person in two different ways (i.e., in terms of a role versus as a unique individual) has led to variations in allocation of resources (Carles & Carver, 1979). All these effects represent acts of *behavior* stemming from initial categorizations. This suggests that behavior-specifying information is linked in memory with category-membership information.

It may be helpful to make two brief digressions at this point. The first bears on the wide range of ways in which the term "cognitive" is used. We have been discussing cognitive processes, but we do not mean to imply in what has been said thus far (or indeed in much of what we will say later) that people always carefully sift through the attributes of an experience and the attributes of their stored knowledge. They *may* do so, particularly when difficulty is encountered in fitting an experience to a knowledge structure. But many instances in which recognition occurs and action is evoked are quite automatic.

The second digression concerns the fact that we have (at least implicitly) broached more here than just cognition. We have brought something else into the picture, something with at least a tenuous connection to affect. What we have introduced here is valuation. If behavioral information is "prescriptive"—that is, says "do this in this context"—it has a positive *value*. It is a behavioral preference, a standard of comparison that one approaches. If behavioral information is "proscriptive"—that is, says "don't do this sort of thing in this sort of setting"—the information has a negative value. It is a standard of comparison that one avoids. Although the valuation associated with a behavioral reference value may not feel particularly affective experientially, it does share with affective experiences that sense of "positive–negative" polarity, along with the associated approach–withdrawal tendency that such a polarity implies.

Let us return now for a moment to the feedback loop with which we began, and consider where we are. Thus far we have attempted to indicate—in the abstract—a way of conceptualizing the evoking of a reference value. And we have asserted that behavioral conformity to such a value increases when self-focus increases. But it should be obvious that there are many kinds of reference values, at many different levels of abstraction. It should also be obvious that many reference values are matched pretty well in behavior with virtually no awareness on the part of the behaving person. For example, a person walking up to a podium to give a speech typically manages to get from the one point to the other successfully, and to do so with little awareness of the process. But the behavior termed "walking" is actually quite an intricate balancing act, entailing the creation of appropriate angles of the components of the legs, rapid shifting of patterns of muscle tensions, all representing the matching of behavior to reference values. Such considerations raise the following additional questions: How are we to conceptualize differences among the various reference values that such a process entails? And how can we account for the fact that so many reference values are matched during this behavior with so little awareness?

A Hierarchy of Behavioral Control

In an attempt to deal with these questions, we turn to a framework suggested by William Powers (1973a, b). The central idea of Powers's approach is relatively simple: Namely, that feedback systems can be ordered hierarchically.[2] Figure 7.2 presents a schematic representation of a hierarchically ordered sequence of

---

[2]We should note here that Powers' approach to hierarchically organized control systems represents only a particular instantiation of a broader class of possibilities (see, for example, discussions of "production systems" by Newell, 1973; Newell & Simon, 1972; Simon, 1975; and of "action identification" by Wegner & Vallacher, 1980). We have chosen to borrow from Powers' model in developing our own theory primarily because of the fit between the nomenclature used in that approach and the types of behaviors that have been of particular interest to us (and of interest to social and personality psychologists more generally).

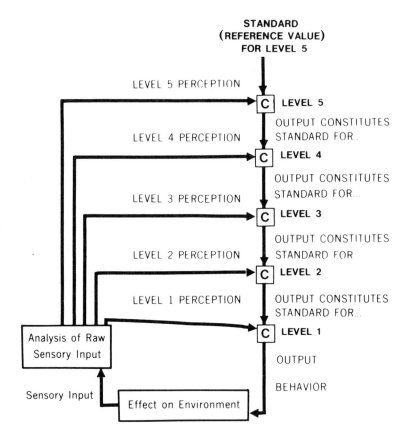

FIG. 7.2.   A hierarchy of feedback loops. The behavioral output of a superordinate loop consists of the resetting of a reference value for the loop at the next lower
level. Goal attainment is monitored at each level via perceptual input information
appropriate to that level (adapted from Carver & Scheier, 1981a).

feedback systems. The boxed ''C'' in each loop represents that loop's comparator. As can be seen in Fig. 7.2, the output of a superordinate loop in a hierarchically organized system is not literally behavior. Rather, the higher-order
loop operates by specifying a goal—a reference value or standard—for the loop
that is immediately subordinate to it. That is, the behavioral output for the one
loop *is* the reference value for the other. That next-level loop, in turn, attempts to
match *its* reference value by resetting standards one level lower in the hierarchy.
As we move downward through the hierarchy, more and more restricted aspects
or qualities of behavior are being specified and controlled.

    At the very lowest level of the hiearchy that Powers proposed, it is easy to see
what is occurring. The reference values being provided to the bottom loop from
the next higher loop are levels of muscle tension. When those tensions are

matched by the lowest-level loops, the result is overt behavior. There is also a fairly intuitive feel for what is happening at the relatively higher levels of control—which have been of the greatest interest to us. Powers gave the term "program control" to self-regulation at one of these higher levels, a level of control that is essentially equivalent to Schank and Abelson's (1977) "script" construct. In a program or script, there is an overall goal, but what component behaviors take place in the process of attaining the goal depends partly on conditions encountered along the way. Control at this level consists of a series of implicit "if-then" decisions.

The level immediately above program control—a level that is also important to personality-social psychology—is termed "principle control;" this is equivalent to Schank and Abelson's "meta-script." Control at this level represents the use of general guiding principles, as the name suggests. This level influences behavior by determining what kinds of programs to engage in, and/or by affecting choices that are made as a program is being executed.

An Illustration.   As a concrete illustration of how this hierarchy would be embodied in a rather ordinary behavioral episode, consider a hypothetical example (see Fig. 7.3). A young man of high school age holds the principle that he should be helpful to his parents without having to be asked. As his family finishes dinner, he seizes an opportunity to fulfill this principle in behavior, by clearing the table and washing the dishes.

In Powers' terms, this set of actions would constitute a program of action, chosen in the service of matching the reference value of helpfulness at the principle level. Note that the principle in question could be realized in a great many types of behavior. This is almost always the case. Principles are relatively content free. The content is provided by a program of action.

The program of dishwashing—like all programs—is not completely specified. That is, what behavior is done at any given point depends partly on the overall goal, partly on what has already been done, and partly on what conditions are encountered along the way. For example, washing the dishes requires that a relationship among objects and oneself be created, a relationship that constitutes "washing." This, in turn, requires that certain actions be taken in *sequence*. For example, water must be poured into the sink, and soap added, before the dishes are scrubbed. Creating the appropriate sequence entails, in turn, the creation of yet more restricted qualities of behavior, culminating in a continually changing flow of patterns of muscle tensions. All these represent lower and lower levels of control. As the young man in this example reaches for another plate or moves the wash cloth, standards are being matched simultaneously by feedback systems all down the hierarchy from the level that is currently superordinate (which may well be the program level or even the relationship level, at this point). The temporarily superordinate level is focal; the lower levels are more automatic and out of awareness.

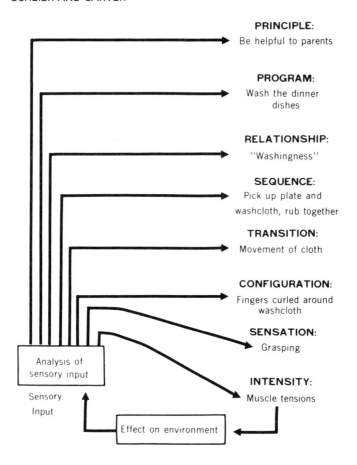

FIG 7.3.   Diagram of the hierarchy implicit in the behavior of a person washing dishes in order to be helpful (adapted from Carver & Scheier, 1981a).

We think that Powers' conceptualization is quite interesting, in that it suggests a way for abstract intentions to be reflected in concrete action. We have not yet attempted to investigate the hierarchical notion empirically, however. Rather, our own studies have implicitly focused on the regulation of behavior at the levels of program or principle control. And the behaviors under scrutiny have been relatively restricted in scope. Before describing that research, however, there is one more facet of the model that must be addressed.

Thus far we have described a system that recognizes and categorizes contexts, decides how to behave on the basis of those categorizations, and then executes the behaviors. What we have ignored thus far is the fact that desired behaviors cannot always be executed. An organism with the processes discussed thus far can strive for goals. But it is incapable of "realizing when it is beaten." It is unable to back out of corners. And for an organism to be pushing steadily onward into a corner is just as maladaptive as it is for the organism to be sitting in a corner lost in thought.

Interruption and Behavioral Disengagement

Our answer to this problem is to assume that the behavior-regulating process can be interrupted by a number of different conditions. The interruption can occur prior to the task attempt if, for example, the person anticipates difficulty attaining a behavioral goal. Or it can occur during the behavioral attempt itself, if something is frustrating that effort (cf. Kimble & Perlmuter, 1970). The frustrating condition can, of course, be either an environmental impediment of some sort, or a deficiency within the person that precludes discrepancy reduction. Regardless of the specific set of conditions underlying the interruption, the interruption itself is presumed to lead to an assessment of outcome expectancy: the subjective likelihood of attaining one's goal given the nature of the situation and the personal resources that are available.

We have assumed that this expectancy judgment represents a binary decision, that it results in a sort of "watershed" effect among potential responses (see Fig. 7.4). That is, behavioral responses to the impediment ultimately appear to reduce to two categories: further efforts, or withdrawal from the attempt. If overt behavioral withdrawal is not precluded, withdrawal may occur behaviorally. If physical withdrawal is difficult for some reason (for example, if the social context does not sanction it), the result may simply be withdrawal of effort, or a mental withdrawal (cf. Heckhausen, 1967; Lewin, 1935). Both renewal of efforts and the withdrawal tendency are assumed to be enhanced by further self-focus.

Though our initial emphasis in considering the assessment process was on the person's *expectancy* that a favorable outcome would occur, it should be obvious that the subjective *importance* of matching a reference value will also have a major impact on the approach–withdrawal decision. We assume that the importance of the goal in question will partially determine the subjective probability at which the watershed occurs. That is, it may take only a small degree of doubt to cause a person to abandon a trivial goal. But for a goal that the same person views as very important, the person may persist in attempting to match the reference value until doubts about being able to do so become overwhelming.

It should also be noted, at least in passing, that the elements that stem from the postulated interruption are not unique to our theory. Indeed, the processes we have described fall squarely in the domain of expectancy-value theories (e.g., Atkinson, 1964), theories that have had a long history in psychology (e.g., Tolman, 1932). Thus expectancy constructs prove to be fully as applicable to a control-theory model of human motivation as to other kinds of models, though a complete description of that fit is beyond the scope of the present chapter (see Carver & Scheier, 1981b, for a more complete description).

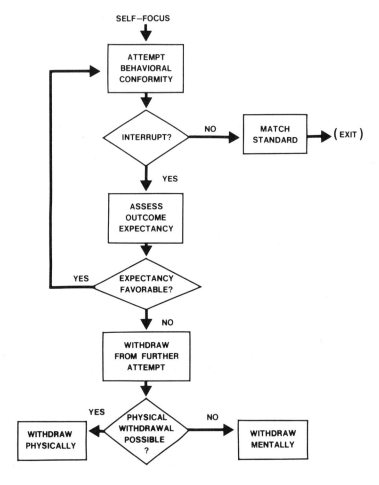

FIG. 7.4. Schematic representation of the approach–withdrawal decision process that occurs when goal-directed behavior is interrupted in some manner (adapted from Carver, 1979).

Interruption: Affective Consequences and Affective Antecedents

Incorporating assumptions into our model about behavioral interruption and outcome assessment allows us to provide a plausible, internally consistent account of the manner in which people back themselves out of corners and withdraw from goals that are unattainable. But such considerations also raise (at least implicitly) some important questions about the role played by affect in the interruption-assessment process.

There are two ways in which affective processes relate to this facet of the model. First, if expectancy assessment represents a cognitive process (and it would seem to), it is also a process that can have affective consequences. That is, the perception that a desired outcome is unlikely—that one cannot shift one's behavior in the direction of the standard—may lead to negative affect. Similarly, the perception that one *can* expect to move in the direction of the standard may lead to positive affect. This, in fact, is exactly how Stotland (1969) defined "anxiety" and "hope" as constructs.

Affective reactions to the assessment process may not be quite so simple, however. We have also argued that the precise nature of the affect experienced in this circumstance will depend on the person's perceptions (i.e., attributions) about the basis for the expectancy. For example, if a favorable expectancy is viewed as being a result of one's own abilities or efforts, the feeling experienced may be one of pride or heightened self-esteem. In contrast, if the favorable expectancy derives from aspects of the person's environment (e.g., powerful or helpful others or a situation that happens to be arranged in a facilitative manner), the feeling generated may be one of gratitude. Similarly, if an unfavorable expectancy is seen as a product of one's own inadequacies or personal shortcomings, the result will be a sense of lowered self-esteem. If the negative expectancy depends instead on environment contingencies (e.g., powerful and hostile others or frustrating situational constraints), the feelings produced are likely to be ones of anger and resentment. (We should note that our position in this regard is very similar to that of Weiner. See his chapter in this volume, and see also Weiner, Russell, & Lerman, 1978, 1979, and Weiner, 1979.)

The second connection between affective processes and the interruption-outcome assessment aspect of the model concerns the potential antecedents of interruption. Specifically, one circumstance that can lead one to interrupt a behavioral attempt, and assess outcome likelihood, is the awareness of rising levels of fear. Put simply, sometimes the things that people try to do are stressful and anxiety provoking. They are threatening. Persons trying to execute such an act face a very real question: Can they cope with their fear well enough to get the behavior done, or can they not? High levels of anxiety, then, constitute a major and important class of events that we assume interrupt ongoing behavior and induce the expectancy judgment process.

RESEARCH EVIDENCE

In the preceding section, we outlined our control-theory approach to behavioral self-regulation. The purpose of the present section is to move from the abstract to the concrete. In it, we describe the results of several studies that investigated one specific aspect of the model just presented (for a more comprehensive review, see Carver & Scheier, 1981a). In one way or another, all the studies that are reviewed in the following paragraphs were intended to examine the idea that ongoing behavior can be interrupted by rising affect—most notably fear—and cause the outcome assessment process to occur.

Some of the studies that we describe used experimental manipulations to vary levels of fearfulness. In others, fearfulness was varied by selecting differing subject groups. Similarly, self-attention was sometimes varied by experimental manipulations. At other times, it was varied by assessing chronic, stable personality differences among persons in their tendencies to be self-attentive. The converging evidence that such disparate methodologies has generated gives us considerable faith in the reliability of the results that have been obtained. The converging evidence has also increased our faith in the imputed underlying processes that the studies were designed to investigate.

Self-Attention and Fear

The first two studies that we conducted were primarily concerned with demonstrating the disruptive behavioral effects of rising fear (Scheier, Carver, & Gibbons, 1981). The studies were less focused on the interaction of self-attention and outcome expectancies, but as is seen, the data bear on this latter issue as well (at least implicitly).

The general rationale underlying the two studies is straightforward. As mentioned earlier, self-directed attention enhances the tendency to conform to salient behavioral standards. Thus, self-attention in the absence of strong anxiety should cause a person to match-to-standard more completely. Self-focus also enhances one's awareness of relatively strong affective states, however (Scheier, 1976; Scheier & Carver, 1977). If fear is intense, then, self-attention should be associated with greater subjective awareness of the fear. This, in turn, should lead to earlier or more frequent interruptions of ongoing behavior. Moreover, to the extent that fear is intense and salient, a person's confidence in effectively dealing with that fear should be diminished, resulting ultimately in quicker withdrawal from the behavioral context.

Self-awareness and Phobic Behavior.   Our first study (Scheier et al., 1981, Experiment 1) attempted to test the validity of this reasoning by selecting subjects who differed in their chronic fearfulness of nonpoisonous snakes and asking them to approach and hold a live snake, under conditions of either high or low self-focus. High-fear subjects had indicated on a questionnaire (from Carver & Blaney, 1977a, b) that they were very afraid of snakes, and that they would probably be unable to pick up and hold a nonpoisonous snake if asked to do so. Low-fear subjects were people who reported being unafraid of snakes and felt that they *could* do the behavior in question.

Several weeks later, each subject participated in an individual experimental session, portrayed simply as a study of the physical aspects of stressful behavior.

TABLE 7.1
Maximum Approach Behavior

	Mirror Present	Mirror Absent
Low fear	9.00	8.65
High fear	5.00	6.88

Note: Higher numbers indicate greater approach (*n* = 17 per group) (from Scheier, Carver, & Gibbons, 1981).

During this session, the subjects were taken to a test corridor, asked to approach an aquarium, uncover it, and remove and hold a 3-foot-long boa constrictor. Thus, approach was established as the salient behavioral goal. The subjects made their attempts only after the experimenter had returned to an observation area out of the subject's view. Self-awareness was experimentally enhanced for some of the subjects in this study by suspending a mirror behind the aquarium at about shoulder height, thus exposing them to their own images during the approach attempt (for empirical evidence regarding the self-focusing effects of mirror presence, see Geller and Shaver, 1976, and Carver and Scheier, 1978). Following the approach attempt, all subjects completed a postexperimental questionnaire that queried them about their experiences during the session.

Nine levels of behavioral approach had been predefined, ranging from (1) approaching to within two feet of the aquarium to (9) holding the snake in the air for 15 seconds. The approach scores are presented in Table 7.1. Analysis of these scores revealed a significant interaction between mirror presence and level of chronic fearfulness. As predicted, high-fear subjects in the presence of a mirror disengaged from their approach attempts significantly earlier in the behavioral sequence than did high-fear subjects run without a mirror. The tendency of the mirror to facilitate approach among low-fear subjects was not reliable, however. (As can be seen in Table 7.1, nearly all the low-fear subjects in both conditions completed the full range of behaviors requested of them.)

Analyses of the postexperimental questionnaire revealed two findings of interest—one negative and one positive. The negative finding was that mirror presence did not lead high-fear subjects to report having experienced greater anxiety in the presence of the snake, as we had anticipated, perhaps because of a psychological ceiling on that dimension. The positive finding was that, consistent with our reasoning, high-fear subjects (overall) reported having devoted more attention to assessing whether their bodily arousal was increasing than did low-fear subjects.

Self-consciousness and Fear. Overall, the behavioral findings generated from this study were quite supportive of our general line of reasoning. Self-

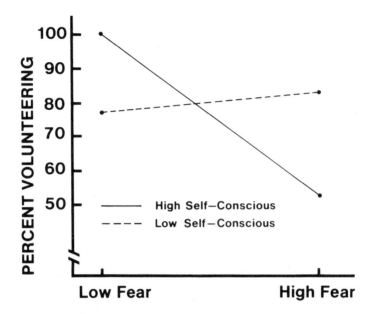

FIG. 7.5.   Percentages of subjects choosing to continue with the experiment, as a function of level of fear induced and degree of private self-consciousness (from Scheier, Carver, & Gibbons, 1981).

attention and level of fearfulness did interact in producing approach behavior, just as we had expected. It seemed desirable to us to document the generality of the findings a bit further, however, because of the somewhat circumscribed nature of the setting from which the findings came. This was the primary purpose of the next study we conducted (Scheier et al., 1981, Experiment 2).

In actuality, our second study extended the generality of the findings in three ways. First, a different type of behavior was chosen. Subjects were asked to receive a series of electric shocks. A standard was established to participate by informing them that the research had important medical implications. Second, rather than assess chronic levels of fear, fear level was experimentally manipulated by telling subjects either that the shocks would be painfully intense or that the shocks would be very weak. Third, rather than manipulate self-focus, the Self-Consciousness Scale (Fenigstein, Scheier, & Buss, 1975) was used to select subjects who differed in dispositional private self-consciousness (the tendency to be aware of one's internal self-aspects—e.g., one's feelings and emotions). The primary dependent variable of interest was whether or not the subject chose to continue with the study.

Subjects' choice behavior is displayed in Fig. 7.5. Analysis of this measure yielded the predicted interaction between fear level and levels of private self-consciousness. As can be seen in Fig. 7.5, when strong fear had been induced, significantly more high than low private self-conscious subjects withdrew from the study. In contrast, when fear was low, persons high in self-consciousness tended to volunteer more frequently than those low in self-consciousness, although this difference fell short of statistical significance.

In addition to indicating whether or not they wanted to participate in the study, subjects were also asked to complete some brief rating scales after their decisions had been made. One of these rating scales assessed the presumed mediator of the anticipated behavioral effects. Specifically, subjects were asked how upset they were at the prospect of receiving shock. Analysis of these ratings revealed a main effect for fear level. Of greater interest, however, was the fact that in the high-fear condition highly self-conscious subjects reported significantly more distress than did less self-conscious subjects. There was no difference between self-consciousness groups, however, in the low-fear condition.[3] These results are entirely consistent with the behavioral findings that were obtained. They are also in line with the reasoning we presented earlier.

Though supportive of our reasoning, the findings of this and the preceding study do not provide a comprehensive picture theoretically. The reason for the limitation involves the experimental situations under investigation. That is, in each study the experimental context was purposely arranged so that interruptions in behavior—which were presumed to result from the awareness of high fear— would be reflected in an increased likelihood of withdrawing from the behavior in question. This was the only way that the interruption could be assessed behaviorally. Such a procedure, however, had the unfortunate side effect of confounding high fear with unfavorable expectancies of being able to cope with the fear. As a result, the data are equivocal with regard to the role played by expectancies in such behavior.

Fear, Expectancies, and Approach–Withdrawal.   As a consequence of this ambiguity, we conducted one further study on the question (Carver, Blaney, & Scheier, 1979). Subjects for this study were chosen only if they reported being moderately fearful of snakes. Thus, unlike the earlier snake study, all subjects in this experiment were *equated* in their self-rated fear of snakes. As in the earlier research, however, the subjects were quite different from each other in terms of their chronic expectancies of being able to overcome their fearfulness and ap-

---

[3]The Self-Consciousness Scale (Fenigstein et al., 1975) also independently measures awareness of what has been labeled the public aspects of self—i.e., an awareness of the self as a social object that creates impressions and has an impact on others (for a more complete discussion of the distinction between private and public self-consciousness, see Scheier & Carver, 1981). When the data from the above study were reanalyzed using personality differences in public self-consciousness, rather than private, no significant effects emerged for either the behavioral or the self-report measures. Thus, the findings that were obtained were related specifically and only to chronic differences in private self-consciousness. The effects of public self-consciousness on the behaviors in question were negligible.

proach and hold a snake successfully. Confident subjects were those who thought they could pick up and hold a snake successfully, if asked to do so. Doubtful subjects, on the other hand, were not at all sure that they could do a behavior like that. Other than these differences in subject selection, the procedures used in the present study duplicated exactly those used in the first study we described. Specifically, subjects were taken to a test corridor and asked to attempt to approach, pick up, and hold a live boa constrictor under conditions of either high or low self-focus (varied again through the presence or absence of a mirror).

Because the predictions made for this experiment differed somewhat from those made for the previously described study, it may be useful to provide a brief description of the rationale behind them. As just mentioned, all subjects in the Carver et al. (1979) study had reported feeling moderately intense anxiety in the presence of nonpoisonous snakes. Because of this, we expected self-focus to enhance awareness of fear among *all* subjects in the study. This, in turn, was expected to result in behavioral interruption among all self-focused subjects. Recall, however, that subjects had also been preselected as varying in their expectancies of being able to cope with their fear successfully. In terms of subsequent behavior, then, we predicted that self-focus and subjects' expectancies would *interact*. More simply, we expected mirror presence to lead to earlier withdrawal from the approach attempt among doubtful subjects. But we expected the mirror to produce an opposite tendency among confident subjects.

In general, the results of the study were quite consistent with these predictions. Table 7.2 presents subjects' approach behavior, as well as some relevant self-report data that were obtained after the approach attempt had been completed. The uppermost portion of the table presents subjects' self-reports about the amount of anxiety they experienced in the presence of the snake. As can be seen there, self-report ratings of the amount of anxiety experienced yielded only a significant main effect for self-awareness condition, as predicted. Confident and doubtful subjects did not differ from each other in self-reported anxiety, but greater anxiety was reported overall in the presence of the mirror than in its absence. The middle portion of the table presents subjects' self-reports of having experienced a momentary sense of inadequacy and fearfulness while approaching the snake. Consistent with our interruption notion, self-focused subjects were significantly more likely to report such a sense of momentary inadequacy than were those whose self-attention was lower. Analysis of subjects' approach behavior, in contrast, yielded an interaction between pretest group and self-focus condition, as can be seen in the bottommost portion of the table. Doubtful subjects withdrew from the approach attempt at an earlier stage of the sequence when self-focus was high than when it was low. As predicted, the means of the confident subject groups were ordered in the opposite direction, though this difference was not reliable.

Additional postexperimental self-ratings lent further support to our reasoning. In particular, subjects were also asked to recall the degree to which they had

TABLE 7.2
Self-Reported Anxiety Experienced in the
Presence of the Snake, Self-Reported
Momentary Sense of Inadequacy and
Fearfulness During the Approach Task, and
Actual Level of Approach Toward the Snake

	Condition	
	---	---
Group	Mirror Present	Mirror Absent
	Self-reported anxiety[a]	
Confident	4.33	3.46
Doubtful	5.25	3.56
	Self-reported sense of inadequacy[a]	
Confident	4.20	3.85
Doubtful	5.38	3.63
	Approach behavior[b]	
Confident	8.47	8.23
Doubtful	6.38	8.31

[a]Larger numbers indicate greater anxiety and felt inadequacy.
[b]Larger numbers indicate greater approach (from Carver, Blaney, & Scheier, 1979).

attended to specific categories of events while engaged in the approach task. One question asked subjects to estimate the amount of attention they had devoted to assessing whether or not their bodily arousal was increasing. A significant interaction between pretest group and self-awareness condition was obtained for this variable. Doubtful subjects reported greater focus on this assessment when self-focus was high than when it was low, whereas the opposite ordering occurred among confident subjects.

A second question asked subjects to indicate the extent to which they had focused on the comparison between their present behavior and the goal (i.e., picking up and holding the snake). Analysis of this variable revealed a slightly weaker but opposite pattern of results: Doubtful subjects tended to report less focus on this comparison when self-focus was high than when it was lower, whereas the opposite was true for confident subjects. In brief, when asked what they were attending to during the approach attempt, doubtful subjects reported attending to their rising arousal (not their behavioral goal), and confident subjects reported attending to their behavioral goal (not their rising arousal). And both of these tendencies were increased by heightened self-focus.

Research Summary.   In the previous sections, three studies were reviewed that tested our reasoning concerning fear-based behavioral interruption. In the first two studies (Scheier et al., 1981), high levels of fear caused subjects to suspend their matching-to-standard attempts and withdraw behaviorally from the situation at hand, presumably because of their negative expectancies of dealing with their fear effectively. Also as predicted, the tendency for fearful subjects to withdraw was greatest among subjects whose attention was self-focused. The third study (Carver et al., 1979) examined the interactive effects of self-attention and coping expectancies more directly. Again, the results were consistent with our theoretical analysis. Self-focus hastened withdrawl, but only when coping expectancies were unfavorable. Among confident subjects, self-attention had the opposite effect. Overall, then, the data offer considerable support for the theoretical position with which we began.

Related Empirical Findings

Before closing this discussion of empricial findings, there are three other relevant studies that should be mentioned, if only in passing. Two of the studies have dealt with test anxiety, one specific direction that we have taken in our most current research. In these studies (Carver, Peterson, Follansbee, & Scheier, 1981), persons high and low in test anxiety were asked to perform a well-defined intellectual task, under highly evaluative conditions. In one case, the task was made insolvable, in order to measure how much persistence subjects showed. In the second case, the task was made solvable, in order to measure task performance. Self-attention was varied in each study during the task attempts by the presence or absence of a mirror. Consistent with the results already presented, self-focus interacted with level of test anxiety in each case. That is, whereas self-focus caused high test anxious persons to be less persistent and perform more poorly on the two tasks, it produced the opposite effects among those low in test anxiety. This, of course, is exactly the pattern of results that our model of behavioral self-regulation would predict.

The final study we would like to discuss was in fact conducted long before our ideas concerning the interruptive effects of rising affect were fully formulated. And in many ways, it can be construed as comprising simply a conceptual analog of the two fear studies conducted by Scheier et al. (1981). It is important, however, because it suggests that the analysis we have presented may be applicable to affective states entirely different from fear.

In this study (Scheier, 1976), subjects were either angered or not angered by an experimental accomplice. Following this, they were free to deliver differential levels of electric shock to the accomplice for errors in a bogus learning task. The effect of self-attention among angered subjects was to cause them to be more responsive to their transient angry affect (i.e., to cause them to give higher-intensity electric shock). More important, self-attention had this effect among all angered subjects regardless of whether they held personal standards that opposed or condoned the use of retaliatory aggression (as assessed by their previously obtained self-reports).

Thus, once again the presence of strong affect coupled with self-attention seems to have led persons to suspend their efforts to regulate their behavior according to higher-order goals and standards, and to become more responsive to their affect. In our current view, this finding represents only another variant of the general set of principles concerning behavioral interruption that we presented earlier. What makes the finding especially noteworthy is the quality of the affect involved—i.e., anger rather than fear. Although not addressed by this research, an interesting question for the future is whether or not such hypersensitivity to angry affect occurs among all persons. The alternative possibility, suggested by our expectancy-based analysis, is that such responsiveness occurs only among those persons who feel unable to cope with their anger effectively.

CONCLUDING COMMENTS: SOME REMAINING CONCEPTUAL ISSUES

This chapter began by describing some general ideas about the regulation of behavior. Specific research findings were then presented that attempted to assess the viability of certain aspects of that reasoning, as it applied to affective experiences. We would like to close the chapter by stepping back a bit from what has been said thus far and comment briefly on the broader question of the nature and function of affect. As already noted, our approach to the research presented in the preceding section was guided more by an interest in overt behavior than by an interest in affect per se. Nevertheless, we have by implication taken a theoretical position on the nature of the emotional process. Several aspects of that position are noteworthy because of their similarity to positions taken independently by others.

First, and perhaps most obviously, we have adopted the viewpoint that rising affect creates an interruption in ongoing behavior. We have focused our research primarily on variables that determine how people *respond* to that interruption. But a reasonable question is *why* emotion has such an effect. What broader function might this interruption serve? Simon (1967) has suggested what seems to be a reasonable answer to this question, in a statement on how emotion might be construed from an information-processing perspective. His position was that emotion causes an interruption of ongoing processing, and *calls for a rearrangement of goal priorities.* More specifically, the presence of a strong emotion seems to represent a call for the goal to which that emotion is relevant to be accorded a higher priority than whatever goal is presently being pursued.

This perspective appears to make a good deal of sense. Fear, for example, is saying that removal of oneself from the present setting is an important goal.

Although our own research would suggest that the presence of an emotion that is sufficiently intense to interrupt behavior may not *invariably* lead to rearrangement of goal priorities, the findings certainly are consistent with a general perspective in which affect serves to induce the person to at least *consider* changing such priorities.

This description of the interrupting function of affect represents a plausible picture. But it leaves many questions unanswered. For example, what touches off the emotion in the first place, before it becomes strong enough to interrupt behavior? The beginning of a response to this question is to assume that affect-specifying information is part of the knowledge structures that develop over time to organize experience. If such structures can incorporate behavioral specifications, why not affect as well? This is essentially the position that has been taken recently by Leventhal (1980). It is implicit in several of the other chapters comprising this volume, and it is implicit in our own reasoning as well (Carver & Scheier, 1981a; see also, Arnold, 1970). According to this perspective, when a schema that incorporates affective information is accessed in the process of perceiving a new stimulus, the affective-response information is evoked along with the other information. Presumably once evoked, the low-level behavioral components of the affective response—that is, facial movements, postural and autonomic changes—are set into motion relatively automatically and immediately.

In examining these components, we find something intriguing. The facial movements that are sometimes associated with emotions—and indeed would seem to be among the most immediate elements of the experience when they *do* occur—appear to represent relatively simple distortions toward emotion-specific stereotypic configurations. This observation suggests that this aspect of the emotional response connects with the hierarchy of *behavioral* control that was described earlier. Moreover, this connection would seem to occur at a relatively low level of abstraction, that is, at the level of control associated with the creation of positional orientations or configurations. This low-level quality of the behavior in question would seem to fit with the observation that emotions somehow seem more "primitive" or basic than do the experiences of reasoning, because reasoning processes would appear to be more likely to connect with the hierarchy at higher levels. Furthermore, though we have not mentioned it previously, events low in a hierarchy of control take place within shorter time scales than do events higher in the hierarchy (see, e.g., Carver & Scheier, 1981a; Power, 1973a). This fact, taken together with the inference just made, would help to account for the observation that affective reactions seem "immediate" and "sudden," particularly when compared to "reasoned" cognitive assessments.

We would note, however, that the emotional experience does not invariably occur immediately upon the presentation of the affect-inducing stimulus. In order for affect to occur, the stimulus must be perceived *at the level of abstraction at which the affect has been encoded.* And if one imagines a hierarchy of levels of abstraction at which a stimulus can be construed, it seems clear that affective reactions can be encoded at virtually any level. Some levels of construal are almost immediately available to perception, but others may require a good deal of processing.

An example may help to clarify this point. Imagine that you are looking at a brass sign located above the entrance to a building. There are many different qualities of this stimulus that are available for your perception. Furthermore, these qualities can be ordered in a rough way in terms of their abstractness. The attributes available to your use include many basic elements—e.g., the intensity of light reflected, the sign's color, the lines and angles of the letters, and so on. But there are also perceptual elements available that represent integrations of these more basic qualities—e.g., "objectness," the fact that the object is a sign, with words on it, and the fact that the words have meaning.

One *could* have an affective response encoded to a simple element such as the amount of light reflected, so that, for example, the fact that this sign is shiny elicits a pleasant reaction. One *could,* alternatively, have an affective response encoded at a higher level of abstraction, for example, to the meaning of the words on the sign—or even to the further *implication* of those words. This particular sign says "men only." And to some people the restrictiveness implied by that phrase elicits a negative affective reaction. Note that the perception of "restrictiveness" is occurring at a higher level of abstraction than is the perception of "shininess," or even the existence of the object as a sign. It is occurring at a relatively "conceptual" or "cognitive" level. To state the point more generally, affects can occur in response to cognitive or semantic evaluations of the *meanings* of objects or events, as well as to simpler qualities, and creating these meanings from the elements of raw experience may require a good deal of processing. In this context, at least, affect follows a good deal of cognition (cf. Zajonc, 1980).

This brings us to a third (and final) point. We have assumed that behavioral discrepancy reduction is relatively free of subjective affect, but that affect is experienced—is generated—when the person steps outside the discrepancy-re-duction attempt to assess "how things are going." If things look bleak, negative affect is induced; if things look good, positive affect is induced. Though we took this position partly on the basis of intuition, others have made statements that are quite similar in form. Pribram (1970), for example, has referred to feelings as "monitors," and many people have noted a kind of complementarity between affect and action (see e.g., Peters, 1970). That is, emotion, while not exactly "passive," may occur when goal-oriented activity is *set* to occur, but is not actually occurring. This raises all sorts of interesting questions about the relationship between affect and action.

We should note, however, that the affective qualities arising from expectancy assessment appear to fit only a restricted set of feelings. At their core, these reactions are all elation and depression. As such, their character is not to *interrupt* and suggest some *new* goal for behavior. Rather, as monitors of progress, they suggest only directions of movement—toward the goal or withdrawal—within the framework of a goal-value that is *already focal*. Interestingly, we have characterized affects that suggest the importance of new goals as interrupting behavior. We wonder whether this distinction might not be important, in that the qualities of the affects involved in each case might differ in some fundamental way.

Perhaps rather abruptly, we have reached our closing point. We have not by any means resolved the problem of conceptualizing the process of affect. But the consistency between our implicit assumptions and the assumptions of others who have focused more closely on the analysis of emotion leads us to be comfortable with at least one general conclusion: that there is a definite place for affective experience in a control-systems approach to behavioral self-regulation.

ACKNOWLEDGMENTS

Preparation of this chapter was facilitated by NSF grants BNS 80–21859 and BNS 81–07236.

REFERENCES

Allen, V. L., & Wilder, D. A. Categorization, belief similarity, and intergroup discrimination. *Journal of Personality and Social Psychology, 1975, 32,* 971–977.

Anderson, J. R. *Cognitive psychology and its implications.* San Francisco: Freeman, 1980.

Arnold, M. B. Perennial problems in the field of emotion. In M. B. Arnold (Ed.), *Feelings and Emotions: The Loyola Symposium.* New York: Academic Press, 1970.

Atkinson, J. W. *An introduction to achievement motivation.* Princeton, N. J.: Van Nostrand, 1964.

Bartlett, F. C. *Remembering: A study in experimental and social psychology.* Cambridge: Cambridge University Press, 1932.

Billig, M., & Tajfel, H. Social categorization and similarity in intergroup behavior. *European Journal of Social Psychology, 1973, 3,* 27–52.

Buckley, W. *Modern systems research for the behavioral scientist.* Chicago: Aldine, 1968.

Bransford, J. D., & Franks, J. J. The abstraction of linguistic ideas. *Cognitive Psychology, 1971, 2,* 331–350.

Cantor, N., & Mischel, W. Traits as prototypes: Effects on recognition memory. *Journal of Personality and Social Psychology, 1977, 35,* 38–48.

Carles, E. M., & Carver, C. S. Effects of person salience versus role salience on reward allocation in a dyad. *Journal of Personality and Social Psychology, 1979, 37,* 2071–2080.

Carver, C. S. Facilitation of physical aggression through objective self-awareness. *Journal of Experimental Social Psychology, 1974, 10,* 365–370.

Carver, C. S. Physical aggression as a function of objective self-awareness and attitudes toward punishment. *Journal of Experimental Social Psychology, 1975, 11,* 510–519.

Carver, C. S. A cybernetic model of self-attention processes. *Journal of Personality and Social Psychology, 1979, 37,* 1251–1281.

Carver, C. S., & Blaney, P. H. Avoidance behavior and perceived arousal. *Motivation and Emotion*, 1977, *1*, 61–73. (a)

Carver, C. S., & Blaney, P. H. Perceived arousal, focus of attention, and avoidance behavior. *Journal of Abnormal Psychology*, 1977, *86*, 154–162. (b)

Carver, C. S., Blaney, P. H., & Scheier, M. F. Focus of attention, chronic expectancy, and responses to a feared stimulus. *Journal of Personality and Social Psychology*, 1979, *37*, 1186–1195.

Carver, C. S., Peterson, L. M., Follansbee, D. J., & Scheier, M. F. *Effects of self-directed attention on performance and persistence among persons high and low in test anxiety.* Unpublished manuscript, University of Miami, Coral Gables, 1981.

Carver, C. S., & Scheier, M. F. Self-focusing effects of dispositional self-consciousness, mirror presence, and audience presence. *Journal of Personality and Social Psychology*, 1978, *36*, 324–332.

Carver, C. S., & Scheier, M. F. *Attention and self-regulation: A control-theory approach to human behavior.* New York: Springer–Verlag, 1981. (a)

Carver, C. S., & Scheier, M. F. A control-systems approach to behavioral self-regulation. In L. Wheeler (Ed.), *Review of personality and social psychology* (Vol. 2). Beverly Hills, Calif.: Sage, 1981. (b)

Duval, S., & Wicklund, R. A. *A theory of objective self-awareness.* New York: Academic Press, 1972.

Fenigstein, A., Scheier, M. F., & Buss, A. H. Public and private self-consciousness: Assessment and theory. *Journal of Consulting and Clinical Psychology*, 1975, *43*, 522–527.

Franks, J. J., & Bransford, J. D. Abstraction of visual patterns. *Journal of Experimental Psychology*, 1971, *90*, 65–74.

Geller, V., & Shaver, P. Cognitive consequences of self-awareness. *Journal of Experimental Social Psychology*, 1976, *12*, 99–108.

Gibbons, F. X. Sexual standards and reactions to pornography: Enhancing behavioral consistency through self-focused attention. *Journal of Personality and Social Psychology*, 1978, *36*, 976–987.

Greenberg, J. Attentional focus and locus of performance causality as determinants of equity behavior. *Journal of Personality and Social Psychology*, 1980, *38*, 579–585.

Hastorf, A. H., Schneider, D., & Polefka, J. *Person perception.* Menlo Park, Calif.: Addison–Wesley, 1970.

Heckhausen, H. *The anatomy of achievement motivation.* New York: Academic Press, 1967.

Kimble, G. A., & Perlmuter, L. C. The problem of volition. *Psychological Review*, 1970, *77*, 361–384.

Kuhn, A. *The logic of social systems.* San Francisco: Jossey–Bass, 1974.

Leventhal, H. Toward a comprehensive theory of emotion. In L. Berkowitz (Ed.), *Advances in experimental social psychology (Vol. 13).* New York: Academic Press, 1980.

Lewin, K. *A dynamic theory of personality.* New York: McGraw–Hill, 1935.

Miller, J. G. Living systems. New York: McGraw–Hill, 1978.

Miller, G. A., Galanter, E., & Pribram, K. H. *Plans and the structure of behavior.* New York: Holt, Rinehart, & Winston, 1960.

Neumann, P. G. Visual prototype formation with discontinuous representation of dimensions of variability. *Memory and Cognition*, 1977, *5*, 187–197.

Newell, A. Production systems: Models of control structures. In W. G. Chase (Ed.), *Visual information processing.* New York: Academic Press, 1973.

Newell, A., & Simon, H. A. *Human problem solving.* Englewood Cliffs, N. J.: Prentice–Hall, 1972.

Peters, R. S. The education of emotions. In M. B. Arnold (Ed.), *Feelings and Emotions: The Loyola Symposium.* New York: Academic Press, 1970.

Posner, M. I., & Keele, S. W. On the genesis of abstract ideas. *Journal of Experimental Psychology*, 1968, *77*, 353–363.

Powers, W. T. *Behavior: The control of perception*. Chicago: Aldine, 1973. (a)

Powers, W. T. Feedback: Beyond behaviorism. *Science*, 1973, *179*, 351–356 (b)

Pribram, K. H. Feelings as monitors. In M. B. Arnold (Ed.), *Feelings and Emotions: The Loyola Symposium*. New York: Academic Press, 1970.

Price, R. H. The taxonomic classification of behaviors and situations and the problem of behavior–environment congruence. *Human Relations*, 1974, *27*, 567–585.

Reitman, J. S., & Bower, G. H. Storage and later recognition of exemplars of concepts. *Cognitive Psychology*, 1973, *4*, 194–206.

Rosch, E. Principles of categorization. In E. Rosch, & B. B. Lloyd (Eds.), *Cognition and categorization*. Hillsdale, N. J.: Larwrence Erlbaum Associates, 1978.

Rosch, E., & Mervis, C. Family resemblances: Studies in the internal structure of categories. *Cognitive Psychology*, 1975, *7*, 573–605.

Rothbart, M., Evans, M., & Fulero, S. Recall for confirming events: Memory processes and the maintaining of social stereotypes. *Journal of Experimental Social Psychology*, 1979, *15*, 343–355.

Rubovits, P. C., & Maehr, M. L. Pygmalion black and white. *Journal of Personality and Social Psychology*, 1973, *25*, 210–218.

Schank, R. C., & Abelson, R. P. *Scripts, plans, goals, and understanding*. Hillsdale, N. J.: Lawrence Erlbaum Associates, 1977.

Scheier, M. F. Self-awareness, self-consciousness, and angry aggression. *Journal of Personality*, 1976, *44*, 627–644.

Scheier, M. F., & Carver, C. S. Self-focused attention and the experience of emotion: Attraction, repulsion, elation, and depression. *Journal of Personality and Social Psychology*, 1977, *35*, 625–636.

Scheier, M. F., & Carver, C. S. Private and public aspects of self. In L. Wheeler (Ed.), *Review of personality and social psychology (Vol. 2)*. Beverly Hills, Calif.: Sage, 1981.

Scheier, M. F., Carver, C. S., & Gibbons, F. X. Self-focused attention and reactions to fear. *Journal of Research in Personality*, 1981, *15*, 1–15.

Scheier, M. F., Fenigstein, A., & Buss, A. H. Self-awareness and physical aggression. *Journal of Experimental Social Psychology*, 1974, *10*, 264–273.

Simon, H. A. Motivational and emotional controls of cognition. *Psychological Review*, 1967, *74*, 29–39.

Simon, H. A. The functional equivalence of problem-solving skills. *Cognitive Psychology*, 1975, *7*, 269–288.

Snyder, M. L., Tanke, E. D., & Berscheid, E. Social perception and interpersonal behavior: On the self-fulfilling nature of social stereotypes. *Journal of Personality and Social Psychology*, 1977, *35*, 656–666.

Srull, T. K., & Wyer, R. S., Jr. Category accessibility and social perception: Some implications for the study of person memory and interpersonal judgments. *Journal of Personality and Social Psychology*, 1980, *38*, 841–856.

Stotland, E. *The psychology of hope*. San Francisco: Jossey–Bass, 1969.

Tolman, E. C. Purposive behavior in animals and men. New York: Appleton–Century–Crofts, 1932.

von Bertalanffy, L. *General systems theory*. New York: Braziller, 1968.

Wegner, D. M., & Vallacher, R. R. *Action identification and self-regulation*. Paper presented at the annual meeting of the American Psychological Association, Montreal, 1980.

Weiner, B. A theory of motivation for some classroom experiences. *Journal of Education and Psychology*, 1979, *71*, 3–25.

Weiner, B., Russell, D., & Lerman, D. Affective consequences of causal ascriptions. In J. H. Harvey, W. Ickes, & R. F. Kidd (Eds.), *New directions in attribution research (Vol. 2)*. Hillsdale, N. J.: Lawrence Erlbaum Associates, 1978.

Weiner, B., Russell, D., & Lerman, D. The cognition–emotion process in achievement-related contexts. *Journal of Personality and Social Psychology*, 1979, *37*, 1211–1220.

Wicklund, R. A. Objective self-awareness. In L. Berkowitz (Ed.), *Advances in experimental social psychology (Vol. 8)*. New York: Academic Press, 1975.

Wicklund, R. A., & Duval, S. Opinion change and performance facilitation as a result of objective self-awareness. *Journal of Experimental Social Psychology*, 1971, *7*, 319–342.

Wiener, N. *Cybernetics: Control and communication in the animal and the machine*. Cambridge, Mass.: M.I.T. Press, 1948.

Wilder, D. A., & Allen, V. L. Group membership and preference for information about others. *Personality and Social Psychology Bulletin*, 1978, *4*, 106–110.

Zadney, J., & Gerard, H. B. Attributed intentions and information selectivity. *Journal of Experimental Social Psychology*, 1974, *10*, 34–52.

Zajonc, R. B. Feeling and thinking: Preferences need no inferences. *American Psychologist*, 1980, *35*, 151–175.

8 The Emotional Consequences of Causal Attributions

Bernard Weiner
University of California, Los Angeles

A set of prevalent emotions, including pity, anger, guilt, pride (self-esteem), gratitude, and resignation (hopelessness) share a common characteristic: Causal attributions appear to be sufficient antecedents for their elicitation. Furthermore, the underlying properties or dimensions of attributions are the significant determinants of these affective reactions.

The evidence supporting these assertions regarding cognition–emotion linkages is examined in this chapter. First, causal attributions and their underlying properties are discussed. The relations between the dimensions of causality and the emotions indicated previously then are presented. This is followed by a brief consideration of the pertinence of this approach to be number of issues within the field of emotion. It will be evident to the readers, as it is to this writer, that a myriad of problems remain to be resolved given this attributional analysis of emotional states. No attempt is made to hide these difficulties. On the other hand, it is hoped that it also will be evident to the readers, as it is to the writer, that this attributional analysis facilitates the understanding of some important emotional experiences.

CAUSAL ATTRIBUTIONS

The guiding principle of attribution theory is that individuals search for understanding, seeking to discover why an event has occurred (Heider, 1958; Kelley, 1967; Weiner, 1980a). Attributional search can be considered one instance of the more general class of exploratory activities, and attribution theory therefore falls within the broad study of cognitive functionalism. It is now recognized that this search is most evident when an outcome is unexpected (e.g., failure when success is anticipated), and when desires have not been fulfilled (e.g., achievement goals are not reached; there is interpersonal rejection; *see* Folkes, in press; Lau & Russell, 1980; Wong & Weiner, 1981).

As intimated earlier, causal search is not confined to any single motivational domain. Individuals desire to know, for example, why their team has been defeated (an achievement concern; Lau & Russell, 1980), why they have been refused for a date (an affiliative concern; Folkes, in press), and why they have lost an election (a power concern; Kingdon, 1967). The number of perceived causes is virtually infinite, although the vast majority of answers to the preceding questions are selected from a rather circumscribed array. In achievement situations, success and failure typically are ascribed to ability (including both aptitude and learned skills), some aspect of motivation (such as short- or long-term effort expenditure, attention), others (friends, family), physiological factors (e.g., mood, maturity, health), the difficulty or the ease of the task, and luck (see Cooper & Burger, 1980). In an affiliative context, acceptance or rejection of a dating request often is ascribed to prior behaviors (e.g., making a good impression, being too forward), physical appearance, and the desires or state of the potential date (wanting to go out, having a boyfriend or prior engagement; see Folkes, in press). And given a political contest, election or defeat tends to be attributed to party identification, the personality characteristics of the candidates, and their stances on issues (Kingdon, 1967).

Inasmuch as the potential list of causes is considerable within any motivational domain, and because the specific causes differ between domains, it is essential to create a classification scheme or a taxonomy of causes. In so doing, the underlying properties of the causes are ascertained and their similarities and differences can be determined. Causes that denotatively differ (e.g., intelligence as a cause of achievement success, physical beauty as a cause of affiliative success, and personality as a cause of political success) may be connotatively quite similar (e.g., intellegience, beauty, and personality, among other similarities, all refer to relatively <u>enduring</u> personal properties). The discovery of these bases for comparison, which are referred to here as causal dimensions, is an indispensable requirement for the construction of a relatively general attributional theory of emotion.

Causal Dimensions

Two methods of arriving at new knowledge, that I somewhat wantonly label dialectic and demonstrative (following Rychlak, 1968), have been used to determine the basic dimensions of causality. The dialectic approach has involved a logical grouping of causes, discovery of an apparent contradiction in reasoning, and the emergence of a new dimension of causality to resolve the uncovered inconsistency. This logical and introspective examination within the attributional domain initiated with a differentiation between causes located within the person, such as intelligence, physical beauty, and personality, and causes outside of the person, such as the objective difficulty of a task, the prior engagement of a desired partner, and the popularity of one's opponent. The internal–external distinction is primarily associated with Rotter's (1966) discussion of locus of control. However, this causal dimension has been captured with various other labels, such as person–environment or disposition–situation, and is evident in contrasts between origin–pawn (deCharms, 1968), intrinsic–extrinsic motivation (Deci, 1975), and freedom–constraint (Brehm, 1966; Steiner, 1970). Within the achievement domain, causes such as aptitude, effort, and health are commonly considered internal causes, whereas objective task difficulty, help from others, and luck are among the perceived environmental determinants of an outcome. Within the affiliative domain, causes such as physical beauty and "charm" are internal, whereas the availability of the desired dating partner is an external determinant of acceptance or rejection. The placement of a cause within a dimension is not necessarily invariant over time or between people. For example, rather than being an external cause, luck can be considered an attribute of a person ("He is lucky."). Given the focus of this chapter, the relative placement of a cause within a dimension is not important. Rather, what is important is that locus, for example, is perceived as a basic property of causes.

A shortcoming of this one-dimensional taxonomy became evident when it was discovered that disparate responses are displayed given causes with an identical locus classification. For example, in achievement-related contexts the perception that an individual has failed because of a lack of effort gives rise to greater punishment than failure attributed to low ability (Weiner & Kukla, 1970). Furthermore, failure perceived as due to lack of ability results in lower future expectancies of success than failure believe to be caused by a lack of effort (Weiner, Nierenberg, & Goldstein, 1976). These disparities show that ability and effort differ in one or more respects, although both are considered properties of the person. A second dimension of causality therefore was postulated; it was labeled causal stability (see Heider, 1958; Weiner, 1979b, 1980a). The stability dimension differentiates causes on the basis of their relative endurance. For example, aptitude, physical beauty, and personality are perceived as lasting, in contrast to mood and luck, which are temporary and can vary within short periods of time. Because ability is believed to be relatively permanent, whereas effort can change from moment to moment, it would be instrumental to reward and punish effort rather than ability. Hence, the postulation of a second causal dimension *apparently* resolves the disparity in punishment given ability versus effort ascriptions for failure. In addition, because ability is perceived as more enduring than effort, prior outcomes ascribed to ability are more predictive of the future than are outcomes ascribed to effort. This accounts for the expectancy differences produced by these two causal ascriptions.

In a similar manner, a third dimension of causality was proposed (see Litman–Adizes, 1978; Rosenbaum, 1972, Weiner, 1979b) when it became evident that some causes identically classified on both the locus and stability dimensions yield dissimilar reactions. For example, failure attributed to lack of effort begets greater punishment than failure ascribed to ill health, although both may be conceived as internal and unstable causes. This indicates that yet another dimension of causality requires identification. Introspection suggested a third causal property, labeled controllability. The concept of control implies that the actor "could have done otherwise" (Hamilton, 1980). Effort is subject to volitional control; one is personally responsible for the expenditure of effort. On the other hand, one cannot typically control inherited characteristics or, in most cases, the onset of an illness. Within the achievement domain, effort is the most evident example of a controllable cause, although so-called traits such as patience or frustration tolerance also often are perceived by others as controllable. Note, then, that ability (aptitude) and effort differ on two dimensions of causality, with aptitude internal, stable, and uncontrollable, whereas effort is internal, unstable, and controllable. The differential punishment given ability versus effort ascriptions for failure is therefore attributable to the stability and/or controllability differences between these causes. On the other hand, disparities in punishment given failure perceived as due to temporary illness versus lack of effort are ascribable only to the controllability dimension.

At present, three dimensions of causality have been identified—locus, stability, and controllability. In most instances, causes such as intelligence, physical beauty, and charisma are perceived as internal, stable, and uncontrollable. This reveals a fundamental similarity between three denotatively different causes that often are invoked to explain positive and negative outcomes in the three motivational domains of achievement, affiliation, and power.

A number of issues remain given this logical analysis. It is not yet determined if there are additional causal dimensions, such as intentionality or "globality" (the generality of a cause; see Weiner, 1979b). In addition, it is uncertain whether the three postulated causal dimensions are orthogonal or even if it is logically possible for a cause to be both external and controllable, for controllability implies internal causation. And it is important to observe that the classification of causes is dependent on the perspective of the attributor. For example, teacher bias is likely to be perceived as a personally uncontrollable cause of failure by an unfairly treated student, whereas an observer may contend that teachers should be able to control their biases. Some of these issues play a role in the discussion of emotions.

Recently, there have been a number of experimental (demonstrative) studies to discover the dimensions of causality (see Table 8.1). Table 8.1 reveals that there is fair agreement between the conclusions of the investigators, although there are some discrepancies. Discussion of the reasons for the inconsistencies falls beyond the scope of this chapter. Suffice it to conclude that the dialectic and the demonstrative procedures have a reasonable degree of convergence; as a working hypothesis, it can be stated that locus, stability, and controllability are

TABLE 8.1
Empirical Studies of Causal Dimensions[a]

Investigator(s)	Motivational Domain	Method	Causal Dimension Found			
			Locus	Stability	Control	Others
Meyer (1980)	Achievement	Factor analysis	X	X	X	
Meyer & Koelbl (1982)	Achievement	Factor analysis	X	X	X	Mood vs. Uncontrollability Anxiety vs. Background Affect vs. Situation
Michela, Peplau, & Weeks (1978)	Affiliation	Multidimensional scaling (MDS)	X	X		
Passer (1977)	Achievement	MDS	X			Intentionality Simple–Complex[b]
Wimer & Kelley (in press)	Many	Factor analysis	X	X	X	Motivation Necessary–Facilitative Common–Unusual Weak–strong Aware–unaware

[a]An investigation by Falbo and Beck (1979) is not included in this summary because it has a number of methodological inadequacies (see Weiner, 1979a).

[b]Distinctions within the dimensions of locus and stability are not included.

189

among the dimensions of causality. These dimensions in part reveal the meaning of a cause and represent the manner in which the causal world is organized.

HYPOTHESIZED DIMENSION-EMOTION RELATIONS

I turn now to the relations between the causal dimensions of locus, stability, and controllability and emotions. The evidence to be presented bears upon the following propositions:

1. *Pride* and *positive self-esteem* are experienced as a consequence of attributing a positive outcome to ego-related aspects of the self, whereas negative self-esteem is experienced when a negative outcome is ascribed to oneself (the causal dimension of locus). This is the case whether the perceived cause is controllable (e.g., effort) or uncontrollable (e.g., aptitude). To paraphrase Kant, everyone can enjoy a good meal, but only the cook can experience pride. Pride and personal esteem are therefore self-reflective emotions.

2. *Anger* is experienced given an attribution for a negative, self-related outcome or event to factors controllable by others. Thus, for example, anger is aroused when one is prevented from studying due to a noisy roommate. In addition, anger is elicited when a negative, other-related outcome or event is perceived as under the personal control of that other. Hence, a pupil failing because of a lack of effort tends to elicit anger from the teacher.

It is believed that *gratitude* is a consequence of a similar configuration of perceived causality (attribution of a personality positive event to factors controllable by others). For example, one would not feel gratitude toward another if this other person was forced to provide help. Of course, the intensity of anger and gratitude will be influenced by many factors in addition to the controllability of the cause, such as the value of the attained or lost goal (Tesser, Gatewood, & Driver, 1968).

3. *Guilt* is experienced when one has brought about a negative consequence for a personally controllable cause. Thus, for example, failure because of insufficient effort tends to elicit guilt within the actor.

4. *Pity* is felt when others are in need of aid or in a negative state due to uncontrollable conditions. Another's loss of a loved one because of an accident or illness (external and uncontrollable) or failure by another because of a physical handicap (internal and uncontrollable) are prototypical situations that elicit pity.

The relations between the causal dimensions of locus and controllability and the emotions of pride (self-esteem), anger, gratitude, guilt, and pity are summarized in Table 8.2. Table 8.2 differentiates the direction or target of the emotion (self- or other-directed), the locus of causality, and the perception of controllability from the perspective of the source of the emotion. Thus, for example, an observer feels pity toward another (an external target) when uncontrollable fac-

TABLE 8.2
Relations of Discussed Emotions to Emotional Target, Locus of
Causality, and Controllability of the Cause

Emotion	Emotional Target		Locus of Causality			Controllability		
	Self	Other	Self	Other	Environ.	By Self	By Other	Uncont.
Pride and self-esteem	√		√			√		√
Anger and gratitude		√		√			√	
Guilt	√		√			√		
Pity		√		√	√			√

tors within that target (other) or uncontrollable factors within the environment have produced a negative state.

I have yet to discuss the relation of emotions to the dimension of stability. Regarding stability, the following propositions are offered.

5. Given a negative outcome, attributions to stable factors give rise to feelings of *helplessness* and *resignation;* that is, if the future is expected to be the same as the past, then helplessness is elicited given a negative state.

6. The affects of anger, pity and perhaps self-esteem are exacerbated when the perceived cause that gave rise to the affect also is stable. For example, pity toward a blind person is anticipated to be greater than pity toward an individual with a temporary eyesight problem. In this case, the stability dimension influences the magnitude, rather than the direction, of the experienced emotion.

A few clarifications of these propositions are offered before turning to the pertinent empirical evidence:

a. It is quite likely that anger and pity can be self-directed. Even in these instances the respective classification of the cause as controllable (eliciting anger) or uncontrollable (giving rise to pity) is anticipated. However, data have not been gathered concerning these possibilities and they are excluded from further consideration.

b. One can feel pride when a relation, a friend, or even one's country has succeeded for perceived internal reasons. Instances of affective experience mediated by personal identification are not considered here.

c. The postulated linked affect does not necessarily follow given the causal cognition. One might engage in a dastardly, controllable deed without guilt; a controllable negative outcome might not produce anger if there are mitigating circumstances; success because of ability could give rise to humbleness or even embarrassment rather than pride; failure of another because of an uncontrollable reason might produce apathy or relief. However, the affects under discussion are quite frequently elicited given the indicated attributional antecedents. Furthermore, given the affect, the linked cause may not be a necessary antecedent. For example, one might experience guilt even though the cause of an event was not controllable; one may feel angry because it has rained; and so on. Note this is similar to current thoughts about the relation between frustration and aggression. That is, there are other antecedents to aggression besides frustration, and frustration need not give rise to aggression.

On the other hand, perhaps feelings of gratitude do require that another has helped you. The postulation of a necessary relation between a particular cognition and a specific affect is a moot and difficult issue. In any case, it can be stated that in many instances we experience pride, anger, gratitude, guilt, and pity, if and only if the hypothesized causal pattern is first perceived.

EMPIRICAL EVIDENCE

In the following pages, evidence bearing upon the six stated propositions is reviewed. The relevant data are contained in research investigations that often also gathered other information; only the data pertinent to causal dimensions and the affects under study here are presented. The research evidence is not equally apportioned across the six propositions: The data concerning pity and anger are most extensive, whereas only two studies contain data applicable to the postulated stability–hopelessness linkage.

The investigations to be reviewed have a number of dissimilarities: Some are simulational, others ask about critical incidents in one's life; some have a free-response or operant format, others are respondent paradigms; some require the ratings of many affects, other examine only one or two emotional responses; some are concerned with reactions in achievement-related situations, whereas others analyze emotions in affiliative or help-giving contexts. But all the discussed studies do rely upon the verbal reports and the judgments of the participants. This may or may not be considered a shortcoming of this research, for linguistic expression often is part of the emotional experience. As Schafer (1976) has remarked: "Without words for it, people in fact remain unprepared to experience much that we ordinarily regard as essential to adult emotional life [p. 355]."

Affective Reactions to Success and Failure

In our initial study of the relations between causal ascriptions and feelings (Weiner, Russell, & Lerman, 1978), we complied a dictionary list of approximately 250 potential affective reactions to success and failure, and we also identified the dominant causal attributions for achievement performance, such as ability, effort, luck, and other people. Then a cause for success or failure was given within a brief story format, the success- or failure-related affects that had been identified were listed, and the participants reported the intensity of the affective reactions that they thought would be experienced in this situation. Responses were made on simple rating scales. A typical story was:

> Francis studied intensely for the test he took. It was very important for Francis to record a high score on this exam. He received an extremely high score on the test. He felt he received this high score because he studied so intensely [or, his ability was high in this subject; he was lucky in which questions were selected; etc.]. How do you think Francis felt upon receiving this score? (Weiner, Russell, & Lerman, 1978, p. 70).

To overcome some of the weaknesses of this simulational and respondent procedure, in a follow-up investigation (Weiner, Russell, & Lerman, 1979) participants reported a "critical incident" in their lives in which they actually succeeded or failed an exam for a particular reason, such as help from others or lack of effort. They then recounted three affects that were experienced.

Both investigations yielded systematic and similar findings. First, there was a set of outcome-dependent, attribution-independent affects that represent broad positive or negative reactions to success and failure, regardless of the "why" of the outcome. "Happy" and "upset" are examples of these reported emotions. In addition, there were emotions uniquely related to particular attributions, such as long-term effort–relaxation and luck–surprise. Finally, and most germane to the present chapter, causal dimensions were reported as influencing affective life. To determine the affects associated with causal locus, the emotions elicited by internal causes such as ability, effort, and personality were compared with the affects elicited by the external causes such as luck, help from others, or task ease or difficulty. It was found that pride and the esteem-related emotions of confidence and competence were linked with internal attributions.

In these experiments the controllability of the cause, such as "others," was not manipulated and could not be determined. Hence, the complex Locus X Controllability interactions that characterize the majority of the hypothesized cognition–emotion relations could not be tested. However, Proposition 1, concerning pride and self-esteem, was fully supported.

In addition, it was found that the perceived continuation of a cause also influenced affective reports. Affects including depression, apathy, and resignation primarily were described given internal and stable attributions for failure, such as lack of ability or a personality deficit. This suggests that only attributions conveying that events will not change in the future beget feelings of helplessness (Proposition 5).

Protecting the Self-Esteem of Others

The prior experiments demonstrated, in part, that attribution of achievement-related outcomes to internal factors is linked with esteem-related affects such as pride and feelings of confidence and competence. That this association also is

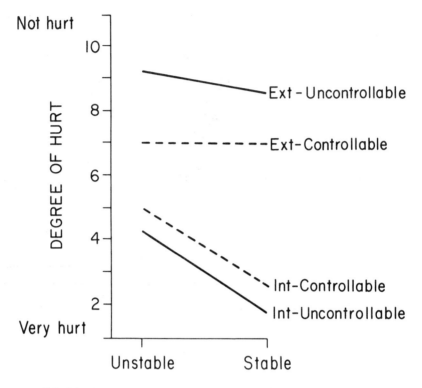

FIG. 8.1.   The actor's estimate of the requester's degree of hurt feelings as a function of the dimensional classification of the cause (from Folkes, in press).

represented in naive psychology is demonstrated in the following experiment (Folkes, in press), which is concerned with feelings in an affiliative context.

Participants were told to imagine that they had rejected a request for a date. Sixteen reasons for the rejection were provided to the subjects, representing causes within the three dimensional causal matrix. For example, the rejection was specified as due to a lack of physical attractiveness (internal, stable, uncontrollable), a negativistic personality (internal, stable, controllable), religious restrictions (external, stable, uncontrollable), and so on. The female participants were asked to reveal what cause they publicly would give to the requester. In addition, the subjects also indicated the extent to which the public and private causes would "hurt the feelings" of the individual asking for a date, if that cause were known to him. It is assumed that this phrase captures the general category of personal esteem.

The relations between expectations of "hurt feelings" and the three causal dimensions are shown in Fig. 8.1. Figure 8.1 indicates that internal reasons for rejection maximize the belief that the other's feelings will be hurt. When the true cause of rejection was external to the requester, the participants reported that they would state that reason 99% of the time. But when the real cause of rejection was internal to the requester, the female subjects indicated that they would lie, stating an external reason over ⅔ of the time. Hence, the behavior of the rejecting females was benevolent, guided by an attempt to protect the self-esteem of the other and mediated by the assumption of a causal locus-self esteem relation. In addition, Fig. 8.1 reveals that a stable cause for rejection when the cause is internal (e.g., "His face and body type are not attractive.") exacerbates these perceived reactions more than does public rejection because of an internal, unstable cause (e.g., "He developed a temporary and ugly red rash.") Similar examples of "affective control" are prevalent in the areas of account-giving and apology.

Affective Reactions to a Request for Aid

In another series of studies (Weiner, 1980b, c), affective reactions and judgments of helping were examined when the cause of the need for aid was manipulated by experimental instructions. In one investigation (Weiner, 1980b), the participants read one of two scenarios:

> At about 1:00 in the afternoon you are riding a subway car. There are a number of other individuals in the car and one person is standing, holding on to the center pole. Suddenly, this person staggers forward and collapses. The person apparently is drunk. He is carrying a liquor bottle wrapped in a brown paper bag and smells of liquor. [Alternate form: The person is carrying a black cane and apparently is ill] [p. 190].

The subjects were asked to assume that they were actually on the subway and to imagine the scene. They then described what their feelings would be in the situation, with three spaces provided for affective descriptions.

A second series of investigations attempted a conceptual replication of this research (Weiner, 1980c). Subjects were given the following two scenarios (as well as another not discussed here) and again were asked to describe their feelings:

> At about 1:00 in the afternoon you are walking through campus and a student comes up to you. The student says that you do not know him, but that you are both enrolled in the same class. He asks if you would lend him the class notes from the meetings last week, saying that the notes are needed because he skipped class to go to the beach. [Alternate form: He needs the notes because he was having eye problems, a change of glasses was required, and during the week he had difficulty seeing because of eye-drops and other treatments. You notice that the student is wearing especially dark glasses and has a patch covering one eye][p. 676].

TABLE 8.3
Percentage of Pity-related and Anger-related
Reactions as a Function of the Story Theme
and the Causal Manipulation (data from
Weiner, 1980b,c)

Emotion	Story Theme			
	Subway (N = 40)		Notes (N = 129)	
	Causal Condition			
	Drunk	Ill	Beach	Eye
Pity	30%	46	6	35
Anger	27	3	40	4

It was initially assumed, and data confirmed this assumption (see Weiner, 1980b, c), that being drunk, just as going to the beach, is perceived as an internal and controllable cause of need. On the other hand, carrying a cane, just as wearing an eye patch, conveys a disability that is internal but uncontrollable.

The reported affective reactions were classified into categories, including a subdivision composed of the reactions sympathy, pity, and concern, and a second subdivision including anger-related negative reactions. The percentage of reported affective reactions in these two categories as a function of the causal manipulation is shown in Table 8.3. Table 8.3 reveals that pity and sympathy dominate the reported feelings given the uncontrollable causes, whereas anger is most prevalent in the beach condition and also is strongly evident in the drunk condition.

In subsequent experiments subjects again received the drunk–ill or the beach–eye scenarios. Following each scenario, they rated the degree to which the causes were perceived as personally controllable, their feelings of pity and sympathy, and their anger-related feelings (Weiner, 1980b, c). Within each experiment there was a strong positive correlation between the judgments of controllability and anger (average $r = .45$) and an even stronger positive correlation between ratings of uncontrollability and pity (average $r = .66$). Within the drunk condition, where the free-response affective reports were most questionable regarding the hypothesized drunk–anger relation, the correlation between controllability and anger-related feelings was $r = .46$, while the correlation between uncontrollability and sympathy was $r = .55$. These data strongly support Propositions 2 and 4.

In a related but independently conceived investigation, Meyer and Mulherin (1980) created eight hypothetical situations in which a person was approached for financial aid. The reason for the need of aid was manipulated and corres-

TABLE 8.4
Mean Affect Factor Scores as a Function of
Stability, Locus, and Controllability of the
Cause (adapted from Meyer & Mulherin, 1980,
p. 205)

	Affective Factor	
Causal Condition (N = 80)	*Anger versus Concern*	*Empathy*
Internal-Stable–Controllable	.83	−.48
Internal-Stable–Uncontrollable	−.79	.48
External-Stable–Controllable	.94	−.31
External-Stable–Uncontrollable	−.67	.53
Internal-Unstable–Controllable	.77	−.42
Internal-Unstable–Uncontrollable	−.66	.57
External-Unstable–Controllable	.03	−.28
External-Unstable–Uncontrollable	−.45	−.10

Note: The higher the number, the greater the anger and empathy.

ponded to each of the eight cells of the Locus X Stability X Controllability causal
matrix. For example, the stimulus person was described as being in need of
money because she did not like to work (internal, stable, controllable) or could
not work because of ill health (internal, stable, uncontrollable). For each condition, the subjects rated the degree to which they would experience each of 25
affects primarily selected from the Multiple Affect Adjective Check List
(Zuckerman & Lubin, 1965).

A factor analysis of the emotional ratings yielded a bipolar factor labeled
anger versus concern and a unipolar factor labeled empathy, which included high
loadings on the emotions of pity and sympathy. Table 8.4 shows the mean
affective factor scores in each of the eight experimental (causal) conditions. The
table reveals that controllable causes gave rise to reported anger, whereas uncontrollable causes elicited empathy (pity). There also is a strong tendency for the
affective loadings to be higher given stable causes, thus providing evidence that
perceived causal stability influences the magnitude of the emotional reactions of
pity and anger.

Pity and Anger Across Situations

The investigations by Meyer and Mulherin (1980) and Weiner (1980b, c) examined the emotional reactions of pity and anger in situations of help giving. In the
following study (Weiner, Graham, & Chandler, in press), reactions of pity and
anger were ascertained in a variety of situational contexts.

Four story themes were created that involved the failure to repay a debt,
committing a crime, failing an exam, and again needing class notes. Within each

of these themes, eight situations were generated providing the reason for the negative event. Again each of these eight reasons represented one cell in the Locus X Stability X Controllability matrix. For example, the external, stable, and uncontrollable cause for each of the respective themes was: "The person cannot repay because a computer breakthrough suddenly made his job unnecessary"; "He committed the crime because he lived in a depressed area where there were no opportunities for employment or adequate schooling"; "The student failed the exam because her math tutor often incorrectly explained answers to problems through the quarter"; and "The student needs the notes because the teacher gave very confusing lectures throughout the entire course." For each of the 32 conditions (4 themes × 8 causes), the subjects rated the degree to which they would feel anger and pity toward the story character.

The general findings across the four themes were quite similar. Figure 8.2 depicts the reports of anger and pity in the causal conditions. Figure 8.2 shows that if the cause is classified as controllable, then reports of anger exceed those of pity, whereas if the cause if classified as uncontrollable, then reports of pity are

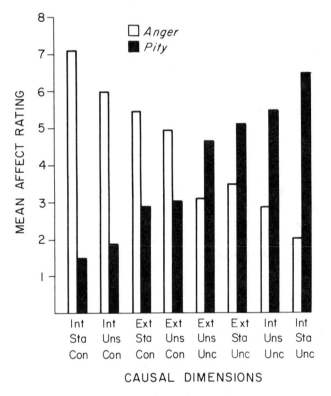

FIG. 8.2.   Ratings of pity and anger, across four themes, as a function of the controllability of the cause (from Weiner, Graham, & Chandler, in press).

greater than those of anger. These relations are particularly true given the internal causes. Furthermore, stable causes maximize feelings of pity given uncontrollable causes and exacerbate feelings of anger given controllable causes. These data are in agreement with the findings already presented and strongly support the hypothesized relations between causal dimensions and emotional reactions. There appears to be a thin line that determines if one will feel anger or pity toward another, and that line is decided by the perceived controllability of the cause. These relations also are known and used in everyday life. For example, when late for an appointment we are likely to give an uncontrollable cause (e.g., heavy traffic) in order to minimize the anger of the waiting party.

Personal Experiences of Pity, Anger, and Guilt

One of the criticisms of some of the reported research is that it is simulational or hypothetical, asking one to report what they might feel if a particular situation were to arise. In a second study conducted by Weiner, Graham, and Chandler (in press), subjects were asked to describe instances in their lives when they experienced the emotions of pity, anger, and guilt. After describing two situations in which each of these feelings were experienced, the concept of causal dimensions was introduced and described. The subjects then rated the cause of the event in question, if applicable, on each of the three dimensions. In addition, two experimenters, one blind to the hypotheses and unaware of the subjects' ratings, classified the cause of the event into the eight dimensional cells (interrater agreement was 94%).

The participants' and experimenters' ratings yielded identical results. Concerning pity, 71% of the causes were rated as stable and uncontrollable, with exactly equal apportionment between the internal and external alternatives. Two quite typical instances were:

1. A guy on campus is terribly deformed. I pity him because it would be so hard to look so different and have people stare at you.

2. My great grandmother lives in a rest home, and everytime I go there I see these poor old half-senile men and women wandering aimlessly down the halls. . . . I feel pity every time I go down there.

Concerning guilt, 84% of the causes were classified as internal, unstable, and controllable. It may be that stable causes arouse greater guilt, but in the majority of reported stories guilt followed an atypical behavior. For example:

1. When I got caught cheating on a math final in high school, I had extreme guilt feelings . . . The bad part was that I was doing well in that class and had no reason whatsoever to cheat. I learned my lesson but I will always feel guilt about the situation.

2. A friend and I studied together and I interfered with her studies by talking, wasting time, etc. On the midterm, I . . . got a strong B, while she got a D. I felt guilty about this.

Finally, for the affect of anger, 86% of the situations involved an external and controllable cause, with the majority of the causes (63%) being unstable. Two typical anger-arousing situations were:

1. My roommate brought her dog into our no-pets apartment without asking me first. When I got home she wasn't there, but the barking dog was . . . . As well, the dog had relieved itself in the middle of the entry.
2. I felt angry toward my boyfriend for lying to me about something he did. All he had to do was tell me the truth.

In sum, these reports clearly reveal the dimension-linked aspects of the emotions of pity, guilt, and anger. In a just-completed study, similar data were reported among children as young as 5 years of age (Graham, Doubleday, & Guarino, 1981). The converging evidence regarding the relations between un- controllability-pity, internal controllable-guilt, and external controllable-anger is rather conclusive.

Inferring Causal Thoughts from Affective Expressions

Thus far it has been documented that causal cognitions give rise to specific affects. It should then follow that, given certain affective displays by others, their associated attributions will be inferred; that is, emotional expression can act as a cue to others, revealing one's causal thoughts. In the following experiment (Weiner, Graham, Stern, & Lawson, 1982) we examined whether knowledge about an actor's emotions, conveyed with verbal labels, enables an observer to infer the actor's causal ascription for an achievement performance.

In this investigation the participants were given scenarios such as: A student failed a test and the teacher became angry. Why did the teacher think that the student failed? Among the affects manipulated were pity, anger, and guilt (along with others not discussed here). The attributions included as possible responses were insufficient effort, low ability, bad luck, and the task was too difficult because of a lack of teacher clarity. The participants indicated on simple scales how much each of the causes was perceived as a determinant of the affective response. The participants also rated the teacher's perceptions of the dimensions of the cause of failure. For example, we asked: If the teacher feels angry, is the cause of the student's failure perceived as internal or external to the student, stable or unstable, and controllable or not controllable by the student?

Figure 8.3 reveals that each of the affects was associated with a particular causal attribution. Given an expression of anger, the implication is that the

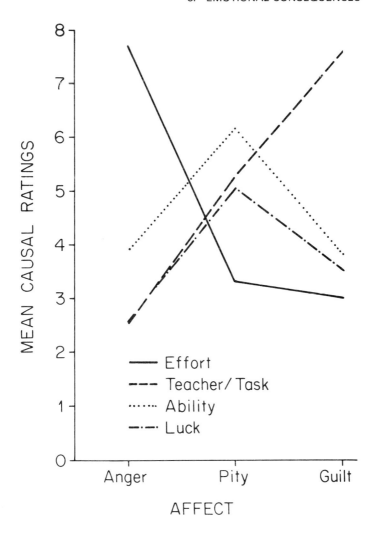

FIG. 8.3. Attributional ratings as a function of the conveyed emotion (from Weiner, Graham, Stern, & Lawson, 1982).

student had not tried sufficiently hard. Anger appears to be an "ought" emotion and often indicates a moral evaluation. Pity, on the other hand, is expressed when lack of ability is thought to be the perceived cause. Finally, guilt is linked with the teacher blaming him or herself.

The causal dimension data are shown in Fig. 8.4. Figure 8.4 reveals that if the teacher feels pity or anger, as opposed to guilt, then the cause of failure is perceived as internal to the student. In addition, the cause for anger is perceived as controllable, whereas the cause is thought to be uncontrollable if the reaction

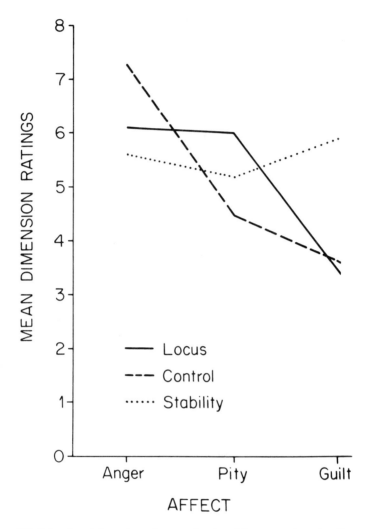

FIG. 8.4.   Causal dimension ratings as a function of the conveyed emotion (from Weiner, Graham, Stern, & Lawson, 1982). High values indicate internal, controllable by the student, and stable.

is pity or guilt. Thus, pity and anger differ in their implications concerning the perceived controllability of the cause. On the other hand, guilt and anger differ in their implications concerning the perceived locus of the cause, which, in these scenarios, also implicated controllability.

Note also the congruence between the specific attributional inferences and the causal dimension ratings. Effort, the perceived antecedent of anger reactions, is internal and controllable; ability, the perceived antecedent of pity reactions, is classified as internal and uncontrollable; whereas teacher clarity, the inferred antecedent of guilt, is external (to the student) and controllable by the teacher. The stability dimension played little role in differentiating among these three affective reactions.

GENERAL ISSUES IN THE STUDY OF EMOTION

The research reviewed in this chapter was not undertaken to resolve basic issues in the study of emotion. Nonetheless, the empirical findings are pertinent to a number of contemporary issues in this field. The following discussion is in part based on these data but also greatly reflects my own theoretical biases. Any criticisms are communicated in a spirit of inquiry and mutual facilitation. It was once confessed (Weiner, Kun, & Benesh–Weiner, 1980) that: "It takes great frustration tolerance and, perhaps, a bent toward self-destruction, to pursue the study of experiential states [p. 112]." Hence, I commisurate with others working in this area and the following comments are offered in the broader context to admiration. I also suggest that nontenured investigators not initiate emotion research.

The Sequence Issue

It has recently been contended that affect often precedes cognition in a variety of psychological phenomena (Zajonc, 1980). The experimental paradigms employed by Zajonc (1980) to support this position are so disparate from the ones reported here that direct comparisons are not possible. Concerning the postulated affect–cognition sequence from an attributional framework, it is entirely possible that in some instances feelings antedate thoughts. For example, in certain situations anger might be a conditioned reaction that then serves as a cue that another is responsible for our failure. Inasmuch as emotional cues can be used to infer the thoughts of others, it is reasonable to presume that these cues also can be used to infer one's own thoughts (see Reisenzein, Weiner, & Morrow, 1981).

Although an affect–cognition sequence is a logical possibility, it is believed to be of secondary importance. There are a number of reasons for not considering this order as fundamental. First, the empirical evidence clearly documents that specific thoughts give rise to particular emotions. Furthermore, affects seem to be changeable solely by altering thoughts. Anger, for example, will readily dissipate when it is discovered that the faulted other is really innocent of wrong-doing. In addition, the affect–thought order does not account for why particular affects, such as anger or pity, are experienced. This is expressly the case when the situational contexts of these disparate reactions are identical.

In sum, it is my belief that cognitions quite typically precede and determine affective reactions (also see Lazarus, 1966). It seems inconceivable that in everyday life we first, for example, experience gratitude and then decide that success was due to help from others. Rather, it is first decided that success is attributable to help from others and, in turn, gratitude is experienced.

Arousal

The concept of arousal is perhaps most conspicuous in this chapter by its absence. This neglect is somewhat in opposition to the prevailing importance given to arousal in the conceptual analyses of emotion (see Mandler, 1975; Schachter & Singer, 1962), although the alleged functions of arousal presently are under question (Marshall & Zimbardo, 1979; Maslach, 1979). In contrast to the position of Schachter and Singer, it is contended that arousal at times follows, rather than precedes, cognitive activity and emotional experience. This presumption is in part based upon evidence that activation or calmness (degree of arousal) following success depend on the perceptions of the causes of that outcome (see Weiner et al., 1978). Investigations by Lazarus (1966, 1968) also indicate that arousal is a product of cognitive appraisal. Lazarus reports that how one interprets a stressful event influences the amount of arousal elicited in that situation.

At present, it is not known whether arousal precedes, accompanies, or follows cognition and emotional expression, or if all or none of these might be true in disparate situations. But, for example, feeling gratitude because of an ascription of success to the volitional help of others, or feeling pride given self-ascription for success, do not appear to require a prior state of arousal that either accompanies the affect or that the individual must interpret prior to an emotional experience. The concept of arousal seems to be entirely superfluous to the attributional analysis outlined here.

There is, in fact, little evidence to support the position that arousal is necessary for emotional experience, or that arousal is a needed concept in the field of emotion (Valins, 1966). In the area of motivation, the concept of arousal (drive) has been abandoned by even most of the animal psychologists (Bolles, 1975). We suggest that issues in the field of emotion are not clarified with an arousal or drive concept. A nondirective drive concept cannot explain the quality or direction of emotional experience and falls prey to all the issues that caused the drive concept to be discarded in the study of motivation. (e.g., Do all the sources of drive or arousal pool into one, as Hull suggested? If they do, then how can different affects be simultaneously experienced? If they do not pool, then drive no longer is a nondirective energizer and the concept of arousal becomes unclear.)

These are but some examples of the kinds of questions and issues that must be addressed and answered for the arousal position to be a viable theoretical option. But surely, is it really likely that we feel aroused prior to a cognitive experience? What, then, causes the arousal? And even if arousal follows, accompanies, or precedes a cognitive interpretation, it still might be an epiphenomenon, not causally related to emotions.

For the affects considered in the prior pages, the antecedent conditions are the particular causal cognitions to which the emotions are linked. The underlying general process that has been implied is that cognitions are sufficient determinants of affect. Arousal is not considered an emotional determinant.

Process versus Content

When psychologists study emotion, they most often are concerned with the emotional process. The search for the emotional process is understandable, inasmuch as the research psychologist typically is interested in laws that transcend any particular emotional experience. But one wonders about the implicit assumption that there is *an* emotional process. This seems unlikely, given the possibility of conditioned emotions, emotions instigated by hormonal conditions, emotions that follow logically from particular cognitions, uncontrollable emotions or "passions," and so on.

The question of specific emotions and their meaning most often is left to philosophers. The differentiation of, for example, gratitude from joy from pride is usually not thought to be an empirically answerable issue. On the other hand, the research that has been presented here is concerned with the nature and the meaning of specific feelings, or the content of emotions. Meaning, it was suggested, is determined by the antecedent conditions and the properties of thought. Furthermore, meaning was ascertained or analyzed by making use of subjects' reports. Mandler (1975) has contended that phenomenological analysis will not lead to an understanding of emotion. That may be correct if he is addressing the emotional process, for most processes, such as learning or perception, are not understood by the experiencers of these processes, and the processes typically are not verbalizable or available as conscious experiences. But if one wishes to study the content of emotions, emotional life, and the meaning of emotions, then one must turn to those who experience these feelings. As the research in this chapter has demonstrated, phenomenological analyses do aid in the understanding and the explanation of emotion.

One disappointment of this author is that in reading about emotion one rarely encounters an emotion. For the naive person, the study of emotions should provide insights about envy, jealousy, love, hate, pride, guilt, and so forth, as opposed to a discussion of the physiological substratum, muscle movements, or other correlates that I believe have attracted disproportionate attention from psychologists. This is not to imply that psychologists must be guided in their work by the layperson, or that these other areas of study are not of great importance. Rather, I think there should be greater attention paid to the emotions experienced in everyday life.

Physiological Correlates

Although the supporting data are quite weak, some psychologists (even cognitive ones) cling to the belief that there will be physiological correlates of emotions; that is, each emotion will have associated with it a particular pattern of internal activity. That seems quite doubtful. For example, assume that someone has just passed an exam and feels happy. Then the teacher communicates that the student received the highest grade in the class. This immediately gives rise to pride. Is it really likely that pride is preceded and/or accompanied by a particular type of internal state? It may be that emotions of great intensity, or emotions that can be represented across species, such as rage or sexual excitement or fear, will have a physiological correlate or some particular internal representation. But this does not seem likely for the vast majority of emotions that are experienced in everyday life, such as gratitude, pride, pity, and guilt.

The Structure of Emotions

An intuitively reasonable belief held by many emotion theorists is that there are some basic emotions, and other emotions are somehow built from or develop out of these more basic feelings. Personality trait psychologists assume a similar conceptual belief and have searched for many years for the basic traits or structures of personality, out of which other aspects of personality are presumed to develop. Unfortunately, the search for a taxonomy of personality has not been successful; there is little agreement concerning how many basic traits there are or what these traits are to be called.

This uncertainty also holds true in the field of emotion. And how complex emotions get built up from more basic ones is a mystery. For example, Plutchick (1962) has argued that pride is a mixture of the primary emotions of anger + joy. Inasmuch as pride relates to achievement success and requires self-ascription, whereas anger often is experienced when there has been volitional interference from others, it is hard to fathom that anger is a component of pride.

It would seem that what are called "basic" emotions should be represented phylogentically, such as fear, rage, anger, and surprise (startle). But what, then, is to be said about affects such as pride, that require self-appraisal and a self-concept? Must any affect that requires higher-cognitive awareness not be considered fundamental? And how are self-reflective affects derived from affects that require less cognitive skills? Indeed, what is "primary" for humans may not be "primary" for infrahumans. But this possibility may render the discovery of the so-called primary or basic emotions quite unlikely.

The Development of Causal Dimensions

It has been intimated in this chapter that affective development awaits the growth of cognitive development, particularly that of causal ascriptions and the underlying meaning or dimensions of the ascriptions. Three causal dimensions have been identified with certainty: locus, stability, and controllability. One might speculate that locus will be the first of the causal dimensions to emerge; many developmental theorists postulate that early in life infants learn to distinguish the me from the not-me, or what has been called the ego or self from others in the social environment. If this is true, then self-esteem and pride may surprisingly be among the early emotions.

Another important aspect of development is coming to understand and to predict the future. This involves the concept of causal stability, which seems to require greater cognitive capabilities (including seriation) than the locus dimension (and probably less than needed for an understanding of intention and volitional control). Feelings of optimism, pessimism, and related affective states such as certain forms of depression and hopelessness might not be experienced prior to the growth of the stability dimension.

The perception of controllability by others, as already stated, relates to principles of justice and "ought," and to the concept of intention. Hence, other-directed affects related to this dimension should develop at a rather late age. As previously suggested, pride therefore should be manifested before guilt.

At this point in time, the sequential development of the dimensions of causality, and how this maturity relates to affective development, are merely speculations. But they are heuristic thoughts to consider.

A Final Note

In this chapter I have attempted to explain some prevalent human emotions, such as pride, pity, guilt, anger, and gratitude. These emotions have been related to antecedent thoughts, called causal attributions. In this endeavor, some underlying beliefs about the study of emotion have been communicated. I think there should be a systematic study of human emotions prevalent in everyday life, partly guided by the phenomenological method, and directed by the belief that cognitions are sufficient antecedents for feeling states.

ACKNOWLEDGMENT

This manuscript was written while the author was supported by a grant from the Spencer Foundation.

REFERENCES

Bolles, R. C. *Theory of motivation* (2nd ed.). New York: Harper & Row, 1975.

Brehm, J. W. (Ed.). *A theory of psychological reactance*. New York: Academic Press, 1966.

Cooper, H. M., & Burger, J. M. How teachers explain students' academic performance. *American Educational Research Journal*, 1980, *12*, 95–109.

de Charms, R. *Personal causation.* New York: Academic Press, 1968.

Deci, E. L. *Intrinsic motivation.* New York: Plenum, 1975.

Falbo, T., & Beck, R. C. Naive psychology and the attributional model of achievement. *Journal of Personality,* 1979, *47,* 185–195.

Folkes, V. S. Communicating the causes of social rejection. *Journal of Experimental Social Psychology* (in press).

Graham, S., Doubleday, C., & Guarino, P. *An attributional analysis of the development of pity, anger, and guilt.* Unpublished manuscript, University of California, Los Angeles, 1981.

Hamilton, V. L. Intuitive psychologist or intuitive lawyer? Alternative models of the attribution process. *Journal of Personality and Social Psychology,* 1980, *39,* 767–772.

Heider, F. *The psychology of interpersonal relations.* New York, Wiley, 1958.

Kelley, H. H. Attribution theory in social psychology. In D. Levine (Ed.), *Nebraska Symposium on Motivation, XV.* Lincoln: University of Nebraska Press, 1967.

Kingdon, J. W. Politicians' beliefs about voters. *American Political Science Review,* 1967, *61,* 137–145.

Lau, R. R., & Russell, D. Attributions in the sports pages: A field test of some current hypotheses in attribution research. *Journal of Personality and Social Psychology,* 1980, *39,* 29–38.

Lazarus, R. S. *Psychological stress and the coping process.* New York: McGraw–Hill, 1966.

Lazarus, R. S. Emotions and adaptation: Conceptual and empirical relations. In W. J. Arnold (Ed.), *Nebraska Symposium on Motivation, XVI.* Lincoln: University of Nebraska Press, 1968.

Litman–Adizes, T. *An attributional model of depression.* Unpublished doctoral dissertation, University of California, Los Angeles, 1978.

Mandler, G. *Mind and emotion,* New York: Wiley, 1975.

Marshall, G. D., & Zimbardo, P. G. Affective consequences of inadequately explained physiological arousal. *Journal of Personality and Social Psychology,* 1979, *37,* 970–988.

Maslach, C. Negative emotional biasing and unexplained arousal. *Journal of Personality and Social Psychology,* 1979, *37,* 953–969.

Meyer, J. P. Causal attributions for success and failure: A multivariate investigation of dimensionality, formation, and consequences. *Journal of Personality and Social Psychology,* 1980, *38,* 704–718.

Meyer, J. P., & Koelbl, S. L. M. Dimensionality of students' causal attributions for test performance. *Personality and Social Psychology Bulletin,* 1982, *8,* 31–36.

Meyer, J. P., & Mulherin, A. From attribution to helping: An analysis of the mediating effects of affect and expectancy. *Journal of Personality and Social Psychology,* 1980, *39,* 201–210.

Michela, J., Peplau, L. A., & Weeks, D. *Perceived dimensions and consequences of attributions for loneliness.* Unpublished manuscript, University of California, Los Angeles, 1978.

Passer, M. W. *Perceiving the causes of success and failure revisited: A multidimensional scaling approach.* Unpublished doctoral dissertation, University of California, Los Angeles, 1977.

Plutchik, R. *The emotions: Facts, theories, and a new model.* New York: Random House, 1962.

Reisenzein, R., Weiner, B., & Morrow, W. *Alteration of perceived responsibility with false anger and sympathy feedback.* Unpublished manuscript, University of California, Los Angeles, 1981.

Rosenbaum, R. M. *A dimensional analysis of the perceived causes of success and failure.* Unpublished doctoral dissertation, University of California, Los Angeles, 1972.

Rotter, J. B. Generalized expectancies for internal versus external control of reinforcement. *Psychological Monographs,* 1966, *80* (1, Whole No. 609).

Rychlak, J. F. *A philosophy of science for personality theory.* New York: Houghton Mifflin, 1968.

Schachter, S., & Singer, J. E. Cognitive, social, and physiological determinants of emotional state. *Psychological Review,* 1962, *69,* 379–399.

Schafer, R. *A new language for psychoanalysis.* New Haven: Yale University Press, 1976.

Steiner, I. D. Perceived freedom. In L. Berkowitz (Ed.), *Advances in experimental social psychology* (Vol. 5). New York: Academic Press, 1970.

Tesser, A., Gatewood, R., & Driver, M. Some determinants of gratitude. *Journal of Personality and Social Psychology*, 1968, *3*, 233–236.

Valins, S. Cognitive effects of false heart-rate feedback. *Journal of Personality and Social Psychology*, 1966, *4*, 400–408.

Weiner, B. *On causes and causal dimensions: A reply to Falbo and Beck.* Unpublished manuscript, University of California, Los Angeles, 1979. (a)

Weiner, B. A theory of motivation for some classroom experiences. *Journal of Educational Psychology*, 1979, *71*, 3–25. (b)

Weiner, B. *Human motivation.* New York: Holt, Rinehart, & Winston, 1980. (a)

Weiner, B. A cognitive (attribution)—emotion—action model of motivated behavior: An analysis of judgments of help giving. *Journal of Personality and Social Psychology*, 1980, *39*, 186–200. (b)

Weiner, B. May I borrow your class notes? An attributional analysis of judgments of help giving in an achievement-related context. *Journal of Educational Psychology*, 1980, *72*, 676–681. (c)

Weiner, B., Graham, S., & Chandler, C. Causal antecedents of pity, anger, and guilt. *Personality and Social Psychology Bulletin* (in press).

Weiner, B., Graham, S., Stern, P., & Lawson, M. E. Using affective cues to infer causal thoughts. *Developmental Psychology*, 1982, *18*, 278–286.

Weiner, B., & Kukla, A. An attributional analysis of achievement motivation. *Journal of Personality and Social Psychology*, 1970, *15*, 1–20.

Weiner, B., Kun, A., & Benesh–Weiner, M. The development of mastery, emotions, and morality from an attributional perspective. In W. A. Collins (Ed.), *Minnesota Symposia on Child Psychology* (Vol. 13). Hillsdale, N. J.: Lawrence Erlbaum Associates, 1980.

Weiner, B., Nierenberg, R., & Goldstein, M. Social learning (locus of control) versus attributional (causal stability) interpretations of expectancy of success. *Journal of Personality*, 1976, *44*, 52–68.

Weiner, B., Russell, D., & Lerman, D. Affective consequences of causal ascriptions. In J. H. Harvey, W. J. Ickes, & R. F. Kidd (Eds.), *New directions in attribution research* (Vol. 2). Hillsdale, N. J.: Lawrence Erlbaum Associates, 1978.

Weiner, B., Russell, D., & Lerman, D. The cognition–emotion process in achievement-related contexts. *Journal of Personality and Social Psychology*, 1979, *37*, 1211–1220.

Wimer, S., & Kelley, H. H. *An investigation of the dimensions of lay causal attribution. Journal of Personality and Social Psychology* (in press).

Wong, P. T. P., & Weiner, B. When people ask why questions and the heuristics of attributional search. *Journal of Personality and Social Psychology*, 1981, *40*, 650–663.

Zajonc, R. B. Feeling and thinking: Preferences need no inferences. *American Psychologist*, 1980, *35*, 151–175.

Zuckerman, M., & Lubin, B. *Manual for the Multiple Affect Adjective Check List.* San Diego, Calif.: Educational and Industrial Testing Service, 1965.

9 Independence and Interaction of Affect and Cognition

R. B. Zajonc
Paula Pietromonaco
John Bargh
The University of Michigan

In part, this paper derives from a recent article (Zajonc, 1980) that reviewed theoretical and empirical evidence suggesting that cognition and affect are separable, parallel, and partially independent systems. One of the purposes of examining the question of whether these two processes are independent is to enable us to better understand how they interact. Clearly, if affect always entails some form of cognitive processing then its influence on other cognitive processes would have to be studied in quite different ways than if it does not, and the problem of the affect-cognition interaction would be formulated in different terms. Of course, the previous paper did not claim that affect is independent of cognition under all circumstances and in all its manifestations. In many cases, perhaps even in most cases of affective reaction, cognition figures as an important factor. There can be no pride, guilt, jealousy, or disappointment without some cognitive participation. But perhaps there can be fear or joy without it. And thus, the argument was that an affective reaction *can* occur without the participation of cognitive processes under *some* circumstances.

Because the idea that affective reactions can occur without the participation of cognitive processes is not without controversy, we shall first review some theoretical and empirical issues touching on the independence of affect from cognition, and then consider some specific aspects of the interaction of these two processes. In particular, we will examine the possibility of studying this interaction at the level of motor representations.

INDEPENDENCE AND AFFECT FROM COGNITION:
THEORETICAL CONSIDERATIONS

The conceptual separation of affect and cognition is, in part, quite arbitrary and it was posited to satisfy certain theoretical purposes (Zajonc, 1980). Any collection of empirical phenomena can be treated, in principle, as one system or as any number of systems. Thus, two people can be treated as a "family," "couple," "group," "duet," "team," and so forth, and thus be analyzed as a unit, that is, as a single system having a definable and specifiable integrity. And the same two people can also be treated as two entirely separate systems if we are interested in their memories or in their kidneys, for example. Many systems that do not occur separately in nature are nonetheless distinguished for conceptual purposes because these distinctions prove analytically useful. For example, one distinguishes quite arbitrarily between learning and performance, short term and long term memory, attention and perception, and so on, although in each case these distinctions are merely different ways of looking at the same phenomenon.

Since affect is not always independent of cognition, it is eventually necessary to specify those circumstances where it is and where it isn't. At the present state of our knowledge, however, no systematic method exists for deciding *a priori* whether cognition would or would not participate in a particular affective reaction. We can only speculate for each case individually. Some clarification can be made, nevertheless, regarding various features of affect as a phenomenon and which of these features might require cognitive participation and which would not.

Zajonc and Markus (unpublished manuscript) have distinguished between the aspects of emotion that form the foci of different theories. On the one hand are theories of affect that derive from the Schachter-Singer (1962) tradition, such as Mandler's theory (1975) or that of Lazarus (1966). They are the *cognitive theories of emotion* because in these theories cognitive processes constitute *necessary* elements. Another class of theories of emotion focuses less on the participation of cognitive processes and more on the participation of somatic processes. These are theories such as Izard's (1977), Leventhal's (1980), or Tomkins (1962, 1963). They are the *somatic theories of emotion.* The cognitive and somatic theories of emotions are not contradictory of each other; they have merely different emphases and interests. Thus, cognitive theories of emotions, since they follow the Singer-Schachter tradition, focus mainly on the explication of the emotional *experience.* In contrast, the somatic theories of emotion are more concerned with the *expression* of emotion. These latter theories seek to determine if there are universalities in emotional expression (e.g., Ekman & Friesen, 1975), or what aspects of the emotional expression allow one individual to recognize the emotion of another.

If we distinguish between the *experience* and *expression* of emotion, we may inquire whether cognition is necessarily involved in both aspects of emotion.

Now one would have to concede that the emotional *experience* cannot occur without some participation of cognition. Since by "experience" we must understand some form of self-perception, the assertion is true by definition. The same is true, of course, of *reported* experiences and of judgments. And thus when Mandler (1982) argues in the present volume that value judgments require cognitive participation, he cannot be contradicted. We are not in disagreement with Mandler on that point when he asserts that "to say that one likes something requires access to stored knowledge".

However, the *expression* of emotion often requires no cognitive processes. A loud noise produces an affective expression, the loss of support or balance also produces an overt emotional reaction, as does extreme heat applied to the body, or extreme pressure. By "expression" of emotion we mean here those aspects of bodily states, changes, and acts that allow one individual to detect the emotional state of another, and often to identify the nature of that state. It is also the case that the administration of a variety of drugs generates a variety of emotional expressions. Alcohol, barbiturates, amphetamines, depressants, and hashish all have clear somatic and expressive consequences. While these expressions and somatic effects may be *accompanied* by cognitive processes, that is, by the experience of emotion, appraisal, or evaluation, they are not necessary for the generation of a variety of emotional reactions that have distinct forms of expression. One needs no labeling or evaluation or appraisal to suffer (or enjoy) the affective consequences of ten ounces of alcohol given unobtrusively.

Needless to say that if cognitive processes do accompany alcohol intake—and they almost always do because they accompany all functions of our life—the emotional reaction caused by the biological consequences of the alcohol content in the blood may take a direction that is influenced and mediated by these cognitions. Thoughts about a rejected manuscript when accompanied by an appropriate dose of alcohol may potentiate depression, whereas thoughts about an impending Caribbean cruise may generate euphoria. In this sense, these cognitive processes give *specific* meaning to certain emergent internal states and supply the *content* of the emotional experience. This proposition agrees with the view of Schachter and Singer about the consequences of cognition for emotion. But it disagrees with their view that cognition is a necessary component. Because we are seldom without *some* thoughts, the question of whether cognition is or is not necessary to emotion may seem quite pointless. It is not. Nearly all objects that fall, fall in the presence of air. Yet laws of acceleration could not have been established without construing conceptual models that had objects fall in the absence of air. Thus, if we imagine a state where an individual had no cognitions whatever, and either was or was not administered alcohol (without knowing, of course), then this individual would express (i.e., show) a different emotional state in one case than in the other. After all, the biological consequences of alcohol do have autonomic, visceral, glandular, and muscular effects that have all the earmarks of an emotion or mood, and they would have these effects regardless of the thoughts that the individual might be entertaining at the moment. Alcohol effects are not "all in the mind."

It is also the case that under some circumstances, still to be understood, the original cognitive bases of certain emotions can be forgotten or dissociated from the affective elements. Yet the object, when reinstated, can produce an emotional reaction of similar content albeit in reduced amplitude. When we meet a friend whom we haven't seen for a long time, the joy is immediate even when we have entirely forgotten why we became friendly or why we came to like the person in the first place. In a variety of pathological cases and under hypnotic suggestion, affect can be aroused by the introduction of a specific stimulus, without the person connecting the one with the other.

The final proposition to be examined in this context is that cognition is *always* a necessary element of emotion, but that sometimes it is unconscious and thus it cannot be detected. This argument unfortunately cannot be disproved. If we find an emotion for which we cannot detect an observable cognitive correlate, then we would simply conclude that some cognitive processes did participate as necessary components, but they were unconscious and, therefore, accessible neither to the actor nor to the observer. Such a theory would have no constraints at all and it would be quite useless. Therefore, the theoretical position taken here is that the independence of affect from cognition holds for cognitions that are accessible to the subject at the time of the emotional reaction or can be otherwise demonstrated (other than by default) to have participated as necessary elements.

If there are circumstances *at all* where affect and cognition are conceptually separate systems, it is useful to treat them as such, so as not to preempt answers to the question of how they interact. We can always collapse them into one system if the benefits of the distinction do not outweigh the benefits of parsimony. But if we start with affect and cognition as one system we will never move beyond it.

INDEPENDENCE OF AFFECT FROM COGNITION: EMPIRICAL EVIDENCE

Even though the independence of affect and cognition is in part a matter of conceptual convenience, empirical support indicating that they are separable systems is not lacking. Suggestive evidence for the independence of affect from cognition is to be found in such results as the inability of generating the same psychophysical space from preference judgments as is generated from similarity judgments, the classical conditioning of aversive reactions, bait shyness, lateralization effects, and the primary and recency effects in impression formation. As early as 1909, Nakashima reported evidence that preference judgments of colors, tones, and geometrical figures are independent of psychophysical judgments made by the same subjects on the same stimuli. He concluded that results for the preference judgments of hues are direct and that they are not mediated by sensory qualities. The same results for the preference judgments of hues were found by Premack and Kintsch (1979), and for the preference judgments of soft drinks (Cooper, 1973). Similarity and preference judgments agree with each other only when the dimensions of similarity are themselves highly evaluative, as is the case in aesthetic judgments (Berlyne, 1975; O'Hare, 1976) or personnel selection (Klahr, 1969).

In a sense, the independence of affect must be assumed for responses to unconditioned aversive stimuli for they are stimuli that the organism had not encountered in the past and that invariably and instantaneously evoke escape or avoidance responses. If cognitive processes mediate the reaction to an aversive UCS then they must be innate, unconscious, and automatic. And in taste aversion, which is a special case of such conditioning, the absence of an association at the cognitive level between the ingestion of food and the subsequent toxic reaction can hardly be disputed. Garcia and Rusiniak (1980) write that "if the rat is allowed to drink a flavored solution and remain alert for about fifteen minutes, perhaps to consolidate the CS memory trace, the delayed nauseous UCS is effective even when presented after cortical functioning has been degraded by anesthesia . . . or by potassium chloride applied to the cortex. . . . Since the emetic UCS is effective when the subject appears partly or wholly unconscious, it is entirely possible that many 'irrational' food aversions may result from adventitious conditioning by a delayed UCS of which the subject has no memory" [p. 151].

Numerous research reports indicate that when cognitive and emotional reactions are called for simultaneously, the emotional reactions are more likely to be controlled by the right brain hemisphere whereas the cognitive reactions are more likely to be controlled by the left hemisphere (Cacioppo & Petty, 1981; Schwartz, Davidson, & Maer, 1975; Suberi & McKeever, 1977). Ross and Mesulam (1979) have examined patients with lesions in the right hemisphere lying directly across from Broca's area. These patients were able to produce intelligible speech. Remarkably, however, their speech was a complete monotone, and devoid of any emotional quality. Thus, for some aspects of emotion and cognition, separate anatomical structures can be identified.

It is a typical finding in impression formation studies (Anderson & Hubert, 1963; Posner & Snyder, 1975) that, whereas affective judgments about a hypothetical target person show primacy effects, the recall and recognition of the adjectives from which these affective judgments are made show recency effects. More recently, Dreben, Fiske, and Hastie (1979) were unable to detect any relationship whatever between the weights that represented the contributions of the adjectives to the overall affective judgment and the recall of these adjectives.

More direct experimental evidence for independence of affect from cognition, however, comes from studies on the so-called mere exposure effect (Zajonc,

1968), that is, the increasing preference for objects that can be induced by virtue of mere repeated exposures. The traditional theory, associated with this phenomenon since the days of Titchener, held that a preference for the repeatedly exposed object was produced by the increasing *awareness of recognition of the object as familiar*. A series of studies in our laboratory (Kunst-Wilson & Zajonc, 1980; Matlin, 1971; Moreland & Zajonc, 1977, 1979; Wilson, 1979), however, has shown that neither objective recognition nor subjective impression of recognition are necessary for the exposure effect, and that a preference for a stimulus object can be enhanced by virtue of repeated exposure alone, independently of whether the person is able or unable to recognize it as familiar. These results were obtained with a variety of stimuli, different methods of presentation, and diverse measures of affect. Nevertheless, they were entirely consistent in showing the exposure effect as being independent of recognition when measured either by subjective report or by objective sensitivity scores (d').

Among the crucial pieces of evidence for the separation of affect and cognition were the studies carried out by Wilson (1979) and by Kunst-Wilson and Zajonc (1980). In the latter study subjects were repeatedly presented with polygons at extremely brief exposures that did not allow for better than chance recognition. Subsequently, they were tested for recognition memory and for liking. Even though they were not capable of distinguishing between objectively old and objectively new stimuli when making "OLD-NEW" judgments, the subjects were able to discriminate reliably between them by means of affective judgments. That is, when two stimuli were presented in test (one old and one new) and the subjects were asked which of the two they liked better, they showed preference for the stimulus that had been presented previously, not for the new one. However, when asked which of the two was old and which was new, their responses did not exceed the chance level.

Mandler (Note 3) was apparently unable in many attempts to replicate the results of the Kunst-Wilson/Zajonc (1980) experiment for reasons that we do not understand. Richard Davidson (Note 4), on the other hand, working independently, and collecting evoked potential data, did obtain results similar to ours and Seamon, Brody, and Kauff (unpublished manuscript) replicated the effect using subliminal as well as supraliminal presentations. And unknowingly, the Kunst-Wilson/Zajonc experiment has followed a study published more than a quarter of a century ago by Littman and Manning (1954) that was performed on smokers of *Camels, Chesterfields,* and *Lucky Strikes.* These researchers also asked for preference and for identification, although not under degraded presentation conditions. Some subjects tasted these cigarettes (blindly) and were required to identify them (i.e., to say whether the cigarette was one they usually smoked or a different one). Another group tasted the cigarettes for preference. The results on cigarette brand identification were inferior to the results on preference. As in the Kunst-Wilson/Zajonc study, subjects preferred their own cigarette brand to others, even though they were not able to identify their own brand when asked about it directly. It thus appears that at least for simple and fundamental affective and cognitive phenomena, an independence between these processes can be safely assumed in a variety of cases.

The Affect-Cognition Interaction

If affect contains significant cognitive components, then the interaction of affect and cognition could be readily studied at that level. And indeed it has been so studied most recently. This approach has been espoused by Bower and his colleagues (Bower, 1981) and by Isen and her colleagues (Isen, Shalker, Clark, & Karp, 1978). In these approaches affect is singled out for its *representation,* and the influence of affect on cognition, such as in selective recall of mood-related words in various mood states, is examined in terms of how these cognitive representations of affect influence the cognitive representations of the words in the list. In short, the interaction of affect and cognition is the interaction of the associative network of the particular affect and the associative network of the particular cognition.

Now, to the extent that these mental representations of affect capture the essence of affect in its entirety, the study of the affect-cognition interaction need not venture beyond these bounds. But if affect has other important correlates and manifestations that can influence cognition, then it may be useful to examine them. And there are a number of reasons to suppose that there is more to affect than its associative network. The danger that an exclusively cognitive approach to the study of the affect-cognition interaction may prove to be limited is especially true of Bower's approach. In all experiments reported by Bower, affect is induced hypnotically *by verbal means.* The subject is told to think about an emotion, to imagine and to recall episodes in which he or she experienced a particular emotion, such as anger or joy, and to try to feel that way. Now, to follow these verbal instructions, a variety of cognitive processes must necessarily be activated and thus become salient. At the same time, it is not at all clear from these experiments if other affective correlates—somatic, visceral, glandular, autonomic—are present as well, or whether the subjects are simply engaged in processing information *about* affect.

This is not the case in Isen's studies where affect is manipulated by more subtle non-verbal methods, for example, allowing the subjects to find dimes, or giving them cookies. In these experiments, too, no independent measures of affective states are taken. It is likely that these measures, if taken, would reveal biological symptoms of affective arousal. But, of course, we need further studies to substantiate this supposition.

Up to now, therefore, the affect-cognition interaction has been investigated by a recourse to the subjective realm. Both affect and cognition were examined for their mutual effects as they occur at the level of mental representations. If one examined how mood influenced the processing of information, it was assumed that mood had some form of mental representation as did the information being processed. It was further assumed that the contact that caused the effects of mood on the processing of the information took place at the level of mental representation.

Affect—and certainly the overt manifestations of affect—one's own and that of others—is a form of information. As such it is represented like other information, although there is no *a priori* reason why all information should be represented in a similar manner. In fact, on *a priori* grounds we would suppose the opposite. When the possibility of representations of different kinds is raised, the question of what these different kinds are is immediately raised, too. Are all representations of the mental and subjective form? Are they either abstract propositions or icons? This question is particularly pertinent if we inquire about the *representation of affect*.

Since affect has such salient and powerful somatic correlates, could not these somatic manifestations have significant representational functions? Since the *expression* of emotion communicates clear content to an observer, why would it not communicate it to the actor? And if it can communicate affect, it can represent and store affect. Surely, affect can be represented by mental and subjective means. But there is nothing preventing the expressive bodily movements, autonomic changes, visceral reactions, glandular secretions, or cardiovascular patterns, to have the capacity of representing affect, too. These events may all have other functions as well, such as to mobilize energy for an adaptive action, release tension, or modulate a particular response to a particular aspect of the environment. But these other functions need not stand in the way of representational functions.

If affect is not represented like most other information, how *is* it represented? In the paper on feeling and thinking, Zajonc (1980) suggested that affect may be processed more like motor skills than like many other forms of information. That is, the somatic constituents and the expressive correlates of affect might themselves—without the participation of symbolic processes—form representations of affect. But this does not mean that affect is processed differently. The possibility of motor representation of all kinds of information, including information about affective phenomena, has been recently explored (Zajonc & Markus, unpublished manuscript). It was suggested in that paper that the motor system can represent information independently of other forms of mental representations.

Let us for the purposes of the argument examine two elementary actions that can be equated respectively with affect and cognition: the action expressing preference and the action expressing recognition. We shall not be concerned with the operational indicators of these two actions, but simply with their abstract and conceptual properties. Both preference and recognition have an object stimulus. Both represent an interaction between an internal state of the organism and the object. In the case of preference we have to do with a predisposition toward or away from the object. In the case of recognition we have to consider the previous encounter between the object and the organism. Predisposition toward the object *Approach-,* *Avoid* means that "I like it", and moving away from the object means that "I dislike it." A previous encounter would let me view the object as "old" whereas the absence of a previous encounter would lead me to believe that it was "new." If the phenomena of preference and recognition are coordinated to affect and cognition, being their prototypical manifestations, it is worthwhile to enquire into the basic and essential differences between these two manifestations. The differences are quite subtle, to be sure, because preference and recognition are enhanced by the same major variable—repeated stimulus exposure. And in overt behavior we may not be able to determine without other knowledge whether a given action expresses preference or recognition. Certainly, in experiments where the subjects push one of two buttons marked "I like it" and "I dislike it" in the case of preference measurement, or "Old" and "New" in the case of recognition memory tasks, the buttons and the behavior topography may be quite identical. Only the label differs. Yet these two actions are clearly not identical from the point of view of the subject, and the correlation between familiarity (objective or subjective) and preference is far from perfect.

In a typical experiment on recognition memory, or on preference, a great deal goes on before the subject responds by pressing one of the OLD and NEW buttons or one of the LIKE and DISLIKE buttons. Some processing of information is required to comprehend the question, and all sorts of computations are carried out after comprehending the question and responding. To come up with a response the subject has to "look inside himself or herself," so to speak, and to indicate this internal state. In the one case the state is one of familiarity with the object, and in the other it is the state of inclination toward it. Although both may well be represented symbolically, it is likely that they are represented in other ways as well. It is, in fact, quite possible that even for these simple states there are a variety of parallel representations (Zajonc & Markus, unpublished manuscript). One such parallel source of representation is to be found in the motor system. In the case of preference, the motor representation may involve a variety of muscular tendencies that the subject may express toward the object. Nearly one century ago Galton observed that interpersonal attitudes could be measured by the physical inclination of people's bodies toward each other (quoted in Pearson, 1924, p. 279), and today's notions of "body language" emphasize the same idea. Suppose then that a distinct posture exists that is associated with preference and another one that is associated with aversion. And suppose further that there are also postures that are associated with reactions to new and old stimuli. How could we distinguish such general postural patterns which signify preference and aversion from those which signify familiarity with an object? We can only speculate. In the case of a novel stimulus, there is also a tendency to approach it, as there is in the case of preference. However, the nature of the approach posture that *is* the expression of preference and the approach posture in reacting to novelty are quite different. While the individual may incline his or her body toward a novel object or approach it, there is simultaneously a considerable orienting activity. There is also caution lest the object turns out to be dangerous. The approach to the novel stimulus is measured and can be aborted readily. In contrast, the approach to a preferred object is calm, relaxed, and confident. There is little exploration because the object is never novel, and there is no hesitation in the posture—the organism need not ready itself for a possible escape. The topography of the two postural patterns, therefore, must be somewhat different and one could document it by EMG recordings.

Note that approach responses are also representations of the organism's reactions to the stimulus. They are of course themselves instrumental or expressive responses, but they have all the properties of other representations as well. They stand in a stable relationship to their referents, they are repeatable, they can be retained, and they can combine with other representations. They are not representations of the stimuli, although some aspects of the stimulus must be invoked to generate these reactions.

In regarding behavior, and especially instrumental and expressive behavior, as having representational and mnestic functions, one begs the question of what is *not* a representation. The answer to this question is that anything *can* be a representation of anything else, either by convention or by usage. The requirement is that one object or one event *stands for* another. Since a one-to-one correspondence or isomorphism are not required (as they are not required of mental or linguistic representations), there may be representations of different degrees of precision and uniqueness. Petting one's cat may be a clearer representation of one's affect toward that animal than feeding it, and both may be less precise than, for example, saying "I love my cat," or the particular pattern of eye fixations coupled with one's facial expression that arise when one sees the cat after a long absence.

Nor is there a need for the representation to be conscious in the sense that we must be aware of the fact that our leaning of our body toward the cat means that we like it. It has certainly not been demonstrated thus far that we are aware of our mental representations. We are aware of some images, of thoughts, and of other mental content. But are they "raw" representations in the strict sense of the word, or are they the *products* of representations? Yet, there is little doubt today among cognitive psychologists that mental representations do exist and perform important functions in information processing.

Thus, the requirement that some event "stand for" its referent in order for that event to be representational must mean only that it must occur repeatedly in similar ways if the object or its surrogate is present. The surrogate of the object may be anything, such as the recollection of the object, a picture of the object, or someone talking about it. Operationally, we can determine if Y is a representation of X by interfering with the occurrence of Y and observing if the information about X (e.g., recall, recognition, detection of X, etc.) was not processed with some impairment. The degree of impairment will tell us something about the importance and uniqueness of Y in representing X. We shall see that such a determination can be more readily established with *motor* representations than with *mental* representations, such as propositions or icons.

There are some indications that a significant internal decoding process that may be considered representational occurs *before* the overt instrumental or expressive response. Thus, for example, Kleinman and John (1975) presented cats with two flicker frequencies. One flicker frequency was associated with food and the other was associated with shock. Evoked potentials were measured and they were found to be distinct for the two stimulus-response couples. In a subsequent test, a flicker frequency was presented that was halfway between the previous two. The question asked was whether the animals would be confused in their instrumental responses and whether the evoked potential patterns would be averages or combinations of the two previously habitually generated potentials. The striking result was that on the occurrence of the flicker of intermediate frequency, the cats did not appear to become confused at all. They either escaped as if to avoid a possible shock or they ran to the feeding box. And their evoked potentials corresponded to these responses. Apparently a sensory motor pattern developed that derived its specificity from the efferent part of the chain and remained fairly flexible with respect to the stimulus process. This had to be so because the onset of the evoked potential was substantially earlier than the onset of the observable instrumental responses. Thus, these evoked potentials together with the associated motor process that must have been initiated to allow the animal eventually to carry out a series of complex acts that led either to escape or to feeding, could be well considered a form of representation of a tendency, such as preference or aversion.

Indications of representations that are evoked early in processing information are to be found in research on subception and perceptual defense. This research has had a controversial history. Nevertheless there is something to be gained by examining its implications for the present purposes. The phenomena of subception and of perceptual defense are said to implicate covert reactions that are not accessible to the individual's awareness. But in our view they can be considered representational. Thus, McGinnies (1949) claimed that when taboo and neutral words are presented for recognition threshold measurement, using the ascending method of limits, GSR taken before recognition are greater to taboo words than to non-taboo words. This work was severely criticized on a number of grounds and it does contain serious methodological flaws (Howes & Solomon, 1950). Although the empirical work itself may be questionable, it is not beyond the realm of possibilities that the hypothesis that McGinnies entertained was in fact correct (Erdelyi, 1974). One of the interpretations of McGinnies' was that individuals experienced conflict when confronted with unseemly words that they had to utter. This conflict suppressed responses thus elevating their threshold to taboo words. At the same time, the conflict exhibited itself in higher pre-recognition GSR's. In an experiment where these possibilities were examined (Zajonc, 1962), the McGinnies procedure was first fully reproduced. Subjects then learned a series of paired associates, where the previously shown stimuli (both taboo and neutral) served as stimulus terms and a new set of taboo and neutral words served as response terms. There were four kinds of pairs. In one set, the stimulus and the response terms were both neutral. In another set, the stimulus and the response terms were both taboo words. In the third set, the stimulus term was neutral while the response term was taboo, and in the last set, the stimulus term was taboo while the response term was neutral. Once the subjects learned these associations to perfection, their recognition thresholds were again assessed to these words while measures of GSR were taken on each tachistoscopic presentation of the words. Again the ascending method was used to replicate the McGinnies conditions. The stimuli previously shown were shown again and recognition thresholds to these stimuli were remeasured. However, this time the subject was instructed to indicate recognition not by reading the word that was presented in the tachistoscope but by saying the word acquired in the previous paired-associates learning session. Thus, in some cases the subject had to indicate his recognition of a perfectly innocuous word by saying a taboo word. At other times he had to indicate recognition of a taboo word by saying a neutral word. Of course, there were words whose recognition was indicated by responses of the same kind. This procedure was used in the expectation that the analysis would reveal whether the elevated thresholds and GSR's were due to what the subjects saw or due to what they said. The thresholds and the GSR measures taken on the recognition trial showed that the major source of variation was indeed due to the responses the subjects used to indicate recognition. The nature of the words shown mattered little. If the word used to indicate recognition was taboo, GSR reaction was elevated and so was recognition threshold. However, the most interesting result for the present purposes was the fact that GSR's taken three trials prior to recognition varied not with the response that the subjects were about to use in indicating recognition, but with the stimulus word shown in the tachistoscope.

There is some indication in these results, therefore, that an affective excitation reflected in autonomic arousal occurred prior to recognition. There also could have been some associated motor patterns—of low amplitude to be sure, but detectable probably with EMG recordings. Some of these subtle motor patterns could have constituted the motor representation of the affective reactions of the individual to the stimuli—hesitation, embarassment, shame, repulsion, aversion, etc.

If it is the case that the affective system avails itself of motor representations to a significant degree, and if we can assume that the cognitive system does the same, then a new arena for the study of the affect-cognition interaction emerges: the arena of motor representations. One of the direct advantages of studying the role of motor representations is that they are more directly accessible, measurable, and manipulable than mental representations. To examine this strategy of research we have recently carried out a number of experiments on the role of motor representations of cognitive material that is heavily affective (Pietromonaco, Zajonc, & Bargh, 1981). These stimuli were photographs of faces and the task was the typical recognition memory task. Recognition memory for faces is much better than for other similar forms of stimuli. It has been suggested that the vast experience that people have with faces and the importance that these stimuli play in one's social life are factors that improve people's face recognition performance. However, some results conflict with this interpretation. Photographs of faces shown upside down are very difficult to recognize—much more difficult than such items as trees, airplanes, or buildings (Phillips & Rawles, 1979). We speculated that the reason for this difficulty lies in the fact that the motor system participates heavily in the perception and processing of faces and that turning a face upside down prevents the individual from engaging this accessory processing apparatus.

When the individual is presented with a face or a photograph of a face, his or her perceptual acts do not consist simply of a passive registration of the stimuli presented. There is a clear reaction, partly affective, and the individual's own face engages a variety of motor responses. Sometimes, when it is a photograph of a smiling face, the subject smiles too. If it is a photograph of an angry face, the subject may furrow his or her eyebrows or purse his or her lips. One of the questions investigated in our research was whether these motor expressions could have representational functions. That is, we sought to determine whether the motor responses of the subject viewing photographs of faces would benefit recognition memory, whether we could augment these motor responses, or interfere with them and thus influence recognition memory performance. If it is the case that motor responses are significantly implicated in face recognition, say there is a specific motor encoding of each photograph and if it is the case that in encoding the photograph the person "mimics" it to some extent, for example, then this possibility is greatly curtailed when the photographs are shown upside down. Note that it is not necessary for a person to reproduce the photographed face faithfully in order to construct its motor representation. In principle, any specific pattern of motor acts that has a consistent relationship with the stimulus face would do, although reproduction might prove to be a most efficient representation. In any event, if a consistent representation is to emerge, some specific features of the photographed face must become connected to some specific and distinct motor reactions. When the face is upside down reproduction is extremely difficult, and most of the motor involvement of the subject is peripheral and orienting in nature. It is directed toward transforming the stimulus face into its right side up orientation. Hence, the specificity and distinctiveness of the motor reactions are restricted, and their representational functions are limited.

Several conditions varying a number of factors were examined in our experiments. In all of these conditions 78 photographs of faces of men were shown during the study period and the same 78 items interspersed among 78 new faces, were shown in the test phase of the experiments. In one of our conditions, during the study phase, the subjects were asked to imitate the stimulus faces in a number of specific ways. They were asked to gaze in the same direction as the face in the photograph, to turn their heads in the same direction, to smile if the face smiled, or generally make the same expressions with their own eyebrows, mouths, and cheeks as in the photograph. A few training trials assured that the subjects could perform this task well. None of the subjects had any difficulties. Another group of subjects was asked to view the 78 faces for the same period of time. However, they were asked to make judgments of the same features that the previous group imitated. Thus, they were asked about the head tilt in the photograph, the eye gaze, and the expression of the mouth, and so forth. Both groups had to pay approximately equal attention to selected features of the faces, but one of these groups engaged their own facial muscles, whereas the other one was not required to do so, although they may have engaged these muscles spontaneously. The imitators scored 73 percent hits, while the subjects who made judgments had only 64 percent hits. Thus, it appeared that recognition memory benefited substantially by engaging the motor system.

Results from other conditions in this and other experiments supported this possibility. In one of the other groups, subjects also viewed the same 78 photographs during the study period but we asked them to chew gum. The purpose of this activity was to interfere with spontaneous encoding movements in which the subjects may engage when looking at the face. We wondered if chewing gum would seriously interfere with face recognition memory performance since all the relevant muscles are occupied. It did. This group had only 59 percent hits. And it was not the muscular effort in itself that was responsible for the decrement in recognition memory performance. If the subject is engaged in another form of muscular activity that does not occupy the muscles that are presumably used in encoding faces, the impairment is not quite as great. Thus, some subjects while viewing the photographs during the study period were asked to squeeze a sponge with their nonpreferred hands in the expectation that this activity was equally effortful to chewing gum, but that it would perhaps not interfere with the motor encoding of the faces. If it was effort alone that impaired performance and conflicted with encoding, then it would not matter whether the subject chewed gum or squeezed a sponge. In fact, since chewing gum is generally better practiced than squeezing sponges, the former should constitute a lesser distraction than squeezing sponges. Yet subjects squeezing sponges achieved 65 percent hits, which was no worse than the group making cognitive judgments. Thus, it was not the muscular involvement *per se* that interfered with face recognition memory but a particular motor involvement—namely that which might otherwise help the individual encode and store face information.

CONCLUSIONS

Clearly, only the possibility that the interaction of affect and cognition may be profitably examined at the level of motor representations has been discussed in this paper. A number of significant questions will no doubt arise when actual empirical and theoretical work gets under way. For example, if it is the case that all motor acts are themselves under the control of cognitive programs (e.g., Adams, 1971; Schmidt, 1975), their representational function may turn out to be only indirect and auxiliary.

Even if it is the case that motor acts are under the control of higher-order programs, it is still useful to consider their possible representational and mnestic functions. Consider, as an example, the study of mood effects on face recognition. If it is the case that the musculature stores some information that is useful for the recognition memory of faces, then certain direct predictions follow. It is difficult for a person to smile when depressed. It would be, therefore, more difficult for that person to reproduce and thus to encode a smiling face than a sad face. The encoding during the study phase could actually be monitored by EMG recordings and compared with the muscle potentials emerging at retrieval. If it is discovered that certain general mood states render certain aspects of motor acts inappropriate for representational purposes, and other aspects especially efficient, we will have discovered a realm of representational processes that are observable, measurable, and manipulable. Experiments of this type are now being carried out in our laboratory and their results will tell us something about the representational role of the motor system and the promise of our approach. It is of some value to note, in this respect, that a similar undertaking cannot be contemplated at all for mental representations at this time.

REFERENCES

Adams, J. A. A close-loop theory of motor learning. *Journal of Motor Behavior*, 1971, *3*, 111–150, 411–418.

Anderson, N. H., & Hubert, S. Effects of concomitant verbal recall on order effects in personality impression formation. *Journal of Verbal Learning and Verbal Behavior*, 1963, *2*, 379–391.

Berlyne, D. E. Dimensions of perception of exotic and pre-renaissance paintings. *Canadian Journal of Psychology*, 1975, *29*, 151–173.

Bower, G. H. Mood and memory. *American Psychologist*, 1981, *36*, 129–148.

Cacioppo, J. T., & Petty, R. E. Lateral asymmetry in the expression of cognition and emotion. *Journal of Experimental Psychology: Human Perception and Performance*, 1981, *7*, 333–341.

Cooper, L. G. A multivariate investigation of preferences. *Multivariate Behavior Research*, 1973, *8*, 253–272.

Davidson, R. J. Personal communication, 1981.

Dreben, E. K., Fiske, S. T., & Hastie, R. The independence of evaluative and item information: Impression and recall order effects in behavior-based impression formation. *Journal of Personality and Social Psychology*, 1979, *37*, 1758–1768.

Ekman, P., & Friesen, W. V. *Unmasking the face*. Englewood Cliffs, N. J.: Prentice-Hall, 1975.

Erdelyi, M. H. A new look at the New Look: Perceptual defense and vigilance. *Psychological Review*, 1974, *81*, 1–25.

Garcia, J. & Rusiniak, K. W. What the nose learns from the mouth. In Muller-Schwarze, D. & Silverstein, R. M. (Eds.), *Chemical signals*. New York: Plenum Press, 1980.

Howes, D. H., & Solomon, R. L. A note on McGinnies' "Emotionality and Perceptual Defense". *Psychological Review*, 1950, *57*, 229–234.

Isen, A. M., Shalker, T. E., Clark, M., & Karp, L. Affect, accessibility of material in memory, and behavior: A cognitive loop? *Journal of Personality and Social Psychology*, 1978, *36*, 1–12.

Izard, C. E. *Human emotions*. New York: Plenum, 1977.

Klahr, D. Decision making in a complex environment: The use of similarity judgments to predict preferences. *Management Science*, 1969, *15*, 595–618.

Kleinman, D., & John, E. R. Contradiction of auditory and visual information by brain stimulation. *Science*, 1975, *187*, 271–273.

Kunst-Wilson, W. R., & Zajonc, R. B. Affective discrimination of stimuli that cannot be recognized. *Science*, 1980, *207*, 557–558.

Lazarus, R. S. *Psychological stress and the coping process*. New York: McGraw-Hill, 1966.

Leventhal, H. Toward a comprehensive theory of emotion. In L. Berkowitz (Ed.), *Advances in experimental social psychology*, 1980, *13*, 139–207.

Littman, & Manning, H. M. A methodological study of cigarette brand discrimination. *Journal of Applied Psychology*, 1954, *38*, 185–190.

Mandler, G. *Mind and emotion*. New York: Wiley, 1975.

Mandler, G. Personal communication, 1981.

Mandler, G. The structure of value: Accounting for taste. In M. S. Clark and S. T. Fiske (Eds.), *Cognition and affect*, New York: Academic Press, 1982.

Matlin, M. W. Response competition, recognition, and affect. *Journal of Personality and Social Psychology*, 1971, *19*, 295–300.

McGinnies, E. Emotionality and perceptual defense. *Psychological Review*, 1949, *56*, 244–251.

Moreland, R. L., & Zajonc, R. B. Is stimulus recognition a necessary condition for the occurrence of exposure effects? *Journal of Personality and Social Psychology*, 1977, *35*, 191–199.

Moreland, R. L., & Zajonc, R. B. Exposure effects may not depend on stimulus recognition. *Journal of Personality and Social Psychology*, 1979, *37*, 1085–1089.

Nakashima, T. Contribution to the study of the affective processes. *American Journal of Psychology*, 1909, *20*, 157–193.

O'Hare, D. Individual differences in perceived similarity and preference for visual art: A multidimensional scaling analysis. *Perception and Psychophysics*, 1976, *20*, 445–452.

Pearson, K. *The life and labours of Francis Galton*. Cambridge: Cambridge University Press, 1924.

Phillips, R. J., & Rawles, R. E. Recognition of upright and inverted faces: A correlational study. *Perception*, 1979, *8*, 577–583.

Pietromonaco, P., Zajonc, R. B., & Bargh, J. The role of motor cues in recognition memory for faces. A paper presented at the Annual Convention of the American Psychological Association, Los Angeles, 1981.

Posner, M. I., & Synder, C. R. R. Facilitation and inhibition in the processing of signals. In P. M. A. Rabbitt & S. Dornic (Eds.), *Attention and performance V*. New York: Academic Press, 1975.

Premack, D., & Kintsch, W. Personal communication, 1979.

Ross, E. D., & Mesulam, M. M. Dominant language functions of the *right* hemisphere: Prosody and emotional gesturing. *Archives of Neurology*, 1979, *36*, 144–148.

Schachter, S., & Singer, J. Cognitive, social, and physiological determinants of emotional state. *Psychological Review*, 1962, *65*, 379–399.

Schmidt, R. A. A schema theory of discrete motor skill learning. *Psychological Review*, 1975, *82*, 225–260.

Schwartz, G. E., Davidson, R. J., & Maer, F. Right hemisphere lateralization for emotion in the human brain: Interactions with cognition. *Science*, 1975, *190*, 286–288.

Seamon, J. G., Brody, N., & Kauff, D. M. Feeling and thinking: Tests of a model of independent processing of affect and cognition (unpublished manuscript).

Suberi, M., & McKeever, W. F. Differential right hemispheric memory storage of emotional and non-emotional faces. *Neuropsychologia*, 1977, *15*, 757–768.

Tomkins, S. S. *Affect, imagery, consciousness,* Vol. I. New York: Springer, 1962.

Tomkins, S. S. *Affect, imagery, consciousness,* Vol. II. New York: Springer, 1963.

Wilson, W. R. Feeling more than we can know: Exposure effects without learning. *Journal of Personality and Social Psychology,* 1979, *37,* 811–821.

Zajonc, R. B. Response suppression in perceptual defense. *Journal of Experimental Psychology,* 1962, *64,* 206–214.

Zajonc, R. B. Attitudinal effects of mere exposure. *Journal of Personality and Social Psychology Monographs,* 1968, *9,* 1–28.

Zajonc, R. B. Feeling and thinking: Preferences need no inferences. *American Psychologist,* 1980, *35,* 151–175.

Zajonc, R. B., & Markus, H. Affect and cognition: The hard interface. Unpublished manuscript, 1982.

10 Comments on Emotion and Cognition: Can there be a Working Relationship?

C. E. Izard
University of Delaware

My charge from the editors was to prepare comments on the chapters of Leventhal, Scheier and Carver, Weiner, and Zajonc. Although these chapters are rich in ideas and empirical data and provide quite sufficient challenge, I wish to make a few general comments.

Because I have spent most of the past 20 years in the study of emotions, this symposium on affect and congnition is of special interest to me. It has to be judged as very timely, a front-runner in a rapidly changing intellectual climate. The topic of the symposium is on an important frontier of the *cognitive sciences,* and that is precisely what makes it extraordinary. (Seventeen years ago, when a different attitude toward emotions prevailed in experimental psychology, a symposium and volume with a very similar title [Tomkins & Izard, 1965] attracted far less attention that I expect for this one.)

There have been similar efforts in psychology, at least some efforts with similar goals, but none of the previous ones were spawned within mainstream experimental psychology, where cognitive models have dominated for almost two decades. Even the emotion theory that penetrated the mainstream was a cognitive model (Schachter & Singer, 1962), but there have been recent failures to replicate the original Schachter–Singer experiment (Marshall & Zimbardo, 1979; Maslach, 1979). The previous symposia on this topic were organized by emotion theorists, and their theory and research remained pretty much on the edge of things until a few years ago. And judging from what was said at this symposium, cognitive and social psychology are still not very well-meshed with the substantial theory and research that belongs mainly to the emotion domain (Ekman, Friesen, & Ellsworth, 1962; Izard, 1971, 1977; Plutchik, 1962, 1980; Tomkins, 1962, 1963). Several events testify to the timeliness of this symposium. Three subdisciplines in the behavioral sciences have engaged emotion theory and produced significant research: developmental psychology (Campos & Stenberg, 1980; Emde, Gaensbauer, & Harmon, 1976; Haviland, 1976; Hoffman, 1980, 1981; Izard, 1978, 1981; Lewis & Rosenblum, 1978; Malatesta, 1980), psychophysiology (Davidson, 1980; Fridlund & Izard, 1982; Schwartz, 1981), and neuropsychology (Tucker, 1981). The Social Science Research Council Committee on social and emotional development has discussed the interface of emotion and cognition frequently over the past 5 years and have a volume on the topic in process. The neurosciences have also made numerous contributions to the understanding of affect and cognition, but these have been rooted mainly in theories of the neural substrates of behavior (MacLean, 1972; Nauta & Domesick, 1978; Papez, 1937).

The 17th Carnegie Symposium on Cognition reflects the considerable involvement of a dozen distinguished cognitive and social psychologists with the topic of emotion. As this volume clearly shows, they have produced some interesting ideas and data, but the research reported in some of the chapters failed to define or measure discrete affective phenomena. In some cases affect was assumed to be the result of an experimental manipulation, without any check on the efficacy or particular meaning of the manipulation. Even in some of the chapters where affect was treated in terms of specific emotions, sometimes as independent variables and sometimes as dependent ones, it was difficult to discern much that enhances the psychology of emotions. We need to continue to advance our knowledge of emotions qua emotions in order to fully understand emotion–cognition interactions.

It is not my intent here to take away from the organizers and contributors of this symposium. On the contrary. I see them as the wave of the future in mainstream psychology. I present these introductory remarks as a friendly challenge to experimental cognitive and social psychologists to join forces with emotion theorists and researchers in the formidable task of operationally defining and measuring discrete emotion constructs so we can better understand the relationships of emotion and cognition. Emotion theorists have sensed the need for this intellectual exchange and collaboration for a long time.

Experimental cognitive and social psychology have sufficient brainpower and person power to subsume emotions and to study emotion–cognition relationships on their own terms with neglect or only passing notice of the developments that have occurred in emotion theory and research especially during the past dozen years. The advances in the cross-cultural, developmental, neurophysiological, and psychophysiological domains are particularly noteworthy (for a summary, see Izard & Saxton, in press). Neglect of these contributions may well hasten the day when we shall need yet another focus or paradigm shift for experimental psychology; careful attention to them should facilitate much needed progress in intellectual exchange among subdisciplines in psychology.

On the Conceptualization of Emotion: Comments on Leventhal's Chapter

It is generally agreed that emotion has three components—neurophysiological, motor-expressive, and what we variously term the subjective experiential, phenomenological, or conscious process. Emotion–cognition interaction can occur in relation to any or all of these components. More on this later.

Cognitive theorists generally think of the neurophysiological component as autonomic arousal. I think of it as activity of the somatic nervous system, including the limbic system and neocortex. These polar opposite views (see Izard, 1977; Mandler, 1975) have not been the source of much of our discussion at this symposium. This is a little less true of our less-varied views of the motor-expressive component.

Most of our deliberations have centered around the third or experiential component of emotion. Leventhal has said that this third component is *meaning* and that each emotion is a form of meaning. This is intuitively appealing to me, perhaps because it differs only in one way from my own view. My own view is that the third component of emotion is a form of *feeling*. It seems an easy step to go from joy-feeling or sadness-feeling to joy-meaning or sadness-meaning. But this difference in conceptualization may be important, for Levanthal can reason that emotion as meaning changes with human development from infancy through old age, and I argue that emotion–feeling is invariant over the life-span.

The *feeling* component of joy in the infant is the same as that in the aged person. What changes is the network of images and memories and anticipations that come to be associated with our emotion–feelings. The bonds between emotion–feelings and cognitions are what I have called affective–cognitive structures, and these, I believe, can be considered as forms of meaning, as well as forms of values and aspirations, which do develop and change over time. I think that Mandler's constructionist view of emotion is really about affective–cognitive structures, not about emotion per se or emotion–feeling. The cognitive-constructivist views of emotion do not deal with emotion as feeling or quality of consciousness. Although Leventhal's theory is not a strictly constructionist one, his concept of emotion as meaning leans toward constructivism and away from the concept of emotion–feeling as a distinct state or process in consciousness. And to fail to come to grips with the emotion state or feeling and its motivational impact on consciousness is to overlook the key process or mechanism in the mediation of emotion–cognition interactions.

In his hierarchical model of emotion activation Leventhal postulates an expressive-motor mechanism for generating primary emotion experience and behavior. I think this makes good sense in an evolutionary-developmental perspective (Izard, 1977), but Plutchik takes an evolutionary stance and argues that cognition is a necessary prerequisite to emotion.

Leventhal goes further than most investigators of emotion–cognition relationships by postulating mechanisms that mediate the relating. He suggests that
emotion is attached more swiftly and permanently to sensory and perceptual
processes than to abstract cognition. This seems quite reasonable in relation to
his model of emotion activation and that of differential emotions theory (Izard,
1977), both of which view sensory processes as fundamental to the generation of
emotion. It might well be that a measure of level of abstraction will index the
intensity of affect in an affective-cognitive structure.

Leventhal's research on pain and illness is quite provocative. The finding that
the monitoring of sensation reduces the subjective experience of pain is a very
neat one. It is an excellent example of how *interest* in and attention to sensory
data can regulate, in this case attenuate, the affective-feeling output of the central
nervous system. This amounts to using one emotion, interest, and one type of
cognitive process, attention focusing, to control or regulate another affect, pain.

Self-Attention and Shame: Comments on Scheier and Carver's Chapter

Scheier and Carver have explicated what should prove to be a useful theoretical
framework, and they have supported their reasoning with a number of empirical
studies. Most of my comments about their chapter make more sense if I first
suggest one additional concept for their theoretical framework. As you might
expect, it is an emotion concept. Acceptance of this concept into their framework
will not change their very nice empirical results, but it may change their way of
interpreting them. It may also open up new avenues for further research, particularly if they should become interested in examining the meaning and significance
of the new concept and its interaction with others already in their framework.

The additional concept that Scheier and Carver might want to consider is that
of shame. A number of emotion theorists, beginning with Darwin (1872; Izard,
1977; Lewis, 1971; Tomkins, 1963), have thought for a long time that heightened self-awareness or self-consciousness is phenomenologically central in
shame. I was very puzzled on reading Duval and Wicklund (1972) and finding
that nowhere in their volume did they mention shame, despite the fact that I was
thoroughly convinced that they had done a pretty nice job of defining it operationally and manipulating it in their experiments. I feel a bit the same way about
Scheier and Carver's work. I believe that they have gone a step beyond Duval
and Wicklund, in that they have made use of both individual-difference measures
and experimental manipulations in order to assess the effects of self-directed
attention.

I am not suggesting that all self-attention activates shame. Scheier and Carver
(1981) have made a distinction between public self-consciousness and private
self-consciousness, and public self-consciousness seems to be a more important
antecedent of shame than private self-consciousness. However, it sets the stage

for shame and I suspect that in their high-fear subjects the fear may have amplified the self-attention, thus inducing shame; and a shame–fear interaction can have a powerful effect on behavior.

I have a few running comments on Scheier and Carver's theoretical statement. I agree with them on their assessment of valuation as a process that shares properties or dimensions with affect. I would go a step further and say that there is no valuation without affect, and that what cognitive theorists generally speak of as appraisal is itself an affective–cognitive process.

I think they are correct in adopting a cybernetic perspective and in utilizing the concept of feedback systems in dealing with affect and in relating affect and cognition. For some time I have felt that an adequate conceptualization of the person requires postulating a grand set of quasiindependent but interrelated feedback and feedforward loops. I also think that their theorizing is enriched by their use of expectancy constructs and by their assumptions about expectancy, which, like anticipation and valuation, is not affectless.

It is reasonable to take the stand that a strong affect can result in the interruption of behavior. I prefer, however, to think of behavior as continually influenced by affect, and that the intensification of ongoing affect or the emergence of a different and strong affect results not simply in interruption of ongoing behavior but in the organization of new behaviors. Another way of saying this is that a change in affect state reorganizes and redirects behavior and mobilizes the energy to sustain it.

I like Scheier and Carver's thinking about affect impinging upon and influencing the course of self-regulatory processes and, in turn, their assumption that self-regulatory processes induce affect. This is a good example of thinking in terms of feedback and feedforward loops.

Regarding their research, I am very pleased to learn about the operational definition and successful measurement of independent factors of private self-consciousness and public self-consciousness. In my view, both probably relate to shame or shyness but on the surface public self-consciousness, concern with how others are viewing and reacting to the self, is probably more closely related to shame. Their finding that self-directed attention enhances the tendency to conform to salient behavioral standards is exactly the effect that differential emotions theory predicts for induced shame. Further, the tendency of high-self-aware people to withdraw more quickly from a feared object is what differential emotions theory predicts as a result of the interaction in consciousness of shame and fear. And their finding that in a high-fear condition highly self-conscious subjects reported significantly more distress than did the less-self-conscious subjects is also consistent with the dynamics of a shame/fear interaction. Fear is a highly toxic emotion and shame a painfully intolerable one.

Finally, I found Scheier and Carver's comments on the facial movements of emotions highly intriguing and would like to hear them elaborate a bit further on this so that I can understand it better. I can certainly agree with the notion that these facial movements (as in emotion expressions) and the regulation of them connects with the hierarchy of behavioral control that they have described.

Emotions Affect Attributions: Comments on Weiner's Chapter

Weiner's basic premise that causal attributions are sufficient antecedents for the activation of emotions appears quite reasonable and intuitively appealing. Any of us can think of numerous instances where we attributed to ourselves some inadequacy and felt shame, or an inability to cope with a threatening situation and felt fear. According to Weiner and the "guiding principle of attribution theory," we make these attributions and experience the consequent emotions because individuals search for understanding, seek to discover why an event has occurred.

Two principles of differential emotions theory suggest that this model of cognition–emotion relationships is quite correct at one level of analysis, but incomplete when viewed from another perspective. Differential emotions theory postulates that emotion is present in consciousness continually. Thus attributional processes are caused or at least affected by ongoing emotion processes. It follows that attributional search is always biased or influenced in some way by affect or emotion. In this conceptual framework, attributional search would be expected to be most objective when the dominant emotion in consciousness is that of interest, and particularly when the interest is directed toward discovery rather than toward the confirmation of an hypothesis rooted in a personal belief system or set of values. I recognize that interest in discovery uninfluenced by personal beliefs and values represents an ideal that may be realized rarely by the individual.

The presence of other emotions in consciousness, whether joy or sadness, anger or fear, will bias or influence the attributional search in specific ways according to the motivational/experiential properties of the dominant emotion. Thus in the sorrow and shame of defeat, a search for the causes of the defeat of one's self or one's own team will likely produce quite different attributions than would the analysis of the same performances by a "disinterested" expert.

Weiner has made an insightful analysis of the dimensions of causality within the framework of attribution theory. An understanding of these dimensions seems to facilitate the prediction of causal ascriptions and the role of particular classes of causal attributions in the activation of specific emotions.

Weiner's discussion of hypothesized dimension–emotion relationships articulates a number of relationships between particular attributions and the subsequent elicitation of specific emotions. I think this is one of the finer heuristics to emerge in social psychology in the past few years. He discusses a number of empirical studies that support these hypothesized relationships. If I understand him correctly, however, the support is in terms of mean responses of subject groups. I think a question of considerable importance for students of emotion-

–cognition relationships is that of individual differences in the likelihood that attribution of a positive outcome to the self will indeed activate positive self-esteem, pride, and joy. Recalling the differential emotions theory postulate that ongoing emotion influences all cognitive processes, including attribution, one might hypothesize that the individual who carried a sad mood into the experimental situation may discount the magnitude or significance of the positive outcome to the self and may experience less or none of the positive emotions reflected in a group mean. The work of Beck (1967) and Kovacs and Beck (1979) and their colleagues have demonstrated that depressives are experts at perceiving a neutral or even a positive event as negative.

A similar argument can be made with respect to the question as to whether anger is experienced following an attribution for a negative self-related outcome to factors controllable by others. Thus whether Student A is angered when prevented from studying by Student B (the noisy roommate) may depend on whether A was studying because of intense interest in the subject, for fear of failure, or with disgust for the reading matter and contempt of his instructor for assigning it to him. The point is that attributions are never unbiased. We find regularity and uniformity in attributional statements when we average across individuals and in effect average out individual differences. I am not trying to detract from the important contributions of attribution theory and research. I am raising a question as to whether this theory and research can be extended by considering the influences of ongoing or prior needs or emotion states. I understand that Weiner now has studies under way that should help answer this question. Attention to individual differences in emotion states in such studies might prove rewarding.

Separate Theories and Separate Systems: Comments on Zajonc's Chapter

I feel I should comment on Zajonc's classification of emotion theories. He placed emotion theories into two broad categories and correctly recognized that the two classes were not entirely independent. His distinction between cognitive theories of emotion and somatic theories of emotion has heuristic value. It quickly draws attention to the fact that there are divergent views regarding the generation of emotion. The traditional cognitive theory of emotion, first articulated in contemporary psychology by Magda Arnold (1960), holds that some kind of perceptual–cognitive process is a necessary prerequisite to emotion. Since then, Lazarus (1968), Mandler (1975), Plutchik (1980), and others have elaborated this view, but in my opinion, none have come so close as Magda Arnold to describing the antecedent appraisal process in such a way as to make it almost compatible with somatic theory. She (Arnold, 1960) characterized the appraisal or antecedent cognitive process as a kind of: "sense judgment" . . . direct, immediate, intuitive, nonreflective [p. 175]. This is pretty close to the somatic theory position that holds that efferent feedback from voluntary muscles (mainly of the face) can lead to emotion without cognition; that is, it is without cognition if cognition is something more than sensory feedback and the cortical–limbic interactions that integrate it. In contrast, Lazarus (Lazarus, Kanner, & Folkman, 1980) describes the cognitive antecedents of emotion as involving: ''learning, memory, perception and thought [p. 192]'' and Plutchik's (1980) model of cognitive emotional functioning involves short- and long-term memory, evaluation, and prediction. In my laboratory we have observed discrete emotion expressions in infants long before we can show that they have anything like short- or long-term memory (Izard, Huebner, Risser, McGinnes, & Dougherty, 1980). There is some evidence that by 10 weeks infants can recognize some aspects of a previously exposed unusual event or stimulus situation, but they do not show object permanence (short-term memory of an object) until about 8 months of age (Kagan, 1978). Thus whatever evaluative process young infants perform prior to their free and frequent expressions of emotions is without much help from Mnemosyne.

In distinguishing between cognitive and somatic theories of emotion, Zajonc suggests that the latter is relatively less concerned with emotion experience. He recognizes that the two types of theory are not dichotomous in this respect, but I would go further and emphasize that somatic theories, at least differential emotions theory, is very much concerned with emotion experience. In fact, this theory defines subjective experience or feeling as one of the three essential components of emotion—the other two being the neurophysiological and motor expressive. In contrasting the two classes of theory, the distinction that I think is much more important is that between emotion–feeling, the experiential component of emotion, and cognition.

Some cognitive theories consider the subjective experience as the ''cognitive'' component of emotion. In contrast, differential emotions theory holds that the third component of emotion is a feeling state or process that can and frequently does exist completely independent of cognition. I like to view the feeling component of emotion in the same way as Suzanne Langer (1967) and Edmund Sinnott (1966), as a phase of the neurophysiological process. It is only when we make this distinction between feeling or emotion-state-in-consciousness on the one hand, and cognition in relation to or about that feeling on the other, that we can concern ourselves productively with the relationship between affect and cognition.

To emphasize this point, crucial to differential emotions theory, let me put it another way. We can have emotion–feeling, meaning that we have awareness of the feeling and thus a particular process in consciousness, without any kind of reflective or symbolic process. Thus we can have awareness of emotion–feeling merely as a function of the neurophysiological processes of emotion, that is, feeling as a phase of the activity of the underlying neural substrates. The process by which neurochemical processes lead to feeling is automatic. If the feeling is gated out or blocked in some way, we do not have emotion because there is no third component . . . we have undifferentiated activation (or arousal in its broader sense) instead.

It is critical for differential emotions theory that we recognize that emotion-–feeling can exist in consciousness at different levels of awareness. At the lowest level of awareness, we are barely conscious of the feeling and may have considerable difficulty articulating it even upon reflection. It is this low-level, unarticulated awareness of feeling that gives rise to the notion of unconscious motivation, for no matter how low the level of awareness, emotion–feeling remains motivational. At the highest level of awareness, the feeling dominates consciousness and we can readily cognize it—symbolize it, ponder it, or try to nurture, attenuate, or suppress it. In these latter processes, the emotion-related cognition can be very important.

One potentially important fallout from Zajonc's classification of emotion theories is that it can draw attention to differences between the two types of theory in their attitude toward the autonomic nervous system. As suggested by the title given to it, somatic theory postulates that the neural substrates of emotion lie within the somatic nervous system. In contrast, the cognitive theories typically view the autonomic nervous system as the neural basis of emotion. Somatic theories see the autonomic nervous system as typically involved in emotion, but as a consequence rather than as an antecedent. Somatic theory considers the autonomic nervous system as an auxiliary system, frequently playing a role in organizing and sustaining coping activities motivated by emotion. (For detailed argument on this issue, see Izard, 1977 and Mandler, 1975.)

Looking Beyond the Arousal–Cognition Model

The arousal-plus-cognition model of emotion activation seems to have been prevalent during much of this symposium as well as during the past 19 years. And I think if there is a place where we need a paradigm shift, this is it, particularly if we are to advance the study of affective–cognitive interaction. There are several serious problems with the postulate that emotion depends on the autonomic nervous system (ANS) and with the arousal-cognition model of emotion.

1. The arousal-cognition model seems to assume that the ANS contains all the neural tissue that relates to emotion. This is very strange in view of the vast body of research linking mechanisms in the limbic lobe and frontal cortex with emotion, and not just linking limbic structures with emotion in general but particular mechanisms with particular emotions. Cognitive theories of emotion generally ignore the various types of cortical arousal that may be orthogonal or inversely related to indexes of ANS arousal.

2. There are no data showing a causal link between autonomic arousal and emotion. There is much data showing correlation or concomitance between various indexes of emotions and ANS arousal. So ANS functions may often be

used to obtain convergent data on emotion, but an index of one or more of the three components of emotion is necessary additional data.

3. The causes of ANS arousal vary widely—from startle to exercise; but I'd like to suggest that the most important determinant of ANS arousal is emotion. So rather than viewing such arousal as an antecedent of emotion, I view it the other way around—ANS arousal is a consequent of emotion, and of other things that require energy mobilization.

4. The arousal-cognition model seems to assume that arousal follows directly from some set of events, which must be subsequently evaluated before there is emotion. The assumption that was very widely held from 1962 to 1979 was that the evaluative process or search for explanation of the arousal was neutral or unbiased. The work of Marshall and Zimbardo (1979) and Maslach (1979) indicates that unexplained arousal leads to a negatively biased search or evaluation.

5. The arousal-cognition model assumes that there is no affect without appraisal, evaluation, or some symbolic process. No evaluative or symbolic process is required for sensing pain or sexual pleasure, or for sensing joy or sadness, anger or fear.

Let me return once more to the all important point concerning the nature of the third component of emotion. Zajonc correctly noted that the representation of affect is generally believed to be in terms of mental structures erected by the cognitive system from images, propositions, etc. I contend that emotion is represented in terms of mental structures only if we conceive of feeling as a mental structure. But these mental structures or feelings are erected by the activities of the neural substrates of emotion. These neural activities are frequently triggered by the cognitive system—by images and anticipations—but they may also arise independently of these latter processes.

REFERENCES

Arnold, M. B. Emotion and personality (Vol. I). *Psychological aspects*. New York: Columbia University Press, 1960.

Beck, A. T. *Depression*. New York: Harper & Row, 1967.

Campos, J., & Stenberg, C. R. Perception, appraisal and emotion: The onset of social referencing. In M. Lamb & L. Sherrod (Eds.), *Infant social cognition*. Hillsdale, N.J.: Lawrence Erlbaum Associates, 1980.

Darwin, C. R. *The expression of emotions in man and animals*. London: John Murray, 1872.

Davidson, R. J. Consciousness and information processing: A biocognitive perspective. In J. M. Davidson & R. J. Davidson (Eds.), *The psychobiology of consciousness*. New York: Plenum Press, 1980.

Duval, S., & Wicklund, R. A. *A theory of objective self-awareness*. New York: Academic Press, 1972.

Ekman, P., Friesen, W. V., & Ellsworth, P. *Emotion in the human face: Guidelines for research and an integration of findings*. New York: Pergamon Press, 1972.

Emde, R. N., Gaensbauer, T. J., & Harmon, R. J. *Emotional expression in infancy*. New York: International Universities Press, 1976.

Fridlund, A. J., & Izard, C. E. Electromyographic studies of facial expressions of emotion and patterns of emotions. In J. T. Cacioppo (Ed.), *Social psychophysiology*, New York: Guilford Press, in press (1982).

Haviland, J. Looking smart: The relationship between affect and intelligence in infancy. In M. Lewis (Ed.), *Origins of intelligence*. New York: Plenum Press, 1976.

Hoffman, M. L. *Social and emotional development in children*. Paper commissioned by the Social Science Research Council for the National Science Foundation's second Five Year Outlook on Science and Technology, 1980.

Hoffman, M. L. The measurement of empathy. In C. E. Izard (Ed.), *Measuring emotions in infants and children*. New York: Cambridge University Press, 1982.

Izard, C. E. *The face of emotion*. New York: Appleton–Century–Crofts, 1971.

Izard, C. E. *Human emotions*. New York: Plenum Press, 1977.

Izard, C. E. On the development of emotions and emotion–cognition relationships in infancy. In M. Lewis & L. A. Rosenblum (Eds.), *The development of affect*. New York: Plenum Press, 1978.

Izard, C. E. An introduction to measuring emotions in human development. In C. E. Izard (Ed.), *Measuring emotions in infants and children*. New York: Cambridge University Press, 1981.

Izard, C. E. & Saxton, P. Emotions. In preparation for the revision of *Steven's handbook of experimental psychology,* in press.

Izard, C. E., Huebner, R. R., Risser, D., McGinnes, G. C., & Dougherty, L. M. The young infant's ability to produce discrete emotion expressions. *Developmental Psychology,* 1980, *16*(2), 132–140.

Kagan, J. On emotion and its development: A working paper. In M. Lewis & L. Rosenblum (Eds.), *Origins of behavior: Affective development*. New York: Plenum Press, 1978.

Kovacs, M., & Beck, A. T. Cognitive–affective processes in depression. In C. E. Izard (Ed.), *Emotions in personality and psychopathology*. New York: Plenum Press, 1979.

Langer, S. K. *Mind: An essay on human feeling* (Vol. 1). Baltimore, Md.: Johns Hopkins University Press, 1967.

Lazarus, R. S. Emotions and adaptation: Conceptual and empirical relations. In W. Arnold (Ed.), *Nebraska Symposium on Motivation*. Lincoln: University of Nebraska Press, 1968.

Lazarus, R. S., Kanner, A. D., & Folkman, S. Emotions: A cognitive-phenomenological analysis. In R. Plutchik & H. Kellerman (Eds.), *Emotion: Theory, research, and experience*. New York: Academic Press, 1980.

Lewis, H. *Shame and guilt in neurosis*. New York: International Universities Press, 1971.

Lewis, M., & Rosenblum, L. A. (Eds.). *The development of affect*. New York: Plenum Press, 1978.

MacLean, P. D. Implications of microelectrode findings on exteroceptive inputs to the limbic cortex. In C. H. Hockman (Ed.), *Limbic system mechanisms and autonomic function*. Springfield, Ill.: Charles C. Thomas, 1972.

Malatesta, C. Z. *Determinants of infant affect socialization: Age, sex of infant and maternal emotional traits*. Doctoral Dissertation, Rutgers University, 1980.

Mandler, G. *Mind and emotions*. New York: Wiley, 1975.

Marshall, G. D., & Zimbardo, P. G. Affective consequences of inadequately explained physiological arousal. *Journal of Personality and Social Psychology,* 1979, *37*(6), 970–988.

Maslach, C. Negative emotional biasing of unexplained arousal. *Journal of Personality and Social Psychology,* 1979, *37*(6) 953–969.

Nauta, W. J. H., & Domesick, V. B. Crossroads of limbic and striatal circuitry: Hypothalamo–nigral connections. In K. E. Livingston & O. Hornykiewicz (Eds.), *Limbic mechanisms*. New York: Plenum Press, 1978.

Papez, J. W. A proposed mechanism of emotion. *Archives of Neurology and Psychiatry,* 1937, *38,* 725–743.

Plutchik, R. *The emotions: Facts, theories, and a new model*. New York: Random House, 1962.

Plutchik, R. *Emotion: A psychoevolutionary synthesis.* New York: Harper & Row, 1980.

Schachter, S., & Singer, J. E. Cognitive, social, and physiological determinants of emotional states. *Psychological Reivew,* 1962, *69*(5), 379–399.

Scheier, M., & Carver, C. Public and private aspects of self. *Review of personaity and social psychology* (Vol. II), Beverly Hills, Calif.: Sage, 1981.

Schwartz, G. Psychophysiological patterning and emotion revisited: A systems perspective. In C. E. Izard (Ed.), *Measuring emotions in infants and children.* New York: Cambridge University Press, 1981.

Sinnott, E. W. *The bridge of life.* New York: Simon & Shuster, 1966.

Tomkins, S. S. *Affect, imagery, and consciousness* (Vol. 1). *The positive affects.* New York: Springer, 1962.

Tomkins, S. S. *Affect, imagery, and consciousness* (Vol. 2). *The negative affects.* New York: Springer, 1963.

Tomkins, S. S., & Izard, C. E. *Affect, cognition, and personality.* New York: Springer, 1965.

Tucker, D. M. Lateral brain function, emotion and conceptualization. *Psychological Bulletin,* 1981, *89*(1), 19–46.

III AFFECTIVE UNDERPINNINGS OF COGNITION

11 Some Factors Influencing Decision-Making Strategy and Risk Taking

Alice M. Isen
Barbara Means
Robert Patrick
Gary Nowicki
University of Maryland

Background

The work to be discussed here deals with the impact of a positive feeling state on the way in which a person goes about making a decision and on the way in which the person responds to risk. This work evolved out of research on the influence of positive affect on social interaction, particularly altruistic or helping behavior. From the earliest, studies that had found that positive affect led to increased helping also expressed concern with understanding the processes underlying this relationship—understanding why and by what means feeling good oneself should lead one to be more generous and helpful to others (e.g., Berkowitz, 1972; Isen, 1970; Isen & Levin, 1972). Using a formulation compatible with that of other work in the area, which had conceptualized helping in emergencies as the product of a decision-making process (Darley & Latané, 1970; Piliavin, Rodin, & Piliavin, 1969), one of these papers suggested that positive affect might have its observed impact on social behavior by influencing this decision-making process (Isen & Levin, 1972). Thus, interest in the processes by which happiness leads to helping produced studies of the influence of affect on decision making and other cognitive processes.

More specifically, in a series of studies it was proposed that positive affect can serve as a retrieval cue for positive material in memory, influencing what comes to mind and thus influencing decision making or judgment (Isen, 1975; Isen & Shalker, 1982; Isen, Shalker, Clark, & Karp, 1978). It has been suggested in another context by Tversky and Kahneman (1973, 1974), that ideas that come to mind first or most easily may influence judgment. Likewise, it may be in this way, through the content of what becomes accessible and comes to mind when one is in the process of weighing the alternatives and deciding on a course of action, that positive feelings can influence the decision to engage in various behaviors.

Before describing our current investigations, we wish to point out three things about the kind of affect state studied in this research. First, we have dealt with low-level "everyday" feeling states, rather than with the relatively intense, dramatic states of emotion written about by others in the field. It is well known that the latter can interrupt and influence behavior, but growing evidence indicates that even the former, low-level general feeling states, are potentially quite influential in directing thought and influencing both social behavior and task performance or problem-solving strategy. Because these states are relatively subtle, and because (being mild or induced by small things) they may occur frequently, the effects that they have on social interaction and cognitive processes may be quite pervasive.

Second, the research we have conducted to date has concentrated on positive feeling states, rather than negative states such as anxiety or anger. Most of the earlier literature addressing the influence of feelings or emotional states on social behavior or intellectual performance has focused primarily on unpleasant states. For example, there are large bodies of work on the influence of frustration or anger on aggression and on the relationship between anxiety and performance. There has also been considerable research on sadness or depression. We have sometimes included negative affect manipulations in our studies, but our primary focus has been on discovering what happens to people's thought processes and social interactions when they feel good. Although we understand the importance of work on negative affect, ever optimistic about the nature of people's most usual feeling states, we believe that work on the effects of positive states will also advance our knowledge in important ways.

Third, it is important to point out that the earlier research has demonstrated that the kind of state we are talking about—an affective state sufficient to influence social behavior and cognitive processes—can be induced by surprisingly small things. As the old saying goes, "it is the little things" in life that make a difference; and our research certainly does not contradict that old saying. We usually arrange for our positive-affect subjects to experience some small success, happiness, gain, or pleasure, and we have found that this can influence their social behavior and certain cognitive processes. For example, it has been shown that finding a dime in the coin return of a public telephone, receiving a free-sample note pad, nail clipper, or package of stationery (valued at about $.29) from a manufacturer's representative, receiving a cookie, winning a game, or hearing positive feedback as to performance on a task of perceptual-motor skills, can lead to increased helping and sociability on the part of positive-affect subjects (e.g., Isen, 1970; Isen & Levin, 1972).

One may ask whether we are sure that these manipulations induced affect, and induced the particular affective state intended by us. The answer, based on these studies in the aggregate, is that we believe so. Because it is not possible to measure internal state directly, we have had to rely on indirect methods to determine that affective state was varied as intended (even a "mood checklist" is an indirect indicator). But we have used a variety of indirect methods—indeed every one that we could think of—to verify the accuracy of our affect inductions, and we believe that we can speak of having induced positive affective states in this research. In various studies we have included "manipulation checks" on the affective state induced—subjects' ratings of their moods or ratings of ambiguous neutral material (e.g., Forest, Clark, Mills, & Isen, 1979; Isen & Nowicki, 1981; Isen & Shalker, 1982). More importantly, however (because one can't be sure about the correspondence between "mood ratings" and feelings), in the studies taken as a group we have triangulated on the concept of affect experimentally by using multiple and divergent methods of mood-induction and noting their convergence as we observed their expected effects on dependent measures of interest. We have also provided for discriminant validation in some studies (Isen & Levin, 1972; Isen & Simmonds, 1978), thereby obtaining further conceptual validation of our hypotheses. We believe that ultimately the greatest strength in arguing for the validity of any manipulation or observed effect arises from this kind of conceptual validation. (See Campbell & Fiske, 1959; Garner, 1954; Garner, Hake, & Eriksen, 1956, for discussion of this and related issues.)

This convergent and discriminant validation has also enabled us, in many cases, to rule out potential alternative interpretations of our findings. Not only does it help to establish that affect was manipulated, as intended, but it also makes less plausible the possibility that the observed effect of feelings in any given case was attributable to extraneous side effects of the particular way in which feelings were induced in that particular case (i.e., that something *in addition* to affect was induced and caused the observed effect).

In addition, we have conducted our research as naturalistically as possible, in an attempt to reduce the potential for alternative influences such as "experimenter demand" or other experimental artifact. Many of the studies described above were carried out in shopping malls, libraries, railroad stations, and street corners, using subjects who did not know that they were subjects in an experiment. This, too, has added to our confidence in the validity of this program of research. All of this in the aggregate leads us to believe that it is affect that has been influenced by our small manipulations and that has produced the observed effects on social behavior.

As noted previously, it has also been found that such manipulations can influence subjects' cognitive processes, such as those involved in memory and judgment. For example, in a study conducted in a shopping mall, people who were unaware that they were subjects in an experiment were approached and given a small free-sample note pad or nail clipper (Isen, et al, 1978). Subsequently, when these subjects encountered a different person taking a consumer-opinion survey and participated in that survey, they evaluated the performance and service records of their major consumer products more positively than did a control group that had not been given the free sample.

Likewise, in several studies, using various means of affect induction, it has been found that positive affect can serve as a retrieval cue for positive material in memory, influencing the subset of material recalled from a memorized list or the speed of recall of a given type of material (Isen et al., 1978; Teasdale & Fogarty, 1979). Positive material seems to be more accessible to people who are feeling good.

Positive Affect and Decision-making Strategy

Now, we turn to the matter that is the primary focus of this chapter—the influence of positive affect on decision-making strategy and risk taking. In addition to the effect described earlier, that of an influence of feelings on cognition and behavior through *content*—that is, through what comes to mind as a function of the feelings being experienced—we now propose that positive affect influences the decision-making *process* itself (the strategies, motivations, and/or criteria influential in making a decision). What we wish to present is a framework (that is, the suggestion that affect may influence cognitive processes and strategies themselves), some general hypotheses, and some preliminary findings that are part of a larger ongoing program of research exploring the influence of positive affect on the processes of decision making and problem solving. As there is relatively little experimental work on this issue at present, our suggestions for particular interpretations of these findings should be considered tentative; our major goal at this time is to begin consideration of the larger area of investigation.

The first hypothesis is that a person in a positive affective state who is asked to make a judgment or solve a problem will tend to reduce the complexity of the judgment or decision task and engage in speedy, simplified kinds of processing. In other words, a person who is feeling good will be more likely to choose the simpler strategy for solving a problem if more than one strategy is possible. In tasks involving many dimensions and possible outcomes, a person who feels good may be more likely to do what Simon (1976) has identified as "satisficing" (taking the first, minimally acceptable, solution based on a simple and low criterion) rather than attempting to optimize (considering many of the possible factors and outcomes, in their proper weights with an eye toward meeting some more-stringent criterion).

This hypothesis, that positive affect makes people tend to reduce the load on working memory, or avoid cognitive complexity, would follow from one of two possible underlying processes[1]: Either that positive affect itself increases the load on working memory, causing subjects to want or have to compensate for the increase by cutting back effort elsewhere; or, if not increasing the load, that positive affect somehow makes subjects more sensitive to and avoidant of "cognitive strain," as Bruner, Goodnow, and Austin (1956) put it.

Consider each of these two possibilities briefly. Positive affect may increase the load on working memory by requiring processing capacity itself in order to be accomplished or maintained. Or it may result in a drain on cognitive capacity, as persons are motivated to think about the positive mood-inducing event or related material rather than about task-related material. People may simply *want* to think about enjoyable things rather than about "work" when they feel good.

The other possibility is that positive affect does not itself increase the load on working memory, but that it makes people more sensitive to cognitive strain and more strain avoidant. This possibility follows from the assumption that positive affect is enjoyable, that people strive to maintain that state once it is induced by avoiding aversive situations as much as possible, and that cognitive overload is aversive. Scholars in the field have noted that decision making can be stressful (Janis & Mann, 1977). Thus, people in a good mood may try to avoid this sense of strain by using strategies to reduce task complexity. There is some evidence in the literature on the relationship between affect and helping that bears on the assumption that happy people try to maintain their positive mood state and are more averse to possible threats to it than are others. In one study, it was found that although positive affect led to increased helping generally, if subjects were led to believe that the particular helping task (assisting a researcher by reading statements designed to put people in a bad mood) would destroy their good moods, they appeared protective of their feeling states and were *less* willing than control subjects to help the experimental confederate (even saying such things as "I'm in too good a mood for that," Isen & Simmonds, 1978). Similarly, people in a good mood may be more likely to avoid cognitive strain in order to preserve their pleasurable feelings.

These two possibilities for the basis of an effect such as we are proposing of positive affect on decision simplification are not exhaustive and are themselves open to empirical investigation. We suggest them in order to illustrate two plausible sets of antecedent cognitive processes that would be compatible with our hypothesis.

A Note on Performance.   Whatever its source, the process that we are proposing implies two divergent possibilities for the performance or judgment of a

---

[1]The actual underlying cognitive processes may be different from these, and empirical work is necessary to investigate this question. The two possibilities presented here are provided only to illustrate the existence of plausible underpinnings for our hypothesis.

person who is feeling good: One, that processing may be more rapid, efficient, and phenomenologically effortless and pleasant, and performance enhanced; but the other, that such processing may be more subject to errors and/or biases (depending on the processes actually used to simplify the situation), and performance impaired. Thus, whether such tendencies will be enhancing or detrimental to task performance itself will depend on certain factors in the task situation, such as the nature and importance of the task, whether feedback on task performance is provided, and the person's history of dealing with affect. We elaborate on this issue a bit later. For the moment, we wish to emphasize that we are focusing on process rather than outcome, and that the process that we are proposing—reducing the complexity of the decision or judgment task—may result in either improved performance (faster, more efficient, more enjoyable performance) or impaired performance (careless or biased performance), depending on the task and other setting conditions.

Empirical Findings

We have sought evidence for these types of affect-related effects on decision making in a series of studies in which we have manipulated affective state, in some of the small ways described earlier, and then administered intellectual tasks. Whereas the tasks have varied widely (from physics-related problems to deciding what kind of car to buy), we have found that they have all been influenced by affective state in ways that are consistent with the general hypothesis outlined here.[2]

In the first of these studies, we selected a task that could be approached in different ways, one of which led to quick solution with relatively little expenditure of mental effort. This might be called an "intuitive" solution. The other possible approach involved more "cognitive strain," as it required keeping more information in mind and mentally manipulating this information in order to solve the task.

The task selected to meet these criteria was a paper-and-pencil timer-tape problem adapted from a puzzle originally used in the Workshop on Physics Teaching and the Development of Reasoning held by the American Association of Physics Teachers. Timer tapes are produced by a mechanism used in physics labs to study motion. A paper tape, which passes through a timer mechanism, is attached at one end to a moving object (say, a weight sliding down an inclined

---

[2]There is also some evidence in the clinical literature that people in whom positive affect has been induced often perform tasks more quickly (Hale & Strickland, 1976, who used the Velten mood-induction procedure, where subjects read statements designed to alter their affective states); and anecdotal reports of the behavior of manic patients also confirms this tendency, though in a bizarre and disordered form, to perform tasks and answer questions quickly. This, of course, contrasts with the behavior of patients in other clinical categories, which is often slowed and cumbersome.

plane). The timing mechanism marks the tape at constant time intervals. Hence, as the object moves faster, dots are marked farther apart on the tape.

In the paper-and-pencil timer-tape problems, the movement of some object is described, and students are shown five possible timer tapes and are asked to select the one that would have been produced by the described pattern of movement (speed). Means (1980) hypothesized that these problems tend to trigger an intuitive type of thinking involving the unexamined assumption that the positive poles of two dimensions (in this case speed and number) vary together. Perhaps for this reason, or perhaps on the basis of perceptual principles, individuals using the intuitive strategy equate the speed of the object with the number of dots on the tape (dots closer together), approaching the problems as a simple perceptual task in which one decides whether dots are becoming more or less numerous as one scans the tape. Because there is actually an inverse relationship between speed and the number of dots produced by the timer mechanism per inch of tape, this intuitive strategy leads to systematically incorrect responses on the timer-tape problems.

Means (1980) found that this intuitive strategy was used by 40% of the college students she tested, whereas about half used the more cognitively taxing logical strategy (entailing coordinating information about the movement of the object, the tape, and the mechanism), and some were inconsistent in their responses. Our hypothesis was that positive affect would increase the tendency of subjects to rely on the intuitive strategy rather than adopting the cognitively more taxing one.

In this study, affect was induced by providing refreshments (juice and cookies) to subjects in the positive-affect condition. Results supported our prediction, as 72% subjects in the positive-affect condition adopted the intuitive strategy (and made systematic errors on the problems), as contrasted with 38% of the control subjects.

Next, we reasoned that this kind of tendency to use mental shortcuts, which we proposed characterizes the problem-solving strategies of people who are feeling happy, might be related to the inclination to employ simplifying heuristics, as described by Tversky and Kahneman (1973, 1974) and others. A heuristic may be thought of as a rule of thumb for solving a problem, in contrast with the more effortful algorithmic application of a rule or with the holding of large amounts of material in working memory. For example, Tversky and Kahneman described the availability (accessibility) heuristic, where persons rely on the ease of retrieving material from memory as a way of estimating frequency of appearance of that material, rather than remembering in some more effortful way or even relying on the thorough use of relevant information such as base rates of occurrence. Heuristics are thought to reduce the complexity of a judgment task, and thus we reasoned that happy persons might display the tendency to employ a heuristic to a greater extent than control subjects.

We began with an adaptation of Kahneman and Tversky's availability-heuristic study, where subjects were asked to listen to a list of 39 names of famous people. Kahneman and Tversky used a list composed of 20 names of relatively less-famous men and 19 names of very famous women (and vice versa, in alternate lists). After hearing a list, subjects were asked whether it had contained more names of males or of females. The authors explained that if subjects were using ease of retrievability as a cue for frequency (the "availability heuristic"), they would respond with the gender that had been represented by the more famous names (rather than with the gender that was truly more numerous), because famous names are easier to retrieve. They found that responding appeared to be guided by this ease-of-retrievability heuristic for a large majority (about 80%) of their subjects.

Because we expected positive affect to increase the tendency to use a simplifying heuristic, we needed to modify the task to decrease the base-rate use of the availability heuristic. We used shorter lists, containing 10 less-famous and 9 more-famous names. Affect was induced in two ways: by means of juice and cookies, and by means of a gift of $1.00 to subjects. Our results revealed no effect of feeling state, as virtually everyone used the heuristic and answered that the more-famous names had been more numerous (even though the more famous had been less numerous by one).

We did learn some interesting things from this study, however. First, that by and large subjects are aware that they are using this heuristic. We asked subjects to describe how they had gone about answering our question, and we were a bit surprised to discover that they were perfectly capable of telling us. They described using the heuristic—trying to recall the names, and basing their decision on those that they could recall. A few even expressed recognition that this process might be influenced by factors other than frequency, but, they said, they had nothing else to go on.

Second, we discovered that positive-affect subjects did differ from control subjects in several ways. They reported having decided on an answer after mentally recalling significantly fewer names (3, in contrast with the control group's mean of 5), although when given a recall test after making their frequency decision they were able to recall as many names on the list as control subjects. In addition, the recall protocols for good-mood subjects contained significantly more intrusions than those of control subjects (who gave virtually none). If positive affect leads to a tendency to accept a response that comes to mind, without laborious checking (assuming that the task itself does not provide feedback), it seems reasonable to expect more intrusions. (Fewer intrusions should be "edited" out before responding.)

Thus, we were encouraged and went on to "titrate" the heuristics study, by examining the effects of positive affect, finally, on a very short list with six names of less-famous people of one sex and three names of very famous people of the other. Under this extreme condition, where there were twice as many names for the sex represented by less-famous people, finally, the majority of subjects give the truly more-numerous gender as their answer. Under this circumstance, it is also possible to see that positive affect does influence the use of this heuristic: Whereas in the control condition only 1 of 21 subjects responded with the gender of the more-famous group rather than the more numerous, in the positive-affect condition 7 of 20 used the accessibility heuristic. This is a statistically significant difference.

The studies described thus far show effects of mood states on performance on tasks where the subjects' decisions are arrived at quite rapidly. In a third type of study, we were interested in decomposing the solution process and seeing how subjects go about performing a more complex decision task. The task that we chose has real-world complexity and application, as it involves the selection of a consumer product from an array of possibilities that vary on several dimensions.

This study examines the influence of positive affect—this time induced by report of success on a task of perceptual-motor skills—on a decision-making task where subjects are asked to choose a car to purchase. There were six fictitious cars and information about each car's ranking on nine dimensions relevant to cars (fuel economy, safety, styling, selling price, etc.). A folder was available for each type of information with a separate color-coded sheet containing the ranking for each car. Hence, subjects could choose to organize information by dimension (folders) or by car (color). The amount of information available clearly exceeded working memory capacity. Subjects were told that they could use as much or as little of the information as they thought they would in a real-life situation, and that they could take notes if they liked. The materials were designed so that there was no clearly superior choice: Each car had both good points and weaknesses. In fact, for a subject who considered all of the information and gave each dimension equal weight (an unlikely assumption, in practice), the six cars were equivalent in expected utility. This study has just been completed, and we are still analyzing some of the data, but we can report some preliminary findings.

So far, we have looked at *how long* subjects took to make a decision and the *amount* of information they used in doing so, as a function of affective state. We are still analyzing the *type* of information that was influential to happy, as contrasted with control, subjects, the *weightings* of various types of factors in the decision processes of each, and the *strategies* that each group employed for dealing with the large amount of information presented. The results thus far indicate that individuals in the positive-affect condition reached a decision significantly more quickly than did control subjects (11.14 minutes as compared with 19.58 minutes for the control group) and were more likely to ignore dimensions that they did not consider important (considering an average of 7.09 dimensions as compared with 8.55 for the control group).

It is also interesting to note that our preliminary analyses of the protocols indicate that control subjects tended to be less efficient than positive-affect subjects, in the sense that they often went back over the same information. On the average, control subjects looked at each piece of information that they considered (e.g., the price of a particular car) twice ($M = 1.94$), whereas positive-affect subjects were significantly less likely to look at the same information repeatedly ($M = 1.28$.) The behavior of our control subjects is consistent with the finding reported by Bruner et al. (1956), that under normal circumstances subjects in problem-solving studies tend to check their answers, often "wasting" trials to confirm hypotheses that they know from their deductions, and the series of previous answers, must be true. Our positive-affect subjects were less prone to such inefficiencies.

Thus, summarizing the results of the series of studies, they tend to support the conclusion that positive affect results in attempts to simplify the decision situation, which result in faster and more efficient decision making, but sometimes biased, incomplete, and incorrect solutions, depending on the nature of the task and the viability of subjects' initial hunches.[3]

Performance

As noted previously, such attempts to reduce the complexity of problem-solving situations may result in either improved or impaired performance, depending on any of several aspects of the task situation. Obviously, where the intuitive hypothesis is correct, or where there is no correct answer or no way of obtaining the correct answer from the information given, this approach will facilitate performance. Not only will happy subjects see and use an intuitive hypothesis, but they will do so with more speed and confidence than will others, allowing them to appear (be) more "decisive" and freeing them to turn to other tasks or think about other things. In cases where the "first hunch" is wrong or leads to incorrect solution, however, performance of happy people is likely to be impaired because they will be less likely to think the problem through or to apply any sort of checking procedure to their first hypothesis. The first hypothesis that occurs to them is likely to be the one on which they will base their answer, unless the task or some other agent provides feedback that this answer is wrong.

---

[3]These studies used different methods of affect induction (refreshments, success)—and the study by Hale and Strickland (1976) mentioned in Footnote 2 found compatible results using still another procedure, the Velten statements—and employed different tasks, as well. Thus, an alternative interpretation of these results as owing to an artifact of one particular method of affect induction—say, that subjects in the positive-affect condition of the first study (timer-tape problem) were not trying as hard because the presence of refreshments made them react to the experimental situation more as a social situation than as a task-achievement situation—therefore is unconvincing. In addition, it might be noted that in the heuristics study, in which affect was also induced by means of refreshments, subjects in the two conditions scored equally when asked to recall the names on the list that they had heard. This finding also renders unlikely an interpretation that providing juice and cookies was distracting to subjects, and that it was this distraction that caused the observed effects in both the heuristics and timer-tape problem studies. If subjects in the positive-affect (juice and cookie) condition had been more distracted than controls, or if, as an artifact of the experimental situation, they had not been trying as hard as controls, it is reasonable to assume that they would have performed less well on the recall task.

This brings us to an important moderator of the affect process that we are proposing here: *feedback on the task*. In all of the tasks described above, subjects received no confirmation that their answers were right or wrong. It is reasonable to assume that if they had known that their first hypotheses had led them to incorrect answers on the timer-tape or frequency-judgment task, they could have corrected their mistakes and improved their performance on subsequent problems. This is an important moderator variable, because in many of the situations of life to which we would wish to apply these results feedback is available or even inherent in the task. For example, in many problem-solving tasks, the solution that one tries either works or it doesn't. If you're trying to figure out how to store your new self-storing storm windows for the summer, and you try a certain combination of moves, you either end up with the storm window stored nicely in place and the window open to the screen, or with the storm window in your arms. You know whether your initial hypothesis about how to store the storm windows was correct.

A good illustration of this point may be had in a study recently completed on the influence of affect on creative problem solving (Isen & Nowicki, 1981). Using the task that Karl Duncker (1945) used in his demonstration of "functional fixedness" (the candle task), and inducing affect by means of exposure to a movie (funny or control), we found that subjects in whom positive affect had been induced were more likely to solve the task than were control subjects.

In this task, subjects are presented with a candle, a box of tacks, and a book of matches and are given the problem of attaching the candle to the wall (a cork board) in such a way that it will burn without dripping wax on the floor or table beneath. The task can be solved if the subject sees that the box can be used separately from the tacks inside it, and that it has the properties necessary to aid in solving the task. The box can be emptied, tacked to the wall, and used as a platform for the candle, which can then be lit and will burn without dripping onto the table or floor. In this case we found that positive-affect subjects were more likely to solve the task than were either of two control groups, one that saw a control film and one that saw no film (75% in contrast with 20% and 13%). The point that we want to stress in this illustration is that the task provides its own feedback.

Watching the behavior of subjects as they worked, one could see that positive-affect subjects got many ideas, rapidly tried them, and rejected inadequate hypotheses, until they came up with the correct solution. Controls tended to stare at the display without trying any solutions, or to perseverate in one mode even after they saw that it did not seem to be working. In another context we have written about this finding emphasizing the flow of ideas that characterizes someone who is feeling good, but the person's responsiveness to feedback is also noteworthy.

Another factor that may moderate the influence of positive affect on the tendency to simplify the decision situation, and make decisions on the basis of limited or biased information, may be the *importance of the task*. None of the studies reported thus far has varied task importance, and this is no doubt a critical factor in how subjects will go about solving the task. It is likely that people who are feeling good, just like people in a neutral mood, will be more cautious on tasks that are very important to them. We have already noted the tendency of positive-affect subjects to protect their good moods, and because failure on an important task would involve loss of positive affect, we would expect that in important tasks the tendency of positive-affect subjects to simplify the task and to "shoot from the hip" would be superceded by processes designed to insure optimal performance. It may be, though, that for happy people the importance of the task may need to be brought home to them more clearly or forcefully than would be the case at another time. We have no direct evidence regarding either of these speculations, but there may be some indirect evidence available in the risk-taking studies described later.

Finally, another moderator variable is one that is beyond the scope of this chapter, but one that we wanted just to mention. This is the variable of an individual's *experience with affect* of various kinds and the ways in which the person has learned to process affect and/or enjoy, capitalize on, or deal with its effects. For example, people who are especially accustomed to feeling happy or who are aware of elation's potential threat to performance on certain kinds of tasks may have worked out strategies for coping with any such effects.

An Application to Behavior: Risk Taking

Now we turn to the question of what impact this processing change—the tendency to reduce complexity—might have on behavior and social interaction in particular. In this context, we describe a few preliminary studies on risk taking of social and nonsocial types. (The social type might relate to susceptibility to social influence or conformity.)

One might assume that judgment strategies of the kind described earlier for positive affect would be associated with risk taking; that the "impulsiveness" or consideration of only part of the evidence, the "jumping to conclusions" or absence of "checking" procedures in the decision-making process, could be equated with bravado or willingness to take risks. The question, however, is whether people who are feeling good are purposely taking risks or merely *appearing* risk prone as they go about considering the evidence differently.

The prediction of risk taking from positive affect is not straightforward. Two lines of thinking and research lead to opposing, or at least complex, predictions for risk taking under conditions of positive affect. First, we know that positive material is more likely to come to mind when someone is feeling good. Thus, we should expect people in this state to be more optimistic and, therefore, more willing to take risks. There is some evidence generally supportive of this prediction in the study involving judgments of one's consumer products, and in other studies finding improved ratings and expectations among positive-affect subjects (Feather, 1966; Isen & Shalker, 1982; Isen et al., 1978; Masters & Furman, 1976; Schiffenbauer, 1974).

On the other hand, a paradox is created by the fact that, at the same time that happiness may increase optimism, as we have seen, it also seems to give rise to a tendency toward mood protection and conservatism under some circumstances (Isen & Simmonds, 1978). This would point to the conclusion that people who feel good might be *less* likely to take risks, especially when the risk directly threatens the affective state, and when the risk is unambiguous and high.

Again, if we look closely we find that the particulars of the circumstances surrounding the decision may make a crucial difference in how people will respond. One of the most important factors may be the ambiguity of the risk situation. Most of the studies that have obtained effects of feelings on evaluation have found these effects to be strongest under conditions of ambiguity (Isen & Shalker, 1982; Schiffenbauer, 1974). In contrast, recall the study where positive-affect subjects given a mood-destroying helping opportunity were less willing than control subjects to help. That study used a procedure that left no doubt whatsoever about the affective consequences that would result from helping, because the helping task involved reading statements described as "designed to put people into a bad mood." Thus it may be that, under conditions where the risk is not clearly present, or where the level of risk or the costs involved are not high, people who are feeling happy will be more willing to take a chance. But in circumstances where risk is clear, or high, they may be less so.

The studies on risk that we describe next support this formulation. In the first of these, subjects who had succeeded on a battery of tests involving tasks, such as color matching and anagrams, showed lessened imitation of confederates' eating patterns in a social situation where refreshments were provided (Isen & Friedman, 1977). That is, while those subjects who had failed tended to match the eating pattern of the experimental confederates, those who had succeeded seemed more independent of the confederates in their choice of whether to take refreshments or not. Success subjects tended to eat regardless of whether confederates took refreshments. Following the behavior of confederates may be thought of as conformity or susceptibility to social influence; and persons who had succeeded displayed less of it.

In this circumstance, where risk (the social risk of eating when no one else is eating, or of not conforming) is either ambiguous or low, people who have been made to feel good do seem to be more willing to take the risk. A second study tried to address the question of social bravery more directly. It varied affect and the factor of whether subjects were provided with their own private bowls of refreshments or only one central bowl for the table, on the assumption that more social risk would be involved in taking refreshments from a central bowl than from individual bowls.

The results of this measure indicate that in terms of willingness to take refreshments, positive-affect subjects again looked more brave, this time, more brave than control subjects as well as those who had failed. That is, success subjects ate just as many crackers whether they had their own bowls or had to reach across the table, while other subjects were quite sensitive to this manipulation, reducing their consumption drastically when there was only a central bowl. The necessity of reaching into a central bowl seemed to inhibit eating in all subjects except those who had just succeeded.

A second kind of risk measure was obtained from subjects in this study. They were asked to compete in a turtle race, and each subject got to choose one of three starting lines for his or her turtle. The line farthest away afforded the best prizes if a turtle was started from it and won, but of course it was described as most risky.

The choice of starting line—which might be seen as more explicit risk taking than the eating measure—showed a different effect of mood. Here, both positive- and negative-affect subjects made significantly *less*-risky choices than did control subjects. They seemed risk-avoidant in comparison with subjects in whom affective state had not been induced.

Several alternative interpretations of these findings are possible (Isen & Friedman, 1977), but the one that seemed most promising was that the crucial difference between these two types of risk (eating in social situations versus choice of starting line) was in the amount of perceived risk. It seemed reasonable, as described previously, that if risk were low or ambiguous, positive-affect subjects would be more likely to take the risk, but that if risk were high, that same group would be less likely to do so.

Thus, we were assuming that risk was low or not perceived in the eating situations, but high in the turtle-race situation. Results of a survey taken on an independent sample of subjects confirmed this assumption. Isen and Friedman (1977) described the situations to subjects, asking them to rate each for degree of risk, on a scale from 1 (low risk) to 10 (high risk). At the same time, these subjects rated two "anchor" risks: that of betting on "red" in a game of roulette and that involved in betting on the number "4" in a game of roulette. The mean ratings were significantly different from each other (red = 5.61; 4 = 9.11; choosing farthest starting line = 6.89; reaching for refreshments = 2.04) and confirm the suggestion that the type of risk on which successful subjects in Isen and Friedman's studies were more willing to take a chance (the "social" risk) was considered a low risk.

In order to test this hypothesis directly and to rule out one or two alternative interpretations of the earlier studies, we are now conducting a third risk-taking study. Here, in addition, affect is being varied by a method not involving success on a task. Subjects in the positive-affect condition receive McDonald's gift certificates. In a study employing a between-subjects design, subjects are then given a chance to bet chips on a roulette bet that is described as either high risk (17% chance of winning), medium risk (50% chance of winning), or low risk (83% chance).

Previous studies such as that of Slovic (1969) have shown that hypothetical and real bets are treated differently by subjects, so we are attempting to make the situation real for our subjects. Subjects receive credit toward a course require- ment in Introductory Psychology for participating in this study, and what they are betting are fractions of this credit for participating. They are handed a stack of 10 chips and are told that their credit for participating is represented by these chips. They don't have to bet any portion of their credit (chips), but they can if they want to. By betting, they can win prizes in addition to receiving their credit for participating, if they win; but if they lose, they will lose all or part of the hour's credit that they would otherwise have gotten for their participation.

Under these conditions, the results so far with approximately eight subjects per condition are tending to support our predictions: In the low-risk condition, people who have been given a free gift are more likely to bet, and bet more chips than do control subjects; but in the high-risk condition; positive-affect subjects are *less* likely than controls to bet and bet significantly fewer chips.

These studies, then, suggest that even though people may be inclined to simplify decision situations when they feel good—and thus they may often look impulsive, or risk-prone—they may not actually be more inclined to take risks per se, unless they are pretty sure that the outcome will be positive. Thus, they may not be any more confident or brave than others, in truly risky situations, although they may seem to be because of their behavior when risk is low.

Just as the influence of affect on task performance depends on the task and particulars of the situation, so its influence on risk taking also seems to depend on factors specific to the judgment or risk situation. We have seen that degree of risk can be an important factor in subjects' decisions to take or avoid a risk. But other issues may be crucial as well and may interact with each other: Type of risk (for example, social or nonsocial risk, risk of money as opposed to risk of life or health, risk of failure, and so on); what and/or how much is at stake; and the way in which the situation or the risk is presented to subjects may be important determinants of the influence of affect on the decision to take the risk or not. For example, as Tversky and Kahneman (1981) have recently suggested, presenta- tions that emphasize costs and those that emphasize benefits may result in differ- ent responses on the part of subjects. It seems reasonable that type of presenta- tion may interact with affective state, as well.

Finally, in studies of the influence of affect on risk taking, a very important aspect of how the choice is presented to subjects may be whether the probabilities are calculated for them, as was the case in our third risk-taking study, or whether subjects themselves must calculate and weigh the potential costs and rewards inherent in the gamble. If, for example, affect influences the processing of costs and benefits differentially, then a situation where subjects must calculate the degree of risk might have a very different outcome from one where these probabilities are precalculated and simply presented to subjects.

In illustration of the potential importance of this point, consider the following: Some might argue that people in whom positive affect has been induced might be less sensitive to potential costs, as compared with rewards, that they may ignore or underweigh such negative factors while they are feeling good. Our data do not encourage this interpretation, because subjects in the positive-affective conditions were quite sensitive to potential cost. When it was high, they avoided betting. Likewise, subjects in the study by Isen and Simmonds (1978) demonstrated sensitivity to potential loss of good mood and avoided helping when they were made aware that helping would destroy their mood states. However, it should be noted that in both of these studies the potential cost was unambiguously explained to subjects. They did not calculate their own chance of winning or of becoming depressed. Thus, these studies do not speak to the issue of whether positive affect leads to underestimating of costs. It may be that where subjects must engage in these kinds of calculations themselves, we would discover some additional effects of feeling state on the process. These possibilities are currently under investigation.

Conclusion

Returning now to the main theme of this chapter, we have proposed that positive affect influences the processes that people use in solving problems and deciding among alternatives. We have suggested one such influence (and there may be others)—that, all else equal, a person who is feeling happy will be more likely than at other times to reduce the load on working memory: to reduce the complexity of decision situations and the difficulty of tasks, by adopting the simplest strategy possible, considering the fewest number of alternatives possible, and doing little or no checking of information, hypotheses, and tentative conclusions. We have also proposed, however, that these effects will be limited by the fact that people try to avoid failure when failure is obvious, and especially when the task is an important one. Thus, where feedback is provided or where the task is extremely important, the performance of people who are in a positive affective state would not be expected necessarily to reflect the kind of processing described here for them in general. We have also seen that the types of processing associated with positive moods can either facilitate or impair performance, depending on the circumstances.

We have explored only a fragment of the territory within which feeling state and decision making interact. In addition to examining the effects of the possible moderator variables mentioned earlier, we need to devise techniques for studying more directly the altered processing modes hypothesized to accompany positive mood. In addition, many more details of the consequences of these processing changes remain to be delineated and explored.

Further, the effects of positive mood on performance can be placed within a wider context once comparable research is conducted on a broader spectrum of affective states: on negative moods, and on both positive and negative affective states of greater intensity than those with which we have dealt. We would argue that it is premature to suggest that negative mood states produce effects parallel (and opposite) to those that we have observed for positive moods; in fact, the weight of evidence suggests that frequently they do not. Many of the recent studies in this and related areas have failed to find symmetrical effects for positive and negative states (Isen, 1970; Isen et al., 1978; Landy, 1981; Leight & Ellis, 1981; Mischel, Ebbesen, & Zeiss, 1976; Teasdale & Fogarty, 1979). In addition, there may be quite different effects for different mood states (such as irritation and anxiety) that are generally lumped together under the heading "negative" or "positive."

Besides valence (positive–negative) and particular quality (for example, anger or anxiety), intensity and arousal may be important dimensions helping to determine the impact of feelings on cognition and behavior. We suspect that really intense emotions may have quite different consequences for cognition than do weaker feelings of the same valence. (Or the situation may be even more complex, with emotional intensity having an impact on performance that depends on whether the emotion in question is positive or negative.) Beyond this, another dimension that may be important is the extent to which an affective state involves arousal (i.e., energizes behavior); that is, in addition to having a particular quality, being positive or negative, and being intense or mild, an affective state may be agitating (stimulating) or depressing (relaxing); and position on this dimension may have important implications for the cognitive consequences of the state. Thus, we suggest that future research consider all four of these dimensions in exploring the impact of affect on cognition.

Our final point is addressed to the overall theme of this volume, the importance of studying affect and cognition in each other's context. Most basic research in cognitive psychology has been conducted within the confines of the experimental laboratory using carefully delineated techniques and tasks. These have resulted in many advances in the study of cognition, but they have also produced some limitations for the field. Although useful for isolating intellectual processes of interest, such tasks and the conditions under which they are administered are not representative of the whole of human thought, and they need to be supplemented by more broadly-based investigations. In natural life situations, reasoning and remembering are carried out in social contexts, where thinking, goals, feelings, and the social context itself all exert influence upon each other. Thus, especially if we hope to apply research in cognitive psychology to practical concerns such as education, clinical treatment, or organization management, we must develop cognitive models that incorporate social and affective variables. We see events such as the present conference as encouraging of such integration, and we hope that such efforts will continue.

REFERENCES

Berkowitz, L. Social norms, feelings, and other factors affecting helping and altruism. In L. Berkowitz (Ed.), *Advances in experimental social psychology* (Vol. 6). New York: Academic, 1972.

Bruner, J., Goodnow, J., & Austin, G. *A study of thinking.* New York: Wiley, 1956.

Campbell, D., & Fiske, D. Convergent and discriminant validation. *Psychological Bulletin,* 1959, *56,* 81–105.

Darley, J., & Latané, B. *The unresponsive bystander: Why doesn't he help?* New York: Appleton, 1970.

Duncker, K. On problem-solving. *Psychological Monographs,* 1945, *58* (Whole No. 5).

Feather, N. T. Effects of prior success and failure on expectations of success and subsequent performance. *Journal of Personality and Social Psychology,* 1966, *3,* 287–298.

Forest, D., Clark, M. S., Mills, J., & Isen, A. M. Helping as a function of feeling state and nature of the helping behavior. *Motivation and Emotion,* 1979, *3,* 161–169.

Garner, W. R. Context effects and the validity of loudness scales. *Journal of Experimental Psychology,* 1954, *48,* 218–224.

Garner, W. R., Hake, H. W., & Eriksen, C. W. Operationism and the concept of perception. *Psychological Review,* 1956, *63,* 149–159.

Hale, W. D., & Strickland, B. R. Induction of mood states and their effect on cognitive and social behaviors. *Journal of Consulting and Clinical Psychology,* 1976, *44,* 155.

Isen, A. M. Success, failure, attention, and reactions to others: The warm glow of success. *Journal of Personality and Social Psychology,* 1970, *15,* 294–301.

Isen, A. M. Positive affect, accessibility of cognitions and helping. In J. Piliavin (Chair.), *Current directions in theory on helping behavior.* Symposium presented at the meeting of the Eastern Psychological Association Convention, New York, 1975.

Isen, A. M., & Freidman, C. H. *The effect of feeling state on susceptibility to social influence and risk taking.* Manuscript, University of Maryland, 1977.

Isen, A. M., & Levin, P. F. The effect of feeling good on helping: Cookies and kindness. *Journal of Personality and Social Psychology,* 1972, *21,* 384–388.

Isen, A. M., & Nowicki, G. P. *Positive affect and creative problem solving.* Paper presented at the annual meeting of the Cognitive Science Society, Berkeley, 1981.

Isen, A. M., & Shalker, T. E. Do you "accentuate the positive, eliminate the negative" when you are in a good mood? *Social Psychology Quarterly,* 1982.

Isen, A. M., Shalker, T. E., Clark, M. S., & Karp, L. Positive affect, accessibility of material in memory, and behavior: A cognitive loop? *Journal of Personality and Social Psychology,* 1978, *36,* 1–12.

Isen, A. M., & Simmonds, S. The effect of feeling good on a helping task that is incompatible with good mood. *Social Psychology Quarterly,* 1978, *41,* 346–349.

Janis, I., & Mann, L. *Decision making.* New York: Free Press, 1977.

Landy, F. An opponent process theory of job satisfaction. *Journal of Applied Psychology,* 1981 *63*(5), 533–547.

Leight, K., & Ellis, H. Emotional mood states, strategies, and state dependency in memory. *Journal of Verbal Learning and Verbal Behavior,* 1981, *20,* 251–266.

Masters, J. C., & Furman, W. Effects of affect states on noncontingent outcome expectancies and beliefs in internal or external control. *Developmental Psychology*, 1976, *12*, 481–482.

Means, B. *Intuitive and logical reasoning approaches to multidimensional problems*. Paper presented at the annual meeting of the AERA, 1980.

Mischel, W., Coates, B., & Raskoff, A. Effects of success and failure on self-gratification. *Journal of Personality and Social Psychology*, 1968, *10*, 381–390.

Mischel, W., Ebbesen, E. & Zeiss, A. Determinants of selective memory about the self. *Journal of Consulting and Clinical Psychology*, 1976, *44*, 92–103.

Piliavin, I. M., Rodin, J., & Piliavin, J. Good Samaritanism: An underground phenomenon? *Journal of Personality and Social Psychology*, 1969, *12*, 289–299.

Schiffenbauer, A. Effect of observer's emotional state on judgments of the emotional state of others. *Journal of Personality and Social Psychology*, 1974, *30*, 31–35.

Simon, H. A. *Administrative behavior: A study of decision-making processes in administrative organization* (2nd ed.), New York: Macmillan, 1957; (3rd ed.), New York: Free Press, 1976.

Slovic, P. Differential effects of real versus hypothetical payoffs on choices among gambles. *Journal of Experimental Psychology*, 1969, *80*, 434–437.

Teasdale, J. D., & Fogarty, S. J. Differential effects of induced mood on retrieval of pleasant and unpleasant events from episodic memory. *Journal of Abnormal Psychology*, 1979, *88*, 248–257.

Tversky, A., & Kahneman, D. Availability: A heuristic for judging frequency and probability. *Cognitive Psychology*, 1973, *5*, 207–232.

Tversky, A., & Kahneman, D. Judgment under uncertainty: Heuristics and biases. *Science*, 1974, *185*, 1124–1130.

Tversky, A., & Kahneman, D. The framing of decisions. *Science*, 1981, *211*, 453–458.

12

A Role for Arousal in the Link between Feeling States, Judgments, and Behavior

Margaret S. Clark
Carnegie–Mellon University

INTRODUCTION

Recently, the question of what feeling states, or moods, are and the processes through which they influence judgments and behavior has received considerable attention. However, most of these discussions have either not mentioned autonomic arousal (Bartlett & Santrock, 1979; Bower, Monteiro, & Gilligan, 1978; Isen, Shalker, Clark, & Karp, 1978; Leight & Ellis, 1981; Macht, Spear, & Levis, 1977; Teasdale & Fogarty, 1979) or have mentioned it just in passing (Bower, 1981; Clark & Isen, 1982). The purpose of the present chapter is to propose a role for autonomic arousal in one model of what feeling states are and how they affect social judgments and behavior (Isen, 1975; Isen et al., 1978; Clark & Isen, 1982) and to present some preliminary evidence for this proposed role.

Clearly, proposing a role for autonomic arousal in affective experience is not a new idea. The relationship of arousal to affective experience has long been of interest to psychologists (e.g., Cannon, 1929; James, 1884; Mandler, 1975; Schachter & Singer, 1962; Zillmann, 1978; and many others). Some of these researchers believe that arousal is an integral part of what an emotion is (e.g. Mandler, 1975; this volume), whereas others have questioned whether arousal is necessary to the experience of emotion (e.g. Weiner, this volume) or have explicitly separated the concept of emotion from that of arousal (Izard & Buechler, 1980). The present chapter does not take a position on these issues. Rather, here it is simply assumed that when a person feels good or bad as a result of some event or thought, that person often experiences increased autonomic arousal. It is on this assumption and its implications for understanding feeling states and their effects on memory, judgments, and behavior that this chapter is based.

Before proposing a role for arousal in feeling states and the processes through which they influence judgments and behavior, some preliminary questions must be answered. What effects *do* feeling states (or moods) have on judgments and behavior? Through what processes are these effects mediated? Indeed, what *is* a feeling state? These questions are addressed in detail in a chapter by Clark and Isen (1982). Here they are reviewed only to the extent necessary for the reader to understand the discussion of the role of autonomic arousal in these processes which follows.

EFFECTS OF FEELING STATES

There is now little doubt that subtle feeling states, or what many researchers have called moods, are capable of influencing a wide variety of judgments and behaviors. To take just a few examples, when we are feeling good, the evidence indicates that we tend to view others more positively (Gouaux, 1971; Gouaux & Summers, 1973; Schiffenbauer, 1974; Veitch & Griffitt, 1976), to give more favorable reports about products we have purchased (Isen et al., 1978), to rate ambiguous slides as more pleasant (Forest, Clark, Mills & Isen, 1979), to have more positive expectations for the future (Feather, 1966; Masters & Furman, 1975), and to give more positive associations to situations in which we imagine ourselves (Clark & Waddell, 1981). In other words, when we are feeling good we tend to behave in a more positive fashion and to perceive the world more favorably than would otherwise be the case.

There is also little doubt that negative moods have pervasive effects on judgments and behaviors. Often, but not always, they have effects that are opposite to the effects of positive moods. For instance, whereas positive moods tend to increase our liking for others, negative moods tend to decrease liking for others (e.g., Gouaux, 1971; Griffitt, 1970; Griffitt & Guay, 1969). Whereas positive moods tend to make us view ambiguous slides as more pleasant, negative moods tend to cause us to view them as more unpleasant (Forest et al., 1979), and clinical depression has been shown to have similar effects. For example, depression seems to lower people's estimates of their future success at a task (Loeb, Beck, & Diggory, 1971).[1]

---

[1] However, it should be recognized that negative moods have sometimes been shown to have different kinds of effects—effects that are actually similar to those of positive moods—for example, both positive and negative moods have been shown to increase adults' willingness to help (Cialdini & Kenrick, 1976). These effects and the processes which may mediate them are addressed in Clark and Isen (1982).

Recently, researchers have addressed the question of what processes mediate the influence of feeling good or bad on judgments and behavior. It is to one model of these processes that we now turn.

THE MODEL

One explanation for why feeling states might influence judgments and social behavior was suggested by Isen (1975). She proposed that these effects may occur because, when people are in a particular feeling state, material stored in memory that is congruent with that feeling state will be more accessible, and consequently more likely to come to mind than it would be at another time. This hypothesis has since been elaborated by Isen and her colleagues (e.g. Isen et al., 1978; Clark & Isen, 1982), and others have discussed the phenomenon of mood increasing accessibility of similarly toned material as well (Bartlett & Santrock, 1979; Bower, 1981). It is necessary to briefly review some of this work before the role that arousal may play in feeling states and the processes through which they influence judgments and behavior can be described adequately.

First, what is meant by increased accessibility of mood-congruent material in memory, and how does this increased accessibility of mood-congruent material influence judgments and behaviors? As pointed out in earlier work (Clark & Isen, 1982), we assume that when something positive or negative happens to a person the feeling tone associated with that experience may be stored in memory associated with the experience. Thus, as illustrated in Fig. 12.1, for someone who lives in Pittsburgh, such as myself, stored along with other memories of the Pittsburgh Symphony, such as where it plays and who conducts it, may be a positive feeling tone.

It is also possible that things that produce a given feeling tone may be linked together in memory as a category, as illustrated in Fig. 12.2. Thus, New En-

FIG. 12.1.   Hypothetical information linked to the symphony in memory.

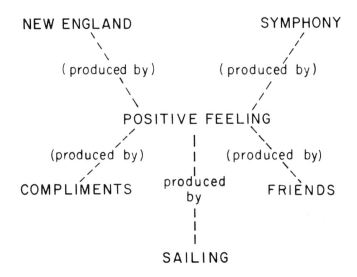

FIG. 12.2.   Hypothetical information linked to positive feelings in memory.

gland, sailing, the symphony, and friends may be stored in memory as examples of things that make me feel good. Of course, this does not mean that all things that produce a pleasant feeling state are linked together in memory. Positive things about one's family may form one category, positive things about work another, and so forth. Returning to the question of what is meant by increased accessibility of material in memory, Clark and Isen (1982) suggest a process of spreading activation such as that described by Collins and Quillian (1972) and Collins and Loftus (1975) as just one possible way to understand this phenomenon. When something positive happens to a person, that person thinks about the event and feels good. To think about an event means that information about the event is activated in memory. The activation may then spread or prime linked material in memory. In this case memories of past experiences that produced similar feeling states should be primed. For example, imagine that something pleasant happens to me. I look over the results of a study I have just finished and they look great. This pleases me and I feel good. Now that I'm feeling good, other thoughts associated with positive feelings may also be activated. Specifically, thoughts about New England, sailing, friends in Pittsburgh, and the Symphony may be "primed." As a consequence, these thoughts ought to be more likely to "come to mind" than they would be at another time.

Now consider the question of how this increased accessibility of mood-congruent information in memory may influence judgments and behavior. When a person feels good, we assume that similarly toned material in memory is more accessible. However, all this information will not necessarily enter conscious-

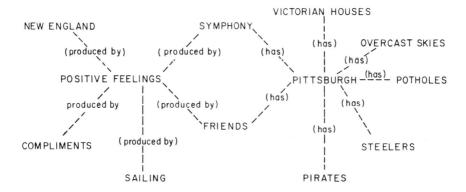

FIG. 12.3.   Hypothetical material primed by a positive feeling state and a question about Pittsburgh.

ness. It may only be when something else primes a subset of that same material that the material will come to mind. To continue the previous example, imagine that, while I'm feeling good as a result of the nice outcome of my study, someone knocks at my office door. It's a friend from out of town who just happens to be in Pittsburgh. She comes in, sits down, and says, "So, how do you like Pittsburgh?" *Because* I'm feeling good, positive thoughts are more accessible than usual. Then when she questions me about how much I like Pittsburgh, and I reflect on Pittsburgh, material about Pittsburgh will also be primed—for example, the type of housing, the weather, and so forth. The material receiving the *most* priming from *both* the positive-feeling state *and* the question about Pittsburgh—that is, thoughts about the symphony and my friends—should be most likely to come to mind, as illustrated in Fig. 12.3. As a consequence, in answer to my friends's question about how much I like Pittsburgh, I may answer that I like Pittsburgh quite well. When I give this answer, I have expressed a judgment that has been "colored" by my feeling state. It is easy to see how my behaviors might be influenced as well. If my friend asked me to join her for dinner that night, the probability of my agreeing might be greater than if I were not in a positive feeling state, because more positive relative to negative thoughts about going to dinner might "come to mind."

The priming processes proposed in this model presumably take place without effort, without awareness, and without interfering with other cognitive processes (Clark & Isen, 1982)—thus we have called them "automatic" processes (Posner & Snyder, 1975). In sum, then, moods may be thought of as the state of feeling good or bad and "automatically" having increased accessibility of similarly toned material from memory—material that, when it becomes conscious, may influence judgments and behavior. Moods or feeling states do not abruptly interrupt ongoing thoughts or behaviors as emotions may, but they may subtly influence many different sorts of judgments and behavior by biasing in a positive or negative direction what thoughts come to mind (Clark & Isen, 1982).

Evidence for the Model

A number of people have now reported results consistent with these ideas. Isen et al. (1978), for instance, have shown that people in positive moods are more likely than are people in no particular mood or in negative moods to be able to recall positively toned words they have previously learned. Isen et al. also found that people who receive a free gift will later report on a consumer survey that their cars and TV sets run better than will people who have not received a free gift. In addition, Teasdale and Fogarty (1979) have shown that being in a particular mood state results in people being able to recall similarly toned material *faster* than would otherwise have been the case, and Clark and Waddell (1981) have shown that the affective tone of our associations to situations tends to be congruent with our mood state. Finally, Bousfield (1950), Bower and his colleagues (Bower, 1981; Bower & Cohen, this volume; Bower et al. 1978); Bartlett and Santrock (1979; Bartlett, Burleson & Santrock, 1982); Laird, Wagener, Halal, and Szegda (1982); Leight and Ellis (1981); Macht, et al., 1977; Nelson and Craighead (1977); and Weingartner, Miller, and Murphy (1977) have also presented evidence consistent with this model. Indeed, Bower and his colleagues have proposed a similar model.

A ROLE FOR AROUSAL IN EXPLAINING THE LINK BETWEEN FEELING STATES, JUDGMENTS, AND BEHAVIOR

Storage of Arousal Imagery as Part of Storage of Feeling Tone

As noted earlier, the preceding reasoning about feeling states leaves out a concept that many psychologists have considered to be crucial to the study of affect—autonomic arousal. It is the intent of the present chapter to propose a role for arousal by integrating some of what psychologists know about autonomic arousal with the model as it now stands.

The present theorizing about autonomic arousal began with the question of what it means to say a feeling tone is stored in memory. To answer this question, one must ask what is distinctive about the effects of the many different events that induce positive (or negative) moods in people. It may be imagery of those distinctive events that is stored in memory and constitutes "storage of feeling tone."

One distinctive characteristic of most mood inducers, both positive and nega-tive, seems to be that they produce autonomic arousal. Certainly the idea that arousal is closely tied to emotion is not new. However, the question of just how the concept of arousal relates to subtle feeling states has not received attention. Here it is proposed that not only does arousal accompany many mood inducers but also that stored in memory linked to other memories of positive and negative experience may be memory of that arousal. In other words, it is suggested that storage of arousal imagery is at least part of what it means to say a feeling tone is stored. (Storage of imagery of facial expressions and body postures may be other parts of what it means to say that a positive or a negative feeling tone is stored, but the emphasis in this chapter is on autonomic arousal.)[2]

In any case, if arousal imagery *is* stored with other aspects of past positive (and negative) experiences, then when something pleasant (or unpleasant) hap-pens to a person and that person is once again aroused, the *arousal* may prime arousal imagery, and material linked to it. In other words, arousal may be *one* tie between positive (negative) feeling states in the present and memories of positive (negative) material from the past.

To determine the plausibility of this idea, it must be established that the kinds of manipulations psychologists have typically used to produce positive as well as negative moods do indeed produce arousal. This is important, for many have considered moods to be milder than emotions and have suggested that they may not be accompanied by autonomic arousal (Buss & Plomin, 1975). Fortunately for the present argument, there is evidence that events very similar and in some cases identical to those that psychologists have used to induce positive and negative moods also produce autonomic arousal.

Evidence of Arousal Caused by Pleasant Experiences

Considering positive mood inducers first, several studies have established that "everyday" positive experiences of just the sort psychologists have often used to induce positive mood—success, free gifts, funny movies—*are* accompanied by autonomic arousal. First consider the evidence that success, something that Clark and Waddell (1981) have demonstrated increases positive moods, elicits arousal as well. In a study recently reported by Mueller and Donnerstein (1981), subjects who received a note saying they had earned $4.50 for writing an essay, a sum exceeding their expectations, and who were told it was "a good, creative essay indicative of intelligence and knowledge," showed significantly greater in-creases in systolic blood pressure than did "neutrally" treated subjects who received an expected $.50 and were told they had written an average essay.

---

[2]Leventhal (1979), Mandler and Kremen (1958), Mandler (1975), and Schachter (1964) have previously suggested that arousal imagery may be stored in memory.

Furthermore, Patkai (1971) found that subjects who played a game of bingo and won small amounts of cash rated their activity as being more pleasant *and* showed significantly greater adrenalin excretion during the game than did the same subjects during a session in which they simply looked through magazines.

Next, consider the evidence that humorous films, something that Gouaux (1971) has used to induce positive moods, elicit arousal. Averill (1969) found that subjects shown the humorous film "Good Old Corn" rated the film as more humorous *and* showed significantly increased palmar conductance, GSR, respiration rate, and respiration irregularity relative to subjects who viewed a control film describing the trip of two amateur zoologists. Furthermore, Levi (1965, 1972) has found that after viewing the film "Charley's Aunt" subjects rated the film as more humorous *and* showed significantly greater increases in urine adrenalin excretion than did the same subjects after viewing a neutral "natural-scenery" film.

Thus, the ideas that: (1) mood inducers may often elicit arousal; and that (2) stored in memory along with other aspects of such positive events may be memories of autonomic arousal seem reasonable.

Evidence of Arousal Caused by Unpleasant Experiences

Perhaps less surprisingly to those who have postulated that negative affect typically involves greater autonomic arousal than does positive affect, there is also evidence that negative experiences of the sort researchers have used to induce bad moods elicit autonomic arousal. Consider negative films first—something that Gouaux (1971) has used to induce negative mood. In Levi's (1965, 1972) research, subjects shown a film chosen to evoke anger ("Paths of Glory") or a film designed to evoke fear ("The Mask of Satan") showed significantly greater increases in adrenalin excretion in the urine than did the same subjects after viewing the neutral "natural-scenery" film. Furthermore, subjects' verbal ratings of the former two films relative to their ratings of the latter film supported the idea that, the former two induced negative feeling states. In addition, Averill (1979) found that after watching "J. F. Kennedy 1917–1963," a film that had previously been shown to evoke sadness (Greenberg & Parker, 1965, as cited in Averill, 1969), subjects showed significantly greater increases in both systolic and diastolic blood pressure than did the same subjects after viewing a control film about two zoologists' trip.

Next, consider other types of negative events that might be expected to induce negative mood states—such as being unable to solve a task or finding oneself in a crowded situation. Jost (1941) has found that both normal children and children being treated for mental health problems showed increases in pulse rate when given a task they could not solve, and Lundberg (1976) has found evidence that feeling crowded produces both increased feelings of "unpleasantness" and increased excretion of catecholamines. He studied train commuters on two trips.

They rated the second trip as more crowded and unpleasant than the first, and measures of their catecholamine excretion obtained from urine samples taken immediately following the second trip were significantly higher than identical measures taken following the previous trip. Furthermore, on both trips, as the train approached its destination, it was rated as being increasingly crowded and unpleasant and boarding passengers had fewer seat selections. These later boarding passengers showed higher catecholamine excretion that did earlier boarding passengers.

Thus, as was the case for positive feeling-state inducers, there is evidence to support the claim that events that put us in bad moods also increase autonomic arousal, and it seems reasonable to assume that stored in memory along with other aspects of these negative moods may be imagery of autonomic arousal.

Given the evidence that both positive and negative mood inducers produce autonomic arousal *and* the assumption that imagery of this arousal is stored in memory, a further proposal may now be made: The greater, or longer lasting, the arousal that accompanies a positive (or negative) event in the present, the greater the possibility that similarly toned emotional experiences from the past will come to mind, and the greater may be the number of such memories that do come to mind. Thus, arousal may be an important component of mood states.

A Potential Problem

At this point one might ask why arousal produced by good fortune in the present is not equally likely to make memories of negative as well as positive events stored along with arousal come to mind. Similarly, why should arousal produced by bad fortune in the present not be equally likely to make positive as well as negative events stored with arousal come to mind? A possible answer is that the arousal states accompanying positive and negative events may differ. There is now considerable evidence that the patterning of physiological events that accompany different emotional states do differ (e.g. Ax, 1953; Funkenstein, 1956; Lacey, Bateman, & Van Lehn, 1953; Regan & Reilly, 1958; Schwartz, Weinberger, & Singer, 1981). However, as Mandler (1975) notes the different physiological patterns that may accompany different emotional states may not be "psychologically functional." He says:

> It is highly unlikely that humans can discriminate slight differences in patterns of autonomic response. More important, it would have to be shown that, given the different patterns of arousal, different emotions will result. At the present time, all I can say about the different physiological patterns in different emotional situations, particularly since they are measured after the onset of the emotional response, is that they are either a response to the environmental conditions that produce differential emotions or they are a response to differential behavior. Nothing in these data shows that the emotional behavior is a function of the physiological pattern [p. 127].

If this is the case, we are still left with the question of why arousal accompanying positive events does not cause negative events to come to mind and vice versa. Therefore, instead of assuming that differential patterning of arousal accompanying positive and negative events will cause priming of *only* similarly toned material from memory, a different explanation is adopted here. This explanation starts with the assumption that arousal accompanying both positive and negative events *does* prime both positively and negatively toned material in memory. After all, as the physiological psychologist Sternbach has stated (1966): "Despite the existence of patterning . . . many different situations produce rather similar activating effects. Increased muscle tension, sympathetic nervous system activity, and EEG desynchronization can be produced by most emotions [pp. 72–73]." But, there is still an important reason why both positive and negative mood inducers should be most likely to cause *similarly toned* material to come to mind; that is, that negative feelings experienced at various times have many attributes in common *in addition to* arousal, and the same is true for positive feelings. For instance, most negative feelings involve similar facial expressions and evaluations of the world. Likewise, most positive feelings result in similar facial expressions and in similar evaluations of the world. Imagery of some of these other shared attributes as well as of arousal may be stored in memory and, as with arousal, their recurrence in conjunction with a current feeling may contribute to priming similarly toned material from memory (see Laird et al., 1982, for evidence that facial expressions may prime related material in memory). Assuming this, it follows that even if arousal accompanying a positive or a negative experience in the present primes both positive and negative material from memory, similarly toned material should receive the *most* priming and should be most likely to enter awareness.[3]

EXISTING EVIDENCE FOR AROUSAL SERVING AS A CUE TO AFFECTIVE MATERIAL IN MEMORY

If the argument thus far is correct, then the greater the amount of arousal a person experiences when something good or bad happens, the more intense or long lasting should be the priming of similarly toned material from memory. Consequently, the greater and/or more long lasting the arousal, the more intense or long lasting should be the resultant mood as well as its influence on social perception and behavior.

Studies originally based on Schachter's (1964) and Schachter and Singer's (1962) theorizing that emotion may be considered a function of experiencing autonomic arousal together with a cognitive label for that arousal are consistent

---

[3]It is also possible that the intensity of arousal accompanying positive states differs from the intensity accompanying negative states, and this is a point that is discussed in detail later.

with this idea. Some of these have tested the idea that subjects may misattribute arousal to their attraction for others (Driscoll, Davis, & Lipetz, 1972; Dutton & Aron, 1974) or have been subsequently interpreted in terms of that idea (Jacobs, Berscheid, & Walster, 1971; Stephan, Berschcid, & Walster, 1971). Some are known as excitation transfer studies (Cantor, Bryant, & Zillmann, 1974; Zillmann, 1971), and still others are studies originally done to test other models, such as a relief theory of humor (Shurcliff, 1968).

This literature is extensive and there is insufficient space to review it all, or even a significant portion of it. However, to illustrate the consistency of previous findings with the present ideas, one misattribution study, one excitation transfer study, and one other study are described and interpreted in terms of the present framework.

Example 1: Misattribution of Arousal to Attraction

Schachter and Singer (1962) originally proposed that emotional states may be considered a function of being physiologically aroused and having a cognition appropriate to labeling this state of arousal. Moreover, they proposed that given a state of physiological arousal for which a person has no immediate explanation, he or she will experience an evaluative need and label his or her state in terms of the cognitions available to him or her. These available cognitions, they imply, are most frequently to be found in the person's immediate environment. As an example of such a process Schachter and Singer (1962) ask their reader to consider a man experiencing unexplained arousal and suggest that: "Should he at the time be with a beautiful woman he might decide he was wildly in love or sexually excited [p. 381]."

Others (Walster & Berscheid, 1974) have elaborated on this idea, and Dutton and Aron (1974) conducted a clever set of studies to test the idea. In one (Dutton & Aron, 1974, study 1), male subjects were approached by a young, attractive female experimenter when they were either on a high, shaky, arousal-producing bridge or on a low sturdy bridge. Subjects who were on the high arousal-producing bridge at the time of the encounter were more likely to call the experimenter later and, when asked to write a story during the study, wrote stories containing more sexual imagery than did the nonaroused subjects. Their two other studies yielded similar results, and, in discussing all three, they cite Schachter and Singer (1962) and propose that their results, like those of Schachter and Singer, were due to cognitive relabeling of their arousal state.

My explanation is not inconsistent with the idea of cognitive relabeling, but it is more detailed and it is distinct in several respects. The present theorizing suggests that, when subjects encountered the attractive, friendly woman, their focus of attention shifted from the bridge to the woman, and thoughts associated with attractive, friendly women were primed. The majority of such thoughts are probably positive. Further, in the high-bridge conditions, the pleasant thoughts may have been intensified by autonomic arousal already present as the result of having crossed the bridge, resulting in the person experiencing a positive feeling state and in bringing to mind even more positive thoughts, presumably those stored in memory with arousal imagery. Positively toned *behavioral* tendencies may also have been more likely to come to mind. This explains the increased sexual imagery in the stories of arousal subjects, as well as their increased tendency to call the woman.

Note that this explanation does not appeal to the construct of an evaluative need on the part of subjects to explain their arousal. Furthermore, the processes, but not the products to these processes, are explicitly assumed to be automatic. In other words, they are assumed to be ones that require no effort, do not enter awareness, and do not interrupt other ongoing cognitive processes. Therefore, I prefer to talk of arousal-priming material from memory rather than of labeling or of attribution of arousal, because the latter two terms might be interpreted as implying the existence of conscious, intentional processes. Finally, the present explanation places a great deal of emphasis on the role that *memory* plays in the process as well as emphasis on cues from the environment, whereas Dutton and Aron (1974), and earlier Schachter and Singer (1962), did not place much emphasis on the role memory might have played in producing the phenomena they observed.

Dutton and Aron (1974, study 1) also predicted and found that arousal would not increase sexual imagery in subjects' stories nor influence subjects' tendency to call the experimenter if the experimenter was a male. This also makes sense from the present perspective. For most male subjects, the sight of a male should not prime sexual imagery nor the desire to phone the other for a date. Thus, arousal plus the sight of a male experimenter should not necessarily have heightened the amount of sexual imagery in their stories. Instead, a tendency for any theme associated with arousal might have been heightened in subjects' stories when there was a male experimenter. For instance, sports themes might have been more common in the aroused-subjects' stories when the experimenter was male.

Example 2: Excitation Transfer

Zillmann (1971, 1978) has proposed a theory of excitation transfer and has conducted many studies that support the theory. As were the results of Dutton and Aron's (1974) studies, the results of these studies are consistent with the present theorizing.

Excitation transfer theory, Zillmann (1978) notes, was derived from Schachter and Singer's work. It is based upon several assumptions. Arousal is assumed to be generally nonspecific, although individuals *are* assumed to be capable of detecting "comparatively gross" changes in level of excitation. Also, individuals are assumed to be able to recall it later. Finally, excitation is assumed to decay rather slowly, and, if excitation from a number of sources is compounded, it is assumed that the individual does not partition it, but rather, according to Zillmann (1978): "tends to ascribe his entire excitatory reaction to one particular inducing condition [p. 359]."

Thus, if a person is aroused as a result of, say, having just watched an erotic film and is subsequently angered by another, the person may ascribe his or her total excitation to that other. In one of his many studies, Zillmann (1971) tested precisely this idea.

To do so, he recruited subjects for a study supposedly on the effect of punishment, in the form of electric shock, on learning. Using an elaborate cover story, he had all subjects participate in the following sequence of events. In a first session, the subject expressed opinions on some issues and a confederate was instructed to indicate agreement by turning on a light or disagreement by shocking the subject. The confederate shocked the subject 75% of the time. Next, the subject watched: (1) an erotic film that had been previously shown to elicit a high degree of arousal; (2) an aggressive film previously shown to elicit a moderate amount of arousal; or (3) a documentary film previously shown to elicit a low amount of arousal. Finally, the subject was told to shock the confederate each time the confederate made a mistake on a learning task and was allowed to choose the intensity of those shocks. The measure of aggression was the intensity of shocks delivered. Zillmann's (1971) results revealed that aggression was greatest following the erotic film that had presumably elicited high arousal, intermediate following the aggressive film that had presumably elicited moderate arousal, and lowest following the documentary film that had presumably elicited low, if any, arousal. He (Zillmann, 1971) explained this by stating that: "communication-produced excitation may serve to intensify or 'energize' post exposure emotional states [p. 431]," or, in other words, arousal from one source could be ascribed to another source that people also recognize as arousal producing.

Again, my position is not inconsistent with his, but it is more detailed and distinct in that it explicitly assumes that the processes involved are ones about which the subject probably had no awareness, and that priming of material from memory plays an important role in the process. Specifically, the effects Zillmann observed may have been due to the sight of the confederate "automatically" priming memories of that person's obnoxious past behavior, and arousal combining with this to prime angry thoughts and a behavioral tendency toward aggression.

I would also note that the present ideas are also consistent with many of Zillmann and his colleagues' other findings, such as those showing that feelings of arousal originally induced by erotic or disgusting stimuli may facilitate enjoyment of music or humor (Cantor, Bryant, & Zillmann, 1974; Cantor & Zillmann, 1973), and that arousal produced by physical exercise can facilitate feelings of anger and aggressive behavior (Zillmann, Katcher, & Milavsky, 1972).

Example 3: "Relief and Humor"

As a final example of past research that is consistent with the present ideas, consider a study by Shurcliff (1968). In this study designed to test the idea that relief enhances humor, Shurcliff exposed subjects to differential levels of anxiety (and, presumably, arousal) by asking them to pick up a docile rat (low anxiety), to pick up a rat and take a blood sample with a syringe (moderate anxiety), or to pick up a rat that might bite them and to take a blood sample (high anxiety). Then, when they went to the cage, they discovered a toy rat. Afterwards the subjects judged how humorous the event was, and a positive monotonic trend was found between degree of anxiety (or arousal) and perceived humor.

Shurcliff (1968) interpreted this result as evidence for a "relief" explanation of humor, but the present theorizing suggests another possible interpretation. Memories of humorous situations and of laughter from the past as well as the behavioral tendency to laugh are probably linked with memories of arousal. (Recall that Levi, 1965, 1972 and Averill, 1969 found that humorous films produced arousal.) Arousal in the present may cue those memories and heighten humor.

A Limitation on the Support that Previous Work Lends to the Present Theorizing

Whereas the research cited above, as well as many other studies, is consistent with the idea that arousal accompanying a mood-inducing event may automatically (without eliciting an "evaluative need" to explain the arousal) prime material stored in memory linked with arousal imagery, they are also consistent with another, equally plausible, explanation; that is, a person may experience an evaluative need and may *consciously* attribute arousal to something occurring simultaneously in his or her environment in an effort to explain that arousal. Therefore, to support the present ideas, it is important to test them in a manner not subject to such an interpretation.

In this regard it is fortunate that the present ideas lead to a prediction to which the above explanation does not. Specifically, the present theorizing suggests the effects of autonomic arousal should *not* be restricted to targets in the environment that seem to be very plausible sources of arousal. Rather, if how to behave or what judgment to make in a situation might be influenced by arousal-related *memories* from the past, then arousal has the potential for influencing that potential behavior or judgment. For example, imagine that a woman has run two blocks to catch a bus to work on a Monday morning. She gets on, notices a friend, and settles in beside her, still aroused as a result of her exercise. Her friend asks how her weekend was. Although it seems unreasonable to assume the woman will attribute her arousal to her friend's question—after all, it is just an ordinary question and besides, the true source of her arousal should be quite apparent—the present theorizing suggests that her answer may *still* be influenced by her arousal. When she reflects upon the question, more emotional experiences might come to mind than usual, so she might be more prone to mention an argument with her husband (instead of some more mundane aspect of the weekend) than would otherwise have been the case.

I (Clark, 1981) have conducted a study to test the idea that autonomic arousal will affect answers to questions that are not reasonable targets to which one might consciously attribute one's current arousal, but which might be influenced by recall of arousal-related material from memory. That experiment is now briefly described.

EFFECT OF A FEELING STATE INDUCTION AND AN AROUSAL INDUCTION ON ANSWERS TO MUNDANE QUESTIONS

In this study (Clark, 1981) subjects either exercised or did not. Then they experienced a positive mood induction or no mood induction, and finally they were asked to answer a series of mundane questions about the quality of faculty, students, and facilities at their university. It was assumed that being asked these questions would not be a reasonable target to which subjects might attribute arousal. However, it was predicted that a positive mood state would make positive material associated with the university more accessible—memories of good grades, good friends, good courses, etc. Further, it was expected that autonomic arousal would contribute to priming the same material. Thus, it was predicted that, given a positive mood state, additional arousal would cause people's judgments about their university to become more positive.

On the other hand, no prediction was made about the effect of arousal in the *absence* of a mood induction. Without knowing what feeling state subjects were in when they began the study, it is impossible to make such a prediction. As noted previously, for subjects in a positive feeling state to begin with, positive associations to the university should already be primed. Additional arousal may provide another cue to the same material, causing it to come to mind and making judgments more positive. However, subjects in negative feeling states to begin with should already have *negative* associations to the university primed, and further arousal may provide another cue to *that* material, causing *it* to come to mind and making judgments more negative. Finally, for subjects in no particular feeling state, the position taken thus far makes no predictions regarding the effects of further arousal. Although there is some evidence that *intense* unexpected arousal produces negative feelings (Marshall & Zimbardo, 1979; Maslach, 1979), there is no evidence that a less-intense arousal state would have the same effects. For these subjects, both positive and negative information might be more likely to come to mind than usually, and these effects might cancel one another's impact on overall judgments.

To test the preceding hypotheses, subjects were recruited for a study on the effects of distraction on memory. Upon arrival each subject was greeted by an experimenter who said the subject would perform a distracting task while listening to a story on tape. Afterwards, he or she would be asked to take a memory test for what had been heard on the tape.

The experimenter told all the subjects that some of the distracting tasks being studied involved physical exercise. Therefore, to be sure no one left the study still feeling the effects of the exercise, she was taking every subject's blood pressure and pulse before doing the task and then again at the conclusion of the study regardless of their assigned condition. She proceeded, then, to take the first set of these measures.

Next, the subject's distracting task was described. For half, those in the arousal condition, it turned out to be stepping up and down on a cinder block. For the remainder, those in the no-arousal conditions, it turned out to be stringing cardboard disks together. All subjects performed their assigned task for 7 minutes while listening to a story and immediately thereafter took a brief memory test. The experimenter then picked up the subject's test, commented that the study was over, and excused herself for a minute to give her supervisor the results, because "She likes to have a look at them." Upon returning, the experi-

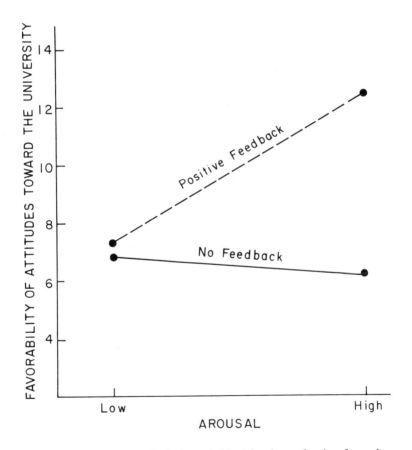

FIG. 12.4.   Favorability of attitudes toward the university as a function of arousal state and type of feedback received.

menter took a second blood pressure and pulse reading, assured the subject he or she was "back to normal" (in fact, however, the exercise subjects were not), and sent the subject into the supervisor's office to be paid or given credit.

Once inside the supervisor's office, a second experimenter, who was unaware of the subject's arousal condition, picked up the subject's test sheet and glanced up at him or her. If the subject had been assigned to the no-mood induction condition, the experimenter commented that she had not had a chance to look over the subject's test results. If the subject had been assigned to the positive mood condition, she said she *had* looked over their results. She told the subject he or she had done very well—way above the norm—and that most people had a very difficult time on the task. She also told the subject he or she should be very pleased, because the ability to remember things when one is distracted is related to general intelligence.

After commenting or not on the test results, the second experimenter began to pay or to give credit to the subject. As she did so, she casually said she wanted the subject to do one more thing. Because the study took such a short time, she was asking everyone to help her research assistant who had been sick the previous semester and who had an "incomplete" in a research methodology course. The subject could help by filling out a survey for her. The subject was then paid or given credit and directed back to the first experimenter's room.

The first experimenter, who was unaware of the feedback manipulation, had the subject fill out a survey on which the subject rated: (1) the quality of university teaching; (2) the quality of teaching in his or her major; (3) how worthwhile courses outside his or her major were; (4) how concerned with students faculty were; (5) how friendly students at the university were; (6) the pleasantness of the campus; and (7) the quality of the libraries. All ratings were made on nine-point scales. The sum of the subject's answers on these questions was the dependent measure for the study.

The results were as follows: The blood pressure and pulse measures revealed that exercise did produce significantly greater arousal in the arousal than in the no-arousal conditions. In addition, the results on the dependent measure, presented in Fig. 12.4, supported the hypotheses about the effects of arousal given success feedback and given no feedback. Specifically, arousal significantly enhanced the favorability of the *success* subjects' judgments about their university. In contrast, arousal had no effect on the favorability of the *no-feedback* subjects' judgments about their university.[4]

---

[4]Success, in the absence of arousal, did not enhance the favorability of subjects' judgments. This may seem puzzling in light of Isen et al's (1978, study 2) finding that a mood induction, by itself, will increase favorability of judgments. However, in that study subjects had been walking in a mall prior to being approached, whereas in the no-arousal conditions of the Clark (1981) study, subjects had been sitting still for 10 to 15 minutes. Thus subjects in the Isen et al. (1978, study 2) study may have been experiencing an arousal level closer to that of the arousal than the no-arousal subjects in the Clark (1981) study.

The results of this experiment are quite consistent with the idea that experiencing arousal in the present will help to prime material previously stored in memory linked with arousal. It was assumed that if positive material were already primed by means of a success manipulation, positive material in memory would be more accessible than at another time. Further, it was assumed that arousal, experienced at the same time, would contribute to priming the same positive material. Consequently, it was predicted that following a positive feeling state manipulation arousal would cause people's judgments to become more positive. This is what was found.

In the absence of a manipulation to make people feel good or bad, however, it was impossible to make a prediction about the effect of arousal on judgment. As noted earlier, for people who began the study in a positive mood, arousal might cause judgments to become more positive. For people who began the study in a negative mood, however, arousal might cause judgments to become more negative, and these effects might cancel one another out. Further, for people in no particular mood to begin with, arousal might prime both positive and negative memories, and these effects might cancel one another out. Consequently, from the present viewpoint, the lack of an effect in the no-mood induction conditions is not surprising.

The results of the present study are difficult to explain in terms of the idea that people experience an evaluative need when they experience unexplained arousal, and that they search the environment for an explanation, or that they attribute their arousal to a target in their environment. Effects of arousal on the subjects' answers to the questionnaire were found, yet it seems implausible to claim that the subjects attributed their arousal to the rather bland questions they were asked.[5] Whereas it is clear that additional studies that more directly implicate priming of arousal-related material from memory are crucial to supporting the present theorizing about arousal and memory, the results of the Clark (1981) study are consistent with the present theorizing. Furthermore, they are difficult to interpret in terms of people consciously labeling their arousal according to cues in the environment. In

---

[5]One might argue that the results might be explained in another way. First, subjects recalled aspects of their university experience in response to the questionnaire; aspects that tended to be positive in the positive-mood condition and neutral in the no-feeling state induction condition. Then they consciously attributed current arousal to those recollections *if* they were emotionally toned, as they tended to be in the positive but not in the no-mood induction condition, thus accounting for the effect of arousal in the positive condition and the lack of an effect of arousal in the neutral condition. However, such an argument seems farfetched. It might also be argued that the results of this study could be interpreted in terms of Hull's drive theory (Hull, 1943; 1952). Positive moods may increase the position in one's behavioral hierarchy of the tendency to make favorable evaluations, and arousal may energize this tendency. This would explain the results in the success conditions. However, even in the no-feedback conditions subjects tended to evaluate their university favorably, yet arousal did not enhance this tendency.

addition, I should note that we *have* very recently conducted two studies which do directly support the idea that arousal cues arousal related material from memory. In these studies material people learned when in a high or low arousal state was best recalled when they are once again experiencing a similar arousal state.

Next I would like to turn to three remaining unanswered questions about arousal and feeling states. First, must enhanced arousal necessarily occur with positive events in order for those events to cue other positive material from memory? Second, does arousal always influence judgments and behavior through the automatic processes discussed thus far? And, finally, might different intensities of arousal result in priming different sets of material from memory?

SOME REMAINING QUESTIONS

Is Elevated Arousal Necessary for Positive Moods to Cue Positive Material from Memory?

Even though in the study just reported the low-arousal-positive-feedback subjects did not give more positive ratings than did the low-arousal-no-feedback subjects, I believe the answer to the preceding question is probably no. As previously mentioned, positive (and negative) experiences share many attributes with one another. Arousal is just one. Others are positive (negative) facial expressions and the evaluation of oneself as a fortunate (unfortunate) person. Thus it should be possible for a pleasant (unpleasant) experience in the present to cue pleasant (unpleasant) material from the past, even if the person is not especially aroused in the present. I only wish to argue that arousal that does accompany pleasant or unpleasant events in the present may make recall of similarly toned memories from the past *more probable,* because it is *one* thing the person's present state has in common with those past, stored states.

Does Arousal always Influence Judgments and Behavior Through the "Automatic" Processes Described Previously?

Thus, far, this chapter has focused on arousal in the present cueing arousal-related material stored in memory through automatic processes that take place without effort, without awareness, and without interfering with other ongoing cognitive processes (Clark & Isen, 1982; Posner & Snyder, 1975). Further, it has been emphasized that these processes can explain many of the effects autonomic arousal has been shown to have on social judgments and behavior without appealing to the existence of an evaluative need to explain arousal. However, this should not be taken to mean I believe that people *never* experience an evaluative need to explain arousal, or that they *never* consciously attribute arousal to a target from their environment or from memory.

Clark and Isen (1982) have discussed a distinction between the kind of *automatic* processes discussed in this chapter and *controlled* processes or strategies that people may intentionally, effortfully use to alleviate negative feelings or to maintain positive feelings. We found this distinction useful in explaining the mixed findings that negative feeling states have been shown to have on judgments and behaviors. In other words, negative feeling states may sometimes cause our judgments and behaviors to become more unlikely or more negative by automatically priming negative material in memory. However, sometimes people may consciously, effortfully try to alleviate negative feelings by thinking positive thoughts or by behaving in a positive fashion. This distinction between automatic and controlled processes may also aid in understanding different types of processes through which arousal may affect judgment and behavior.

Automatic processes such as those described in this chapter may often mediate the influence of arousal on judgments and behavior. However, sometimes arousal may influence judgments and behavior through more effortful controlled strategies. The question of when arousal will have an impact on judgment and behavior through each type of process is briefly elaborated upon in the following section.

When Arousal Will Tend to Influence Judgments Automatically.   Every day, people experience elevations in autonomic arousal, sometimes due to physical exercise, sometimes due to emotional events such as being complimented, doing well on a test, watching a horror movie on TV, or going to the dentist. Experiencing arousal as a result of these sorts of events should not give rise to an evaluative need nor a conscious search for the source of that arousal. We *know* from past experience with exercise and with emotional events what caused the arousal.

However, in spite of already having an explanation, the arousal may automatically prime arousal-related material from memory. As a consequence it may influence subsequent judgments and behavior. For example, in the case of arousal produced as a result of emotional experiences, it may contribute to inducing a similarly toned ongoing mood state. Or, as in an example given earlier in this chapter, it may result in a person including more emotional experiences in a description of what her weekend was like, etc.

When Arousal Will Tend to Influence Judgments through Controlled Processes.   Despite the fact that throughout this chapter I have focused on arousal influencing judgments and behavior through "automatic" processes, it is obvious that arousal may sometimes influence behavior through very different sorts of processes—effortful, conscious, controlled processes. Two types of situations in which this may occur are briefly outlined below.

First, as Schachter (1964) suggested long ago, when a person experiences arousal *that has no obvious cause,* the person may experience an evaluative need and may consciously and effortfully search for an explanation. In such cases, "controlled" rather than "automatic" processes are mediating the effects of arousal on judgments and behavior. One example of such a situation is, of course, the situation in which the subjects in Schachter and Singer's (1964) classic experiment who were unknowingly injected with adrenaline and who received either no explanation or who were actually misinformed regarding its effects found themselves. Similarly, a person who has drunk coffee and who later that night has forgotten about the coffee but cannot fall asleep due to the arousal may feel a need to explain that arousal. People in such states may then consciously search the environment and/or memory for an answer—perhaps hitting on the correct answer, perhaps on an incorrect one—and their answer may influence their judgments and behavior. For example, if the person who cannot fall asleep consciously decides that his or her arousal and subsequent insomnia is due to some noise from a neighbor, he or she may call the neighbor to complain. In any case, it is important to note that a controlled process such as this is a different sort of process than the automatic processes that have been the primary focus of this chapter. As noted in an earlier chapter (Clark & Isen, 1982), controlled processes may "override" the automatic processes through which arousal may influence feeling states. However, I believe that the effects of arousal on judgments and behavior are far more often mediated through automatic processes than through controlled processes elicited in the kind of situation just described.

There is also a second type of situation in which controlled processes may mediate the effects of arousal on thoughts and behaviors. If a person finds him or herself in a very aroused state, for whatever reason, that person may intentionally behave in a manner aimed at alleviating that arousal. For instance, a shy person may be very aroused because he or she has to give a speech before a large audience. The person, knowing full well that anticipation of the speech is causing the arousal, may intentionally focus his or her thoughts elsewhere, perhaps by reading the newspaper or talking to a friend. Once again, this idea is not new. Piliavin and Piliavin (1972), for example, have proposed that such processes may influence whether or not a person helps in an emergency. They propose that as arousal in an emergency situation increases, the probability of observers making *some* response in order to alleviate the arousal increases. That response may either be to help or to escape from the situation, depending upon other factors.

Might Different Intensities of Arousal Cue Different Sets of Material From Memory?

People talk of different types of positive and negative states that intuitively involve different levels of arousal—of states of serenity and of elation, for example, or of states of depression and of extreme irritability. In addition, Russell (1980) has recently conducted some research supporting the claim that affective experience varies both in terms of how positively or negatively toned it is *and* in terms of the degree of arousal it involves.

If different mood inducers do involve different levels of arousal, and if people can detect such differences, a proposition that may not be true, there are some important implications for the present arguments. Positive or negative mood inducers that elicit low arousal may be more likely to elicit memories associated with similar, low amounts of arousal than with memories associated with high arousal and vice versa. Thus, a quiet, beautiful boat ride might be more likely to cue memories of watching a beautiful sunset than memories of participating in an enjoyable and invigorating athletic contest. Similarly, participating in that contest may be more likely to cue positive memories of dancing than memories of the beautiful sunset. In other words, mood states may vary in terms of how much arousal they involve as well as in terms of whether they are pleasant or unpleasant, and material congruent with *both* aspects of any given mood state may be most accessible to a person in that mood state.

It may also turn out to be the case that unpleasant events typically involve greater arousal than pleasant ones. This may be another reason, in addition to those discussed earlier, why arousal accompanying positive states is more likely to prime positive memories than negative memories and vice versa.

FINAL COMMENTS ON AROUSAL AND FEELING STATES

Before summarizing this chapter, I would like to make two final observations about mood states and to speculate on how the notion of arousal fits with these observations. The first has to do with the duration of feeling states, and the second with the unexpectedness of most mood-inducing events.

Duration of Feeling States.   Feeling states have been discussed thus far as being states of feeling good or bad and of having increased accessibility of similarly toned material in memory, presumably due to priming. Yet, priming, as studied by cognitive psychologists (e.g. Meyer & Schvaneveldt, 1971; Neely, 1976), is not considered to be a phenomenon that takes place over 10 to 20 minutes. Why, then, should feeling states and their effects on judgment and behavior endure for such periods of time? Part of the answer may lie in their being large quantities of similarly toned material in memory, so that one positive thought may prime others that prime still others and so forth. Another important and perhaps related part of the answer may lie in the nature of physiological arousal. Physiological states of arousal often endure for periods of, say, 10 minutes, and *throughout* that time arousal may contribute to the priming of affectively toned material in memory. In other words, arousal may serve to support the chain of one positive thought leading to another and so forth, by contributing to the activation of the *same* material that other aspects of the positive thoughts are priming. Thus priming involved in feeling states may be a special sort of priming distinct from the priming phenomena observed by cognitive psychologists by virtue of the involvement of physiological states of arousal.

Expectancies.   Another idea that follows from the reasoning in this chapter is that unexpected positive (or negative) events ought to be more likely to produce ongoing positive (or negative) feeling states than should expected positive (or negative) events. Unexpected events have been shown to produce increases in autonomic arousal (Berlyne, Craw, Salapatek, & Lewis, 1963), and the Clark (1981) study demonstrates that arousal that accompanies a positive event exaggerates the effect of that event on subsequent judgments. Thus, a high school student who expects he or she will be accepted at a college to which he or she has applied should be less likely to be put in a positive mood when an acceptance letter arrives than should a student who did not expect to be accepted. Similarly, a person who expects his or her application for a job to be turned down should be less apt to be put in a negative mood when that happens than should a person who does not expect his or her application to be turned down.

SUMMARY

The intention of the present chapter was to integrate the concept of autonomic arousal with a current model of how feeling states influence judgments and behavior (Clark & Isen, 1982; Isen et al., 1978). It has been suggested that storage of arousal imagery in memory is part of what it means to say that a feeling tone is stored in memory. Further, it has been suggested that the experience of arousal in the present, as the result of a similarly toned emotional experience, exercise or whatever, may prime memories linked with arousal imagery, making them more likely to come to mind and to influence behavior. Although it is noted that further studies directly implicating priming of arousal-related memories in the processes through which feeling states in general (and arousal in particular) influence judgments and behavior is needed, some preliminary evidence (Clark, 1981) to support the preceding ideas has been presented. Furthermore, it has briefly been noted that two studies directly implicating memory on the processes proposed here *have* very recently been completed.

In addition to proposing a role for arousal in the links between feeling states, judgments, and behavior, the implications of this idea for understanding the duration of feeling states and the impact of people's expectancies for positive or negative events on possible ensuing mood states has been discussed. Finally, it has also been noted that not *all* the effects of arousal on judgments and behavior are necessarily mediated through the automatic processes, which have been the primary focus of this chapter. When a person experiences uncertainty about the source of his or her arousal or when the arousal state is particularly intense, the effects of arousal on judgments and behavior may be mediated by controlled strategies.

ACKNOWLEDGMENTS

Preparation of this chapter was facilitated by a Ford Motor Company Research Fund grant. I thank Sheldon Cohen, Susan Fiske, Lynne Reder, Michael Scheier, and Daniel Wegner for their helpful comments on the material in this chapter.

REFERENCES

Averill, J. R. Autonomic response patterns during sadness and mirth. *Psychophysiology*, 1969, *5*, 399–414.
Ax, A. F. The physiological differentiation of fear and anger in humans. *Psychosomatic Medicine*, 1953, *15*, 433–442.
Bartlett, J. C., Burleson, G., & Santrock, J. W. Emotional mood and memory in children. *Journal of Experimental Child Psychology*, in press.
Bartlett, J. C., & Santrock, J. W. Affect-dependent episodic memory in young children. *Child Development*, 1979, *50*, 513–518.
Berlyne, D. E., Craw, M. S., Salapatek, P. H., & Lewis, J. L. Novelty, complexity, incongruity, extrinsic motivation, and the GSR. *Journal of Experimental Psychology*, 1963, *66*, 560–567.
Bousfield, W. A. The relationship between mood and the production of affectivity toned associates. *The Journal of General Psychology*, 1950, *42*, 67–85.
Bower, G. H. Mood and memory. *American Psychologist*, 1981, *36*, 129–148.
Bower, G. H., & Cohen, P. Emotional influences on learning and cognition. In M. S. Clark & S. T. Fiske (Eds.), *Affect and cognition*. Hillsdale, N.J.: Lawrence Erlbaum Associates, 1982.
Bower, G. H., Monteiro, K. P., & Gilligan, S. G. Emotional mood as a context for learning and recall. *Journal of Verbal Learning and Verbal Behavior*, 1978, *17*, 573–578.
Buss, A. R., & Plomin, R. *A temperament theory of personality development*. New York: Wiley, 1975.
Cannon, W. B. *Bodily changes in pain, hunger, fear and rage*. New York: Appleton, 1929.
Cantor, J. R., Bryant, J., & Zillmann, D. The enhancement of humor appreciation by transferred excitation. *Journal of Personality and Social Psychology*, 1974, *30*, 812–821.
Cantor, J. R., & Zillmann, D. The effect of affective state and emotional arousal on music appreciation. *Journal of General Psychology*, 1973, *89*, 97–108.
Cialdini, R. P., & Kenrick, D. T. Altruism as hedonism: A social development perspective on the relationship of negative mood state and helping. *Journal of Personality and Social Psychology*, 1976, *34*, 907–914.
Clark, M. S. *Enhancing the link between feeling states and judgments through arousal*. Unpublished manuscript, Carnegie–Mellon University, 1981.
Clark, M. S., & Isen, A. M. Toward understanding the relationship between feeling states and social behavior. In A. Hastorf & A. M. Isen (Eds.), *Cognitive social psychology*. New York: Elsevier, 1982.

Clark, M. S., & Waddell, B. *Explaining the link between feeling states, helping, attraction and acquisition of information.* Unpublished manuscript, Carnegie-Mellon University, 1981.

Collins, A. M., & Loftus, E. F. A spreading-activation theory of semantic processing. *Psychological Review,* 1975, *82,* 407–428.

Collins, A. M., & Quillian, M. R. How to make a language user. In E. Tulving & W. Donaldson (Eds.), *Organization of memory.* New York: Academic Press, 1972.

Driscoll, R., Davis, K., & Lipetz, M. Parental interference and romantic love: The Romeo and Juliet Effect. *Journal of Personality and Social Psychology,* 1972, *24,* 1–10.

Dutton, D., & Aron, A. Some evidence for heightened sexual attraction under conditions of high anxiety. *Journal of Personality and Social Psychology,* 1974, *30,* 510–517.

Feather, N. T. Effects of prior success and failure on expectations of success and subsequent performance. *Journal of Personality and Social Psychology,* 1966, *3,* 287–298.

Forest, D., Clark, M. S., Mills, J., & Isen, A. M. Helping as a function of feeling state and nature of the helping behavior. *Motivation and Emotion,* 1979, *3,* 161–169.

Funkenstein, D. H. Nor-epinephrine-like and epinephrine-like substances in relation to human behavior. *Journal of Mental Diseases,* 1956, *124,* 58–68.

Gouaux, C. Induced affective states and interpersonal attraction. *Journal of Personality and Social Psychology,* 1971, *20,* 37–43.

Gouaux, G., & Summers, K. Interpersonal attraction as a function of affective state and affective change. *Journal of Research in Personality,* 1973, *7,* 254–260.

Griffitt, W. B. Environmental effects on interpersonal affective behavior: Ambient effective temperature and attraction. *Journal of Personality and Social Psychology,* 1970, *15,* 240–244.

Griffitt, W., & Guay, P. "Object" evaluation and conditioned affect. *Journal of Experimental Research in Personality,* 1969, *4,* 1–8.

Hull, C. L. *Principles of Behavior.* New York: Appleton-Century Crofts, 1943.

Hull, C. L. *A Behavior System: An Introduction to Behavior Theory Concerning the Individual Organism.* New Haven, Conn.: Yale University Press, 1952.

Isen, A. M. Positive affect, accessibility of cognitions and helping. In J. Piliavin (Chair.), *Current directions in theory on helping behavior.* Symposium presented at the meeting of the Eastern Psychological Association, New York, 1975.

Isen, A. M., Clark, M., & Schwartz, M. F. Duration of the effect of good mood on helping: Footprints on the sands of time." *Journal of Personality and Social Psychology,* 1978, *36,* 1–12.

Isen, A. M., Shalker, T., Clark, M., & Karp, L. Positive affect, accessibility of material in memory and behavior: A cognitive loop? *Journal of Personality and Social Psychology,* 1978, *36,* 1–12.

Izard, C. E. Emotion and cognition: Can there be a working relationship? In M. S. Clark & S. T. Fiske (Eds.), *Affect and cognition.* Hillsdale, N.J.: Lawrence Erlbaum Associates, 1982.

Izard, C. E., & Buechler, S. Aspects of consciousness and personality in terms of differential emotions theory. In R. Plutchik & H. Kellerman (Eds.), *Emotion: Theory, Research, and Experience* (Volume 1). New York: Academic Press, 1980.

Jacobs, L., Berscheid, E., & Walster, E. Self esteem and attraction. *Journal of Personality and Social Psychology,* 1971, *17,* 84–91.

James, W. What is an emotion? *Mind,* 1884, *9,* 188–205.

Jost, H. Some physiological changes during frustration. *Child Development,* 1941, *12,* 9–15.

Lacey, J. I., Bateman, D. E., & Van Lehn, R. Autonomic response specificity: An experimental study. *Psychosomatic Medicine,* 1953, *15,* 8–21.

Laird, J. D., Wagener, J. J., Halal, M., & Szegda, M. Remembering what you feel: The effects of emotion on memory. *Journal of Personality and Social Psychology,* 1982, *42,* 646–657.

Leight, K. A., & Ellis, H. C. Emotional mood states, strategies, and state-dependency in memory. *Journal of Verbal Learning and Verbal Behavior,* 1981, *20,* 251–266.

Leventhal, H. A perceptual-motor processing model of emotion. In P. Pliner, K. R. Blankstein, &

I. M. Spigel (Eds.), *Advances in the study of communication and affect* (Vol. 5): *Perception of emotion in self and others.* New York: Plenum Press, 1979.

Levi, L. Sympathoadrenomedullary responses to "pleasant" and "unpleasant" psychosocial stimuli. In L. Levi (Ed.), *Stress and distress in response to psychosocial stimuli: Laboratory and real life studies on sympathoadrenomedullary and related reactions.* Stockholm: Almquist & Wiksell, 1972.

Levi, L. Urinary output of adrenalin and noradrenalin during pleasant and unpleasant emotional states A preliminary report. *Psychomatic Medicine,* 1965, *27,* 80–85.

Loeb, A., Beck, A. T., & Diggory, J. Differential effects of success and failure on depressed and nondepressed patients. *The Journal of Nervous and Mental Disease,* 1971, *152,* 106–114.

Lundberg, U. Urban commuting: Crowdedness and catecholamine excretion. *Journal of Human Stress,* 1976, *2,* 26–32.

Macht, M. L., Spear, N. E., & Levis, D. J. State-dependent retention in humans induced by alternations in affective state. *Bulletin of the Psychonomic Society,* 1977, *10,* 415–418.

Mandler, G. *Mind and Emotion.* New York: Wiley, 1975.

Mandler, G. The structure of value: Accounting for taste. In M. S. Clark & S. T. Fiske (Eds.), *Affect and cognition.* Hillsdale, N.J.: Lawrence Erlbaum Associates, 1982.

Mandler, G., & Kremen, I. Autonomic feedback: A correlational study. *Journal of Personality,* 1958, *26,* 388–389.

Marshall, G., & Zimbardo, P. G. Affective consequences of inadequately explained physiological arousal. *Journal of Personality and Social Psychology,* 1979, *37,* 970–988.

Maslach, C. Negative emotional biasing of unexplained arousal. *Journal of Personality and Social Psychology,* 1979, *37,* 953–969.

Masters, J. C., & Furman, W. Effects of affect states on noncontingent outcome expectancies and beliefs in internal or external control. *Developmental Psychology,* 1975, *12,* 481–482.

Meyer, D. W., & Schvaneveldt, R. W. Facilitation in recognizing pairs of words: Evidence of a dependence between retrieval operations. *Journal of Experimental Psychology,* 1971, *90,* 227–234.

Mueller, C. W., & Donnerstein, E. Film-facilitated arousal and prosocial behavior. *Journal of Experimental Social Psychology,* 1981, *17,* 31–41.

Neely, J. H. Semantic priming and retrieval from lexical memory: Evidence for facilatory and inhibitory processes. *Memory and Cognition,* 1976, *4,* 648–654.

Nelson, R. E., & Craighead, W. E. Selective recall of positive and negative feedback, self-control behaviors, and depression. *Journal of Abnormal Psychology,* 1977, *86,* 379–388.

Patkai, P. Catecholamine excretion in pleasant and unpleasant situations. *Acta Psychologica,* 1971, *35,* 352–363.

Piliavin, J. A., & Piliavin, I. M. Effect of blood on reactions to a victim. *Journal of Personality and Social Psychology,* 1972, *23,* 353–361.

Posner, M. I., & Snyder, C. R. Attention and cognitive control. In R. L. Solso (Ed.), *Information Processing and Cognition: The Loyola Symposium.* Hillsdale, N.J.: Erlbaum, 1975.

Regan, P. F., & Reilly, J. Circulating epinephrine and norepinephrine in changing emotional states. *Journal of Nervous and Mental Disease,* 1958, *127,* 12–16.

Russell, J. A. A circumplex model of affect. *Journal of Personality and Social Psychology,* 1980, *39,* 1161–1178.

Schachter, S. The interaction of cognitive and physiological determinants of emotional state. In L. Berkowitz (Ed.), *Advances in Experimental Social Psychology.* New York: Academic Press, 1964.

Schachter, S., & Singer, J. Cognitive, social, and physiological determinants of emotional state. *Psychological Review,* 1962, *69,* 379–399.

Schiffenbauer, A. Effect of observer's emotional state on judgments of the emotional state of others. *Journal of Personality and Social Psychology,* 1974, *30,* 1, 31–35.

Schwartz, G. E., Weinberger, D. A., & Singer, J. A. Cardiovascular differentiation of happiness, sadness, anger, and fear following imagery and exercise. *Psychosomatic Medicine,* 1981, *43,* 343–364.

Shurcliff, A. Judged humor, arousal, and the relief theory. *Journal of Personality and Psychology,* 1968, *8,* 360–363.

Sternbach, R. *Principles of Psychophysiology.* New York: Academic Press, 1966.

Stephan, W., Berscheid, E., & Walster, E. Sexual arousal and heterosexual perception. *Journal of Personality and Social Psychology,* 1971, *20,* 93–101.

Teasdale, J. D., & Fogarty, S. J. Differential effects of induced mood on retrieval of pleasant and unpleasant events from episodic memory. *Journal of Abnormal Psychology,* 1979, *88,* 248–257.

Veitch, R., & Griffitt, W. Good news—bad news: Affective and interpersonal effects. *Journal of Applied Social Psychology,* 1976, *6,* 69–75.

Walster, E., & Berscheid, E. A little bit about love: A minor essay on a major topic. In T. L. Huston (Ed.), *Foundations of Interpersonal Attraction.* New York: Academic Press.

Weingartner, H., Miller, H., & Murphy, D. L. Mood-state-dependent retrieval of verbal associations. *Journal of Abnormal Psychology,* 1977, *86,* 276–284.

Zillmann, D. Excitation transfer in communication-mediated aggressive behavior. *Journal of Experimental Social Psychology,* 1971, *7,* 419–434.

Zillmann, D. Attribution and misattribution of excitatory reactions. In J. H. Harvey, W. Ickes, & R. F. Kidd (Eds.), *New directions in attribution research* (Vol. 2). Hillsdale, N.J.: Lawrence Erlbaum Associates, 1978.

Zillmann, D., Katcher, A. H., & Milavsky, B. Excitation transfer from physical exercise to subsequent aggressive behavior. *Journal of Experimental Social Psychology,* 1972, *8,* 247–259.

13

Emotional Influences in Memory and Thinking: Data and Theory

Gordon H. Bower
Paul R. Cohen
Stanford University

INTRODUCTION

We have investigated emotional influences on human memory, perception, judgment, and thinking. We find powerful effects of people's feelings upon their cognitive processes. Our first group of results show how a person's feelings act like a selective filter that is tuned to incoming material that supports or justifies those feelings; the filter admits material congruent with the perceiver's mood but casts aside incongruent material. Feelings cause congruent stimuli to become more *salient,* to stand out more, arouse more interest, cause deeper processing and greater learning of congruent material. This filtering is important insofar as it determines what gets stored in memory in the first place.

Second, we find that people's feelings affect what records they can retrieve from memory. People can best retrieve events originally learned in a particular mood by somehow reinstating or returning to that same mood. We have several demonstrations of this "mood-state-dependent retrieval."

Third, we find emotional influences upon thinking and judgments. People's social perceptions as well as their imaginative fantasies are subjective; they are easily influenced by their feelings at the moment. These influences occur when people evaluate their friends, themselves, their possessions, and their future.

We propose a preliminary theory to explain these empirical results. This theory assumes that memories of events are recorded into a semantic network, and that different emotions can be represented by different units or nodes in this same network. When active, an emotion will become associated with coincident events. Memories, concepts, and perceptual categories are retrieved by the spreading of activation from the current emotion unit as well as from the units corresponding to the explicitly presented retrieval cues.

Whereas this network theory suffices to account for our results in a general way, it is incomplete in not addressing how emotional reactions are evoked by events. We introduce the "blackboard" control structure to model how the person combines several knowledge sources in arriving at an emotional interpretation of a situation. This enables us to deal with certain theoretical puzzles such as reappraisals of earlier emotional experiences and hot versus cold uses of emotional terms.

Experimental Background.   Most of our experiments use a common methodology that is quite effective. We induce emotional states (happiness, sadness, or anger) in our college-student volunteers via hypnotic suggestions. We first select volunteers who are highly hypnotizable. After hypnotizing them, we suggest that they place themselves in a specified emotional state by remembering an appropriate scene from their life and reliving that emotional experience in their imagination. Their happy scenes are typically moments of success or personal intimacy; sad scenes are usually moments of failure, loss, or rejection. After getting into the specified mood at a moderate level, subjects are asked to maintain it while they perform our experimental tasks. The tasks require 5 to 20 minutes, during which we typically remind subjects to refresh and maintain their mood. The hypnotic moods seem quite genuine and produce results comparable to mood effects obtained by naturalistic means. With this background, we now describe some of our results. Some of these were described earlier (Bower, 1981), although several new findings are reported here.

Selective Filtering and Learning

The basic hypothesis is that people's feelings cause certain environmental stimuli to become more salient, to stand out, to evoke deeper processing and better memory. We have not yet carried out experiments that would provide the most straightforward tests for emotional effects in selective observation.

We do have demonstrations of selective learning of happy versus sad material in a narrative by subjects who were happy or sad at the time they read it. One story was about two college men getting together and playing a friendly game of tennis. Andre is happy—everything is going well for him—whereas Jack is sad—nothing is going well for him. The events of the two men's lives and their emotional reactions are vividly described in the story, which is a balanced, third-person account. After reading, our subjects were asked who they thought was the central character and who they identified with. We found that readers identified more with the character who was in their mood, thought the story was about him, and thought the story contained more statements about him.

The subjects recalled the text the next day while in a neutral mood, with the results shown in Fig. 13.1. Subjects recalled more facts about the character with whom they had identified. Eighty percent of the facts recalled by the sad readers

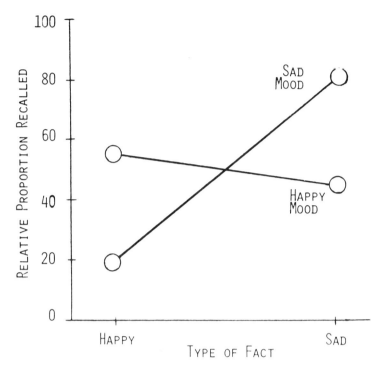

FIG. 13.1.   Relative percentages of recall of facts about the happy character versus the sad character by readers who were happy or sad (from Bower, 1981).

were about the sad character; 55% of the facts recalled by the happy readers were about the happy character. This is mood-congruous selection according to the character the statement was about. It differs from state-dependent memory (to be discussed shortly), because these subjects were in a neutral mood during recall.

In another experiment (Bower, Gilligan, & Monteiro, 1981) we had subjects read some simulated psychiatric interviews, in which a psychiatrist led a patient through several sessions of hypnosis-induced age regression. The patient in the narrative briefly described a series of unrelated happy incidents and sad incidents from his life. The subjects were made to feel happy or sad while reading this by posthypnotic suggestion. Later they recalled the narrative with the results shown in Fig. 13.2.

Here again, people learned more about incidents congruent with their mood. Happy readers recalled about one and one half times as many happy incidents as sad incidents, whereas sad readers recalled about one and one third times as many sad as happy incidents. So the mood-congruity effect occurred for happy versus sad incidents related by a single character.

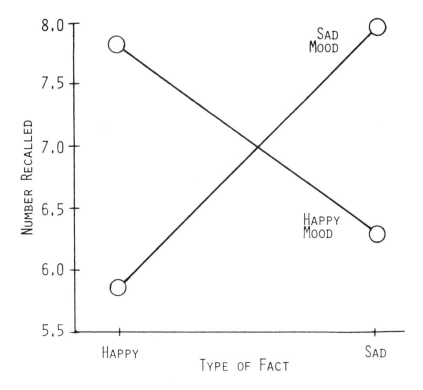

FIG. 13.2.   Number of happy versus sad story incidents recalled by readers who were happy or sad. (One character in the story described both types of personal incidents, from Bower, 1981).

How are we to explain the mood-congruity effect? Without describing details here, we note that we are investigating three complementary explanations of mood-congruous learning. The first hypothesis is that subjects semantically *elaborate* more on mood-congruous material; the second is that mood-congruous narrative events are more likely to *remind* subjects of an autobiographic event; the third is that mood-congruous material causes a more *intense* emotional reaction than does incongruous material. Any or all of these immediate effects could plausibly cause greater memory for mood-congruous events. Space limitations preclude our describing this research here.

Selective Retrieval

Besides selective storage, emotion also influences which memory records are easily accessed in memory. Here, we find emotion "state-dependent" memory: People can best retrieve a memory by reinstating the emotion they were experiencing when they originally stored it. Thus, subjects who are happy can thereby recall better some experience stored when they were happy. The effect is not "all–or–none" but "more–or–less" recall, similar to other context changes such as altering a person's environment between learning and recalling.

State dependency may be illustrated with an early experiment by Bower, Monteiro, and Gilligan (1978). Subjects were taught to free recall two lists of 16 words, one list learned while they were happy, the other learned while they were sad. Later they recalled both lists when they were in one mood or the other. (The second entry into a mood was always achieved by remembering a different happy or sad experience than used originally.) The results are shown in Fig. 13.3. People who were tested sad recalled more of the list they had learned while sad, whereas people who were tested happy recalled more of the list they had learned while happy. Relative to control subjects who learned and recalled both lists in a single mood, subjects who learned the lists in different moods showed interference when recalling a list in its "wrong" mood, and facilitation when recalling it in its "right" mood. The results are explicable by assuming that subjects'

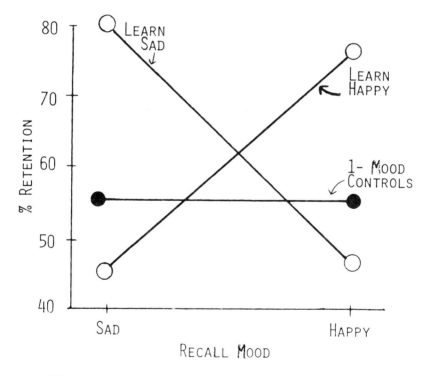

FIG. 13.3.   Percentage retention scores depending on the match between learning mood and recall mood. The sloping lines refer to subjects who learned the two lists under different moods (from Bower, 1981).

mood becomes associated to the learning items, that these associations facilitate recall when the test mood matches the mood under which the targets were learned, but they interfere with recall (retrieving competing items) when the test and input moods mismatch.

This mood dependency in free recall has been replicated several times in our laboratory. We find state dependency in recall of emotional events that people have recorded in personal diaries; similarly, mood exerts a selective influence on recall of pleasant versus unpleasant childhood experiences.

State dependency does not require hypnotically induced moods, as shown by two other results. Bartlett, Burleson, and Santrock (in press) produced mood-state dependent learning with happy versus sad moods in kindergarteners and third-grade children. For inducing the moods, the experimenters simply asked the child to reimagine (and retell to the experimenter) for several minutes either a very happy or very sad experience they have had. A mood check found this was quite effective. The subjects learned two lists in different moods and were tested in one of the moods (using a different evoking experience), as in our earlier experiment. The authors reported that when happy, children recalled more of the items learned while happy (.60) than the items learned while they were sad (.49). Conversely, sad children showed the reverse pattern of recall of the two lists (sad list .58, happy list .43). Kindergarteners and third graders did not differ in the amount of state dependency shown.

A second, striking example of mood state-dependent memory was reported by Henry, Weingartner, and Murphy (1973). Psychiatric patients with bipolar manic–depressive swings were observed over several months. At several sessions throughout this period patients were asked to generate 20 free associations to each of two novel stimulus words; 4 days later patients would be asked to reproduce the same 40 words they had generated before. In addition, clinicians rated the change over the 4 days in the patient's affective state, using several mood dimensions such as degree of activation and euphoria–depression. Henry et al. found that the greater the change in patients' affective states—from mania to depression or vice versa—the more they forgot the target associations generated 4 days previously.

These several examples suggest that mood-dependent retrieval is a genuine phenomenon, whether the mood swings are created experimentally or by endogenous factors in a clinical population.

The Semantic-Network Theory

What kind of theory can explain these mood state dependent effects? Bower (1981) proposed a theory of emotion that viewed it within a semantic network model of memory similar to those common in cognitive psychology (Anderson, 1976). We excerpt the description Bower (1981) wrote before:

First, let me provide some background. Human memory can be modeled in terms of an associative network of semantic concepts and schemata that are used to describe events. An event is represented in memory by a cluster of descriptive propositions. These are recorded in memory by establishing new associative connections among instances of the concepts used in describing the event. The basic unit of thought is the proposition; the basic process of thought is activation of a proposition and its concepts. The contents of consciousness are the sensations, concepts, and propositions whose current activation level exceeds some threshold. Activation presumably spreads from one concept to another, or from one proposition to another, by associative linkages between them. A relevant analogy is an electrical network in which terminals correspond to concepts or event nodes (units), connecting wires correspond to associative relations with more or less resistance, and electrical energy corresponds to activation that is injected into one or more nodes (units) in the network. Activation of a node can be accomplished either by presentation of the corresponding stimulus pattern or by prior activation of an associated thought.

To illustrate, a simple event such as "Mary kissed me at a specific time and place" would be recorded in memory, as shown in Fig. 13.4, in terms of new labeled linkages between my prior concepts of Mary, myself, and kissing. The links are labeled S to denote the subject and P the predicate of the proposition. Learning consists of establishing these associations and increasing their strength.

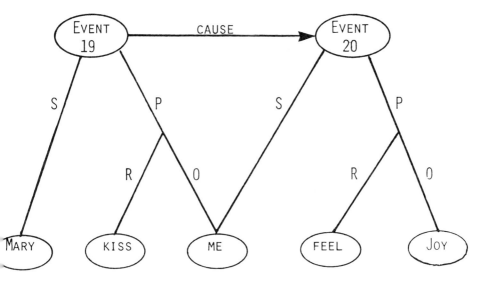

FIG. 13.4.   A semantic-network encoding of a proposition ("Mary kissed me") and an emotion it causes. Lower circles, or nodes, represent preexisting concepts, and lines represent new associations, S = subject; P = predicate; R = relation; and O = object (from Bower, 1981).

Later when asked, "What did Mary do?" activation of the Mary concept will transmit activation to the Event 19 node and thence to its branches, causing the model to retrieve the other links and thus recall that "Mary kissed me."

Figure 13.4 also shows a causal link from the event to an emotional reaction—namely, the emotion of joy. The emotional interpretation of an event that creates such links is itself largely molded by cultural or personal rules of intricate subtlety—but this is not the place to elaborate on that (author's note: see the last part of this chapter). The network encodes the fact that Event 19 caused Event 20, and the latter involves a primitive node for the emotion of joy.

The semantic-network approach supposes that each distinct emotion such as joy, depression, or fear has a specific node or unit in memory that collects together many other aspects of the emotion that are connected to it by associative pointers. In a recent paper, Clark and Isen (in press) have proposed a similar conception. Figure 13.5 shows a schematic for a small fragment of the many connections to a emotion node—say, sadness for Emotion 3. Collected around this emotion node are its associated autonomic reactions, standard role and expressive behaviors (that is, the way we display sadness), and descriptions of standard evocative situations which when appraised lead to sadness. Also included are the verbal labels commonly assigned to this emotion such as sadness, depression, and the blues. Some of these various linkages are innate, while others are learned and elaborated through acculturation.

In addition, each emotion unit is also linked with propositions describing events from one's life during which that emotion was aroused. This was illustrated in Fig. 13.4 with the Mary-kissing incident that caused joy. The emotion aroused at that

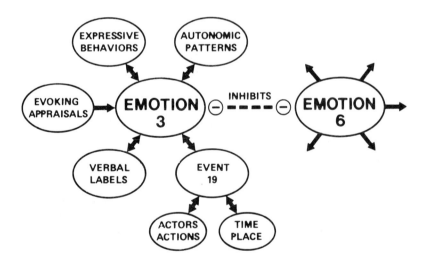

FIG. 13.5. Small fragment of the connections surrounding a specific emotion node or unit. Bidirectional arrows refer to mutual exchange of activation between nodes. An inhibitory pathway from Emotion 3 to Emotion 6 is also shown (from Bower, 1981).

time became associated by contiguity and causal belongingness with the evoking event. As a second example, the grief felt at the funeral of a friend would be associated with a node containing a description of things noticed at the funeral.

These emotion nodes can be activated by many stimuli—by physiological or symbolic verbal means. When activated above a threshold, the emotion unit transmits excitation to those nodes that produce the pattern of autonomic arousal and expressive behavior commonly assigned to that emotion. Each emotion may reciprocally inhibit an emotion of opposing quality, as fear inhibits joy and sexual arousal. If two emotion nodes are activated at once and they are not mutually inhibiting, then the subjective impression and expressive behavior pattern may be a blend or mixture of the two pure patterns. For example, sadness mixed with surprise may blend into disappointment (see Plutchik, 1980a,b).

Activation of an emotion node also spreads activation throughout the memory structures to which it is connected, creating subthreshold excitation at those event nodes. Thus, a weak cue that partially describes an event, such as "kindergarten days," may combine with activation from an emotion unit to raise the total activation of a relevant memory above a threshold of consciousness. Thus, the sad person becomes conscious of thinking about, and will recall some sad event from, his or her kindergarten days. This recall constitutes reactivation of a sad memory and sends feedback excitation to the sadness node, which will maintain activation of that emotion and thus influence later memories.

Network Theory of State-dependent Retrieval

The network view of emotional behavior has several implications. Of immediate interest is that it explains mood-state-dependent retrieval. The relevant associative connections for this process are isolated and emphasized in Fig. 13.6, which illustrates a part of the associative network encoding the learning of materials used in one of our experiments. The subject learned brief adjective–noun phrases such as "dying dog," "lost money," and "happy days" in the context of learning List 1 while experiencing Emotion 1 (see Gilligan & Bower, 1981). During learning the phrases became associated to the unit describing Context 1 and to the emotion unit active at that time. Later, when asked to recall events that occurred in Context 1, the subject activates the Context 1 node in memory, and activation spreads out from it as the subject searches for relevant items. But Context 1 is a weak, overloaded cue because it is associated with many things, so any one connection is subject to heavy interference. Suppose, however, that during recall the subject is returned to the same distinctive emotional state he or she was in during learning. Then, activation from that Emotion 1 node also will spread along its associative links to the target items, where it will summate with the activation spreading from the Context 1 cue to the items. The summation of activation at the intersection nodes causes the target events to become more accessible to recall when testing occurs in the same mood as learning. In contrast, if the mood is altered between learning and recalling, say to Emotion 2, recall suffers because the benefits of intersection from two search cues are absent; moreover, the search from the different emotion node will call up interfering associations that will compete with recall of the correct target items.

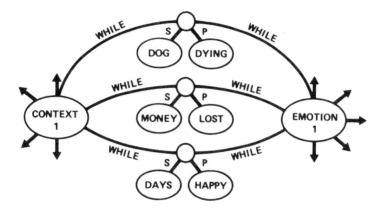

FIG. 13.6. The crucial connections for explaining mood-state-dependent retrieval. The subject has studied many adjective–noun phrases (dying dog, lost
money, happy days, etc.) in Context 1 while feeling Emotion 1. The associations
indicated (and many others) are weakly formed (from Bower, 1981).

This theory works more or less the same for recall of experimental items or of
real-life eipsodes from the recent past or from one's childhood. The specification of
the material to be recalled is partly contained within the Context 1 node as either
"List A learned today" or "last week's events" or "childhood incidents."

Network theory also explains a significant qualification about state-dependent
learning. This qualification is that the state-dependent effect occurs best with free
recall, when minimal cues are given for retrieval of the targets, but the effect is
greatly reduced when memory is tested with more adequate cues such as occur in
strongly cued recall or recognition tests. To illustrate, if recall were prompted with
a predicate of a phrase, such as "dying" for recall of "dying dog," recall would
be much higher than free recall, and the state-dependent effect would be reduced.
We have found this result, and so have Jim Eich and his associates (Eich, 1980;
Eich, Weingartner, Stillman, & Gillin, 1975) in several studies with drugs. Figure
13.6 suggests why this is expected: A strong cue like the predicate of a phrase—
say, "dying"—will retrieve the stored event relatively directly, because that cue is
close to the target noun (of "dog") and that pathway has no competing associations. With such a cue, the memory-search process starting from the weak Context
1 cue, which otherwise would have to occur in free recall becomes unnecessary,
and it was that search that we facilitated by reinstating the emotional mood of
learning. Thus, the search clue provided by mood reinstatement is unnecessary
when adequate retrieval cues are provided for the memory targets, so the matching
of moods between input and output has relatively little effect [p. 134–136].

Face Recognition Memory

Eich's generalization that state dependency is eliminated by recognition memory
tests is indeed impressive. However, as professional skeptics, we felt called upon

to put it to a severe test. Consequently, Randy Gellerman and Bower searched for state-dependent memory using recognition memory for faces. We thought that of many possible stimuli the human face would be most likely to be subject to emotional biases in encoding. For example, Schiffenbauer (1970) found that, compared to neutral-mood controls, subjects induced to feel disgust or anger (from listening to a tape recording) described a set of facial photographs using many more negative than positive emotional labels. In our experiment subjects were induced to feel happy or angry as the background emotion while they studied and were tested for recognition of slides of men's faces. The slides were taken from three high-school yearbooks (supplied by Tony Bower) and were of 160 male Caucasian twelfth graders, excluding faces with highly discriminable features such as long hair, eye glasses, scars, or facial hair. Subjects were placed in a happy or angry mood, were presented 40 slides to study at a 3-second rate, then were shifted to the opposite mood and presented with a second set of 40 slides for study. Ten minutes later, subjects were returned to a happy or sad mood, took half (80) the tests, then returned to the alternate mood for the remaining tests (80). Half the test slides in each test block were distractors, a quarter had been represented earlier while the subject was angry, a quarter had been presented before when the subject was happy. Each input slide was tested either in the same or its opposite mood according to a 2 × 2 design.

If a person's facial expression is an important part of the total encoding of an event, as Zajonc (this volume) suggests, then recognition memory for a picture should suffer when the subject's test mood (and expression) differs from the learning mood for that picture. Conversely, if Eich's generalization is right, then we should find no mood-dependent memory effects on recognition memory.

The percentage correct recognition responses are shown in Table 13.1. These results showed no differences whatsoever in recognition memory according to the input mood or the output mood or their interaction. Thus, contrary to the intuition that face encoding would differ according to the mood of the perceiver, we confirmed Eich's generalization: There is no state-dependent retrieval effect

TABLE 13.1
Percentage Correct Recognitions of Faces
According to Their Input Condition and Test
Condition

		Test Mood	
		Happy	Angry
Learning	Happy	64	65
Mood	Angry	59	57
	*Distractor	83	85

with recognition measures of memory. Thus, this prediction of the model in Fig. 13.6 is confirmed.

Emotional Influences on Thinking and Judgment

The network theory expects several cognitive effects when emotions are strongly aroused. Concepts, words, themata, and inference rules connected to the aroused emotion should be primed and more available. We have examined a few instances of how emotion influences thought processes, concentrating more on fantasies or reveries rather than goal-directed problem solving.

Free Associations.   One line of work examined verbal free associations. Subjects who were happy or angry generated chains of free associations to neutral words, which often reflected their mood. The network theory implies this by supposing that the prevailing mood acts as a constant source of activation so that the most activated word associations lie on intersection points in the network between the mood and the stimulus word. Thus, the associates typically satisfy joint constraints suggested by the mood and the stimulus words.

Imaginative Fantasies.   Because concepts related to the prevailing mood are primed into readiness, mood should bias the interpretation of ambiguous scenes. Because of this, and because mood also affects associations, one expects mood to influence imaginative fantasies. We have investigated how happy, sad, or angry subjects tell stories about what was happening in scenes depicted in cards of the Thematic Apperception Test (TAT). Using judges' ratings of content, we have found that the content of TAT stories frequently reflects the subject's mood; that is, happy subjects usually tell happy stories, angry subjects tell angry stories, and so on.

Snap Judgments.   The network theory implies that mood will influence "snap" judgments about familiar people or objects about which the subject has stored heterogeneous impressions. Isen, Shalker, Clark, and Karp (1978) found that subjects who were feeling good after receiving a small gift were more positive in rating the performance of their TV's and their cars for a mock consumer survey. Following that lead, we had our subjects give "thumbnail personality sketches" of familiar people in their lives (e.g., cousin, uncle, teacher); some characters were described while the subjects were happy and others while they were angry. We found that their judgments were strongly influenced by their passing mood. Angry judges are merciless, faultfinding; happy judges are charitable, loving, generous.

Assuming heterogeneous impressions have been stored about familiar persons, we may suppose that one's current mood causes retrieval of primarily positive or primarily negative memories and opinions of a familiar person. In this way, the summary evaluation is biased by the availability of the positive versus negative features that come to mind. This is just a state-dependent memory effect in disguise.

Probability Estimates of Future Events. A cornerstone of rational behavior is the idea that one chooses an optimizing action by combining the utilities of prospective outcomes with their subjective probabilities. Rationality requires that the probability estimates be unbiased, or at least as objective as possible. In collaboration with William Wright, Bower has investigated how happy versus depressed moods influence subjective probabilities of future events. Subjects read two 12-item questionnaries comprised of possible future events and were asked to estimate the "objective probability" of each event on a 0-to-100 scale. Half the future events were blessings, half were disasters; within each set, half referred to personal events, and half to national or world affairs. Sample items asked the subjects to estimate the probability that within the next 3 years they would take a vacation in Europe, that in the next 5 years they would be in a serious automobile accident, and that within the next 10 years there would be a major disaster at a nuclear power plant in California. Our hypnotized subjects were placed into a happy or/depressed mood, filled out one questionnaire, then were placed in the opposite mood, and completed the second questionnaire. The order of the moods and the questionnaires was counterbalanced over subjects. Subjects were asked to try to be objective as possible in their estimates, and all sincerely believed their estimates were factually based and not influenced by their moods.

Nonetheless, people's mood dramatically influenced their subjective probability estimates compared to estimates given by control subjects in a neutral mood (see Table 13.2). When happy, subjects elevated their probability estimates of positive future events and reduced estimates of negative future events; on the other hand, depressed subjects did just the reverse, increasing their probability estimates of catastrophes and lowering their estimates of blessings. These mean differences were present on 22 of the 24 event questions, despite wide scatter of the estimates and small numbers of subjects in each comparison. Here,

TABLE 13.2
Average Estimated Probabilities over Many
Positive and Negative Events According to
Estimator's Mood

	Event Type	
Mood	*Positive*	*Negative*
Happy	.52	.37
Neutral	.44	.43
Depressed	.38	.52

then, is the optimism of the happy person and the pessimism of the depressed person.

To explain this result, one must first note that the methods people use to make probability estimates are diverse and domain specific. A predominate strategy is to use the event in the question (say, about auto accidents) to try to remember either relevant media news programs or specific autobiographic episodes that involve such events or similar ones—accidents you have had or your friends have had. A relative frequency estimate would then be made from this available sample and extrapolated as one's future estimate. Because of mood state-dependent retrieval, memories of mood-congruent episodes would appear to be very available, hence probability estimates would be drastically biased in the expected direction (see Tversky and Kahneman, 1973). Other estimating strategies (e.g., building causal scenarios) would seem also to be similarly influenced by mood. Subjects' introspective reports were consistent with this analysis.

Although we prefer to interpret the preceding four experiments as showing the *automatic* influence of emotion upon thinking, an obvious alternative is that the hypnotic subjects are simply complying with what are the "emotional-role behaviors" implicitly demanded by the mood induction; that is, angry mood induction may be just a suggestion to play the role of an angry person in all the tasks. Elsewhere, Bower (1981) has marshalled the arguments and evidence against this demand–compliance interpretation of the results. Space limitations prevent our recounting them here.

Social Judgments.   We believe that judgments about interpersonal actions are largely subjective and can be distorted by the mood of the judge or perceiver. Social acts are often ambiguous, and perceivers have to read the intentions hidden behind people's words and actions. In that reading, the emotional premise from which they begin strongly influences how they interpret behavior. Is this student sticking to his point of view with admirable persistence, or is he being pigheaded? Is this soldier's action boldly daring or is it reckless? Clearly, the judgments we make depend on how the event impacts on our goals and how we feel about the actor. Happy people tend to be charitable, loving, positive in their interpretation of others. Depressed people are quick to notice any signs of flagging friendship, to exaggerate the slightest criticism, to overinterpret remarks as personal, denigrating, and pitying. Angry people have a chip on their shoulder, tend to be uncharitable, ready to find fault, to take offense. They may "take out their anger" on an innocent bystander who had nothing to do with arousing their ire; this is the basis for "scapegoating."

These emotional influences on judgments apply just as well when people are judging themselves and their own behavior. For instance, psychiatrically depressed patients are notorious for castigating themselves for what they perceive as their incompetent, despicable actions.

Joseph Forgas, Susan Krantz, and Bower investigated whether emotion could influence subjects' moment-by-moment perception of their own behavior. Specifically, we asked whether normal college students would naturally *see* themselves as incompetent and negative if they looked at themselves while feeling socially rejected. Conversely, we wanted to see whether people would *see* themselves as behaving with positive prosocial actions if they looked at themselves while feeling happy. This required a 2-day experiment. On the first day, pairs of subjects were interviewed together for about 20 minutes about personal topics, and this was videotaped with their knowledge and consent. The next day they returned and learned how to score videotaped interviews for prosocial, positive or antisocial, negative conversational behaviors. Examples of positive behaviors were smiling, leaning forward, contributing friendly remarks; negative behaviors were frowning, looking away, grimacing, and so on. Subjects learned to score such behaviors every 10 seconds while watching two persons in a video. Following this, subjects were hypnotized. Half of them were asked to remember and replay in imagination a moment of social success when they performed spectacularly well and felt good about themselves. The remaining subjects were asked to recall and replay a moment of social failure, when they had felt embarrassed and socially rejected because of something awkward or shameful they had

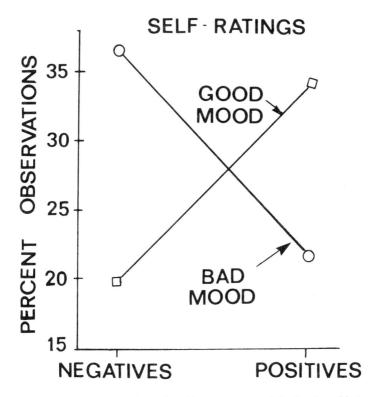

FIG. 13.7. Self-observations of positive and negative behaviors by subjects feeling good or bad about themselves.

done. Subjects were asked to maintain their mood while they looked at the 20-minute videotape of themselves being interviewed together with their partner. Every 10 seconds they were to mark at least one positive or negative behavior they observed in themselves or in their partner. Note that these are almost moment-by-moment perceptual judgments, not retrospective evaluations from memory.

The primary results are shown in Fig. 13.7 for self-ratings. Because different subjects gave varying numbers of marks, Fig. 13.7 depicts the percentages of all so-called "observations" that fall into various categories. The results show that people who felt socially rejected perceived themselves (by their "objective counts") in the videotaped interview as exhibiting more negative, socially inept acts than positively skilled acts. In contrast, subjects in a good mood perceived more positive, prosocial actions than negative actions in themselves. These differences are all "in the eye of the beholder"; neutral judges rated the two groups of subjects as exhibiting roughly equal proportions of positive and negative behaviors. The results illustrate just how ambiguous "body language" is,

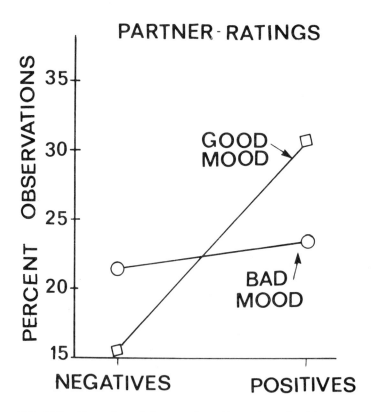

FIG. 13.8.   Observations of the partner's positive and negative behaviors by subjects feeling good or bad about themselves.

because, as noted, these are moment-by-moment perceptual judgments, not retrospective evaluations. It appears that social behavior is almost a blank canvas onto which perceivers project a picture according to their moods.

The subjects' perception of their partner's behavior is shown in Fig. 13.8. Happy people see more positive, prosocial actions than negative actions being performed by their partner. Socially rejected subjects see fewer positive actions in their partner, but still their positive attributions exceed their negative ones. Thus, people who are feeling socially rejected were inclined to castigate themselves but not others; those who were feeling the glow of social success had a Pollyanna bias to see the good qualities in others as well as in themselves.

Such emotional influences on social judgments can be explained, at least roughly, by the semantic network theory. The perceiver's mood activates and primes into readiness mood-congruent concepts, hypotheses, and inference rules; and these are used in expectation-driven (top-down) processing to classify and assimilate ambiguous interpersonal actions.

To summarize these last few findings, we have shown emotional influences on several kinds of judments and thinking. This includes free associations, TAT stories, snap judgments of personality, probability estimates of future events, judgments of others and of one's own actions. We now consider an incompleteness of the network theory.

Extending the Network Theory of Affect

Parsimony recommends the idea that emotional reactions to experiences should be stored along with nonemotional features in the same memory medium, according to the same storage principles, and retrieved by the same principles. Similarly, the spreading activation mechanism is attractively familiar: An aroused emotion spreads out activation, priming into readiness related concepts, words, themata, and inference rules. This enables the model to react differently to the same situation depending on its current emotional state. Further, the idea that an emotion becomes associated to coincident events and can later act like a retrieval cue suffices to explain mood state-dependent memory.

Whereas the network theory deals with the cognitive consequences of an emotion after it has been aroused, its major incompleteness is that it does not address how emotions are aroused in the first place. Figure 13.6, for instance, depicts "evoking appraisals" that feed excitation into the emotion node, but that part of the system was unanalyzed. That was because in earlier work Bower and his associates were interested in the cognitive *consequences* of emotional states, not their antecedent *causes*. Nonetheless, we feel that the "pattern-recognizing" aspects of emotional arousal should be addressed, and so we propose the "blackboard" control structure described following.

A theory about cognitive consequences of emotion needs to deal with emotional appraisals for several reasons. A first reason is that one major consequence of emotion is to change the way people appraise or evaluate situations. This was our point about mood affecting social judgment. To explain such results, then, one must model the appraisal process.

A second reason to deal with appraisal is to enable the model to assess properly its emotional attitude toward people, objects, and issues. Consider an illustration: We witness an argument that culminates when a bully, Sam, beats up a smaller child, Johnny. The model will store a description of that event in memory linked to the emotion it felt at the time, such as anger. Later we ask the memory model how it feels about Johnny. Can the system calculate how it feels about a person or entity by simply averaging the evaluations linked to episodes in which that entity occurs? This "inheritance of affects" strategy gives the wrong answer in this case, because the model should not feel angry at Johnny. The model needs a more discriminating appraisal system in the first place, one that will assign praise or blame appropriately to the participants in an emotional episode. Thus, an appropriate model would store anger with the bully (Sam), sympathy with the victim (Johnny), and perhaps distress at the episode of Sam's hitting Johnny. But that "assignment of responsibility" uses capabilities beyond the initial network theory. Our blackboard appraisal approach can deal with such examples.

A third reason for elaborating the control structure that uses the network data base is to distinguish "hot" versus "cold" uses of emotion concepts. The former network approach basically had one node for each emotion, say "fear," and any reference to or use of that concept would somehow "turn on" that fear node in the network. But that is also the operation the model identified as "feeling afraid" subjectively. So that leads to the absurd implication that people always feel afraid when they refer to the concept. But surely, people discourse cooly about emotions many times without feeling the emotion at all. Consequently, we should distinguish the node corresponding to the concept of fear versus the node for experiencing fear itself. But then the model needs a control structure and a pattern recognizer to decide which node to activate in different circumstances.

Fourth, a control structure and appraisal system is needed to deal with the phenomena of hot versus cold *replaying* of an emotional memory, and *reinterpretation* or reappraisal of earlier emotional memories. Consider the replaying of memories in imagination. We are impressed by the fact that for many emotional memories this can be done either *with* feelings or *without* feelings. How does a model of the mind account for the difference in these cases? A plausible conjecture is that the feelings arise as you unpack, develop, and recreate your thoughts at the original experience rather than skimming over an abstract summary of the episode. Our blackboard model deals with this by supposing that to reexperience the emotion of an event the system must recreate as closely as possible from memory the state of the "blackboard" at that time, then appraise that "blackboard situation" again as though it were fresh, and then "turn on" the appropriate emotion nodes. But to do this, one must have a mechanism for appraisals.

Reinterpretation should perhaps better be called reappraisal. People often review earlier experiences and modify their emotional appraisal of the events. Thus, a spouse's remark that upset us at the time may be reappraised later as an innocent remark designed to comfort us; a stream of pleasing flattery may be later reappraised as an insincere manipulation to benefit the flatterer. We change emotional appraisals for several reasons: First, different facts may come to light that alter *cognitions* about some person or event (e.g., facts that prove their innocence); second, we may change our basic *values* or attitudes (e.g., toward marijuana smoking) between the original experience and the reappraisal; third, we may change the *importance* assigned to the event because our goals or priorities change; fourth, the passage of the event replaces our anxious *uncertainty* with calm hindsight about its outcome; fifth, our *mood* may change from, say, anger to charitable benevolence, so in reappraisals this new, charitable light is cast upon events. These five causes of reappraisal—changes in evidence, in values, in importance, in uncertainty, in moods—are discussed later within our expanded blackboard model. The key idea is that the reasons for an initial emotional appraisal of an event are stored in memory along with the event and its appraisal. This data structure permits the model to reexperience the event by replaying one's original emotional reaction to it, or to replay the event and reinterpret it using modified appraisal rules, perhaps even incorporating new facts into the second appraisal. This new appraisal may then be linked as an update to the old event structure in memory. This process then permits the model to say things like "I used to like Bill's flattery. But then I learned that he was an insincere manipulator, so now I feel ashamed that I was duped."

Having listed some incompletenesses of the former network theory of emotion, we now introduce a general framework for modeling emotional appraisals.

The Blackboard Control Structure

We believe that a model of how people arrive at emotional appraisals must be complex because it requires integration of several knowledge sources. Consequently, any model will require a control structure that facilitates the coordination of many knowledge sources. In artificial ingelligence programs like HEARSAY II and CRYSALIS, this coordination is carried out using a "blackboard" control structure. The blackboard control structure is well-suited for interpretations that develop as multiple knowledge sources contribute their advice opportunistically and asynchronously. The blackboard model develops interpretations of a situation incrementally; interpretations gain support from the several knowledge sources. The partial interpretations produced by knowledge sources are called hypothesis elements. Typically, the input to a knowledge source is the output of another knowledge source; for example, a situation might have to be identified cognitively by one expert before its emotional significance can be appraised by other experts.

The blackboard is also a model of the focus of attention; the model's attention is focused on the hypotheses on the blackboard. Several competing hypotheses may be under consideration simultaneously. However, attention eventually focuses on that hypothesis for which the evidence is greatest; thereafter, the alternative hypotheses slowly fade from the blackboard. In this respect, the blackboard has many of the properties of short-term memory or working memory. In fact, no misunderstanding will arise if psychologists think of the blackboard as their construct of working memory.

We think of the contents of the blackboard as separated for the moment from the knowledge sources that use it. However, in a system like ACT (Anderson, 1976), working memory is just the activated portion of the long-term memory network plus some activated rules. To recast the blackboard model within ACT would require that the "blackboard" be considered to be those long-term memory nodes (concepts or propositions) whose activation level exceeded a certain threshold. We do not attempt this translation here. ACT and the blackboard model may be notational variants of one another, but we find the "blackboard" level of description easier to follow.

Emotional Knowledge Sources

We believe that people interpret a situation cognitively and then appraise that cognitive interpretation in arriving at the type and level of emotional reaction they will have. Thus, any model must begin with cognitive "pattern-recognition" knowledge, which enables it to recognize objects, people, events, and so on. This "cognitive interpretation" (C-I) knowledge is applied to material on the blackboard to arrive at internal symbolic representations of the external environment. We model C-I knowledge in terms of interlocking sets of productions, as in HEARSAY-II. Cognitive interpretation is shown as the early phases diagrammed in Fig. 13.9. Cognitive interpretation itself is a multistage process moving from sensory–feature extraction to conceptual meaning interpretation. The cognitive interpretation may vary in its level of refinement and detail as more processing occurs, and an emotional response can be triggered at any level or stage in processing.

The second kind of knowledge assigns an emotional appraisal to the cognitive interpretations; we call this "emotional interpretation" or E-I knowledge. We model this also in terms of productions called E-I rules. Because this is the central component of our model, we postpone its discussion for the moment.

Third, Fig. 13.9 shows that the intensity of the emotional reaction posted on the blackboard is adjusted depending on the personal importance of the event. Importance assignment requires knowledge of the person's goals and basic values. Once goals are known, then a partial ordering of importance of subgoals can be constructed. As a further factor, intensity of an emotional reaction may be adjusted by the uncertainty of the event. Unexpected events usually generate

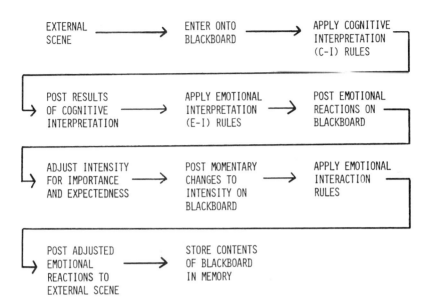

FIG. 13.9.   Changes to the state of the blackboard result from knowledge sources posting hypotheses during appraisal of an emotional situation.

stronger emotional experiences than expected ones. We say little about either of these knowledge experts except to note that they are clearly needed by the model.

Fourth, Fig. 13.9 indicates that the emotional reaction is modulated by its interactions with other emotions that are either ongoing or evoked by the event in question. Thus, a sad or frightening event will decrease one's happiness, anger may intensify one's depression, and so on. For convenience, we formalize these interactions by rules that adjust an ongoing emotion in light of a temporary emotional change created by an incoming event. The rules in these cases could just as well have been implemented as inhibitory or excitatory connections among emotion nodes, like a system of lateral inhibition. One's choice on this implementation issue has certain implications. For instance, explicit rules about emotional interactions provide declarative knowledge that the model can refer to and reason about (e.g., to manipulate others' emotional reactions). Conversely, an inhibitory link between two emotion nodes is like tacit procedural knowledge that "does its job" but cannot be reasoned about or altered. We prefer the rule formulation because the model requires flexibility to change interpretations due to experience.

Emotional-Interpretation Rules.   The most important part of the appraisal system is the emotion interpretation knowledge, which we formalize as many E-I rules or productions. These specify for a given cognitive interpretation an appropriate emotional appraisal. Each rule has a left-hand side (LHS) that represents a cognitive interpretation, and a right-hand side (RHS) that specifies an alteration of one or more emotions. Such E-I rules may have sophisticated conditions and outcomes. Whereas highly specific E-I rules describe individual events (such as a bully hitting a victim) in their LHS's, we believe that as some E-I rules are generalized, their LHS's come to specify goals and motives. We believe that there is a class of events, called "goal events," that includes goal achievement, goal blocking or frustration, goal abandonment, plan interruption, goal conflict, and so on. These goal events are present in the LHS's of general E-I rules, and emotion results when they are instantiated. We believe that individuals maintain a large set of background goals, such as "preserve well-being," as well as more specific goals activated as they work on a specific problem. One's goals may perhaps be organized into hierarchies along the lines described by Carbonnell (1979). The importance of goals is that they direct processing in the system. When goals are achieved or thwarted E-I rules should turn on the appropriate emotion. For instance, if while pursuing a top-level goal you notice that a required subgoal is already true in the world, then you should feel happy. An appropriate production is:

> IF a subgoal is discovered to be true,
> THEN increase happiness.

Similarly, if a goal is frustrated, the emotion of frustration or anger results.

The left-hand side of such rules can be generalized by replacing constants by variables or by deleting restrictive clauses. Similarly, a rule may be specialized or refined by the reverse operations, adding clauses or specifying a variable to be a particular constant. For instance, a more specific version of the earlier rule would be:

> IF you're starting on an auto trip and you find that your friend
> already filled your car with gasoline,
> THEN increase happiness.

A generalization of the earlier rule would be

> IF you reduce any difference between your
> current state and the goal state,
> THEN increase happiness.

The E-I rules may be hierarchically organized according to the generality of their triggering conditions, their LHS's. They can also be organized by the sophistication of cognitive interpretation required to match their LHS's. For example, an unexpected loud noise provides an immediate stimulus for which even infants have an emotional production; on the other hand, snide social remarks require sophisticated processing to determine whether one has been complimented or insulted.

The LHS's of E-I rules are partial descriptions of some state of the world, so cognitive interpretation is needed to produce this information. The knowledge involved in cognitive interpretation maps from external stimuli to an internal representation of the world; E-I rules map from these internal representations to emotional reactions. The knowledge used in cognitive interpretation tells us what is going on in the world; E-I rules tell us how we feel about it. Interestingly, cognitive interpretations can be disputed in a way that emotional interpretations cannot; one's perceptions can be denied, but not one's feelings. Emotional interpretation is subjective. Although some common, general, E-I rules exist, individuals surely differ to a large degree in their stock of E-I rules.

Most E-I rules are learned, and some are idiosyncratic. However, we expect that many primitive and adaptive behaviors can be modeled by innate E-I rules. For example, almost anyone—from infants to adults—will become upset by very loud, unexpected noises; similarly, everyone experiences frustration when a goal is thwarted. Between the idiosyncratic E-I rules and the "hardwired" ones is a range of rules that are culturally learned. For example, events that caused our grandmothers to shrink in horror, such as the wearing of skimpy bathing suits, are commonplace today, and those that were commonplace then, such as slaughtering and cleaning chickens, are repugnant to most of us today.

We think that E-I rules should not specify a complete emotional state in their RHS's, but rather an adjustment to the current level of a specified emotion, such as "increase fear," or "decrease happiness." A person's current emotional state may be described as the activation level of a set of N emotions like fear, anger, happiness, sadness, disgust, and so on. We may then conceive of any state as a 1 × N vector of intensity values, varying, say, on a 0 to 1.0 scale. An E-I rule increases or decreases one or more emotions, say, by an associated linear operator.

By admitting N emotion values at differing levels, the model can deal with the phenomena of ambivalence and mixed, conflicting emotions. We assume that the central processor can report the activation level of any emotion, and momentary behavior will be selected usually by the stronger emotion. If several emotions can be satisfied by one behavior, then that behavior will be favored by the sum of their strengths. As noted, conflicting emotions interact; for example, fear inhibits joy, fear inhibits anger, etc. Thus, when the cognitive situation changes and one emotion is increased, a dynamic adjustment process may be launched as the other emotions adjust to the perturbation.

Importance, Unexpectedness, and Emotional Intensity.   The RHS's of E-I rules adjust the intensity of a mood; for example, they "increase happiness" or "decrease fear." Two other factors that influence the intensity level of an emotion are importance and unexpectedness. These "scale" the adjustments to intensity specified by E-I rules. For example, consider an E-I rule that specifies an increase in intensity of anger of, say, 40% in response to seeing a bully attack a weakling. This increase should be scaled upward even further if the weakling is especially important (e.g., if he is a member of your family), and it should be scaled downward if he is unimportant (e.g., if it is a random act of violence on TV news). Similarly, the unexpectedness of an event scales the intensity of one's emotional response to it; a surprising event is assumed to adjust intensity upward, whereas an expected event would produce lower activation.

It is difficult to specify the rules that adjust intensity depending on importance, because what is important is domain specific. For example, in social relations, truthfulness (or the lack of it) is important, in chess, control of the center of the board is important, in medical diagnosis, accurate tests are important, and so on. Although there may be no domain-independent rules for assigning importances, some rules are plausible for a general domain like planning. For instance, the importance of a goal would depend on the number of subgoals it subsumes in a plan. A distinction is made between conjunctive goals that must all be achieved for a plan to work, and disjunctive goals, any of which will allow the plan to work. Conjunctive and disjunctive subgoal trees show contrasting asymmetries in the importance attached to success or failure of individual subgoals. In a disjunctive tree, the success of any subgoal increases with the number failed previously. In a conjunctive tree, the failure of any subgoal has equal importance and is to be avoided, whereas the importance of a subgoal success increases with the number of subgoals previously achieved.

Expectedness and unexpectedness also scale intensity. In general, unexpected events lead to more intense emotions. A blackboard model can judge unexpectedness because it continuously posts top-down hypotheses about the state of the world. Thus, rules for judging unexpectedness are of the form:

> IF the blackboard does not contain a top-down
> hypothesis for this event,
> THEN the event is unexpected.

Clearly, more sophisticated rules can be formulated that deal with partial matches and degrees of surprise, but this rule illustrates the general principle.

The modulation of emotional intensity by expectedness is illustrated by our reactions to jokes and suspense stories when they are novel instead of overly familiar.

Interaction Rules.   Interaction rules also modulate the intensity of emotional reactions. The LHS's of these rules contain at least one clause describing an emotional interpretation, and optional clauses describing other emotions and cognitive interpretations. An example of an interaction rule is the following:

> IF intensely happy, and
> an emotional interpretation of sadness is posted for
> an event,
> THEN decrease the intensity of ongoing happiness by 10%,
> cut the increment in sadness by 50%.

The intensities of emotions that are posted are scaled for their importance as described earlier, so if the sad event were very important its intensity would be reduced less than that of happiness.

A second function of interaction rules is to specify an intuitive progression as emotions are aroused in sequence by events. For example, if one experiences fear but then discovers that there was nothing to be afraid of, he will feel relief followed perhaps by a feeling of shame or foolishness.

A third function of interaction rules is to "calm down" the emotions after instigating circumstances are removed. A simple rule for dissipating emotion is this:

IF emotion E is active, and
the emotional interpretation that evoked E is no
longer active on the blackboard,
THEN decrease the level of intensity of E by 50%.

To summarize our comments, Table 13.3 cites the knowledge sources and specifies their input–output relationships. We have discussed cognitive interpretation (C-I) rules, emotional interpretation (E-I) rules, importance and unex-

TABLE 13.3
Input–Output Relations Among Four Kinds of Knowledge Involved in
an Emotional Appraisal

Rules	Input	Output
Cognitive Interpretation (C-I)	Sensory Stimuli, or RHS of C-I rules	Symbolic representation of external environment
Emotional Interpretation (E-I)	RHS of C-I rules	Adjustment of current emotion
Importance and Unexpectedness	RHS of C-I rules	Adjustment to intensity of an emotion
Interaction	RHS of E-I, and (RHS of C-I rules)	Adjustments among emotions, Adjustments to intensities of emotions

Examples

C-I: IF you see squiggles of a certain type on an EEG record,
      THEN infer an ongoing petit mal seizure

E-I: IF you discover you have epilepsy,
      THEN increase fear

Importance: IF A and B are disjunctive methods of achieving G, and A has a lower cost than B,
      THEN A is more important than B

Interaction: IF you are happy, and a frightening stimulus occurs,
      THEN decrease happiness.

pectedness rules, and interaction rules. All these interact on the blackboard to influence the intensity and quality of emotional reactions to either an external situation or replaying of a memory or imagined scene played out on the blackboard.

Emotional Situations and E-I Rules

In a chapter describing a model for recognizing emotional situations, we should try to characterize generally situations that cause emotional reactions. This is difficult because the evoking situations vary so widely. Nonetheless, some tentative remarks are in order about a taxonomy of emotional situations.

A first type of event that arouses emotion is unexpected, intense, startling stimuli. This class includes painful stimuli. Equally arousing are physical events like slipping, falling, or losing one's balance. These events will have innate E-I rules for turning on the emotions of surprise, pain, and/or distress.

A second source of emotions are cues that have become conditioned to these intense or painful events, which lead to feelings of apprehension.

The third and largest source of emotions are events surrounding the achievement, interruption, or thwarting of motivated, goal-directed activities. Evolution has equipped us with a set of homeostatic mechanisms for regulating our bodily needs, to obtain enough oxygen, food, water, benign temperatures, and so on. Deprivation arouses the relevant need state that motivates actions to reduce the need, with goal achievement accompanied by excitement, satisfaction, and pleasure. These are the prototypic ''positive reinforcers'' that traditional learning theory talks about.

Learning theorists such as Hobart Mowrer (1960) believed they could extend the previous two categories of positively or negatively valenced reinforcers, thus classifying any stimulus presentation as pleasantly positive or aversively negative. Emotions were then conceived as reactions to the presentation or removal of these positive or negative events, or as reactions to cues signalling the imminent presentation or removal of these events. Thus, in Mowrer's scheme, joy results from getting an ongoing positive activity leads to frustration and anger, loss of a sustained positive relationship causes sadness or anger; presentation of an aversive event leads to pain, distress, and perhaps anger; anticipation of an aversive event leads to fear or anxiety; removal of an aversive event causes relief; anticipation of that removal leads to hope.

A basic problem with this classification is that it presupposes a prior classification of events as positive or negative. But that classification surely varies according to individuals' goals and cognitions. For instance, achieving a top-level goal like losing weight may require obese people to alter their customary evaluation of eating sweets or sitting in very hot steambaths.

Another problem with Mowrer's scheme is that it misses the point that humans' emotional reaction to an event varies with their explanation of the causes of the event. This is illustrated clearly in Weiner's research reported in this volume. People have elaborate theories for explaining their positive events (successes) or negative events (failures) along the causal dimensions of internal versus external factors, controllable versus uncontrollable factors, and stable versus unstable factors. Thus, a success attributed to one's own efforts or ability leads to pride, whereas failure ascribed to lack of effort or ability leads to depression. A negative, controllable event that one attributes to others causes one to feel anger. Guilt occurs when one causes a negative outcome for a friend when it could have been prevented. One feels pity toward others who are in a negative state due to uncontrollable factors. One feels gratitude toward others when one receives positive events due to their personal control.

Weiner's taxonomy of causal factors leading to different emotions fits neatly into the E-I rules envisioned for our blackboard model. One can easily write productions whose left-hand sides are values of the several causal attributes of an event, and the right-hand side is an emotional interpretation. For instance,

IF someone acts in a negative way
and the factors causing the act are
internal, stable, uncontrollable,
THEN feel pity at $\Theta = .7$
and feel anger at $\Theta = .2$.

IF someone's action leads to a positive event
for you and that outcome was under under his control,
THEN feel gratitude at $\Theta = .6$
and feel happiness at $\Theta = .4$.

The point is that taxonomies of social situations that generate emotions (such as Weiner's or Roseman's, 1979) can easily be translated into our model as E-I rules that turn on emotions appropriately depending on the cognitive appraisal of the social situation. Of course, such E-I rules are learned during acculturation of each individual and vary somewhat across cultures.

Having discussed briefly the range of situations that lend to emotional reactions, we now turn to illustrating the blackboard model for emotional evaluation.

An Illustration of the Blackboard Model's Operation

To illustrate the blackboard system, we walk through an example supplied by a friend; call him Fred. His apartment had been burglarized a week ago, and the police told him just today that the burglars were in fact murderers escaped from prison. The event in question occurs late that night when Fred is awakened by a noise in the hallway outside his apartment. Initially, he thinks the noise was caused by burglars, experiences fear, considers telephoning the police. But then he hears singing, infers the noise and singing is coming from his friendly neigh-

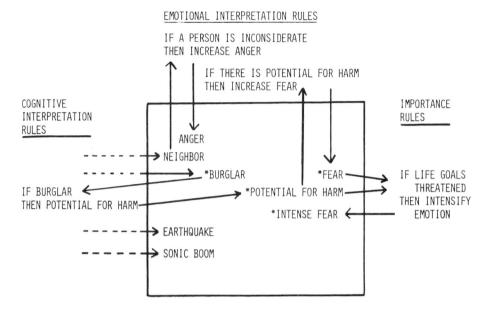

FIG. 13.10.   The state of Fred's blackboard after interpreting a noise as a burglar.

bor, Bill, who's staggering home after drinking too much. Fred then feels angry at Bill for inconsiderately frightening him in the middle of the night.

Figure 13.10 shows the state of Fred's blackboard after he has just heard the noises. Cognitive interpretation rules provide several possible explanations—a burglar, a neighbor, a sonic boom, an earthquake (this is California)—and E-I rules assign an initial emotional interpretation to each. We use concept names like "burglar" as shorthand for an existential proposition like "There is a burglar out there." Some of these hypotheses have only a fleeting life. The sonic boom and earthquake hypotheses are quickly discarded when Fred localizes the noise as coming from within his building. That leaves the blackboard containing two competing hypotheses about the noise. At this point top-down expectations tilt the balance toward the burglar hypothesis. The knowledge that generates these expectations is not shown in Fig. 13.10; however, Fred's learning about the murderers that day will have primed a class of hypotheses about burglars and the fear they should provoke.

The burglar interpretation is temporarily favored over the neighbor interpretation, but both remain on the blackboard. The "importance" source assigns a large intensity increment to the fear felt on this occasion because burglars are potentially dangerous. By focusing attention on the burglar interpretation, the model now becomes biased to interpret ambiguous stimuli as evidence of a burglar. Thus, small, metallic sounds would be interpreted as the burglar trying to pick a locked door in the hallway.

At the next juncture in the episode, Fred hears singing and interprets it as Bill's drunken song. The Bill interpretation gains prominence over the burglar interpretation. In so doing, the emotional interpretation of anger gains prominence over that of fear. Although the new evidence makes the neighbor interpretation dominant, there is still a residue of the burglar interpretation, so that fear persists for a while.

Upon identifying the noise as drunken Bill, Fred becomes very angry. We explain this emotional adjustment in terms of interaction rules. These rules cause Fred to become more angry than he would have if he hadn't been frightened at first.

Selection and Application of E-I Rules

The E-I rules are organized in a generalization hierarchy according to their LHS's. This hierarchy sits in long-term memory, with each rule "looking down upon" the blackboard for its triggering conditions. Figure 13.11 shows a portion of the E-I hierarchy for interpreting and reacting to simple acts of aggression. The LHS of each E-I rule is represented as a ACT network. The notation at the terminal leaves of the rules are explained shortly.

The cognitive system produces a description of an external situation as a set of propositions such as "Sam hit Johnny" and "Sam is older and bigger than Johnny." We assume that such event descriptions are output by the perceptual parser and are entered onto the blackboard as ACT-like tree structures. (This is no substantive restriction because ACT structures are expressively equivalent to the first-order predicate calculus.) The next step is to try to match some left-hand–side of an emotional interpretation rule to this event description on the blackboard. As noted, the LHS's of E-I rules are ACT-like network structures or Boolean combinations of them, as illustrated in Fig. 13.11. When an E-I rule is instantiated, the RHS assigns emotional reactions to the event as a whole and to the participants in the event. The E-I rule itself tells the system how to assign the appropriate emotional charges. It does this by linking one or more central emotion nodes (say, anger and sympathy) with designated intensities into designated spots in the matching conceptual structure. This action is carried out by the links from the terminal nodes of the E-I structures. Once these linkages are made, activation flows over them and "turns on" the appropriate emotion node.

We think of E-I rule selection as pattern matching of LHS's of rules to the blackboard event or its immediate inferences. More precisely, we view rule selection as a three-part search process. The first part partitions the space of E-I rules into at least two categories: mood-congruent E-I rules and E-I rules that are not mood congruent. The second phase of search produces a list of all mood-congruent E-I rules that match the event on the blackboard. If this process fails to

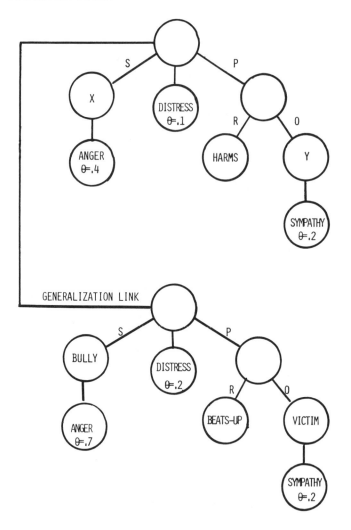

FIG. 13.11.   A specific rule and its generalization, replacing some constants by variables. The modulator nodes for emotion are connected to the main concepts.

find any matching mood-congruent rules, it searches the category of nonmood-congruent rules. The third phase of search ranks the rules found in the second phase, effectively narrowing the list down to a single rule. The choice of criteria for picking one rule from several applicable rules is a strategic one. We favor picking the maximally specific E-I rule, that is, the one that binds to the greatest number of constants in the event on the blackboard. For example, if the event is "Sam hit Johnny," then the third phase of search should favor an E-I rule that specifies "Sam hit someone" over one that says "Someone hit someone"; and it should prefer both to a rule that says "X hit Y."

The first phase of the selection process is consistent with the network model of state-dependent memory; that is, it can be implemented by spreading activation in a network of E-I rules. The space of E-I rules is easily partitioned into mood-congruent and nonmood-congruent rules by spreading activation from the currently active emotion node to all rules that mention the emotion in their RHS's. This elevates the activation level of mood-congruent rules so that the system favors them over others.

The goal of the second phase of rule selection is to list those E-I rules whose LHS's match the event on the blackboard. Because this phase of rule selection considers mood-congruent matches before those that are not mood congruent, the search process will perpetuate the current mood if possible.

This matching phase is complicated by a number of factors. First, complete and literal matches are relatively rare; instead, a LHS may be a partial match to the event on the blackboard, or it may match variables to constants, or both. For example, a complete, literal match to the blackboard event "Sam hit Johnny with a stick" is simply "Sam hit Johnny with a stick"; a partial match is "Sam hit Johnny"; a matching of variables to constants is "Sam hit someone." Another reason that matching is complicated is that we intend matches to be made not only to blackboard events but also to immediate inferences from them. For example, we want to infer from the facts that "Sam hit Johnny" and "Johnny is much smaller and weaker than Sam" the conclusion that "A bully hurt a weakling." We assume that this reasoning is done by cognitive interpretation (C-I) rules, and that the conclusions are posted on the blackboard, where they are matched by the LHS's of E-I rules.

Figure 13.12 shows the structure that results from matching an E-I rule (P238) to "A bully hurt a weakling." The E-I rule makes assignments of emotions to the components of the event; it associates anger at a certain intensity with Sam, the bully, sympathy with Johnny, the weakling, and distress with the episode as a whole.

We have several comments about the data structure in Fig. 13.12. First, the emotional assignments have been determined in this instance by a general rule; the event need not have happened for the model to have predicted how it *would* feel should an event of this type arise. Second, the model is being told to feel three different emotions at once—anger, distress, and sympathy—although these have different evoking objects. Whereas the more strongly aroused affect will tend to dominate thought and action, the lesser emotions are nonetheless present and produce mixed or alternating feelings depending on the focus of the model's attention.

Third, this data structure with its emotional assignments is what will be stored in long-term memory about this episode—specifically, the event with its emotional assignments will be stored with a token of the E-I rule used in this appraisal. Later we discuss the benefits of such memory records.

Fourth, the nodes in Fig. 13.12 with emotion labels are called "modulator" nodes. They are three-way links. One link is made upon this occasion directly to

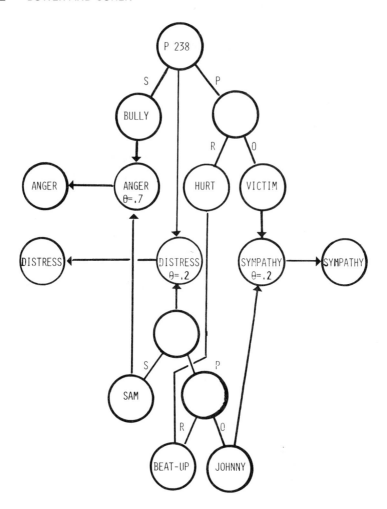

FIG. 13.12.   The episode "Sam beat up Johnny" is matched to an E-I rule
"Bully hurts victim." Emotional reactions to the elements of the episode are
specified by modulator nodes.

the parent emotion node such as anger or sympathy. The second link goes to the
abstract variable in the E-I rule that has been instantiated in the instance (for
example, "bully" or "weakling"). The third link goes to the specific concepts
of the event that instantiated particular roles of the E-I rule (Sam and Johnny).
We think of modulator nodes as gates or valves that let activation flow from the
active nodes on the blackboard (namely, Sam and bully) through the modulator
gate over to the parent emotion node, thus causing that node (anger here) to be
aroused at a specified level. This results in a token of that emotion being placed
on the blackboard.

Fifth, the Θ values on the modulator nodes in Fig. 13.12 summarize the *intensity* of the emotional impact of the event upon each of its component concepts. We represent the intensity of activation of an emotional node on a scale from 0 to 1.0. Then the impact of an event occurring at time t in increasing an emotion of level e_t is represented by the linear operator $e_{t+1} = e_t + \Theta(1 - e_t)$. Here, Θ is a fraction between zero and one that determines how much the designated emotion changes toward its maximum value. One would expect that more important E-I rules would have larger associated values of Θ.

Let us assume that the activation coming from the variable in the E-I rule and its instantiated concept (i.e., from bully and Sam) add to a constant, say, one unit. Then the Θ value on the modulator valve tells us how much to increase the activation arriving at the parent emotion node (anger in this example) from the event in question. Thus, if the ongoing level of anger were .2 before this event, then the new anger level immediately after this event would be $.2 + .7(1 - .2) = .2 + .56 = .76$, which is a high level of anger. A built-in feature of an incremental emotion operator is that the model can accumulate a series of small provocations until it "boils over," as the parent anger node gains ascendancy over inhibiting emotions.[1]

Applications of the Model to Some Emotional Phenomena

We have now set forth the blackboard model, sketched how it arrives at an emotional appraisal, and illustrated the data structure it stores in memory about an emotional event. Let us now show how the model accounts for several emotional phenomena noted before.

State-Dependent Retrieval. Memory records emotional events along with instantiated E-I rules in data structures like that shown in Fig. 13.12. This system automatically indexes such data structures by the emotions felt at the time. Thus, if the person for any reason returns to the indicated emotional state (say, with

---

[1] The principle illustrated assigns "importance" to the E-I rule or participants in it. A complementary approach is for the system to have assigned importance weightings (in advance) to conceptual objects such as people ("Johnny"), property ("my car"), and aggregations ("my nation, church, race"). When activated, all concepts transmit a certain level of activation. One might suppose that this activation increases with the importance of the concept. On this account, the idea of one's self, spouse, or children would just automatically send out more activation once it was triggered, thus simulating greater "attentional demand." If so, and if this activation gets shunted via a modulator switch (see Fig. 13.12) into an emotion node, this means that more important concepts could lead to greater levels of emotional response when they participate in involving an E-I rule. Thus, in Fig. 13.12, if Johnny is especially beloved by the model, it should feel even greater sympathy. We have not yet thought through all the consequences of this "concept importance" approach to calculating emotional arousal. It seems to have some obvious good points as well as some flaws.

high-intensity activation of the parent anger node), the anger modulator valve in Fig. 13.12 will pass that activation into the memory record shown. Thus, the "Sam beat up Johnny" incident will be partially activated. The new insight here is that a given episode may be retrievable by cuing with either of the emotions (sympathy, anger or distress) felt toward the participants in the scene.

Priming Emotional Interpretations. Let us examine the consequences of activating a particular parent emotion node like anger. An obvious consequence is that this will send activation to all E-I rules that have anger as one of their modulator nodes. This amounts to "priming" those E-I rules into readiness for use in interpreting the next cognitive situation. Priming facilitates the system searching the E-I rules in order of their current level of activation, and selecting the first E-I rule that can be instantiated in the cognitive situation.

This priming causes the model to interpret ambiguous situations in a manner congruent with its prevailing emotion. Thus, the angry model has a "chip on its shoulder," is quick to take offense, is ready to find fault. Thus, if Sam were now to smile at the model who is angry at him, the model would interpret the smile as a mocking smirk and worthy of further anger.

An implication of this theory is that mood-congruent situations should be identified more quickly than mood-incongruent situations. For example, when judging the emotion displayed in a photograph of a face, the anger viewer should "see anger" quicker than sadness, whereas the sad viewer should "see sadness" quicker than anger.

Emotional Content of Fantasies. Our TAT results showed that people's feelings influenced the content of the imaginative stories they told. Although we are unable to develop a complete model of story construction, it is clear that a crucial early stage will be the storyteller's selection of a *theme,* such as achievement, or romance, or aggression and murder. Such high-level themes are linked to the parent emotion nodes. Thus, when the story constructor is feeling angry, themes reflecting frustration or aggression are primed and selected to control story construction.

Replaying an Emotional Memory. People can replay to some extent their original emotional reaction using the memory of a real or imagined event. How can this be explained? Our model says that to re-experience an emotion exactly, one must duplicate exactly the state of the blackboard at the time of that earlier experience. The more closely one can approximate the original state—the other ongoing feelings, the uncertainties of that moment—the more faithful will be the replay of that emotion. In replaying a memory, a propositional network structure like that in Fig. 13.12 is reactivated, placed on the blackboard, and the emotions designated in that memory record (by its modulator nodes) are "turned on."

The extent to which the parent emotion nodes are turned on again will depend on several factors that may have changed since the original experience. The most conspicuous change is in people's uncertainty about what an event signified (e.g., how badly was Johnny hurt by the bully?); they were uncertain during the original experience, and that contributed to their arousal level then, but later we know the consequences of the event, so we cannot become so aroused by the event.

Reinterpreting While Replaying a Memory.   When a memory is posted on the blackboard and replayed, that is the occasion for the model to automatically try to interpret the event once more. Although the event's memory record refers to an original E-I rule (P238 in Fig. 13.12), the system nonetheless searches for any E-I rules that will match the propositions contained in the memory record (i.e., that "Sam hit Johnny"). Under what circumstances will a reexamination of that event now come up with a different emotional interpretation? We consider several ways this can happen in the model:

1. Changed Mood.   If the model is now feeling happy and loving, E-I rules refering to charity and forgiveness will be primed and will become available for quick matches to blackboard events. Thus, Sam's actions may be matched by an E-I rule that interprets Sam's hitting as part of a playful prank of exuberant children.

2. Changed Facts.   Suppose the model has learned that Sam is a retarded person who has been picked on repeatedly by Johnny who is a nefarious scoundrel. Then the intermediate inferences of Fig. 13.12 are all wrong now. So a different E-I rule should now be instantiated, namely, one that causes one to feel satisfaction at retribution for injustice. That will cause the model to feel glad to see scoundrel Johnny get what he deserves.

3. Changed Importance.   The model may have been upset originally at the incident because it liked Johnny and assigned importance to events affecting his welfare. Suppose that that liking changes into neutrality or even dislike. Then reevaluation of the hitting event in memory will lead to a greatly reduced emotional reaction. As a contrasting example, when Fred labeled his burglars as "murderers," his replaying of the burglary of his home would evoke greater discomfort.

The other component of importance was uncertainty: the initial hitting incident may have aroused more emotion because the model was uncertain how much harm was being done to Johnny, but this uncertainty is no longer present.

4. Changed E-I Rule.   People occasionally change their E-I rules perhaps through some "conditioning" or "extinction" experiences or social influences (e.g., religious conversions). Thus, if the model joins the Nazi party and learns to admire strong superman and hate the weak, then new E-I rules will be learned. (Rule learning is modeled in ACT by different "strengths" of frequently reinforced versus neglected E-I rules.) In this case, when the model replays its memory of Sam hitting Johnny, that should now find a match to the LHS of a different E-I rule, which causes the model to feel admiration for Sam and contempt for Johnny. We have shown how in replaying a memory the model will search for an E-I rule with a matching LHS. When a match occurs, a token of that rule will be instantiated (if it is the same rule as before, this is a second instantiation of it). This invocation and instantiation of an E-I rule by a proposition on the blackboard is one of the causes of emotion in the model. If the E-I rule invoked during this reappraisal is different than originally, then different emotions will be evoked (partly at the same time as the old ones are replayed). Significantly, this new interpretation and its E-I rule will be stored in memory now with that old memory record. This gives the model the ability to update its feelings—to say of an event "That used to upset me, but it no longer does."

Conflicting Emotional Interpretations. Conflicting emotional interpretations may give rise to "mixed feelings" in many situations. For example, imagine that a beloved aunt dies and leaves you $5000; you are likely to feel grief over her death and happiness over your windfall. In our theory, this is represented simply as two events (the death and the inheritance) with two concurrent emotional interpretations. Because the interpretations give rise to different emotions, the intensity of each will be descreased by the other.

"Mixed feelings" are represented by simultaneously active and conflicting emotional interpretations. A related situation involves an active emotional interpretation that conflicts with remembered emotional interpretations. For example, if you hear that "Sam hit Johnny," but you like Sam very much, then you will moderate your anger toward him. There are several ways that this can happen. First, you may fail to infer that Sam is a bully, in which case the E-I rule that specifies anger toward bullies will not apply. This is quite plausible, especially given the powerful effect of mood on selective recall and inference. On the other hand, if you are already angry when you hear that Sam beat up Johnny, you may experience mixed feelings: anger toward Sam for his violence to Johnny, but also happiness from recalling one or more positive things about him.

Hot Versus Cold Cognition. It appears necessary that the long-term memory should have one unit or node that is the emotional feeling itself, another unit that is the concept of the emotion, and a third unit that is the name of that concept. See Fig. 13.13 for a diagram of this. The first node is responsible for the subjective emotional experience, the autonomic and expressive behaviors, and the cognitive influences; the second node collects together the meaningful connections of the concept (and points to the first node as its referent); and the third node (the "name") is used to talk about the concept and its referent emotion. The name of the concept can be activated and used without in the least turning on the referent feeling. This is done when we discourse dispassionately about an

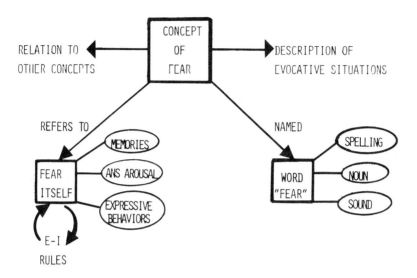

FIG. 13.13.   Relations among network nodes representing an emotion, the concept of it, and words naming the concept.

emotion. The only natural way to "turn on" the feeling node is through instantiation of an E-I rule by a blackboard situation. (An unnatural method is to directly stimulate an emotion center with a brain electrode.); that is, natural emotions cannot be turned on directly but only through matching an E-I rule to an actual, imagined, or remembered situation represented on the blackboard. People cannot just feel sad or angry in the abstract; rather, they must activate a memory or imaginary scene that will lead them into sadness or anger.

This method for arousing emotions seems right intuitively. The technique is well-known among acting teachers (e.g., Stanislavski, 1936) and every fledgling actor or actress collects a set of emotional memories that they can press into service to stimulate the emotions their stage roles demand.

Reasoning about Emotional Memories.   Recall that an emotional experience causes a data structure like that in Fig. 13.12 to be recorded in memory. This stores the event (Sam hit Johnny) along with the pattern of emotional reactions evoked and a token of the E-I rule whose instantiation led to that emotional reaction. In Fig. 13.12, the top-level node is a token of E-I rule P238 about bullies hurting weaklings.

This memory structure may be compared to that proposed in the earlier, simpler theory (see Fig. 13.4); that earlier theory would have just associated one emotion, say anger, with the whole episode by a direct linkage. The new approach provides for a more discriminating assignment of emotional reactions to participants in the episode. Perhaps more importantly, the new scheme permits the model to reason about or give justification for its emotional interpretations. We believe this is an important advantage that warrants further comment.

A first advantage of storing the instantiated E-I rule with the event's memory is that it enables one to reinterpret the event emotionally in case his E-I rules change. Thus, someone can replay an upsetting memory, notice that it is now best interpreted by an altered E-I rule, and thus store this new emotion with the event memory. The former memory model did not have the capability of "understanding" (giving reasons for) any such changes that the model would record.

Second, the "examined life" to which a culture exhorts its members requires that they be able to *justify* their acts, attitudes, and emotional reactions. Our new data structure can do this because it points to the E-I rule justifying its emotional reaction to the original event. Moreover, this particular E-I rule is itself located within a generalization hierarchy (imagine Fig. 13.11 generalized). Thus, a childhood bully hitting a weaker child is just a special case of a powerful person taking advantage of a weak one, which in turn is a special case of an act that exaggerates a preexisting inequity of happiness or utility (i.e., the strong get stronger). Thus, if asked repeatedly to justify its wrath at bully Sam, the model can be "backed up" its belief hierarchy, where it will provide ever more general rationales for its indignation. In moral arguments, people are often called upon to justify their moral ("emotional") judgments in just such abstract terms.

Third, this generalization hierarchy of emotional rules gives one a way to conceptualize how cognitive therapy affects emotional disorders. For example, in rational emotive therapy as practiced by Albert Ellis (1962), the maladjusted patient is conceived to have certain irrational beliefs, expectations about himself, other people, and their relationship to him. Sample irrational beliefs can be represented as very general rules such as:

IF I'm not perfect,
THEN I am worthless and should be depressed.

IF everyone doesn't love everything I do,
THEN I am worthless and should be depressed.

IF everything doesn't go well,
THEN I'm to blame and should feel guilty.

In rational emotive therapy and in Beck's (1976) cognitive therapy, much therapeutic effort is concentrated on unearthing the patient's irrational beliefs, then challenging and changing them, replacing them with less-self-defeating beliefs. The basic premise of the therapy is that emotional appraisals can be viewed as the application of abstract rules to specific situations, and that it is possible to change these rules directly and thus effect therapeutic changes in maladaptive emotional syndromes. The therapy is undeniably effective in many instances.

Our theory of an E-I rule hierarchy provides a way to discuss the effect of such "attitude" therapy. The problem encountered in such therapy is also predicted by the theory, namely, that a general rule freshly taught by the therapist will be short-circuited (not applied) by the client reverting to specific, low-level E-I rules of long, strong standing. Much guided practice *in vivo* in using the new emotional interpretation rules is needed to bring about therapeutic changes.

Affective Similes and Metaphors. The hierarchical organization of E-I rules permits one to compare episodes and note their similarity in terms of the general E-I rule and pattern of affect they evoke. Thus, a man beating his dog is like Sam hitting Johnny, and both are like someone pulling the wings off a butterfly. All are instances of E-I rules that identify various forms of cruelty, and the specific E-I rules are collected under a common, generalized cruelty E-I rule. Because of their common affective response and invocation of common E-I rules, one of these episodes may remind us of another. Thus, the Wehrmacht army's blitzkreig into Belgium in 1940 may remind us of a bully's overpowering a defenseless opponent. These sorts of remindings by affective similes occur frequently in literary metaphors and in everyday conversations.

To summarize this section, by storing instantiations of reasoning rules with the episodes in which they are used, the model can reason intelligently at a later time about the episode. It can explain how it felt, and can justify its feelings at several levels of abstraction. It can compare one emotional episode to another, even if they do not share concepts, on the basis of common or related E-I rules. Importantly, it can also say why it feels differently about an episode at a later time; for example, if it learns that the man was not actually beating the dog but was only pretending to beat it for a circus routine, the model can reinterpret the episode and by comparing the original E-I rules with the more recent ones, it can say why it feels differently.

These conditions do not detract in any way from the advantages of the original semantic network model. Those network ideas are still used to account for state-dependent memory and selective learning by the usual mechanisms of cuing and spreading activation. The new model adds capabilities for appraising emotional situations and reasoning about those appraisals.

Final Comments

Let us summarize briefly what we think we have accomplished. First, we reviewed experimental results showing diverse influences of emotion upon selective learning, selective retrieval, and emotionally biased judgments and interpretations. The effects are strong, wide-spread, and intuitively understandable. Second, we reviewed the earlier semantic network theory of emotional memories that sufficed to explain roughly most of those experimental results. Third, we noted incompletenesses in that theory and pointed to the need for an emotional appraisal system. Fourth, we introduced the blackboard control structure for coordinating the knowledge sources we believe are involved in emotionally appraising situations. We described some of the knowledge sources and sketched briefly how they might interact on the blackboard in arriving at an emotional interpretation. Fifth, we then applied this blackboard model to several complex phenomena in emotion such as replaying and reinterpreting one's earlier emotional experiences.

We would emphasize that these latter ideas are in an early stage of development, and we would feel more secure if we had an operating computer program that implements our verbal ideas. We are impressed by the difficulty of the problems to be faced by any theory of emotional behavior. We hope that we have contributed in some measure to the clarification or resolution of some of the problems.

ACKNOWLEDGMENT

This research was supported by Grant MH–13950 from the National Institutes of Mental Health to G. H. Bower.

REFERENCES

Anderson, J. R. *Language, memory and thought.* Hillsdale, N.J.: Lawrence Erlbaum Associates, 1976.

Bartlett, J. C., Burleson, G., & Santrock, J. W. Emotional mood and memory in young children. *Journal of Experimental Child Psychology,* in press.

Beck, A. T. *Cognitive therapy and the emotional disorders.* New York: International Universities Press.

Bower, G. H. Mood and memory. *American Psychologist,* 1981, *36* (No. 2), 129–148.

Bower, G. H., Gilligan, S. G., & Monteiro, K. P. Selectivity of learning caused by affective states. *Journal of Experimental Psychology: General,* 1981, *110,* 451–473.

Bower, G. H., Monteiro, K. P., & Gilligan, S. G. Emotional mood as a context for learning and recall. *Journal of Verbal Learning and Verbal Behavior,* 1978, *17,* 573–585.

Carbonell, J. G. *Subjective understanding: Computer models of belief systems.* New Haven, Conn.: (A.I. Tech. Rep. 150), Yale Computer Science Dept. 1978.

Clark, M. S., & Isen, A. M. Toward understanding the relationship between feeling states and social behavior. In A. Hastorf & A. M. Isen (Eds.), *Cognitive social psychology.* Amsterdam: Elsevier, 1982.

Eich, J. E. The cue-dependent nature of state-dependent retrieval. *Memory and Cognition,* 1980, *8,* 157–173.

Eich, J. E., Weingartner, H., Stillman, R. C., & Gillin, J. C. State-dependent accessibility of retrieval cues in the retention of a categorized list. *Journal of Verbal Learning and Verbal Behavior,* 1975, *14,* 408–417.

Ellis, A. *Reason and emotion in psychotherapy.* New York: Lyle Stuart, 1962.

Gilligan, S. G., & Bower, G. H. *Emotional mood and remembering one's autobiography.* First draft of manuscript, Department of Psychology, Stanford University, 1981.

Henry, G., Weingartner, H., & Murphy, D. L. Influence of affective states and psycho-active drugs on verbal learning and memory *American Journal of Psychiatry,* 1973, *130,* 966–971.

Isen, A. M., Shalker, T. E., Clark, M. & Karp, L. Affect, accessibility of material in memory, and behavior: A cognitive loop? *Journal of Personality and Social Psychology,* 1978, *36,* 1–12.

Mowrer, O. H. *Learning theory and behavior.* New York: Wiley, 1960.

Plutchik, R. *A psychoevolutionary synthesis.* New York: Harper & Row, 1980. (a)

Plutchik, R. A language for the emotions. *Psychology Today,* February 1980, *2,* 68–78. (b)

Roseman, I. *Cognitive aspects of emotion and emotional behavior.* Paper presented at the meeting of the American Psychological Association. New York: September 1979. (Unpublished manuscript, Department of Psychology, Yale University.)

Schiffenbauer, A. I. *The effects of a judge's affective state upon his judgment of the emotional state of others.* Unpublished doctoral dissertation, Department of Psychology, Stanford University, 1970.

Tversky, A., & Kahneman, D. Availability: A heuristic for judging frequency and probability. *Cognitive Psychology,* 1973, *5,* 207–232.

14 Comments

Herbert A. Simon
Carnegie-Mellon University

AFFECT AND COGNITION: COMMENTS

Over the past three days we have heard about a dozen papers on the relations between affect and cognition, presenting to us much new experimental evidence and both old and new theories to explain the experimental facts. Fortunately, my assignment does not require me to comment on this whole panoply of ideas, but only upon the segment of it that has occupied today's sessions. That is task enough, but, to perform it adequately, I must make some reference to what has gone before. I will start, therefore, with some general remarks, and then focus more closely on the three papers we have heard today.

Representation and Process

Terminological problems are important, not because there are usually right and wrong answers to them, but because unless we settle them we will not understand each other. George Mandler, in his opening paper on Friday, objected to confounding cognition with thinking processes. "Representation," he said, "and not process, is at the heart of cognition."

Now I must take exception to the exclusiveness of that proposal. We do not have to choose between viewing cognition in terms of representation or viewing it in terms of process. The two views are wholly compatable. There is no representation without process, and no process without representation.

For example, when we represent something, whether in computer memory or human memory, as a list, we imply that there exists some process, "Find the Next," that allows us, given an item on the list, to access the following item. We imply that there exist other processes, too—Insert, Delete, Transpose—that allow us to manipulate and alter the list. In any information processing system, representation and process are inextricably interwoven, so that if our research teaches us something about one of them, it inevitably teaches us something about the other. In my comments, therefore, I will feel as free to discuss affective and cognitive processes as to discuss the representation of affect and cognition—indeed, I will generally talk about both at the same time.

The Meaning of "Affect"

Turning now to "affect," the other term in the title of our symposium, I encounter a different difficulty. Here I have some impression, in moving from one paper to the next, that we are indeed the traditional blind men, now touching one part of the elephant, now another. Affect is a word of everyday language that is subject to the imprecision of all such words—perhaps to more imprecision than most. Its various meanings are connected—that's how they arose in the first place—but not synonymous. If our science is to advance, we must identify these nuances and both construct and adhere to a vocabulary that makes the necessary distinctions in a consistent way. Let me, then, comment on what I see as the several aspects of affect that must be distinguished.

1. The human nervous system that we are trying to understand has a central component that is serial in its operation, its ability to carry on several tasks simultaneously being severely restricted by the bottleneck of attention, or short-term memory. Indefinite survival of such a system in a world where danger may appear suddenly or where nonpostponable demands (for air, water) may arise requires some means for interrupting the attentional mechanism and directing attention to the present danger or requirement (Simon, 1967).

In the human organism, interruption may originate in sensory stimuli (detection in peripheral vision of a rapidly moving object, detection of a loud noise), in stimuli coming from the autonomic nervous system (hunger pangs), or by evocation of affect-tinged items in long-term memory (recall of an embarrassing experience). The interruption redirects attention and also usually causes arousal of the autonomic nervous system and endocrine systems. Some of what we call affect and emotion is associated with this constellation of events, particularly emotions like surprise, fear, and anger.

2. Arousal of the autonomic and endocrine systems can occur at a more diffuse and subtle level, without obvious interruption of attention. Again, ordinary language includes these phenomena in the orbit of affect and emotion, although when the state is not acute and interruptive, the terms "mood" and "feeling" will often be applied instead of "emotion." Typical examples are sadness and happiness.

Mood, like affect that interrupts, can originate in internal stimulation and arousal (e.g., from the effects of drugs upon the endocrine system), but also in evocations of long-term memories that cause autonomic or endocrine arousal. The effects of moods, as shown in several of the experiments reported today, are to establish contexts that influence and direct cognitive activities—for example bias memory retrieval processes toward certain long-term memory contents and away from others. Hence, moods operate, in some ways, rather like cognitively established goals.

3. People make cognitive evaluations of all sorts of things and events, and may store these evaluations in long-term memory. As George Mandler has reminded us, such evaluations have two different sources. On the one hand, evaluations may be memories of affect associated with the object and event on some occasion or occasions when we experienced it. We may remember that we were sad, or happy, or frightened when some particular event or kind of event occurred, and the memory may or may not also reinvoke the original emotion. On the other hand, we may simply have learned in our social environment to associate a particular cognitive evaluation with a particular object or event: beef is good food, but lizard flesh is bad food.

We may make choices (e.g., between beef and lizard) on the basis of our evaluations, with or without any accompanying affect. The only connections between cognitive evaluations and affect is that the former may be (but need not be) initially caused by the latter, and because the former may be associated with and evoke the latter. (If I have learned, socially, that lizard meat is not proper food, it can easily induce nausea when it is served to me.)

Failure to distinguish between cognitive evaluation and the affect that may or may not accompany it can cause great confusion. Some jurors may be able to make a cognitive evaluation that a convicted criminal should be sentenced to death without experiencing particular affect while arriving at the decision. Other jurors may find such dissociation between evaluation and affect almost incomprehensible. Probably, a great deal of mutual misunderstanding among human beings arises from the great variety, among us, of patterns of association between cognitive valuations and affect.

Since long-term memory can be the repository of interrupting, mood-arousing, and value-laden symbols, affect and cognitive evaluations can enter consciousness suddenly—that is, by the ordinary processes of recognition and resulting evocation.

From a theoretical standpoint, therefore, we can employ such terms as affect, emotion, mood, valuation to designate states and processes in long-term memory, the attentional system and its interrupter, the autonomic nervous system, and the endocrine system. I personally prefer to employ *affect* as a generic term, *emotion* to refer to affect that interrupts and redirects attention (usually with accompanying arousal), *mood* to refer to affect that provides context for ongoing thought processes without noticeably interrupting them, and *valuation* to refer to association of cognitive "labels" attributing positive or negative valence to objects or events. I will try to stick to this terminology in the remainder of my remarks.

Although I believe, from evidence of their other writings, that the authors of today's symposium papers would agree with my terminological proposals, most of the reports of experiments that we have heard here define affect operationally in a quite different way. Instead of referring explicitly to theoretical constructs, they refer to the particular experimental manipulations that were used to induce affect. This is a perfectly acceptable procedure, and certainly one that accords well with established methodological traditions in psychology, but we must never forget that it leaves one essential task undone. Having employed certain sadness-generating manipulations, say, for one condition of an experiment, we must verify not only that the manipulations produce effects of one kind or another, but also that they do, in fact, induce the mood of sadness. That is, we must have some relatively direct way of assessing the presence or absence of the mood of sadness. Without such a measure, we cannot guarantee the equivalence, even approximately, of our independent variables or experimental manipulations across different experiments. Few of the experiments reported here included such an independent measure of the emotion or mood induced by the experimental manipulations, although in some instances separate studies have demonstrated the mood-inducing efficacy of these stimuli.

Relations between Affect and Cognition

When one considers the interaction of affect and cognition in mental functioning, one is struck by the qualitative incongruity between these two domains, and one is initially puzzled as to how two such disparate kinds of processes can influence each other at all.

Affect is diffuse, hard to describe and harder to differentiate and classify. There are degrees of sadness, but are there also kinds? And how many emotions are there, and what are they? Cognition, by contrast, is highly specific, mostly representable by strings or structures of symbols. Especially in formal domains like mathematics, it can have exquisite precision and can distinguish minute nuances.

Affect is susceptible to continuous gradation in degree, like something that can be scaled by real numbers or modeled by an analogue device. Cognition is digital in character; symbol structures can be discriminated by yes–no tests from other symbol structures.

Affective states change not only continuously, but usually relatively gradually—proverbially, one must count to ten before anger subsides. Cognitive structures succeed one another in short-term memory at rapid rates, the minimal intervals between them being tenths of seconds rather than tens of seconds.

How can two languages that are so radically different, not only in vocabulary and syntax but in their very units of meaning, communicate with each other? To my mind, the most plausible answer to that question is given by postulating mechanisms of *interruption* and *arousal*. Interruption is the setting aside of the current focus of attention, defined by the contents of short-term memory or, other formulations, by the activated subset of long-term memory. Arousal is the stimulation of the autonomic nervous system and endocrine system, which may, in turn, cause interruption of attention and/or modify the levels of activation of particular areas in LTM. There is nothing very novel about this theory, and it is supported by a good deal of physiological as well as behavioral evidence. I have described it in greater detail elsewhere (Simon, 1967) and provided references to its antecedents.

The mechanisms of interruption and arousal provide two-directional causal paths between affect and cognition. First of all, certain sensory stimuli, for example, seeing a rapidly moving object in peripheral vision or hearing a loud noise, readily interrupt ongoing trains of thought, and at the same time may arouse the endocrine system and bring into action "weak methods," like flight or attack, for dealing with a situation.[1] Here the causal arrow runs from sensation to emotion (anger, fear) and thence to change in cognitive focus of attention.

This same interruption process may begin, not with a sensation, but with the evocation of an affectively charged element of LTM, or with stimulation of the autonomic nervous system (e.g., by pain or hunger). What all of these chains of events have in common is the intermingling of a shift of attention with endocrine arousal and detection of signals coming from the autonomic nervous system.

Second, it appears that arousal, however initiated, can have relatively long-term effects upon the activation of memory, with the result that it can establish or modify context for the ongoing cognitive processes. What are postulated here are not two different mechanisms, but a distinction of degree between a relatively abrupt break in attention (in which case we speak of "emotion"), and more subtle influences on context (in which case we speak of "mood").

I do not think that we need a more complex set of mechanism than this to account for the possibility of affect and cognition interacting, or to explain the kinds of interactions that are demonstrated by the experiments in today's papers or the papers presented at the other sessions. Most of the papers reported here follow this causal path in one direction: that is, from emotion or mood, as the independent variable, to change in cognition, as the dependent. If we were

---

[1] I borrow the term "weak methods" from artificial intelligence to refer to programs that may be applicable to many situations, do not demand much information for their execution, but may be correspondingly inefficient.

interested in symmetry, we could easily produce effects in the opposite direction. Every novelist depends on cognitive processes applied to the printed page being able to evoke mood and emotion. Outside of literature, a simple sentence will often suffice: "Your slip is showing," or "You are a stupid ass."

As a matter of fact, if we look at the structure of the experiments reported here, we see that, although the object of the experiment is to show that affect can influence the course of cognition, the operations used to produce the affect act upon the cognitive processes. Thus Gordon Bower and his colleagues induce subjects to feel happy or sad by having them read about happy or sad events. Alice Isen's and Margaret Clark's subjects become happy when they find a dime, receive a cookie, or win a game, or receive success feedback regarding their performance on a task. So the experiments we are discussing here demonstrate the influences of affect on cognition, but depend for their efficacy on the fact that cognition may create affect.

Mood and Memory Retrieval

Many of the experiments that are reported here describe effects of mood upon memory. Bower and Cohen review a number of experiments reporting such "mood congruity" effects, and others are described in the papers by Isen and Clark. The effects appear both in experiments on learning (those aspects of stimuli are more likely to be learned that are congruent with the mood of the learner) and in experiments on retrieval ("People can best retrieve a memory of an event by reinstating the emotion they were experiencing when they originally stored the event (Bower and Cohen)").

It is not hard to postulate mechanisms to explain the learning effect—Bower and Cohen propose several. The one that appeals most strongly to me, more on grounds of parsimony than because there is direct evidence for it, is that mood focuses attention on those aspects of the stimulus that are congruent with the mood. This hypothesis follows rather directly from the notion of interruption postulated earlier.

Explaining the facilitation of retrieval by mood congruity is more difficult, especially since the facilitation appears only in recall tasks and not in recognition tasks. (The explanation for this difference provided by Bower and Cohen seems to me ad hoc and unconvincing.)

The model of memory used in all of the papers of this session postulates a large associative net together with a spreading activation process that makes particular portions of the net selectively accessible for recall. Nothing is said in these models about the paths used to access the memory, except the associative paths that may be followed once an initial access has been achieved. This model of memory, ignoring the access paths, seems to me seriously incomplete. To recall a metaphor I have proposed elsewhere, human memory operates like a large, unalphabetized encyclopedia, which is, however, provided with an index.

(In computer science terminology, such a memory is referred to as "content addressed.") The body of the encyclopedia itself has many cross-references (i.e., it is an associative net). Once initial access is obtained to more or less relevant information, the associative links can be used to obtain related information, and it is easy to see how the search might be biased by varying levels of activation of the different nodes.

Initial access to the encyclopedia must be gained, however, by recourse to the index—that is, by an act of recognition of a sensory stimulus or a symbol held in STM. (See Simon, 1979, Sections 2 and 3, for an elaboration of this model.) The distinction between "index" and "text"—between recognition processes to provide access to LTM and associative processes that permit it to be searched—provides a basis for understanding why different effects may be observed in recall experiments, which may involve considerable search as well as recognition, from those observed in recognition experiments, which do not generally require associative search of memory once it has been accessed. In particular, if activation is a process that operates on the associative structures of LTM, but not upon the access routes, the index, then we can account for the effect of mood upon learning and recall, but the absence of an effect upon recognition.

Another serious difficulty remains in the explanations. The spreading activation model will produce the effects described in these experiments only if there is a nearly direct connection between the "mood" nodes in memory and all of the cognitive memories that were tinged with those particular moods. For if the memory of sad events is to be enhanced by a sad mood, then the sadness must raise the activity levels of all the nodes referring to sad events. This seems to suggest an inordinate amount of "wiring" emanating from the nodes that represent the moods (Bower and Cohen refer to this difficulty as the fanout problem), but perhaps a clever architect of circuits could suggest how this could be accomplished plausibly. In view of the antiquity of those parts of the brain that are implicated in the emotions, there is nothing implausible in a hypothesis that they are connected in different ways to the "cognitive" nodes than the latter are to each other.

All of this, while highly speculative, does suggest some directions for the future. In particular, it suggests that a picture of a homogenous long-term memory, with nothing but associative links and spreading activation, is overly simple. We must distinguish between recognition processes (the index) and associative processes (in the text) of that memory, and we probably must postulate that the structures storing affect and connecting it with cognitive contexts are somewhat different (closely related to the diffuse character of affect) from those that operate solely within cognitive structures. I would hope that as Bower and Cohen elaborate the model they have sketched into a fullblown computer program, they will experiment with the utility and plausibility of distinctions of these kinds.

The basic phenomena to be accounted for by these mechanisms—the influence of affective "context" on cognition—are made eminently clear by the experiments that have been described at this session. What is needed, as the authors of the session's papers have emphasized, is to pin down and make operational that term "context."

Some Comments on Specifics

Before concluding my remarks about today's session, I'd like to add some specific comments about particular points in the papers. The comments can be rather brief because the papers were all on the same wave length, expressing generally compatible views about the relations of affect and cognition. As my previous remarks indicate, I am in almost full agreement with these views, and full of admiration for the excellent experiments that our speakers have reported, aimed at testing them.

Affect and Strategies.   Professor Isen illustrated with her experiments the important point that the arousal of affect not only may influence, selectively, the retrieval of information, but may also bias the selection of strategies for the performance of problem-solving tasks. This general effect is certainly predictable from the kinds of models we have been entertaining, but the exact nature of the influence in particular experiments is not at all predictable. Moreover, I find Professor Isen's explanations for these specifics somewhat unconvincing. At least I can conjure up alternative explanations that seem to me just as plausible.

In one set of experiments, where positive affect has been induced in subjects by serving them lemonade and cookies, these subjects used simpler cognitive strategies for tasks than did control subjects. Professor Isen suggests that positive affect, requiring attention, may place a load on STM, or that subjects in a pleasant mood may be motivated to avoid cognitive strain. Of course, an alternative interpretation is that the lemonade and cookies did more than induce positive affect. They may also have led subjects to reinterpret the situation as less a test situation than a social (or "sociable") situation, and hence to reduce their motivation to perform well. There is nothing in the experimental manipulation that prevents ramified cognitive changes in the state of mind of the subject beyond the mere induction of a pleasant mood. Further experimentation will be needed to rule out this alternative explanation, which, I confess, appeals to me as the more likely.

The plausibility of this alternative interpretation is enhanced by Professor Isen's experiments on risk taking. Subjects who had been successful in a task were more willing to take a "social risk" (i.e., to behave in a relatively unrestrained fashion in a social situation) than other subjects. But surely this result can be explained by the association in our culture, and I believe in most others, between status and behavioral freedom. Winning induced not only pleasure but also a self-perception that allowed the successful subjects to take initiative in social interaction. In neither of these sets of experiments do we need to postulate a special effect of pleasant feelings upon cognitive processes. Instead, relatively well understood social variables can serve as mediators.

Autonomic Arousal.   In Professor Clark's interpretations of her experiments, it is the role she attributes to autonomic arousal that gives me pause. I am not sure that I can wholly distinguish her interpretation of the experiment in which exercise (and consequent arousal) magnified the effect of positive affect from the usual interpretations in terms of misattribution. I have always interpreted the misattribution hypothesis (at least in the form in which it was used by Schachter) to mean simply that autonomic arousal is too global a set of phenomena to propel behavior in any particular direction. Hence, its interpretation by the subject, and its effects on his behavior, must depend on the cognitive context in which it occurs. Arousal in a context that is "funny" may lead to slightly manic behavior; while arousal in a context where anger would be appropriate may lead to angry behavior.

The experimental evidence deals mainly with how the subject behaves in a given cognitive context and under a particular condition of arousal. How aware the subject is of either context or arousal state is not the central question. Misattribution theories, in contrast with Professor Clark's explanation, speak of subjects as "interpreting" their arousal state in terms of a particular cognitive context. But in the absence of direct evidence that the subject is aware of either arousal or context, it would be as accurate to describe the subject as interpreting the context in terms of his or her arousal state. The behavioral consequence in either case is that the two interact, with or without awareness, to produce the altered behavior. Hence, I do not see as wide a gap between Professor Clark's explanation and misattribution explanations as she does, although her demonstration that memory as well as environmental context can influence the interpretation of arousal seems to be entirely new.

The Blackboard Model.   Finally, I should like to raise a question about the "blackboard" concept employed by Bower and Cohen. As their references indicate, the blackboard mechanism has had some utility in artificial intelligence. In fact, Allen Newell and I made use of it there and, I believe, were the first to christen if not to discover it. Its application to the modeling of semantic memory is another matter. In the particular use that Bower and Cohen make of it, it does not seem to me to perform any function that was not already being performed by the spreading activation mechanism.

The whole idea of spreading activation is that the course of the cognitive processes must be responsive to context—they cannot respond indifferently to the total contents of LTM. The activated portion of LTM defines the (momentary) context. But this is precisely the task that Bower and Cohen assign to the blackboard. Hence, the blackboard mechanism seems not to add anything to their scheme, and parsimony would suggest that it be omitted.

Implementation of the Bower-Cohen scheme (with or without the blackboard) would go far toward testing whether the general approach to the interaction between affect and cognition that I have outlined in this chapter and that has been set forth in alternative, but largely compatible, language by all three papers in this session, can in fact account for the phenomena. We will need many more experiments of the ingenious sorts that have been described here, but we will also need large-scale modeling to determine whether these kinds of plausible theoretical proposals would really deliver as promised in the context of a very large and complex system of interactions.

CONCLUSION

Cognitive psychology has lived for several decades essentially without affect, attending to its narrower task of explaining ''cool'' thinking. The papers of this symposium remind us of the important interactions between affect and thought that are characteristic of most real life situations. The evidence presented in the symposium papers is very encouraging to the prospects of our gaining a better understanding of these interactions. First of all, the papers demonstrate that it is not hard to create experimental manipulations of the relevant variables sufficiently powerful to produce large observable effects. Second, there already appears to be a considerable measure of consensus about the kind of theoretical framework that needs to be built in order to accommodate both affect and cognition in the same head.

ACKNOWLEDGMENTS

This research was supported by Research Grant MH-07722 from the National Institute of Mental Health.

REFERENCES

Simon, H. A. Motivational and emotional controls of cognition. *Psychological Review*, 1967, *74*, 29–39.
Simon, H. A. *Models of thought*. New Haven, CT: Yale University Press, 1979.

Author Index

Weingartner, H., 268, *289,* 296, 300, *330, 331*
Weiss, R. L., 46, *54*
Werner, J. S., 31, *36*
White, R. W., 56, *77*
Wicklund, R. A., 158, *181, 183,* 232, *238*
Wiener, N., 158, *183*
Wierzbicka, A., 5, *36*
Wilder, D. A., 80, *109,* 161, 162, *180, 183*
Wilkes-Gibbs, D., 27, *35*
Williamson, R. C., 46, *54*
Wilson, H. K., 129, *149*
Wilson, W. R., 27, *36,* 216, *227*
Witkin, H. A., 130, *154*
Wolford, G., 18, *34*
Wong, P. T. P., 186, *209*
Woodworth, R. S., 128, *154*
Word, C. O., 74, *78*
Wundt, W., 6, *36*
Wyer, R. S., Jr., 161, *182*

X, Y, Z

Yekovich, F. R., 115, *118*
Zadney, J., 161, *183*
Zajonc, R. B., 6, 19, 24, 27, *36,* 55, 56, 57, 58, *78,* 112, *118,* 124, 147, *154,* 179, *183,* 203, *209,* 211, 212, 215, 216, 218, 219, 221, 222, *226, 227,* 301, *331*
Zanna, M. P., 71, 74, *78,* 113, 114, *118*
Zeiss, A., 259, *261*
Ziff, P., 12, *36*
Zillmann, D., 129, *154,* 263, 273, 274, 275, *286, 288, 289*
Zimbardo, P. G., 129, *151,* 204, *208,* 277, *288*
Zimmerman, R., 138, *151*
Zola, I. K., 138, *154*
Zuckerman, M., 197, *209*

Subject Index

M, N

Match, 61–68, 70, 72, 73–75, 116
Memory (see Arousal; Faces, memory for;
    Mood; Selective effects on recall vs.
    recognition; State-dependent memory),
    56, 58–61, 265–286, 338–342
  for emotional events, 327–329
  initial access to, 338–339
  and recall, 338–339
  and recognition, 338–339
  storage of arousal imagery in, 268–272,
    283–285
  storage of feelings in, 265–272, 285
Mental withdrawal, 167
Mere exposure effect, 27–28, 215–217
Metaphors and similes, 329
Misattribution, 273–274
Mood (see Feeling states; Variability), 80, 92,
    100–101, 102–103, 214, 217–218, 225,
    263–286, 334–335, 338–342
  and accessibility of mood congruent
    information, 265–269, 273–281,
    284–285
  and attraction, 264, 273–275
  definition of, 335–337
  duration of, 284–285
  effects on judgments and behavior, 263–268,
    277–281
  and learning, 338–339
  and memory retrieval, 335, 338–342
  negative, 265–268, 270–272, 284–286
  positive, 264–268, 269–270, 272, 277–281,
    284–286
  protection, 254, 255
  relation to expectancies, 285
  storage of, 263–286
Mood congruity, 291, 293–294
Motor representations of emotion, 211,
    218–224
Nausea, 122, 215
Negative feedback loop, 159–161

O, P

Optimizing, 246
Outcome expectancy, 167, 169
Pain, 124–125, 133, 134, 136–137
  phantom, 132–133, 134
Perceptual defense, 221

Perceptual-motor model, 121, 127–128
  expressive-motor processing in, 128–129,
    130–131
  and illness cognition, 140–149
  interaction of processing mechanisms in,
    135–140, 142–143
  role of conceptual memory in, 128, 129,
    134–135
  role of schematic-emotion mechanism in,
    128, 129, 130–133, 144–145
Perceptual processing system, 122–123
Performance, 244, 247–248, 252–254, 259
Person perception, 58, 66, 73
Physical illness (see Perceptual-motor model),
    106, 123–150
Piecemeal models, 58–60, 64–65, 71, 74–75
Pity, 185, 190–192, 196, 197–203, 206, 207
Polarization, 87–88, 91–92
Political cognition, 66–70
Preference, 7, 30
Pride, 185, 190–192, 193, 204, 205, 206, 207,
    211
Priming (see Accessibility; Spreading
    activation), 266–267, 269, 272,
    274–277, 280–282, 284–285
Public versus private self-consciousness, 173

R, S, T

Rearrangement of goal priorities, 177
Reassertion efforts, 167
Relational structures, 3, 9, 20
Representation (see Schemas; Mood, storage
    of), 3, 4, 6, 9, 16, 26, 28, 31, 32,
    81–106, 211, 218–225
Risk, 243, 254–258
Sadness, 334–336
Satisficing, 246
Schema (see Match; Perceptual-motor model;
    Representation; Value), 3, 6, 8, 10, 13,
    15–20, 22–24, 25, 26–27, 28–30,
    31–32, 60–61, 81, 112, 128, 136, 140,
    143, 147
  consensual, 66–74
  deficiencies in schema-based theories, 115
  idiosyncratic, 62–66
  (in) consistency, 62–73, 74
  theory, 3, 27
Scripts, 134, 138, 140